D1766116

004008

# THE EUROPEAN LAW OF COMMERCIAL AGENCY

This is the third edition of the leading work on European commercial agency, by two practising lawyers who have been involved in many of the leading cases since the adoption of the European Directive on self-employed commercial agents. Since the previous edition there have been a string of important cases which have helped to clarify previously confused issues but even now some of the case law remains unsatisfactory. In this third edition of their work, Randolph and Davey have once again drawn out the consistent threads in the case law to predict the likely approach of the courts, both at UK and EU level, to those issues which still remain undecided. The approach adopted in the earlier editions of tackling difficult issues head-on and suggesting concrete answers to practitioners has once again been carried through into the third edition.

As well as including references to all the relevant cases in the text, the work now includes a new chapter on the valuation of businesses by Dr Ruth Bender of the Cranfield School of Management, as well as an up-to-date version of the chapter on French law by Dr Séverine Saintier of Sheffield University and on German law by Dr Michael Reiling, Rechtsanwalt, Noerr LLP.

# The European Law of Commercial Agency

## Third Edition

Fergus Randolph QC
and
Jonathan Davey

·HART·
PUBLISHING

OXFORD AND PORTLAND, OREGON
2010

Published in the United Kingdom by Hart Publishing Ltd
16C Worcester Place, Oxford, OX1 2JW
Telephone: +44 (0)1865 517530
Fax: +44 (0)1865 510710
E-mail: mail@hartpub.co.uk
Website: http://www.hartpub.co.uk

Published in North America (US and Canada) by
Hart Publishing
c/o International Specialized Book Services
920 NE 58th Avenue, Suite 300
Portland, OR 97213-3786
USA
Tel: +1 503 287 3093 or toll-free: (1) 800 944 6190
Fax: +1 503 280 8832
E-mail: orders@isbs.com
Website: http://www.isbs.com

British Library Cataloguing in Publication Data
Data Available

ISBN: 978-1-84113-850-3

Typeset by Foreword Ltd, Oxford
Printed and bound in Great Britain by
TJ International Ltd, Padstow, Cornwall

# Contents

# Table of Cases

**EU**

# France

## Germany

## United Kingdom

# Table of Legislation

**EU**

*Directives*

## United Kingdom

### *Primary Legislation*

### *Secondary legislation*

---

[1] Scottish implementing regulations

# Table of International Treaties and Conventions

# 1

# Introduction,
# Trends and
# Emerging Issues

## 1.1 INTRODUCTION

U NTIL THE START of 1994 the relationship between agents and their principals was not subject to any specific legislation in the UK. Other EU countries, notably France, Germany and Italy, had for many years provided statutory protection to agents. There was a view that the different levels of protection afforded to agents by the different systems of law within the EU might disadvantage businesses in some areas of the EU or result in distortions of competition.

For these reasons specific rules in the form of an EU directive were proposed, requiring EU Member States to change their systems of law so as to provide a uniform level of protection for commercial agents. These proposals were the subject of lengthy and detailed negotiation and comment within the UK and in other EU Member States before Directive 86/653 ('the Directive') was finally adopted in 1986.

It is the Directive, and the Commercial Agents (Council Directive) Regulations 1993 (as amended)[1] ('the Regulations') which implement the Directive into English law, which are the specific subject of this book. A copy of the Regulations as amended, together with the Directive, can be found in Appendices 1 and 6, respectively. There is separate implementing legislation for Northern Ireland.[2]

---

[1] SI 1993/3053: these Regulations have been amended twice: first by the Commercial Agents (Council Directive) (Amendment) Regulations 1993 (SI 1993/3173) and secondly by the Commercial Agents (Council Directive) (Amendment) Regulations 1998 (SI 1998/2868). The latter amended the provisions of the Regulations dealing with jurisdictional maters following representations from the European Commission. See further ch 4.4.

[2] SR 1993/483.

## 1.2 WHY ARE THE REGULATIONS IMPORTANT?

The Regulations are important because their adoption marked a fundamental change in English law relating to agents. In particular, the Regulations gave the following new rights to agents for the first time:

— a right to compensation or to an indemnity payment when the agreement comes to an end (even where this is as a result of the death, disability or retirement of the agent);
— a right to be paid commission in certain circumstances even where the principal's contract with the customer has not been concluded;
— a right to commission on certain transactions in circumstances where the existing agency agreement does not give the right to commission;
— a right to commission on transactions concluded after the agency agreement has terminated in some cases;
— a right to a written statement of the terms of the agency contract;
— a right to extracts from the principal's books of account to check the amounts of commission due; and
— minimum notice periods on termination of the agency contract.

## 1.3 CONTINUING UNCERTAINTY

As the authors and others predicted, the novel nature of the Directive and of the Regulations, coupled with the lack of effective guidance, has made the process of determining the exact scope of the rights and obligations of agents and principals a long drawn-out and expensive one. Specifically, the exact scope of the definition of 'commercial agent', the basis on which compensation is to be calculated and a host of other issues have all been determined through expensive litigation by the parties involved in individual disputes.

A number of key issues under the Regulations could be said still to be undecided or still to be the subject of uncertainty: examples would be the exact parameters of the indemnity and the definitive position on secondary activities.

As was also predicted at the time of adoption, because the amounts in dispute are often small[3] it has therefore been the case that disputes have not been considered by the appellate courts in more than a handful of cases.

It is undoubtedly the case that the adoption of the Directive and implementation of the Regulations and the consequent uncertainty for principals has resulted in the termination of a large number of agency agreements.

Continuing uncertainty has, in the authors' experience, also resulted in principals deciding to utilise other structures (such as employment of sales personnel) in preference to agency.

---

[3] As will be seen in ch 9, the amount in dispute in the leading case of *Lonsdale v Howard & Hallam* [2007] UKHL 32, was no more than £15,000.

It must be concluded that all of this has had a significant distorting effect on the market and on business: less efficient structures will have been adopted, or agencies may not have been granted at all, where there was concern as to the impact of the Regulations.

## 1.4 TRENDS AND EMERGING ISSUES: DIRECTION OF CASE-LAW

Looking specifically at the UK case-law since the introduction of the Regulations, a few things are immediately apparent.

First, it is clear that, as judges have increasingly become familiar with the concepts introduced by the Directive, and as a firm base of case-law has progressively developed, the courts have become more adept at dealing with these concepts.

A second discernible trend is the increasing importance of the concept of goodwill in the case-law. As will be seen in chapter 9, goodwill is now the touchstone for the calculation of compensation according to the House of Lords in the leading case.[4] Goodwill has also been present in the case-law as a concept in the context of indemnity (unsurprisingly) since 1998[5] and as regards compensation[6] and secondary activities[7] since 2003.

The emergence of the concept of goodwill as perhaps the core concept in UK case-law on commercial agents is surprising for a number of reasons:

(a)  the word 'goodwill' is not used in either the Directive or the Regulations;
(b)  it may be that the origins of references to goodwill are in German law as it is (as will be seen in chapter 10) a key concept in the German law on indemnity. But if this is the origin of references to goodwill, it is questionable whether this concept should have found its way into considerations relevant to compensation. It will also be seen in chapter 9 that the English courts have in a number of cases (and in contrast to the approach taken by the Scots courts) sought to move away from reliance on a review of French law in determining the proper scope of the agent's rights to compensation. If French law is not to be considered in determining the proper parameters of compensation, why is German law any more relevant to a consideration of the Regulations, particularly where compensation is concerned?

There may be a logical conflict between the use of goodwill in the context of determining whether an agent's activities are secondary (see *Gailey v Environmental Waste Controls*[8]) and its use in the context of calculating compensation:

---

[4] *Lonsdale v Howard & Hallam* [2007] UKHL 32.
[5] *Moore v Piretta PTA Limited* [1999] 1 All ER 174.
[6] *Tigana v Decoro* [2003] EWHC 23.
[7] *Gailey v Environmental Waste Controls* [2003] ScotCS 300.
[8] See n 5 above; the court determined whether the agent's activities involve increasing goodwill in the principal's business as part of a consideration of whether or not the agent's activities are secondary.

in *Gailey* the Court saw the schedule to the Regulations as requiring that 'good-will should attach to the sale of the particular goods in question'.[9] This is at best confusing and at worst contradictory: an individual is not a commercial agent for the purposes of the Regulations unless he is engaged in building up good-will in the principal's business, but compensation is based not on the goodwill developed for the principal but on the goodwill which the agent 'possessed in the agency'.[10]

It therefore remains to be seen whether the approach taken by the House of Lords in *Lonsdale v Howard & Hallam*[11] will survive scrutiny should its approach to valuation of the agent's business ever be considered by the European Court of Justice (ECJ). It may, however, be the case that the Court concludes that the details of calculation of compensation or indemnity are matters properly to be determined by the national court.

---

[9] Conversely, in calculating compensation, the court looks at the goodwill built up in the agent's business.

[10] To quote His Honour Judge Harris QC at first instance in *Lonsdale v Howard & Hallam*.

[11] [2007] UKHL 32.

# 2

# The European Dimension

## 2.1 OUTLINE

THIS CHAPTER GIVES a brief outline of the general EU legislative framework, how EU directives in particular are incorporated into the UK legal order and the availability of remedies in the domestic courts for breaches of EU law. More in-depth analysis of the position can be found in the traditional EU law textbooks.

On 1 December 2009, the Lisbon Treaty came into force. The Treaty and its long adoption process has garnered much publicity. It will have wide impact on the development of the EU, most of which is outside the scope of this work. However, one result of the Lisbon Treaty is that the name of the EC Treaty has changed to the Treaty on the Functioning of the European Union (TFEU). Another result is a renumbering of the previous EC Treaty provisions. Thus, the two Treaty articles which form the legal basis for Directive 86/653 have changed from Articles 47 and 94 EC Treaty to Articles 53 and 115 TFEU, respectively. It should also be noted that the European Court of Justice will be known as the Court of Justice of the European Union and the previously named Court of First Instance will be known as the General Court. The TFEU article governing preliminary references is now Article 267.

## 2.2 THE SCOPE OF THE EUROPEAN DIMENSION

In these days of constantly changing boundaries, one can be forgiven for not being completely sure of what exactly the European dimension comprises.

At the time of writing, the EU comprises 27 Member States: Austria, Belgium, Bulgaria, the Czech Republic, Cyprus, Denmark, Estonia, Finland, France, Germany, Greece, Hungary, Ireland, Italy, Latvia, Lithuania, Luxembourg, Malta, the Netherlands, Poland, Portugal, Romania, the Slovak Republic, Slovenia, Spain, Sweden and the UK. However, the *acquis communautaire* or the established law of the European Union covers more than just the 27 Member States. Under the terms of the Agreement on the European Economic Area (EEA), which came into force on 1 January 1994, many of the legislative provisions of the European Community are to be binding upon the parties to the Agreement. Aside from the EU Member States, Iceland, Liechtenstein and Norway are parties to the Agreement. The effect of the Agreement is that many EU provisions will now be applicable in the countries and the Directive is one of them—see Annex VII.E of the Agreement on the European Economic Area, where the Directive is specifically described as being applicable in the EEA states. Switzerland is a party to the European Free Trade Agreement (EFTA), but voted against joining the EEA. Its relations with the EU are governed by a bilateral agreement and in particular the provisions of the Directive are applicable.[1]

## 2.3 OVERVIEW OF THE COMMUNITY LEGISLATIVE ORDER

There are three forms of binding Community legislation: regulations, decisions and directives.

### 1. Regulations

Regulations have general application, are binding in their entirety and are directly applicable in all Member States: see Article 288 TFEU (formerly Article 249 EC Treaty). They thus become law in the Member States without any need for implementation by the national legislatures.

Regulations may be of direct effect. This means that they may confer rights on individuals which the national courts must protect, but this will depend on whether the particular provisions relied upon are sufficiently precise and unconditional.

### 2. Decisions

Decisions are binding in their entirety upon those to whom they are addressed: see Article 288 TFEU. They are not intended to have general application but are directed at specific Member States or specific undertakings.

Decisions may be of direct effect if unconditional and sufficiently precise. Those who may take advantage of this will be not only those to whom the decision is addressed but also those affected by the decision: see Case 9/70: *Grad v Finanzamt Traunstein* [1970] ECR 825.[2] Where a decision is addressed to a

---

[1] See Annex III.E.28 of the Agreement between the European Community and the Swiss Confederation on the free movement of persons: OJ [2002] L114/6: 30 April 2002.

[2] See most recently in this connection, Case C-18/08: *Foselev Sud-Ouest SARL v Administration des Douanes et Droits Indirects* [2009] 1 CMLR 30; see also as regards the direct effect of decisions, the Opinion of AG Trstenjak in Case C-80/06: *Carp Snc di L Moleri e V Corsi v Ecorad Srl* [2007] ECR I-4473 at points 55 et seq.

Member State, the same considerations, relevant to directives and set out below, will apply.

## 3. Directives

Directives are binding as to the result to be achieved, on each Member State to which they are addressed, but they leave to the national authorities the choice of form and methods: see Article 288 TFEU. They therefore do not have to be addressed to every Member State, but if they are, they must now be published in the Official Journal: Article 297(2) TFEU—this provision merely translated what was long-standing practice into a formal duty. Usually Member States are given a specified period within which to implement the provisions of any given directive. Thus, most Member States were given until 1 January 1990 to implement the Directive, whilst the UK and Ireland were given until 1 January 1994 to implement it because of the substantial difference between the existing common law position in those countries and the new regime imposed by the Directive.

The issue of direct effect of directives is more complex than for regulations, but should be examined because agents and principals may have rights pursuant to the Directive which must be safeguarded by the national courts. The reason for this complexity is that all directives are addressed to Member States and therefore it might be assumed that the issue of direct effect does not arise. However, the Court of Justice of the European Union has made clear that directives can be relied upon by individuals before the national courts in certain situations and that, in any event, domestic legislation must be interpreted in the light of the relevant provisions of an applicable directive, thereby giving rise to the indirect direct effect of those provisions[3]. However, that exercise is not without restriction. The national courts are required to act by way of interpretation not rewriting; accordingly, the national courts are not required to impose an artificial or strained interpretation of national law.[4] If they need to, national courts will disapply the provisions of the incompatible national law. Thus, in the present context, agents and principals may have rights arising from the provisions of Directive 86/653 which can be safeguarded in national courts through the mechanism of direct effect.

The general principle is that directives may have direct effect but only in certain respects. In other words, restrictions have been placed on the direct effect of directives, which are not present for regulations. For example, directives are not

---

[3] See eg Joined Cases C-397/01 to C-403/01: *Pfeiffer* [2004] ECR I-8835; Joined Cases C-378/07 to C-380/07: *Angelidaki*—judgment of 23 April 2009 [2009] 3 CMLR 15. The same position has been taken by the Court of Justice of the European Union in the context of Directive 86/653—see case C-456/98: *Centrosteel Srl* [2000] ECR I-6007.

[4] See in this connection the remarks of AG Sharpston in Case C-432/05: *Unibet* [2007] ECR I-2271 at para 55, as accepted by Blair J in *Wilkinson v Fitzgerald & Others* [2009] 3 CMLR 33 at para 65.

capable of being directly effective between individuals.[5] The only rights which may be relied upon are those which an individual has against the Member State (or an emanation of that state) in question. The Member State in this context can be acting as employer or public authority.[6] Further, in order for an individual to be able to rely on a directive or individual provisions therein, the time-limit for implementation of the directive must have expired without the full and correct implementation of that directive.[7] Finally, it should be noted that, as with regulations, the provisions relied upon in a directive must be sufficiently precise and unconditional if they are to be directly effective.

Even where provisions in a directive are not directly effective or the question of direct effect does not arise, national courts must still interpret the national law implementing the directive in question in conformity with the terms of the directive implemented.[8] This is so even where the national implementing legislation was adopted prior to the directive in question.[9] The House of Lords has confirmed that, although this concept was confined to legislation and could not be extended to cover contracts made between individuals, nonetheless as a matter of English domestic law, national courts were obliged to interpret such agreements in the light of the relevant directive.[10]

## 2.4 INCORPORATION OF COMMUNITY LAW INTO THE UK LEGAL ORDER

The EEC Treaty, as it was called then, was incorporated into UK domestic law by the European Communities Act 1972. This Act came into force on 1 January 1973. Section 2(1) of the Act provides:

> All such rights, powers, liabilities, obligations and restrictions from time to time created or arising by or under the Treaties, and all such remedies and procedures from time to time provided for by or under the Treaties, as in accordance with the Treaties are without further enactment to be given legal effect or used in the UK shall be recognised and available in law, and be enforced, allowed and followed accordingly; and the expression 'enforceable Community right' and similar expressions shall be read as referring to one to which this sub-section applies.

The above provision should be read together with section 2(4) of the Act, which makes it clear that in the event of a conflict between domestic and EU law, the latter should take precedence. Thus, the doctrine of the supremacy of Commu-

---

[5] See eg Case 152/84: *Marshall v Southampton South West Hampshire Area Health Authority* [1986] ECR 723 and Case C-201/02: *Wells v Secretary of State for Transport, Local Government and the Regions* [2004] ECR I-723.

[6] See Case C-188/89: *Foster & Ors v British Gas plc* [1990] ECR I-3313.

[7] See Case 148/78: *Publico Ministero v Ratti* [1979] ECR 1629.

[8] See Case 14/83: *Von Colson & Kamann v Land Nordrhein-Westfalen* [1984] ECR 1891.

[9] See Case C-106/89: *Marleasing v La Comercial Internacional* [1990] ECR I-4135.

[10] See *White v White and the Motor Insurers' Bureau* [2001] 1 WLR 481. This case has been reviewed by Flaux J in *Byrne v. MIB and Others* [2007] QB 66.

nity law is enshrined in the UK legal order. In practice, this means that if the national provisions implementing the Directive conflict with those of the Directive itself, the national implementing provisions are to be ignored in favour of the Directive's provisions.

### 2.5 OVERVIEW OF REMEDIES AVAILABLE UNDER COMMUNITY LAW

Although the doctrine of direct effect provides that individuals may rely on Community rights before the national courts, the specific remedies available to enforce those rights are not prescribed by EU law. This is because the Court of Justice of the European Union has taken the view that in general the remedies to be available in the national courts are for the laws of the particular Member States to determine.[11]

The Court of Justice of the European Union has, however, stressed the need for effective remedies at the national level in order to protect Community law rights.[12] It has also held that, as a matter of EU law, Member States may be required to compensate individuals for damage caused by an infringement of Community law for which the Member State is responsible.[13]

In so far as the UK is concerned, the position is as follows: a distinction has been drawn by the courts between private and public law remedies.

### 1. Private Law Remedies

In terms of private law claims, damages are available for breach of a directly effective provision of Community law, the cause of action generally being treated as a breach of statutory duty.[14] It follows under English procedural law that, where such actions are brought, injunctions may also be sought and granted where damages will not be an adequate remedy.[15]

---

[11] Case 33/76: *Rewe-Zentralfinanz eG & Rewe-Zentral AG v Landwirtschaftskammer für das Saarland* [1976] ECR 1989.

[12] Case C-213/89: *R v Secretary of State for Transport, ex parte Factortame* [1990] ECR I-2433.

[13] Cases C-6/90 and C-9/90: *Francovich, Bonifaci & Ors v Italy* [1991] ECR I-5357. In the case of *Byrne*, the English Court of Appeal held that the relevant criteria had been met and that therefore the UK was liable in damages to the claimant.

[14] *Garden Cottage Foods v Milk Marketing Board* [1984] AC 130. See also the judgment of the Court of Justice of the European Union in Case C-453/99: *Courage v Creehan* [2001] ECR I-6297.

[15] *Cutsforth v Mansfield Inns Ltd* [1986] 1 WLR 558.

## 2. Public Law Remedies

In so far as concerns remedies for breach of EU law by a Member State or an emanation thereof, the Court of Justice of the European Union has laid down the following guidelines:

— Liability for loss and damage caused to individuals as a result of breaches of Community law attributable to a national public authority constitutes a principle inherent in the system of the EC Treaty which gives rise to obligations on the part of the Member States.
— It is for each Member State to ensure that individuals obtain reparation for loss and damage caused to them by non-compliance with EU law, whichever public authority is responsible for the breach and whichever public authority is in principle, under the law of the Member State concerned, responsible for making reparation.[16]
— In order for a Member State to be required to make reparation for loss and damage caused to individuals as a result of breaches of EU law for which that Member State can be held responsible, three conditions must be met: the rule of law infringed must have been intended to confer rights on individuals; the breach must have been sufficiently serious; and there must be a direct causal link between the breach and the loss or damage sustained.[17]

The House of Lords applied these guidelines when finding that the UK was liable in damages to a number of foreign, mainly Spanish, fishermen for breaches of their fundamental Community law rights.[18]

### 2.6 RIGHTS AGAINST THE UK FOR FAILURE TO IMPLEMENT CORRECTLY THE DIRECTIVE

Despite the fact that the *Francovich* case was concerned with the total failure of a Member State to implement a directive, it is clear that its findings are relevant to a situation in which a Member State has failed to implement correctly a given directive. If an individual can show that criteria referred to above are met, then in principle, damages would be available.

It should be noted that no action has been taken by the Commission against the UK for failure to implement the Directive properly. This does not mean that such action could not arise in the future, especially if the national courts were to interpret provisions such as those relating to secondary activities in a way which could be considered to be incompatible with the provisions of the Directive.[19]

---

[16] See Case C-302/97: *Konle v Austria* [1999] ECR I-3099.
[17] See Joined Cases C-46/93 and C-48/93: *Brasserie du Pecheur and Factortame* [1996] ECR I-1029.
[18] See *R v Secretary of State for Transport, ex parte Factortame and Others* [2000] EuLR 40.
[19] However, this is thought unlikely in the light of the examination of that particular issue by the English High Court in *Crane v Sky In-Home Service Ltd* [2007] 2 All ER (Comm) 599.

It should also be noted that, following Commission intervention, the domestic legislation implementing the Directive was amended in so far as its scope was concerned.[20]

---

[20] See ch 4.

# 3

# Development of the Directive and the Regulations

## 3.1 INTRODUCTION: WHY CONSIDER THE DRAFTING PROCESS?

T HIS CHAPTER TRACES the drafting and development of the Directive up to the time of its adoption, and then looks at ministerial thinking and the drafting of the Regulations following adoption of the Directive. This account is included because it may be of assistance to practitioners and others in understanding why certain provisions are included in the Regulations and why they are phrased as they are. As a note of caution, however, although the courts will look to drafts of the Directive to interpret its spirit and purpose, the English courts are not generally entitled to look at drafts or other documents which form part of the domestic legislative drafting process.

## 3.2 THE LEGISLATIVE BACKGROUND TO THE DIRECTIVE

At first sight, the need to analyse the legislative background to the Directive might not seem readily apparent. We are, after all, concerned with the finished Directive. Why is it necessary to look at the early proposals and previous drafts? The need to do so becomes clear once the way in which Community law is interpreted is understood.

Community law is interpreted in a contextual and purposive way, rather than literally. The reason for this is twofold. First, because Community legislation is published and equally authentic in all the official languages of the EU (23 at present) and because translation is not an exact science, variations arise. It is essential in such cases that courts have the possibility to interpret the law freely rather than be tied to the literal interpretation of the text. Secondly, much EU legislation is expressed in less specific terms than would be the case normally with UK legislation.[1]

---

[1] In the case of *King v Tunnock* [2000] EuLR 531, the Inner House of the Scottish Court of Session described some of the drafting of the Directive to be 'in the eyes of UK lawyers . . . at the best somewhat clumsy'.

Because of the lack of specificity, it is essential that the courts are able to reach their decisions on particular interpretations using as wide a basis as possible. The European courts defined the way in which EU law should be interpreted as follows:

> [E]very provision of Community law must be placed in its context and interpreted in the light of the provisions of Community law as a whole, regard being had to the objectives thereof and to its state of evolution at the date on which the provision in question is to be applied.[2]

In placing the Directive in its context and in order to have regard to its objectives, an examination of inter alia the proposals and drafts of the Directive should therefore be undertaken. An in-depth analysis of individual provisions in the proposals and drafts will not be carried out here but rather in the relevant parts of chapters 5–9 inclusive, where they can be analysed in conjunction with the relevant provisions of the Directive as adopted.

## 3.3 THE LEGISLATIVE CHRONOLOGY OF THE DIRECTIVE

The first formal proposal made by the Commission for a directive co-ordinating the laws of the Member States relating to self-employed commercial agents was submitted to the Council of Ministers on 17 December 1976. To this proposal was appended a very useful Explanatory Memorandum from the European Commission. Despite the fact that the adopted Directive has changed markedly since this initial first formal proposal, the Explanatory Memorandum is still of assistance in interpreting the more general aspects of the present Directive. Thus, for example, the Memorandum contrasts commercial agents with salaried or wage-earning commercial travellers; it makes clear that the eventual Directive should apply to situations not only including two or more Member States, but also to those involving only a single Member State; it also states that the eventual Directive should be seen in effect as a codification of the law. A copy of this document is given in Appendix 4, appearing as an Annex to the Law Commission Report.

This proposal was then submitted by the Council to the Economic and Social Committee on 11 January 1977 for its opinion. This body has advisory status and, pursuant to the then EC Treaty, the Council had to seek its opinion on, for example, matters relating to internal market harmonisation measures, of which the Directive was one. The Committee consists of representatives of the various categories of economic and social activity (Article 257 of the TFEU—formerly Article 193). In practice, it consists of three groups: employers, workers and others. The Committee issued its opinion on the Commission's proposals on 24 November 1977.[3]

---

[2] Case 283/81: *CILFIT v Italian Ministry of Health* [1982] ECR 3415, 3430.
[3] [1978] OJ C59/31.

The Commission proposal was also submitted to the European Parliament for its opinion. This opinion was delivered and subsequently published on 9 October 1978.[4]

Despite the fact that the Parliament's opinion is also advisory, it has more power to affect proposed legislation than the Economic and Social Committee. This difference in importance can be seen by the fact that the Commission amended its original proposal to take into account more of the Parliament's suggested amendments[5] than those of the Economic and Social Committee.

The Commission's amended proposal was submitted to the Council on 29 January 1979. Thus, up to this stage, the legislative process had taken just over two years.

This momentum was then lost, for there was then a wait of nearly eight years before the final text was published as Council Directive 86/653 on 31 December 1986. Although the authors have not had sight of the Council Minutes, it is clear that most of this delay can be attributed to the fact that the Member States were not agreed on the draft Directive and that as this period was prior to the Single European Act the differences could not be dealt with by qualified majority voting.

## 3.4 THE 1977 HOUSE OF LORDS SELECT COMMITTEE REPORT (APPENDIX 5)

As will have been noted above, the original Commission proposal for a directive concerning commercial agents was submitted to the Council at the end of 1976. It was thus from that time that the Member States, which comprise the Council, first became formally aware of the Commission's proposal. It is therefore not surprising that soon thereafter came the first response from the UK in the form of a House of Lords Select Committee Report dated 27 July 1977. The purpose of the Report was to determine whether there was any justification in principle for introducing such a directive at all. The conclusion of the Select Committee was that there was no such justification. In particular, and based on evidence which had been presented to it, the Committee found there was a 'variegated pattern of agencies' in the UK and that there was no justification to impose a single body of inflexible legal rules, such as those contained in the Directive, on such a pattern. The Committee felt that a better solution would be to provide flexibility which would enable the parties to an agency contract to arrange terms which suited their respective needs. The Committee was further of the view that if rules favouring commercial agents were imposed, then principals would find other means of selling.[6] The Committee concluded by stating that it noted with concern a tendency by the Commission to interfere, in ways which

---

[4] [1978] OJ C239/17.
[5] [1979] OJ C56/5.
[6] A proposition which has indeed been borne out by the facts—as noted in ch 1.

were not altogether judicious, with particular segments of the national legal systems. Such systems, or the segments thereof, had not come into existence by accident; rather they had arisen from the local circumstances, habits and sentiments of the people. Changes thereto should, in the Committee's opinion, only be effected with care and where real need was demonstrated.

## 3.5 THE 1977 LAW COMMISSION REPORT

Following swiftly on from the above-mentioned House of Lords Select Committee Report, the Law Commission reported on the Commission's proposal in October 1977. The Report is not only of interest in so far as it comments on the draft Directive, but also in so far as concerns its annexes, which comprise the draft itself, the Commission's Explanatory Memorandum thereto,[7] and a copy of the 1953 German law and the Report provisions which were at the basis of much of the Commission's proposal. These annexes, together with the Report, are reproduced at the end of this book (Appendix 4).

As to the Law Commission's views on the Commission's proposal, perhaps unsurprisingly they do not differ markedly from those expressed by the House of Lords Select Committee. However, it does produce a very useful synthesis of German law and its links to the Directive. The main findings of the Law Commission were as follows:

— The proposed legislation was intra vires the EC Treaty, in that it was possible to contend that differences in the laws of the Member States relating to commercial agents did affect the functioning of the Common Market in that they inhibited the commercial agent's freedom of establishment within the Community and could interfere with the agent's freedom of movement of goods and services between Member States.
— The term 'commercial agent' had no precise connotation in English law; it did not represent a category of persons who had a common legal characteristic.
— The provisions of the proposed Directive were clearly based on German commercial law and in particular on sections 84–92c of the German Commercial Code; those sections related to a special category of agent who had to perform certain functions permanently in commerce and for a principal who had to be a standing client; the same sections made clear that a commercial agent was identifiable as a member of a particular social group with special social and economic needs—he was apparently a quasi-employee who, whilst retaining some independence, was substantially dependent on his principal and therefore required protection.
— The goodwill indemnity provisions in the draft Directive reflected similar provisions in the German Commercial Code and were intended to compensate the agent for the fact that as a rule the agent's work increased the goodwill

---

[7] Referred to in s 3.3 above.

of the principal and not that of the agent and that on termination of the agency, the principal derived a benefit from the accrued goodwill whilst the agent suffered a corresponding loss; as to this indemnity payment, the Law Commission stated that 'it is difficult to see why in general the agent should receive a payment, for which he has not bargained, when the contract terminates. This is particularly so where the agency contract is for a fixed period and makes no provision for such a payment.'

— The proposed Directive would not remove the uncertainties that existed over the content of commercial agents' rights; rather, the proposal was likely to create uncertainty whenever there was a conflict between the provisions of the Directive and what the parties had in fact agreed. The recurring theme was that even if the policy behind the proposal was sound, which was doubtful, its provisions were likely to produce great uncertainty across a very wide area.[8]

— The proposed rules were full of uncertainties, gaps and inconsistencies and in many respects offended against basic principles of the English law of agency; the provisions depended for their operation on a corpus of law which was not stated in the Directive and their introduction would necessitate the distortion of the common law of agency and of other areas of commercial law.

Overall then, it can be seen that the UK establishment was not in favour of the Commission's proposal. However, as with many things, such opposition was not sufficient to block the proposal; all it did was delay it for over ten years.

## 3.6 THE DTI GUIDANCE NOTES

After the Directive was published on 31 December 1986, at least two important Guidance Notes were put out by the Department of Trade and Industry (DTI) describing the provisions and indicating the UK government's position on their implementation into domestic law. Although such Guidance Notes are not binding, they are of interest to practitioners. To that end, the two most important Notes—those published in July 1987 and in 1994—appear at the end of this book in Appendices 2 and 3. A brief overview of the 1987 Guidance Notes will be given below. In so far as concerns the 1994 Guidance Notes, these will be referred to in later chapters when specific provisions are being analysed.

It could have been expected, given the relatively prompt production of the Notes, that a draft of the Regulations would have been available in 1988, allowing a substantial period for consultation and redrafting, but a first draft was not available for public comment until May 1990. No doubt submissions were received following the publication of the Notes, but details of those responses have not been published.

---

[8] In this at least, the Law Commission has been proved to be correct, as an increasing number of frustrated practitioners can testify.

### 3.7 EFFECT OF THE DELAY

As already mentioned, the Directive is unclear in several important respects, and the DTI noted the fundamental changes in the English law of agency which would result from implementation of the Directive. Although the DTI subsequently advised against acting on the basis of drafts (*Financial Times*, 15 December 1993), given the effective retrospectivity of the Regulations in various respects, it was inevitable that from the moment the Directive was adopted (or before that time), well-briefed clients and their advisers would be actively considering the terms of the Directive and its likely effect both in making the decisions considered in chapter 1 and in determining the likely costs of termination of agency relationships.

Given this, it is unfortunate that the time between the publication of the 1987 Note and the making of the Regulations themselves—a period of almost six and a half years—was not used to finalise the form of the Regulations and to implement them well in advance of the 1 January 1994 deadline with a long transitional period, so as to give principals and agents ample time to adjust their relations and to take the Regulations into account. It is likely that much of the uncertainty and ensuing litigation which resulted from the late introduction of the Regulations would have been avoided had this course been adopted. In the event, the Regulations were made on 7 December 1993 and laid before Parliament on the following day, a period of only three weeks before the date when they would apply to all new and existing agency agreements.

### 3.8 THE 1987 EXPLANATORY AND CONSULTATIVE NOTE

Much of the 1987 Note consists of a description of the terms of the Directive and this is not repeated here. However, section C of the Note is of interest as it considers the various options allowed to Member States by the Directive, these being as follows:

— Article 2(2) allows Members States to exclude from the scope of the Regulations persons whose activities are deemed by national law to be 'secondary'. The DTI noted that there was not yet any such definition in UK law but that it was the government's intention to define and exclude such activities. Paragraph 51 of the Note stated that individuals whose activities as commercial agent were not their primary 'business' occupation and also individuals who sell from mail-order catalogues were to be excluded. Although the Regulations deal expressly with the latter (see paragraph 5 of the Schedule) the remainder of the Schedule to the Regulations takes a different tack in that it looks at the purpose of the arrangement between agent and principal, rather than business activities as a whole.

— Article 4(3) deals with the obligation on the principal to communicate with the agent regarding transactions procured by the latter. The Directive did not provide a specific option here, but the DTI noted that the government did not intend to stipulate that the principal must inform the agent of the execution of commercial transactions.

— Article 7(2) (right to commissions where the agent is either entrusted with or has an exclusive right to a specific geographical area or group of customers): the DTI noted that the government's initial preference was for the latter and the Regulations mirror this choice.

— Article 13(2): Member States are entitled pursuant to the Directive to provide that an agency contract is not valid unless evidenced in writing. The DTI invited comments from interested parties, but was clearly not inclined to stipulate that agency contracts must be in writing. In fact, this provision of the Directive is something of an oddity since questions as to the validity of the agency contract are most likely to arise when the agent wishes to claim compensation on termination; given that the purpose of the Directive is to protect agents, it is noteworthy that this provision of the Directive seems likely (where adopted by Member States) to operate against the agent's interests.

— Article 15(3) (minimum periods of notice): Member States were entitled to provide that in the fourth, fifth and sixth years, the minimum notice period would be four, five and six months, respectively. The DTI noted that the government did not propose to take up this option since the three-month notice period would be sufficient. It would be open to the parties to agree longer periods if they wished to do so. Although the sufficiency of the three-month notice period is not questioned, it could be considered that the DTI's logic is somewhat flawed in that the whole purpose of much of the Directive is to override any written agreement on certain matters which might be made between principal and agent.

— Article 15(4) stipulates that where longer notice periods are agreed, the notice period for the agent must not be longer than that for the principal. In fact there may be very good commercial reasons why the principal requires longer notice from the agent than he is required to give: for instance, in distant markets or in areas where consents and registrations are necessary for a new agent, the principal may require some time to find a suitable replacement agent and to deal with any necessary formalities. The same logic does not necessarily apply where the principal wishes to dispense with the agent's services: he may already have identified a suitable individual and started the necessary registration processes.

— Article 17 (the choice between the indemnity and compensation routes upon termination of the agency contract): the DTI noted that 'Member States are required to include one of these options in their implementing legislation.' The Note stated that the government favoured the compensatory route, but the Regulations in fact allow the parties to choose the indemnity route in their agreement and this possibility was only added in the final version of the draft Regulations.

— Article 17(2)(a), indent 2: this entitles Member States to provide that the application or otherwise of a restraint-of-trade clause could be taken into account in deciding whether the payment of an indemnity was equitable. Again, the DTI merely requested views from interested parties. Although the indemnity option was subsequently incorporated in the Regulations, this option was never specifically included. There is, however, nothing in the Regulations which prevents a court taking this issue into account in deciding what is equitable.

These comments were largely confirmed by a minister in response to a question raised in the House of Commons in 1989 (*Hansard*, 15 March 1989, question answered by Humphrey Atkins, Chancellor of the Duchy of Lancaster). The minister also made it clear that the Regulations would not be made before 1992.

## 3.9 THE FIRST DRAFT OF THE REGULATIONS

Whilst it is not proposed to go through every provision of each of the drafts, there are interesting differences reflecting changes in thinking and approach between the two drafts and the Regulations, and some of these are explored below:

— The draft contained a definition of 'quarter' for the purposes of payment of commission under what is now Regulation 10(3), but the final form of the Regulations leaves it to the parties to determine the start and finish dates of quarters.
— There was a lengthy list of individuals who would not be considered to be commercial agents for the purposes of the Regulations. Secondary activities were described briefly in paragraph 2 (compare the tortuous provisions of the Schedule in the Regulations). Bizarrely, the first draft excluded from the definition of commercial agents persons who were wholly involved in other activities! The question of the territorial application of the Regulations and its interaction with choice of governing law and jurisdiction is a difficult issue, as can be seen from chapter 4. The first draft merely stated that the Regulations would apply to any agency contract whose applicable law was the law of England and Wales or Scotland and that the Regulations could apply to protect agents not established in a Member State if the parties so agreed.[9]
— The draft attempted to recast the duties of principal and agent as set out in Articles 3 and 4 of the Directive.
— Paragraph 7 stated that the question of whether there was customary remuneration in the absence of an agreement on commission was to be tested both in the area in which the commercial agent operates and in the area in which his office is situated.
— Transactions on which commission is due: the first draft omitted the wording

---

[9] This issue has now been the subject of an amendment to the Regulations and case-law—see ch 4.

from Article 7(1)(a) of the Directive regarding 'concluded as a result of his action' and replaced this with the words 'conclusion of the transaction was effectively caused by the act of the commercial agent'.

— The draft omitted the words 'as soon as and to the extent that' in Article 10 of the Directive: those words suggest that, where the contract between principal and third party requires delivery/payment by instalments, commission will also be payable by instalments.

— The draft replaced the word 'executed' which appears in Articles 10 and 11 of the Directive with the expression 'carried out', which is no clearer.

— One of the most fascinating elements of the draft is paragraph 14. Chapter 8 deals with the question of the extent to which the provisions of Articles 7–10 are mandatory or non-mandatory, but (contrary to the view of most writers on the subject and the DTI's own Guidance Note published in 1994), paragraph 14 stated that a term would be void insofar as it conflicted with paragraphs 11–13 (ie in its entirety)—these are the provisions mirroring Articles 10–12. Neither the Regulations nor the second draft make any reference to this issue.

— Compensation: paragraph 18 of the first draft differs in several important respects from the relevant provisions of Article 17 of the Directive. The problematic expression 'compensation for . . . damage' from the Directive was replaced with the words '[compensation] . . . for losses, liabilities, costs and expenses' which the agent has incurred. The difficulties raised by the former expression are referred to in chapter 9.

— Similarly, as regards the second paragraph and indents in Article 17(3), rather than being stated to be circumstances in which damage will be deemed to have occurred particularly, the draft stated that 'in particular the compensation shall take into account' the matters set out in those indents, but the indented expressions themselves are not faithfully reproduced, these amendments being an attempt to clarify words and expressions in the Directive which were of uncertain meaning.

— The draft did not reproduce faithfully the provisions of Article 18 of the Directive, attempting instead to state the situations in which compensation would be payable.

— The Directive's reference to default justifying immediate termination became a reference to breach entitling the principal to terminate under the general law, and rather than merely referring to the death of the agent, referred to frustration of the contract including the agent's death.

— Restraint of trade: this was more narrowly defined in the first draft and extended only to a clause in an agreement restricting the right of a commercial agent to act as a commercial agent following termination, whereas the Directive refers to an agreement restricting the business activities of a commercial agent. In addition, paragraph 19(b) of the first draft is not reflected in the Regulations—this stated that a restraint-of-trade clause would be valid only if it was reasonable from the point of view of the principal and the commercial agent and their common customers—perhaps an (inaccurate) attempt to summarise the English law on restraint of trade generally. In any event, the Directive and the Regulations state that other rules of national law which impose restrictions on the validity of restraint-of-trade clauses are unaffected. Therefore, even though a two-year covenant may be non-problematic from the point of view of the Directive and the Regulations, if it would be void by reason of the restraint-of-trade doctrine, then the relevant provisions of the Regulations and the Directive will not save it.

In almost all cases, the Regulations have reverted to the wording from the Directive, leaving it to the courts to determine the meaning of these words at the expense of litigants. This is one of the particular reasons why uncertainty is likely to persist notwithstanding the making of the Regulations and the DTI's Guidance Note.

The authors' view is that the DTI was discouraged from attempting to clarify the position by the *Francovich* decision referred to in chapter 2. Since it is established that in certain circumstances a failure to implement, or to implement properly, a directive can result in liability upon the Member State concerned, the DTI may have decided that the risk of such actions would be reduced as much as possible by merely reflecting the wording of the Directive in the Regulations.

The danger is, however, that in so far as the English courts determine the meaning of unclear expressions in the Regulations and this diverges from any subsequent interpretation by the European Court of Justice, the government is likely to be held to have failed to implement correctly in any event and will therefore be open, arguably, to actions based upon the *Francovich* principle. The authors suggest that it would have been advisable for the DTI to conduct detailed discussions with the Commission with a view to ascertaining the Commission's view and minimising this risk. Whether such discussions took place is not known.

## 3.10 THE SECOND DRAFT OF THE REGULATIONS

This was issued under cover of a letter of 4 June 1993. The covering letter stated that the second draft took into account comments received during the initial consultation. The reason for the delay in excess of three years in producing this revised draft is not clear, but whereas the period for consultation on the first draft was in excess of seven months, the consultation period on the second draft only lasted just over seven weeks.

The principal features of the second draft were as follows:

— The definition of commercial agent expressly excluded the agent who acted as agent in respect of services, but it was not clear from the draft whether this would exclude agents who acted as agent in respect of any services whatsoever, or would only exclude the services element of the contract.

— Definitions of 'agency contract', 'commission', 'goods', 'quarter' and 'restraint of trade clause' were included. Only definitions of 'commission' and 'restraint of trade clause' have survived into the Regulations. The definition of goods was different from that in the first draft, but the reason for this is not clear.
— Governing law and jurisdiction: paragraph 3 of the first draft was deleted and replaced with a simple statement that the Regulations extend to Great Britain (compare Regulations 1(2) and 1(3)). In addition, a new paragraph 23 was added, stating that where the agreement did not require the agent to carry on any activity on behalf of his principal within the EC, the Regulations would not apply unless the parties agreed otherwise. This seemed to be a logical compromise between the government's clear antipathy towards the Directive and the aim of harmonising UK laws with the laws of other Member States. Paragraph 23 does not appear in the Regulations.
— Derogation: paragraph 5 was new and set out in detail those provisions from which derogation was not permitted. It stated that terms which were inconsistent with paragraph 3 and 4 (duties of principal and agent) would be void and that certain other provisions could not be excluded, varied or restricted to the detriment of the agent. Although the list of such provisions is unsurprising in itself, it provides a pointer to the question (discussed in chapter 8) of the ability to exclude, for instance, the terms of Articles 7 and 8 of the Directive. Certainly, the suggestion in the second draft is that Articles 7 and 8 are capable of exclusion. Article 5 is also relevant to the question of the status of inconsistent terms.
— Paragraph 12 included a definition of 'books and papers' in connection with the agent's rights to review the principal's records.
— Paragraphs 21 and 22 of the second draft were completely new. Paragraph 21 stated that a contract could be entered into before 1 January 'in terms which are in accordance with these Regulations' (presumably entitling the parties to incorporate the Regulations into their contract even before the implementation date), stating that nothing in the Regulations would affect the rights and liabilities of an agent or principal which had accrued before 1 January 1994 (but seemingly leaving it open to a court to calculate the notice period by reference to the total duration of the contract and to look to the period before 1 January in calculating compensation). Paragraph 21 also stated that the Regulations would apply after 1 January 1994 to a contract made before that date and that accordingly provisions which were less favourable than the mandatory provisions of the second draft were to be read as if they were in accordance with the appropriate Regulation or if they could not be so read would be void.

As with the first draft, the Regulations largely forsake the novel provisions of the second draft in favour of tracking the wording of the Directive.

### 3.11 COMPLIANCE COST ASSESSMENT, PERCEIVED EFFECT ON BUSINESS AND LIKELY COSTS

The DTI produced the required compliance cost assessment as part of the production of the Regulations.

In the earlier editions of this work, the authors pointed out some gaps and inconsistencies, particularly in DTI's assessment of likely costs. However, these have now all been overtaken by reality. The authors' view is that the uncertainty and consequent legal costs caused by the lack of clarity or guidance surrounding the questions of compensation or indemnity (which was only resolved as regards compensation in the *Lonsdale* case)[10] have resulted in significant costs to business. In addition, the uncertainty has led to distortion of markets as principals favour distribution strategies less efficient than agency out of fear of the potential cost of compensation and this must inevitably have had (perhaps continues to have) a cost for the economy.

---

[10] [2007] 1 WLR 2055.

# 4

# Choice of Law and Scope
# of the Regulations

## 4.1 OUTLINE

MANY COMMERCIAL AGENCY agreements are either oral or very brief. As such, there is often no express agreement between the principal and commercial agent in relation to the law governing the contract. This chapter will set out briefly the relevant legislation which will have to be examined on a case-by-case basis in order to determine, in cases where there has been no express provision as to applicable law, what that law is. For more detailed treatment, reference should be made to one of the standard works listed in the bibliography. This work assumes, except where specifically stated to the contrary, that the courts of England and Wales have jurisdiction.

This chapter will also examine the scope of the Regulations. For example: what is the position of an agent carrying out activities not only in Great Britain but also in other EU Member States? Do the Regulations apply to agents whose activities are carried on entirely outside the EU? What is the position of an agent who is established in the UK but whose activities are carried on outside of the UK or the EU?

## 4.2 APPLICABLE LAW

Regulation (EC) No 593/2008 of the European Parliament and of the Council of Ministers dated 17 June 2008 came into force on 17 December 2009.[1] It replaces the 1980 Rome Convention on the law applicable to contractual obligations ('the Rome Convention'), which was ratified by the UK pursuant to the Contracts (Applicable Law) Act 1990, and applies to contracts (including those between a principal and commercial agent) concluded as from 17 December 2009 ('relevant contracts'). The domestic statutory instrument disapplying the Rome Convention in relation to England, Wales and Northern Ireland and applying the provisions

---

[1] [2008] OJ L177/6.

of Regulation (EC) 593/2008 as regards relevant contracts is the Law Applicable to Contractual Obligations (England and Wales and Northern Ireland) Regulations 2009.[2] Given that many commercial agency contracts concluded before 17 December 2009 will still be effective as at the date of publication of this work, relevant extracts of both the Rome Convention and Regulation (EC) No 593/2008 will be set out below.

Article 3.1 of the Rome Convention provides that

> [a] contract shall be governed by the law chosen by the parties. The choice must be demonstrated with reasonable certainty by the terms of the contract or the circumstances of the case. By their choice the parties can select the law applicable to the whole or a part only of the contract.

This provision demonstrates the importance given to the parties' express choice of applicable law. However, that importance is tempered by Article 3.3, which provides that

> [t]he fact that the parties have chosen a foreign law, whether or not accompanied by the choice of a foreign tribunal, shall not, where all the other elements relevant to the situation at the time of the choice are connected with one country only, prejudice the application of rules of the law of that country which cannot be derogated from by contract, hereinafter called 'mandatory rules'.

The principle behind Article 3.3 of the Rome Convention has been used, implicitly at least, to disapply express choice-of-law provisions in two cases involving commercial agents. In the first, *Ingmar*,[3] the then ECJ held that provisions in Directive 86/653 relating to a commercial agent's right to post-termination indemnity or compensation were applicable even though the agreement specifically stated that the applicable law was that of California. The ECJ held that a principal in such a situation could not evade his obligations under the Directive by the simple expedient of the choice-of-law clause in question. In the second case, *Accentual Limited v Asigra Inc*,[4] reliance was placed on the case of *Ingmar* in order to disapply an arbitration clause which required all disputes to be settled by arbitration in Toronto; the agreement which was the subject of the dispute in question was governed by the laws of Ontario and the federal laws of Canada.

Article 3.1 of the Rome Convention has not been altered by Regulation (EC) No 593/2008. However, Article 3.3 of the Rome Convention has been changed somewhat. The relevant provisions of Regulation (EC) No 593/2008 are Articles 3.3 and 3.4.

Article 3.3 provides that

> [w]here all other elements relevant to the situation at the time of the choice are located in a country other than the country whose law has been chosen, the choice

---

[2] SI 2009 No 3064.

[3] Case C-381/98: *Ingmar v Eaton Leonard Technologies Inc* [2000] ECR I-9305.

[4] [2009] EWHC 2655 (QB), decision of Tugendhat J in the English High Court of 30 October 2009 (not yet reported).

of the parties shall not prejudice the application of provisions of the law of that other country which cannot be derogated from by agreement.

Article 3.4 provides that

[w]here all other elements relevant to the situation at the time of the choice are located in one or more Member States, the parties' choice of applicable law other than that of a Member State shall not prejudice the application of provisions of Community law, where appropriate, as implemented in the Member State of the forum, which cannot be derogated from by agreement.

It is not thought that the changes to Article 3.3 of the Rome Convention will materially affect the position of parties to commercial agency contracts in the light of the existing case-law referred to above.

The position where the parties have made no choice as to the applicable law is less clear. Article 4.1 of the Rome Convention provides that '[t]o the extent that the law applicable to the contract has not been chosen in accordance with Article 3, the contract shall be governed by the law of the country with which it is most connected'.

Article 4.2 seeks to elucidate the position thus:

Subject to the provisions of paragraph 5 of this Article, it shall be presumed that the contract is most closely connected with the country where the party who is to effect the performance which is characteristic of the contract has at the time of conclusion of the contract, his habitual residence, or, in the case of a body corporate or unincorporate, its central administration. However, if the contract is entered into in the course of that party's trade or profession, that country shall be the country in which the principal place of business is situated or, where under the terms of the contract the performance is to be effected through a place of business other than the principal place of business, the country in which that other place of business is situated.

Article 4.5 provides that

[p]aragraph 2 shall not apply if the characteristic performance cannot be determined, and the presumptions in paragraphs 2,3 and 4 shall be disregarded if it appears from the circumstances as a whole that the contract is more closely connected with another country.

Accordingly, where there is no choice of applicable law, the key issue in the context inter alia of a commercial agency agreement will be to determine the place of its characteristic performance. The characteristic performance of an agency agreement will be that carried out by the agent. The place of that characteristic performance will, in the light of Article 4.2, be the place where the agent is established, which will not necessarily be the place where the agent's work is performed.[5]

Regulation (EC) No 593/2008 has sought to tidy up the position. Article 4.1

---

[5] See *Bowstead and Reynolds on Agency*, 18th edn, para 11-006.

sets out specific rules for specific types of contract. Article 4.1(b) provides as follows:

> To the extent that the law applicable to the contract has not been chosen in accordance with Article 3 and without prejudice to Articles 5 to 8, the law governing the contract shall be determined as follows: a contract for the provision of services shall be governed by the law of the country where the service provider has his habitual residence.

At least one leading textbook[6] opines that this provision should cover agency contracts, and that for that purpose, the agent will be the service provider. The authors see no reason to disagree with that analysis. However, where an agency agreement relates exclusively to the sale of goods, it could be argued that Article 4.1(b) might not be applicable.[7]

To the extent that an agency agreement did not fall within the scope of Article 4.1(b), the catch-all provisions in the Article are of relevance. Article 4.2 provides that

> [w]here the contract is not covered by paragraph 1 or where the elements of the contract would be covered by more than one of points (a) to (h) of paragraph 1, the contract shall be governed by the law of the country where the party required to effect the characteristic performance of the contract has his habitual residence.

Article 4.3 continues as follows:

> Where it is clear from all the circumstances of the case that the contract is manifestly more closely connected with a country other than that indicated in paragraph 1or 2, the law of that other country shall apply.

Article 4.4 concludes, stating that, '[w]here the law applicable cannot be determined pursuant to paragraphs 1 or 2, the contract shall be governed by the country with which it is most connected'.

## 4.3 CHOICE OF LAW AND THE REGULATIONS

Regulations 1(2) and 1(3) as amended set out the position as regards applicable law, where there is a choice-of-law clause and that choice is an EU law. If the parties chose English or Scottish law, then the Regulations will apply irrespective of where in the EU the agent carries out its activities. This follows Regulation 1(3)(b) as amended, which provides:

> A Court or tribunal shall (whether or not it would otherwise be required to do so) apply these regulations where the law of another member State corresponding to these regulations enables the parties to agree that the agency contract is to be governed

---

[6] See Dicey, Morris and Collins, *The Conflict of Laws*, 3rd Cumulative Supplement to the 14th edn (2006), para 33R-404.

[7] See, by way of analogy, the position taken by AG Mazak in Case C-381/08: *Car Trim GmbH v KeySafety Systems Srl* of 29 September 2009.

by the law of a different member State and the parties have agreed that it is to be governed by the law of England and Wales or Scotland.

Regulation 1(3)(b) arose by way of amendment to the original Regulations, pursuant to the Commercial Agents (Council Directive) (Amendment) Regulations 1998.[8] As the amendment itself is not overly clear, the Explanatory Note to the relevant Statutory Instrument comes as welcome relief through its brevity and clarity. It provides in relevant part as follows:

> Following representations made by the EC Commission to the effect that the earlier regulations did not deal with the case where the parties expressly agreed that the law of any part of the United Kingdom was to apply to the contract between them and that a court in the United Kingdom was to have jurisdiction but the activities of the agent were to be carried out elsewhere in the Community, these regulations seek to put the matter beyond doubt in relation to Great Britain. Whether or not it would otherwise be required to do so, a court or tribunal is required to apply the regulations in the case mentioned above, provided that the law of the other member states so permits.

Thus, as long as the EU law of the place of performance allows for another applicable law to be chosen by the parties, then the Regulations will apply in such a situation. If, on the other hand, the parties chose the law of another Member State, then the Regulations will not apply and the implementing provisions of the Directive in that other Member State will apply instead. This arises from Regulation 1(3)(a) which provides:

> A Court or tribunal shall apply the law of the other member State concerned in place of regulations 3 to 22 where the parties have agreed that the agency contract is to be governed by the law of that member State.

## 4.4 THE SCOPE OF THE REGULATIONS

At first sight, Regulation 1(2) seems to be clear and unambiguous. It simply defines the scope of the Regulations as being applicable to the activities of agents in Great Britain—Great Britain is the relevant territory because of the constitutional need to provide separate legislative measures for Northern Ireland. As noted above, this provision must now be read in conjunction with the amended Regulation 1(3)(a) and (b). However, certain problems arise, as follows:

— What constitutes activities?
— What is the position of a commercial agent who carries out activities not only in Great Britain but in other Member States? Do the Regulations only apply to the activities carried out in Great Britain and not to those carried out elsewhere in the EU?[9]

---

[8] SI 1998 No 2868, which came into force on 16 December 1998.

[9] It should be noted that by amendment to the original Regulations, reference to Member States in the Regulations includes Contracting States to the EEA Agreement—see the Commercial Agents (Council Directive) (Amendment) Regulations 1998 (SI 1998/2868).

— What is the position of an agent who carries out all of its activities outside the territory of the EU?
— What happens if the agent has activities both within Great Britain and outside the EU?

The Directive is of little help on the above issues as, by its very nature, it sets out the co-ordinating measures to be implemented across the EU and does not (and indeed could not) address the issue of the scope of the individual Member States' implementing legislation. That is a matter for the national implementing legislation. However, it raises a problem inherent in the use of directives as a means of harmonising legislation throughout the EU. All Member States must implement directives fully and correctly. This does not mean that they will all implement a particular directive in exactly the same way. Thus, differences may and often do exist between the different national implementing measures for a particular directive. Such differences should eventually be ironed out by the Court of Justice of the European Union, but this may take some considerable time. In the meantime, different Member States may have different views of the same directive. It is interesting to note that earlier versions of the Regulations did not contain a provision similar to that at Regulation 1(2). Indeed, it was only in the final draft of the Regulations that this provision was brought in. Prior to that, the only clause that had an impact on this issue was contained in paragraph 23 of the second draft. This provided that the Regulations did not apply when an agent's activities would not take place within the European Community. The Regulations are much narrower, applying only where the agent's activities take place within Great Britain.

The UK authorities have taken a standpoint on the problems mentioned above. This is contained in this guidance notes published by the DTI, which can be found in Appendix 3. However, those guidance notes pre-date the above-mentioned amendment to the Regulations and therefore must be read with that fact firmly in mind. The DTI makes it clear that the views expressed in the notes should not be taken as binding authority and that the final arbiter in such matters is the ECJ/Court of Justice of the European Union. The Court of Appeal also made it clear that the DTI Notes were not admissible for use by the courts to interpret the Regulations.[10]

## 4.5 THE CARRYING ON OF ACTIVITIES WITHIN GREAT BRITAIN

Given the increasing use of electronic communications between businesses, in particular via the Internet, the question of where an agent's activities are carried out is of some importance. If, for example, an agent were to be physically situated

---

[10] *Ingmar v Eaton Leonard Technologies Inc* [1999] EuLR 88 at 92a–b.

in France, but sought clients and/or sales of goods in Great Britain through electronic media, there should be no reason why the Regulations could not apply.[11]

It should be noted that in order for the Regulations to apply, it is not necessary for the principal to be established in a different Member State to that of
the agent. Although there is specific mention in the Directive of the difficulties
posed by principals and agents being in different Member States, the ECJ has
made it clear that the national implementing legislation can (and indeed should)
apply even when both parties to a commercial agency agreement are within the
same Member State.[12]

## 4.6 ACTIVITIES WITHIN THE EU

Where an agent carries out its activities both in Great Britain and in other
Member States, the view of the DTI is that the Regulations govern the agent's
activities in Great Britain but do not cover the same agent's activities anywhere
else in the EU.[13] This view has been overtaken by the above-mentioned amendment to the Regulations and, accordingly, if English law is the applicable law
of the agreement, then the Regulations will apply to all the agent's activities
within the EU.

## 4.7 ACTIVITIES OUTSIDE THE EU

If all of the agent's activities take place outside the territory of the EEA, the DTI's
view follows the principle established in the first and second drafts—that is to
say that the Regulations will not apply, even where the parties to the relevant
contract have agreed that the agreement is to be governed by English law. However, the parties could agree specifically to include in their contract some or all
of the provisions contained in the Regulations. This again follows the principles
of earlier drafts of the Regulations. It should be noted that the draft paragraph
containing the relevant provisions on non-EU activities was not included in the
final text. Accordingly, there is no guidance on the issue apart from what was in
the previous drafts and the DTI's views on those drafts. However, it is thought
that this represents a sensible position, given that one of the stated aims of the
Directive is to remedy the impact of differences in national agency laws on the
conditions of competition within the EU.

---

[11] For support of the stance taken by the authors, see Dicey, Morris and Collins, above n 6, para
33-418; cf Bowstead and Reynolds, above n 5, para 11-012.
[12] See Case C-215/97: *Bellone* [1998] ECR I-2191.
[13] This view is shared by Bowstead and Reynolds, above n 5, para 11-012.

## 4.8 ACTIVITIES BOTH WITHIN AND OUTSIDE THE EU

It is the authors' view that only those activities taking place within the EU should be covered by the Directive. This position appears to have received support from Advocate General Leger in the *Ingmar* case, in which he stated that

> [t]he existence of a territorial link—either through the actual presence of one of the economic operators in the territory of a Member State, or through the pursuit of an economic activity in that territory—thus imposes Community jurisdiction on the legal relationship in question.[14]

Interestingly, this approach would permit the Directive, and therefore the Regulations, to apply to a situation in which the principal was established in Great Britain with the agent being established and active outside the EU.

## 4.9 THE NON-EXCLUSION OF REGULATIONS 1, 2 AND 23

It should be noted that Regulation 1(3)(a), as amended, only relates to Regulations 3–22. Thus, where the law of another Member State applies, Regulations 1, 2 and 23 may continue to apply. These provisions are not lacking in importance. For example, Regulation 2 determines which commercial agents shall be covered by the Regulations and which shall not. It is thus crucial to any situation affected or potentially affected by the Regulations.

It must follow (and indeed the DTI takes this view) that the deliberate exclusion of Regulations 1, 2 and 23 in Regulation 1(3)(a) means that the question of the scope of the Regulations is still to be determined pursuant to the Regulations and in particular Regulation 2, even though another law has been chosen as the law governing the contract. As the DTI points out in its 1993 Guidance Notes, this approach assumes that the other Member State in question, whose law has been chosen to govern a particular contract, has properly implemented the Directive.

---

[14] AG Leger's Opinion in Case C-381/98: *Ingmar* of 11 May 2000 at para 37, [2001] 1 CMLR 9.

# 5

# Regulation 2(1):
# Commercial Agents

## 5.1 OUTLINE

T HIS CHAPTER DEALS with the central question of which agents are covered by the Regulations, including the issue of whether the Regulations apply to commercial agents dealing in both goods and services.

## 5.2 WHAT IS A COMMERCIAL AGENT?

The definition of a commercial agent is of central importance to the interpretation and understanding of the rest of the Regulations. As noted in chapter 3, it has been the subject of considerable thought by the DTI, although the Regulations in fact largely replicate the terms of the Directive.

Regulation 2(1) defines a commercial agent, but as will be seen in the next chapter, Regulation 2(2) then excludes certain categories of agent from the Regulations.

## 5.3 DEFINITION

A commercial agent is defined as a self-employed intermediary who has continuing authority to negotiate or to negotiate and conclude the sale or purchase of goods[1] on behalf of and in the name of another person. Each of the elements of this definition merits separate consideration.

---

[1] Although buying agents are rare, note that the agent in *Page v Combined Shipping and Trading* [1997] All ER 656 was both a buying and selling agent.

## 5.4 'SELF-EMPLOYED INTERMEDIARY'

Some writers have been misled by the expression 'self-employed' to conclude that the Regulations do not apply to companies.[2] This is incorrect. This expression is taken from Articles 49–55 of the Treaty on the Functioning of the European Union (and specifically Article 53), which relate to the adoption of directives for the co-ordination of laws in Member States concerning the taking up and pursuit of activities as self-employed persons by EU nationals. The distinction is not, however, between natural and legal persons. Indeed the draft Directive which was the subject of the Commission's Explanatory Memorandum of 14 December 1976, appended to the Law Commission Report, expressly allowed the exclusion of certain of the agent's rights where the paid-up share capital of the agent exceeded a given figure, clearly indicating that corporate entities will fall within the definition of commercial agent. It is unclear whether the word 'intermediary' adds anything—its presence in the Directive is probably merely a reflection of the fact that these words are a term of art in other Member States.

## 5.5 'CONTINUING AUTHORITY'

Clearly, what is contemplated is something more than authority to act on a single occasion for a particular principal.[3] The DTI's 1994 Guidance Notes suggest that if an agent is appointed on a temporary basis or for a specified number of transactions, then the Regulations would not apply. Is this correct? Does 'continuing authority' mean the authority to conclude an unlimited number of transactions? It would be a strange result if it were possible to avoid the Regulations by appointing the agent to conclude a specified but large number of transactions. In *Poseidon*, the ECJ indicated that the number of transactions *concluded* by an intermediary was normally an indicator of continuing authority but was not the sole determining factor.

Regulation 7(2) contemplates the agent being granted exclusive rights to a specific group of customers. Why should an agent who is granted exclusive rights in respect of a handful of customers be covered by the Regulations when an agent who is granted authority for a limited number of transactions is not? Further, suppose that an agent is given an exclusive right to ten named customers pursuant to an agency agreement entered into for a period of three years and the agent successfully negotiates a long-term supply contract in excess of three years with each of those customers: should the question of whether the Regulations apply depend upon whether the contract stated that the agent would only have authority to act in respect of ten transactions?

The authors believe that the better view is that where an agent has authority for more than one transaction, this authority should be seen as 'continuing'. The

---

[2] See eg T Brennan and C Jones, 'Compensatory Measures' *The Gazette* 6 January 1994.
[3] As confirmed by the ECJ in Case C-3/04 *Poseidon* [2006] ECR I-2505.

authority continues up to the point when the second transaction is concluded and that authority is (in the absence of other provisions) of indefinite duration even if of limited scope. The authors do not believe that it is safe to assume that limiting authority to a specified number of transactions will take the arrangement outside the Regulations. In *Poseidon*[4] the ECJ held that in circumstances where a single contract was repeatedly extended, there was continuing authority only if the principal actually conferred authority on the agent to renegotiate successive extensions.

## 5.6 PRECEDENT CLAUSES

The precedent clause set out at (a) below might be utilised where there is to be authority for only one transaction. The precedent set out at (b) below is a provision which might be incorporated for the avoidance of doubt in arrangements which are in reality distribution agreements or other relationships and where there is to be no agency relationship. By way of caution, it should be noted that the court will look at the factual question of whether or not there is continuing authority: the mere inclusion of such a provision will not change the facts and advisers should be careful in counselling clients on this fact.[5] The authors also believe that it is unlikely that the effect of the Regulations can be avoided by entering into a series of contracts, each of which relates to a single transaction: the courts are likely to look through such a relationship and to find that there is in fact continuing authority, the agent reasonably assuming that he will be granted authority for a further transaction when he has concluded one transaction. In *Moore v Piretta PTA Limited*,[6] the Court construed the phrase 'the agency contract' in Regulation 17 as referring to the entirety of the agency relationship between principal and agent and not merely to the latest in a chain of contracts between them.

The suggested precedent clauses are as follows:

(a) The Parties agree that the Agent has been appointed solely for the purpose of concluding a single transaction between the Principal and the Customer and that accordingly the Agent shall not have nor be deemed to have any continuing or other authority to negotiate or to negotiate and conclude any other transaction on behalf of the Principal.

(b) The parties agree that the Distributor is acting as an independent trader

---

[4] *Ibid.*

[5] See eg *AMB Imballaggi Plastici SRL v Pacflex Limited* [1999] All ER (Comm) 249. Note, however, that the Court of Appeal in *Mercantile International Group v Chuan Soon Huat* [2002] EWCA Civ 288 gave great weight to the written form of the agreement between the parties in deciding that M was a commercial agent, and explained away unusual aspects of the relationships and discrepancies between the documentation and operation of the agreements in practice as potentially constituting 'side agreements'. The Court of Appeal was clearly of a similar mind in *Sagal v Bunz* [2009] EWCA Civ 700.

[6] *Moore v Piretta PTA Limited* [1999] 1 All ER 174, 180.

in purchasing the goods from the Manufacturer and selling those goods to its own customers at prices and upon terms determined solely by the Distributor. Accordingly, it is agreed that the Distributor shall not have nor be deemed to have any continuing or other authority to negotiate or to negotiate and conclude any transaction for the sale of goods or otherwise for or on behalf of the Manufacturer nor to pledge the credit of or bind the Manufacturer in any other way.

## 5.7 SUB-AGENTS

The position of sub-agents is not fully worked out in English common law, and the Regulations add a confusing additional factor into this equation.

Where a sub-agent is properly appointed, his acts bind the principal as if they had been performed by the agent. Does this mean that the sub-agent has continuing authority to negotiate or negotiate and conclude on behalf of the principal?

There is no privity of contract (ie no contractual link) between a principal and a sub-agent as a matter of course. Contractually, therefore, in the absence of an agreement between principal and sub-agent, the common law provides the sub-agent with rights against the agent but not against the principal. The definition of 'commercial agent' in Regulation 2(1) talks of 'continuing authority' but does not state that that authority has to be the result of a contract between principal and subagent.

This question was the subject of a reference to the ECJ by the English High Court in *Pace Airline Services Limited v Aerotrans Luftfahrtagentur GmbH*,[7] but it is understood that the case settled before the ECJ considered it. It has, however, now been definitively answered by the Court of Appeal in *Light and others v Ty Europe*.[8] At first instance, the judge found that there was authority for the sub-agents to act on behalf of the principal and that there was no need for this to be on the basis of contract. The Court of Appeal disagreed, citing the numerous references throughout the Regulations to 'the agency contract' and fearing 'chaos and confusion' were sub-agents to be allowed to bring claims against the principal. The Court of Appeal noted that the intermediate agent might well have a claim for compensation and Tuckey LJ saw 'no reason why as [the intermediate agent's] agents the [sub-agents] should not have been able to establish a stake in the [intermediate agents] compensation claim'.[9] However, the sub-agents would, it seems, have no claim under the Regulations against the intermediate agent, and will often have no contractual claim. Accordingly, the authors prefer the view of the first-instance judge. In particular:

---

[7] *Pace Airline Services Limited v Aerotrans Luftfahrtagentur GmbH* Case C-64/99, [1999] OJ C121/123.

[8] *Light and others v Ty Europe* [2003] EWCA Civ 1238.

[9] See para 35.

1. whatever 'contract' means in the context of the Regulations, it is an EU law concept, not an English law one;
2. the definition of 'commercial agent' does not refer to a contract, and the key phrase in Regulation 17 is 'termination of . . . relations with the principal';[10]
3. the authors' view is that there should be no difficulty in principle for the Court enquiring as to the structure of the agency network and determining compensation accordingly. Particularly in the light of *Lonsdale v Howard & Hallam*,[11] why should the value of each sub-agent's business not be separately calculated?

## 5.8 'GOODS'

Why was the Directive limited so as only to apply to agencies for the sale of goods? In the Scottish case of *Gailey v Environmental Waste Controls*,[12] the Court of Session, seeing goodwill as the touchstone for answering a number of questions concerning the Regulations, suggested that this may be because principals in supply of services cases are more likely to come into contact with the customer and therefore have a better moral claim to the goodwill generated than is the case with goods agencies.[13]

As regards the definition of 'goods' itself, the first and second drafts contained definitions of goods by reference to other statutes. There is no definition in the Regulations, but the DTI's Guidance Note suggests that these words should be interpreted in accordance with EU law generally.

The DTI's view was that the definition in section 61 of the Sale of Goods Act 1979—excluding land and money—would be a reasonable guide. It is reported that the High Court judge in the unreported Pace case[14] considered that cargo space on aircraft could be 'goods' for this purpose. It seems to the authors that this argument is difficult to sustain.

In *Tamarind and others v Eastern Natural Gas and Eastern Energy*[15] it was accepted that gas was goods and there seems to have been a suggestion from the judge that he also considered electricity to be goods.[16] There were in the past rumours that the Commission might at some stage publish a draft directive extending protection to agents who deal in the supply or purchase of pure services. No draft ever emerged and it is unlikely that this will now happen. It might

---

[10] Regulation 17(6). Regulations 17(1) and (7) do refer to the agency contract.

[11] *Lonsdale v Howard & Hallam* [2007] 1 WLR 2055.

[12] *Gailey v Environmental Waste Controls* [2004] EuLR 423 at 436B.

[13] Note, however, that some Member States have chosen to implement the Directive but also to extend its protection to agents who represent principals in relation to services.

[14] S Sidkin, *Commercial Lawyer* February 1999, 101.

[15] *Tamarind and others v Eastern Natural Gas and Eastern Energy* Commercial Court [2000] EuLR 708.

[16] The judge referred to 'selling electricity or other products': see para 41.

be questioned whether such a measure would affect any significant number of agents in the EU.

In *Crane v Sky In-home Services and others*,[17] it was noted that it was common ground between the parties that an agency relating to the sale of Sky television digital packages related to services, not goods, and was therefore outside the scope of the Regulations.

## 5.9 ARE AGENTS WHO DEAL IN GOODS AND SERVICES PROTECTED BY THE REGULATIONS?

The second draft included the words 'but not services', but these words have not been included in the Regulations. The interesting question which this raises is the status of an agent who deals in both goods and services. If, for instance, the agent is seeking orders for major items of capital equipment on behalf of a principal, it is likely that the principal will agree to provide consultancy services, or to install and commission the equipment, or to provide guarantee or maintenance services, through the agent. This issue may have some bearing on the question of whether the agent's activities are 'secondary' (see chapter 6.3),[18] but also raises the question of the status of the services element of such an arrangement. If the agent has been paid commission on the consultancy/installation and commissioning/servicing and maintenance aspects of the transaction with the customer (which may be a substantial part of the price):

— Do the rules regarding the payment of commission apply to these elements?
— Are these elements of commission to be taken into account for the purpose of calculating compensation or an indemnity payment?
— If not, what happens if, because the principal quotes a single global price for all the services provided, it is not possible to ascertain what element relates to the goods and what element to the services?

The DTI did not address the issue in its Guidance Notes, but the authors' view is that the reference to goods is merely a matter of defining the status of the commercial agent and that, unless his activities in relation to services render his activities as an agent in respect of the sale of goods secondary, the Regulations will apply.

The Scottish Courts have held that an agent acting on the sale of conservatories was not an agent for the sale of goods.[19] The contracts concerned were not a series of separate contracts for, on the one hand, the supply of materials and, on the other hand, the supply of building works, but an entire contract for the

---

[17] *Crane v Sky In-home Services and others* [2007] EWHC 66 (ChD) at para 11.

[18] Which is the basis on which it was considered by the Scottish Court of Session in *Gailey v Environmental Waste Control* [2004] EuLR 424 at 437A.

[19] *Marjandi v Bon Accord* [2007] Scot SC 55.

supply of all goods and works required, and as such were not to be considered as contracts for the supply of goods.

But do the Regulations apply in respect of the whole of the sum due to the agent by way of commission and will the whole amount payable be taken into account in calculating compensation or the indemnity payment? If the answer is that the whole consideration is taken into account, then this raises an interesting drafting question. If the draftsman is faced with a situation where the agent is likely to act in respect of both goods and services, what is the effect of drafting two separate agreements (which could be tied together through cross-default provisions to ensure that for certain purposes they would work as if one single agreement)? If the relationship is to be viewed as one of commercial agency since the goods element outweighs the services element, then separating the two may mean that the compensation/indemnity payment is lower and that the principal escapes some of the other mandatory provisions of the Regulations in relation to the services element. However, if the inclusion of services within the agreement would render the agent's activities in relation to the sale of goods secondary, then the effect of separation would be to ensure that the Regulations applied to part of the relationship when combining the two would have taken the whole of the relationship outside the Regulations.[20]

This points to an interesting inconsistency. If an agent earns 55 per cent of his commission in relation to services, then his activities as an agent in respect of the sale of goods may be viewed as secondary, whereas if the proportions were reversed the Regulations might apply with their full weight to the whole of his commission payments.

If the proportion changed during the course of the contract, could an agent be within the terms of the Regulations for part of the duration of the contract and outside the Regulations for the remainder? If so, the parties may be unaware that the relationship has ceased to be subject to the Regulations, or conversely has become subject to them. In such circumstances, would the Court apply the Regulations only if and for so long as the Regulations apply in calculating compensation or indemnity, and should it discount the period during which the agent's activities in relation to the sale of the goods are secondary? This is not as fanciful a set of circumstances as might first appear: if an agent is seeking to procure orders for major items of equipment from customers at the outset and is successful, then in the latter part of the term of the contract it may well be that the bulk of income[21] ceases to be earned from equipment sales, but relates principally to maintenance or guarantee services, training and so forth. This is

---

[20] Given the view expressed by the Court in *Moore v Piretta PTA Limited* (see s 5.5 above), it may be that the Court would ignore form and view this as a single agency even if it consisted of two separate contracts.

[21] Indeed, it is unclear whether any such balance would be struck on the basis of volume or value of transactions effected; in this example, value would likely point in one direction, volume in the other!

an issue that neither the Directive nor the Regulations address, and the Schedule to the Regulations is ill-suited to resolving this question.[22]

This issue has, however, been addressed at a senior appellate level in the Scottish Courts in *McAdam v Boxpack Limited*[23] which stated that, in the context of determining whether an agent's activities were secondary, it was necessary to look at the position at the inception of the contract. Similarly, in *Crane*[24] the Court chose to answer questions regarding secondary activities at inception, noting with seeming disapproval that the agent might 'drift in and out of qualifying commercial agency during the currency of the arrangement'. The authors are not convinced by this approach. Would the Court have reached the same conclusion if a relationship were to shift from not being an agency to being an agency during its life?

## 5.10 'AGENTS FOR UNDISCLOSED PRINCIPALS'

There was previously some doubt as to the status of agents who act for undisclosed principals. The wording of the Directive and of the Regulations seemed to exclude them by referring to negotiating and concluding contracts 'on behalf of and in the name of' that person. This approach has been confirmed by the ECJ in *Mavrona*[25] and by the Court of Appeal in *Sagal v Bunz*.[26] The reason for this approach may be explained by the goodwill issue addressed elsewhere,[27] and also the class of agents known in civil law systems as 'commission agents' whom the ECJ determined did not fall within the definition of commercial agent. Compare this decision with that in the *Mercantile* case.

It is also clear that, where the Court concludes that the agent is negotiating for itself rather than the principal, it will conclude that the relationship is not an agency for the purposes of the Regulations.[28]

---

[22] But see ch 6.3 below.
[23] *McAdam v Boxpack Limited* [2006] SLT 217 at para 20.
[24] [2007] EWHC 66 (Ch) at para 77.
[25] Case C-85/03 [2004] ECR I-1573.
[26] *Sagal (trading as Bunz UK) v Atelier Bunz GmbH* [2009] EWCA Civ 700 at para 13.
[27] Ch 9.
[28] A rather thin distinction to this effect was entered in *AMB Imballaggi Plastici SRL v Pacflex Limited* [1999] All ER (Comm) 249. The Court had no difficulty in concluding that the relationship in that case was not one of commercial agency; although the contract allowed for agency dealings, dealings were in fact conducted on a sale and resale (distributorship) basis with the agent determining resale prices. The above-mentioned case was reviewed in *Mercantile International Group plc v Chuan Soon Huat Industrial Group* [2002] 1 All ER (Comm) 788, a judgment of Andrew Smith J in the Commercial Court, in which it was held that an arrangement for remunerating by way of 'mark-up' rather than by commission was not inconsistent with agency. The judgment has been upheld on appeal (see [2002] EWCA Civ 288).

## 5.11 'NEGOTIATE'/'NEGOTIATE AND CONCLUDE'

'Negotiate and conclude' is less problematic than 'negotiate'—an agent who has continuing authority to negotiate and conclude transactions is clearly the type of agent referred to in chapter 1, who actually has power to bind the principal to transactions. Unfortunately, at least in the UK, this type of agent is very much rarer than his counterpart, the agent who funnels orders and business back to the principal but does not have or purport to have any authority to bind the principal to contracts. Is this type of agent (referred to in chapter 1 as a 'marketing agent') within the scope of the Regulations at all? What is the meaning of the word 'negotiate' when used on its own?

## 5.12 DO THE REGULATIONS APPLY TO MARKETING AGENTS?

If 'negotiate and conclude' is taken to mean the power to bind the principal to transactions, then 'negotiate' must mean something less than actual or apparent authority to bind the principal. But how far need the agent be authorised in order to be 'negotiating'? In what sense can someone be said to have power to negotiate when he does not have power to conclude? Where the 'agent' does not have 'authority' to take any part in the process leading up to contract formation, the agent cannot be said to be 'negotiating'—so, an 'agent' who merely circulates literature or samples does not in the authors' view 'negotiate'. However, if the agent has a greater role—for instance it presents price lists or standard terms of trading, liaises with the principal and so forth—it is negotiating and therefore falls within the scope of the Regulations. The test is not a difficult one to satisfy.

It is clear that this expression includes most, if not all, 'marketing agents'. The reality is that the agent is likely to act as the point of contact between principal and customer, at least at the outset. It will be the agent who (either directly by visiting the customer's premises, or through advertisements and the general creation of product image for the principal's goods in the territory) acts as the catalyst to orders for the principal in most cases. Normally the agent will visit the customer alone and present product brochures, specifications, the principal's price list. The agent will ascertain the customer's requirements and advise the principal of these, even if it is doing so with a view to asking whether a particular modification can be made or a particular discount granted. It is often the agent who communicates the principal's response to the customer, but even if principal and customer enter a dialogue direct, the catalyst for this will have been the agent. In the broader sense, the agent is 'negotiating'. Certainly, he is doing all that he could do on behalf of the principal without actually 'concluding'. This view has received judicial approval in the case of *Nigel Fryer Joinery*

*Services Ltd v Ian Firth Hardware Ltd*,[29] referring to *PJ Pipe & Valve v Audco*[30] and in turn to *Parks v Esso Petroleum Company Limited*[31] to the effect that the word 'negotiate' has a meaning broader than simply to negotiate a sale. In *Fryer*, the Court held that an agent who introduced customers, suggested indicative prices and encouraged a customer to place orders at the prices agreed or specified by the principal to customers came 'well within the ordinary meaning of "negotiate".[32]

The Law Commission Report notes that

> [B]y far the majority of commercial agents in the member states are at the present time authorised only to negotiate on behalf of their principals, the conclusion of the actual agreement for the transaction being a matter for the principal himself. The Directive reflects this situation.[33]

This specific issue has been considered by the English courts in at least two cases relating to petrol station attendants and in two other cases. In the earlier, unreported case of *Elf Oil UK Limited v Pilkington* (1994), the Court held that the crucial issue was whether the 'agent' negotiated or merely managed: only in the former case would he be a commercial agent for the purposes of the Regulations.

In the other case, *Parks v Esso Petroleum Company Limited*,[34] the Court of Appeal considered a number of grounds of appeal by Mr Parks against the decision of the Vice Chancellor. The Court of Appeal had to consider whether he was a commercial agent for the purposes of the Regulations and whether his activities as a commercial agent were secondary so as to take him outside the scope of the Regulations. It decided that he was not a commercial agent on the basis that he did not negotiate. Whilst not questioning this decision on its facts, the authors believe that the approach taken by the Court of Appeal is flawed and may lead to incorrect decisions if followed in other cases. In asking whether Mr Parks negotiated, the Court was directing itself to the wrong question; what it should have asked was whether Mr Parks had authority to negotiate.[35] The reality in many mature commercial agencies is that the agent does little negotiating day to day. Long-established customers secured for the principal by the agent use fax, phone or e-mail to communicate repeat orders on the basis of a published price list. There is no ongoing negotiation here in any meaningful sense. But the agent undeniably has authority to negotiate.

The third case, also unreported, is *Hunter v Zenith Windows*,[36] in which the

---

[29] *Nigel Fryer Joinery Services Ltd v Ian Firth Hardware Ltd* [2008] EWHC 767 (Ch).

[30] *PJ Pipe & Valve v Audco* [2005] EWHC 1904 (QB).

[31] *Parks v Esso Petroleum Company Limited* [2000] Eu LR 25.

[32] At para 20.

[33] This view was confirmed by the expert evidence given in *PJ Pipe & Valve Co Limited v Audco* [2005] EWHC 1904 (QB) at para 13.

[34] [2000] EuLR 25.

[35] For other criticisms of the *Parks* case, in particular in comparison to similar cases in Germany with different results, see an article by Sellhorst and O'Brien in *International Business Lawyer* July/August 2000, 320.

[36] Unreported, Norwich County Court 13 June 1997.

Court decided that an agent whose role was principally to train and co-ordinate the activities of other agents[37] was nevertheless to be viewed as having authority to negotiate. The agent's claim failed, however, on the basis that his activities as agent were secondary.[38] It seems that the judge's reasoning revolved in part around a view that the agent was negotiating even though he was doing so through the medium of sub-agents.[39]

In *PJ Pipe & Valve Co Ltd v Audco*, the Court cautioned against a limited or restricted interpretation of the word 'negotiate' that would exclude agents who had been engaged to develop goodwill for the principal.[40]

### 5.13 SPECIFIC EXCLUSIONS

Regulation 2(1) goes on to exclude three types of persons specifically from the definition of 'commercial agent', namely:

— company officers;
— partners; and
— insolvency practitioners (the earlier drafts referred to receivers, liquidators and others).

The first of these is presumably only of potential relevance in so far as the company officer is not an employee.

### 5.14 OTHER DEFINITIONS

Regulation 2(1) also defines 'commission' and 'restraint of trade clause', and these definitions are dealt with in the sections to which they relate.

---

[37] Described in ch 6.14 as a 'super-agent'.
[38] See ch 6.3 below.
[39] Contrast this with the views expressed in ch 5.7 above regarding sub-agents.
[40] See para 155 of the judgment.

# 6

# Regulations 2(2)–2(5): Commercial Agents Outside the Scope of the Regulations

## 6.1 OUTLINE

THIS CHAPTER EXAMINES the types of commercial agents which are specifically excluded from the scope of the Regulations. It also covers those situations where the activities of commercial agents are secondary to other activities and which accordingly cause the agents concerned to fall outside the ambit of the Regulations.

## 6.2 WHICH TYPES OF COMMERCIAL AGENT ARE SPECIFICALLY EXCLUDED FROM THE REGULATIONS?

Regulation 2(2) stipulates that certain persons who fall within the definition of 'commercial agent' will nevertheless remain outside the scope of the Regulations. These include:

— commercial agents whose activities are unpaid;
— commercial agents when they operate on commodity exchanges or in the commodity market (note that the definition of 'commodity market' from the first draft has not been reproduced in the Regulations); and
— Crown agents.

None of these is surprising, but it is important to note that certain persons will be viewed as commercial agents, as follows:

— Agents appointed on a 'trial basis'. Comparison will be made below between the position of employees on the one hand and commercial agents on the other. In UK law, an employee has no right to an unfair dismissal or redundancy payment for a period of one year following commencement of employment and no right to redundancy payments for a period of two years following commencement of employment. There is no such 'honeymoon'

45

period with agents and the Regulations apply with their full force from the first day of the relationship;
— Agents who do not have a written agreement with the principal. Regulation 13 gives each party a right to receive from the other a signed written document setting out the terms of the agency contract. Clearly, then, agents without written agreements are nevertheless within the terms of the Regulations.
— Agents operating on the basis of non-exclusive agency contracts as well as exclusive agency contracts, the only difference being in relation to the payment of commission (see below).

### 6.3 WHICH TYPES OF ACTIVITIES ARE DEEMED TO BE SECONDARY?

Regulation 2(3) together with the Schedule is important in that it helps to define the scope of the Regulations as a whole. Clearly if a person's activities as a commercial agent are secondary, then the Regulations will not be applicable. However, there are very few types of agency contracts which are specifically excluded from the Regulations. Apart from those set out in Regulation 2(2), the Schedule only specifically deals with two types of contract, preventing them from coming within the scope of the Regulations, namely those involving mail-order catalogues for consumer goods and those involving consumer credit agreements (paragraph 5 of the Schedule). It should be noted that even for these types of contract, the reference to them in the Schedule amounts only to a rebuttable presumption that they fall outside the Regulations as they will be secondary to other activities. The Schedule is poorly worded, unclear and usually unhelpful.[1] Regard should also be had to the judgment of Morison J in *Tamarind International Ltd and Others v Eastern Natural Gas (Retail) Ltd and Others*,[2] in which the court held that the concept of a commercial agent whose activities are secondary under the Schedule was not one which had any meaning in English law and it was not a term of art common throughout mainland Europe. The court continued, stating that there was therefore no yardstick in the common law which measured and defined those agents whose activities were secondary and those whose activities were not. Given this lack of specificity it is important to examine the various early drafts of Directive 86/653, the Directive itself and the early drafts of the Regulations to see whether any help can be gained from such provisions.

---

[1] See the *obiter* remarks on the Schedule's lack of clarity by Lord Justices Waller and Peter Gibson in *AMB Imballagi Plastici SRL v Pacflex Ltd* (CA) [1999] 2 All ER (Comm) 249.
[2] *Tamarind International Ltd and Others v Eastern Natural Gas (Retail) Ltd and Others* [2000] EuLR 709.

## 6.4 THE COMMISSION PROPOSAL FOR THE DIRECTIVE

Article 3 of the Commission's proposal of 17 December 1976 excluded four specific types of intermediary from the scope of the Directive:

— those who were employed;
— those who acted in their own name;
— those who were appointed to act for a specified transaction or a specified number of transactions;
— those who acted in the insurance or credit fields.

Further, Article 4(1) of the Commission's proposal of 17 December 1976 gave Member States the right not to apply provisions relating to remuneration and compensation to persons acting as commercial agents but by way of secondary activity only. The draft made it clear that the question of whether an activity was secondary or not was one which was to be determined in accordance with the commercial usage of the relevant Member State. It also provided that Member States could apply, if they so wished, the provisions of the Directive to persons who were not commercial agents, but who could be assimilated by them.

## 6.5 THE OPINION OF THE ECONOMIC AND SOCIAL COMMITTEE

In its Opinion on the Commission's proposal, the Economic and Social Committee suggested with regard to the scope of the Directive that the list of the specified types of intermediary excluded from the Regulations should be amended to read '[those] who carry out their activities in the insurance field or on behalf of credit institutions'—see paragraph 2.3.2 of the Opinion. Further, the Committee suggested that another type be added to the list, namely those who work for firms engaged in mail-order or doorstep selling. The Opinion also made the following comments which should be noted:

— The explanatory memorandum states that the Commission intends to submit a draft Directive co-ordinating the laws of the Member States on agents working in the field of insurance and on behalf of credit institutions. (paragraph 2.3.3 of the Opinion)

— Article 4 gives Member States the right not to apply certain legal provisions of the agency contract to persons who act as commercial agents 'by way of secondary activity only'. It also empowers Member States to apply the Directive to other persons who can 'be assimilated to commercial agents' (eg women who collect bulk orders for mail-order establishments or who organise collective sales in their own homes). (paragraph 2.3.4 of the Opinion)

— The Committee considers that Article 4 gives Member States too much latitude and this might make it difficult to define the scope of the Directive precisely. Article 4 should, therefore, be deleted. The proposed fifth indent to Article 3 reinforces the case for deletion. Mail-order agents account for the bulk of the category referred to in Article 4(1) (paragraph 2.3.5 of the Opinion).

As to the draft Directive on insurance intermediaries and credit institutions, instructive reference can be made to Directive 64/224 concerning the attainment of freedom of establishment and freedom to provide services in respect of activities of intermediaries in commerce, industry and small craft industries (OJ 1964 L69/64). The second recital to that Directive provides that:

> Whereas certain activities of intermediaries are not covered by this Directive, either because they belong to branches of activity for which separate Directives are to be adopted or because, in accordance with the General Programmes, they are to be liberalised at a later date.

Thus, at Article 4 of Directive 64/224, the following types of intermediaries' activities are excluded from the scope of the Directive:

— insurance of all kinds (in particular insurance agents, brokers and assessors);
— banks and other financial establishments (in particular foreign exchange dealers, stockbrokers, mortgage brokers and the like);
— matters concerning immoveable property (in particular estate agents and brokers);
— transport undertakings (in particular shipbrokers, forwarding agents, customs agents and travel agencies).

Reference to Directive 64/224 is useful in that it demonstrates why certain activities of commercial agents are outside its own scope. Can the same reasoning not be applied to Directive 86/653? Commentators have followed this approach as far as exclusions are concerned. Further, Directive 86/653 specifically refers to Directive 64/224 in its opening recital.

## 6.6 THE OPINION OF THE EUROPEAN PARLIAMENT

In its opinion on the Commission's proposal, the European Parliament suggested two additions to the specified types of intermediaries excluded from the scope of the draft Directive. The first addition was to cover part-time agents involved primarily in mail-order sales to consumers from catalogues published periodically, at least twice a year, offering a wide range of goods for sale by cash or hire purchase. It can be seen that this is similar to the amendment suggested by the Economic and Social Committee. The second addition was to cover intermediaries who carried out their activities in the aviation sector.

## 6.7 THE COMMISSION'S AMENDED PROPOSAL

The Commission amended Articles 3 and 4 of its original proposal without taking into account the suggestions of the Economic and Social Committee and the European Parliament. The Commission's amendment added a further category of intermediaries to be exempt from the Directive. The amendment was in the following terms:

> . . . to intermediaries who, according to the practice prevailing in the State in which they habitually carry on their activities, are regarded as doing so by way of secondary activity only.

In its amended proposal, the Commission also deleted Article 4(1) but kept Article 4(2).

## 6.8 THE DIRECTIVE AS ADOPTED

In the text of the Directive as adopted, the Council reshaped the original Article 3 fundamentally. The original specified types of intermediaries to be excluded were deleted and the following were inserted:

— commercial agents whose activities are unpaid;
— commercial agents when they operate on commodity exchanges or in a commodity market;
— Crown agents for overseas governments and administrations (Article 2(2) of the Directive).

As to the issue of secondary activity, the Council followed the amended proposal of the Commission and extended the original proposal so that the whole of the Directive was excluded for those persons whose activities as commercial agents were considered secondary by the law of the Member State in question (Article 2(3) of the Directive).

It should be noted that, despite the fact that the proposals from the Economic and Social Committee and the European Parliament were not taken up by either the Commission or the Council, the UK legislative authorities made use of the suggestions with regard to mail-order agents and included them in paragraph 5 of the Schedule. This is a good example of why draft European legislation should be examined when conducting an exercise such as the present one. Such drafts may also indicate a position to take on a given point, which position is not clear from the wording of the final text itself.

## 6.9 THE DRAFT REGULATIONS

The first draft of the Regulations was published in 1990. Regulation 2(2) listed those persons who should not be deemed to be a commercial agent. The list included many more categories than set out in the Directive, including those persons wholly or mainly engaged in a business of selling or buying goods on their own behalf, those persons engaged in selling goods from mail-order catalogues, and those persons who were wholly or mainly engaged in activities other than those of a commercial agent. The Directive, it will be recalled, set out a finite number of types of commercial agent to which the Directive did not apply. It can thus be seen that there was a fundamental difference between the first draft of the Regulations, which set out certain persons not deemed to be commercial agents and who were not therefore affected by the Regulations, and the Directive, which listed those activities of commercial agents deemed not to be covered by the provisions of the Directive. It was this dichotomy which led, it is presumed, to a redrafting of the proposed Regulations. Thus, the second draft carefully followed the text of the Directive as to which types of commercial agent were not to be covered by the Regulations. It also removed the categories which were not provided for in the Directive (referred to above) and placed them in a new section dealing with secondary activities. The list of commercial agents' activities deemed to be secondary appeared to be exhaustive. From the perspective of correct implementation of a directive, it appeared that as far as these latter provisions were concerned, the UK authorities had carried out their task correctly. However the position changed dramatically between the second draft and the Regulations as adopted.

## 6.10 THE REGULATIONS AS ADOPTED

The Regulations kept the position the same with regard to the three types of commercial agents who were excluded from the scope of the Regulations. However, with regard to the provisions on secondary activities, the previous draft provisions were rejected in favour of an extensive schedule. It is assumed that this was done in order to give more flexibility to the concept of secondary activities and to get away from the exhaustive list that it replaced. The result is, however, rather nebulous, which may widen the opportunities for agreements to be categorised as falling outside the scope of the Regulations, but which has a rather negative effect on legal certainty.[3] It should be noted that consumer credit agents are deemed by the Schedule to fall outside the scope of the Regulations. This category of agent was not referred to in the any of the earlier drafts, but it will be recalled that the proposals by the Commission sought to exclude agents who carried out activities in credit fields.

## 6.11 THE DETERMINING FACTOR ACCORDING TO THE DTI

According to the DTI's 1994 Guidance Notes, the determining factor in deciding whether activities are secondary, and therefore whether a given agency contract comes within the provisions of the Regulations, is whether the agent is required

---

[3] See, by way of example, the different conclusions reached by the courts in the cases of *Hunter v Zenith* and *Tamarind v Eastern National Gas* (see section 6.3 above) on the specific question of whether procuring one transaction was likely to lead to further transactions.

to keep, as his own property, a considerable stock of the product. This test is taken from the Commission Notice on Exclusive Dealing Contracts with Commercial Agents.[4] That Notice (now superseded) deals with the application of the EU competition rules to agents. In the Notice, the Commission states that Article 81(1) of the EC Treaty (formerly Article 85(1))[5] does not apply to situations in which an agent is not acting as an independent trader with regard to the principal. The Commission states that if an agent is required to keep as his own property a considerable stock of the product, then that agent is likely to be treated as an independent trader rather than a commercial agent.[6]

It is thought that the choice of such a determining factor is misleading for the following reasons:

— The test used in the Commission Notice is to determine matters relating to competition law. The Regulations have nothing to do with competition law.
— The test was used by the Commission to determine whether an agent was an independent trader. The issue at stake in the Schedule to the Regulations is what constitutes secondary activity. The two are not the same or even similar.
— The test as used by the Commission was not the only criterion set out in the Notice. There were two other alternatives: first whether the agent was required to organise, maintain or ensure at his own expense a substantial service to customers free of charge, and secondly, whether the agent could or did in fact determine prices or terms of business. Neither of these two further alternatives were relied on by the DTI.
— The reliance on the single test marks an obvious move away from the DTI's position as set out in the 1993 Guidelines. There, the DTI stated that the existence of any one of the criteria set out in the Commission Notice would not in itself be inconsistent with an agent's commercial activities being secondary—see paragraph 23.

In the authors' opinion, the DTI would have done better to keep to its statement in the 1993 Guidelines that there existed '*no readily apparent test or tests to apply* in order to determine the matter of secondary activity' (see paragraph 24).

### 6.12 A CHANGE DURING THE CONTRACT TOWARDS SECONDARY ACTIVITIES

If activities of an agent are deemed to be secondary at the start of a contract, does that mean that if the relevant activities become more important, then this factor is not taken into account? Whilst it would seem from a common-sense

[4] OJ 1962/139.
[5] Now Art 101 TFEU.
[6] See also Commission Notice 2000/L291/01, *Guidelines on Vertical Restraints*, where the relevant determining factor is that of financial or commercial risk borne by the appointee. At the time of writing, revised Guidelines were under review.

point of view that the test should be a continuing one, even though this may lead to the Regulations being applied to a particular contract which was clearly outside their scope when it began operating, the courts have, as has already been noted, decided this issue in favour of an application of the test solely at the inception of the relationship.[7]

## 6.13 SECONDARY ACTIVITIES IN PRACTICE: THE CASE-LAW TO DATE

Unsurprisingly, judges have struggled with the Schedule, and what the court in *Crane*[8] described as the 'elusive concept of secondary activities'. By way of cautionary notes:

— applying the Schedule and reviewing the issue of secondary activities will always be heavily fact-dependent and advisers should beware of extrapolating too far from the case-law; and
— while some issues can be considered as decided law in the light of the cases over the past few years, that is not universally the case.

The following principles are discernible from the cases:[9]

— one should look at the position at inception, not on termination;[10]
— it is initially for the agent to show that his activities are not secondary;[11]
— the touchstone is whether this agent has been engaged to develop goodwill in the principal's business, which goodwill the agent cannot realise for his own benefit.[12] In particular, it will be recalled that the House of Lords in that case answered an intervention on behalf of the Winemakers' Federation of Australia to the effect that a valuation of an agent's business would take into account the portability of an agent's goodwill. It is strange that the case-law has adopted this approach without a single express reference to goodwill in the Schedule.

There are a number of other factors arising from the cases which are noteworthy but can probably not yet be described as settled law, as follows:

— where the goods are identified in the market with the supplier/manufacturer

---

[7] See ch 5.9 above.

[8] See *Crane v Sky In-home Services Limited and others* [2007] EWHC 66 (Ch) at para 59.

[9] Particularly *Gailey, McAdam v Boxpack, Crane v Sky In-Home Service, Marjandi v Bon Accord*, and *Edwards v International Connection (UK) Limited* (Central London County Court) (2005 WL 3804444) (as well as the earlier case of *Tamarind*). *Gailey, McAdam* and *Marjandi* are Scottish cases, and despite the fact that the English and Scottish courts have not always agreed on issues arising out of the Regulations, the authors believe that significant weight should be accorded to them, particularly the appellate decisions in *Gailey* and *McAdam*.

[10] See *McAdam*, para 20. The authors would reiterate their doubts as expressed at ch 5.9 above.

[11] *Gailey*, para 40; *Crane*, para 51.

[12] See *McAdam*, para 22, approving the approach in *Gailey* and in *Tamarind*.

rather than with the principal, the agent's activities would be secondary.[13] This is a surprising conclusion, but springs again from a consideration of good-will; and because it goes to goodwill, the court considered that 'its presence or absence is of considerable significance';

— it is unclear how the 'tailpiece' to paragraph 2 of the Schedule relates to the remainder, or how and when paragraphs 3 and 4 are to be applied.[14] It seems to the authors that to commence by reviewing paragraph 2 is the right course, although it is unclear whether it ultimately makes any difference;

— it was suggested in *Gailey* that a full-time agent had a greater moral case to compensation than someone who was part time.[15] The authors consider this view questionable and it does not stand up well to a comparison with the position under EU employment law;

— the meaning of the word 'secondary': as will be seen from the above dis-cussion, the courts have concluded that this is not simply a question of numerical comparison. The ultimate expression of this reasoning is to be found in *Gailey*;[16]

— again from *Gailey*,[17] that if the principal's business is not predominantly one involving the sale of goods, the agent's activities are 'necessarily secondary'.

All of the above considerations regarding the complexity and uncertainty hang-ing over secondary activities cause the authors to conclude that a rewriting of the Schedule is long overdue—either to capture the issues addressed in the case-law and on which the Schedule is vague or silent, or to correct the increasing tendency of the courts to look to issues of development of goodwill (as opposed to those things expressly referred to in the Schedule) as the critical factor.

## 6.14 WHAT IS THE POSITION OF 'SUPER-AGENTS'?

An explanation may be called for at the outset: by a 'super-agent' the authors mean to refer to an individual who manages or controls a force of independent individuals engaged in selling for the principal either as sub-agents or under direct contract from the principal.

As has already been seen, the view of the Court is that sub-agents themselves are outside the scope of the Regulations. In the unreported County Court case of *Hunter v Zenith Windows*, it was apparently decided that a 'super-agent' was not within the protection of the Regulations because his activities were second-ary, by reference to paragraph 2(b)(ii) of the Schedule. In contrast, the Court in *Light and others v Ty Europe* expressed the view, *obiter*, that the 'super-agent'

---

[13] *Gailey* at 442 A-C.
[14] See discussion of these issues in *Marjandi v Bon Accord* [2007] Scot SC 55 at para 64.
[15] At para 37.
[16] At 437 A-D.
[17] At 443 B-E

would have a claim under the Regulations[18] despite having concluded that much or most of what the super-agent did seemed to be mere sales administration.[19]

### 6.15 WHAT IS THE POSITION AS REGARDS NORTHERN IRELAND?

As mentioned above, the Regulations do not apply to Northern Ireland, for which there is a separate implementing Regulation (SR 1993/483). It was made on 17 December 1993 and came into force on 13 January 1994, a little after the due implementation date. Detailed reference should be made to that Regulation, but it largely mirrors SI 1993/3053. The comment in chapter 4 regarding Regulations 1(2) and (3) is of relevance in determining whether an agent who operates for the whole of the UK need make two separate claims for compensation/indemnity or only one claim, in circumstances where his or her agreement with the principal is governed by English law.

---

[18] Para 35.
[19] Para 11.

# 7

# Regulations 3, 4 and 5:
# Rights and Obligations of
# Agent and Principal

## 7.1 OUTLINE

THIS CHAPTER DEALS with the duties of a commercial agent to his principal and the duties of a principal to his commercial agent. Since 2002, the main area of development has been in the domestic courts, with very little added by the ECJ. This is unsurprising, given that the Court's approach to other areas of the Directive has been to hold that the Member States have a substantial degree of discretion.[1] Accordingly, analysis of, for example, the principle of good faith in France may prove to be of little assistance to an English court. The issue of whether these Regulations operate to imply terms into particular contracts or should be viewed as overlying statutory obligations is still at large, but following the decision in the case of *Janet Mann v Flair Leisure Product plc*,[2] it is certainly arguable that they fall into the latter category, with all the consequences that would follow from that.

## 7.2 THE AGENT'S DUTIES

As can be seen from the wording of Regulation 3, the duties of a commercial agent set out in that Regulation essentially mirror the fiduciary duties imposed on agents by English law, which were reviewed in chapter 1. They also reflect the ordinary common law duties arising under English law of being obliged to obey reasonable instructions and to exercise reasonable care, skill and diligence. Accordingly, the duties set out in Regulation 3 add little, if anything, to English law as regards the agent's duties but serve to codify obligations which already existed at common law.

---

[1] See eg its judgment in *Honyvem*; see also the Advocate General's Opinion in Case C-348/07: *Semen* (not yet reported).

[2] Birmingham District Registry Mercantile Court, judgment of HHJ Alton of 15 December 2005.

However, there is one area which does call for some further examination—
that of acting in the interests of the agent's principal and in good faith. It is
clear, at least insofar as concerns the Regulations, that an agent is entitled to act
for other non-competing principals. That can be seen from the Schedule to the
Regulations, which provides inter alia that one of the indications that an agent's
activities are not secondary is that 'the agent devotes substantially the whole of
his time to representative activities (whether for one principal or for a number
of principals whose interests are not conflicting)'.[3]

Less clear is the position regarding competing principals. An agent will
generally be bound by the fiduciary duty not to put himself into positions of
conflicting interest. That duty will not of course be broken where the agent
informs the principal of his intention to act for a competitor and the principal
gives the agent permission to do so. However, in the absence of such authorisation, does Regulation 3 prohibit an agent from acting for competing principals?
The question will depend to a large extent on the definition to be attached to the
notion of 'good faith'. This concept has not been defined by the ECJ, and given
the latter's approach to Member State's discretion in determining other matters
under the Directive, it is to be presumed that national courts will retain a similar discretion in so far as concerns notions such as 'good faith'.[4]

The DTI in its Explanatory Note on the Regulations stated that the agent's
duty of good faith as contained in Regulation 3 simply restated the duties owed
at common law by an agent to his principal. However, the accuracy of the DTI's
position must be questioned given its position on a principal's corresponding
duty of good faith under the Regulations. The DTI suggested that the principal's duties in this regard merely amplified the position at common law. That is
clearly wrong, given that there is no such duty of good faith on the principal at
common law.

It has been suggested that in fact the notion of good faith should be interpreted in a radically different manner to the position taken in the past in English
law.[5] The suggestion is that because good faith is now mutual as between agent
and principal, the duty on both parties extends to ensuring not only that the
other party's interests are protected but also that the joint interests of both parties must be protected. This approach is apparently consistent with the French
approach to commercial agency. However, for the reasons already expressed, it is
not clear that English courts (as opposed to their Scottish counterparts) would
wish to adopt the position in France.[6] If however, that were to be the position
taken by the English courts, then it would open up the possibility for an agent
to argue that its duty of good faith was not just limited to safeguarding the

---

[3] Para 3(c) of the Schedule to the Regulations; see also the judgment of Scott Baker LJ in *Smith
v Reliance Water Controls Ltd* [2003] EuLR 874 at para 26.

[4] See eg the ECJ's judgment in Case C-465/04: *Honyvem Informazioni Commerciali Srl v Mariella
De Zotti* [2006] ECR I-2879.

[5] See Saintier and Scholes, *Commercial Agents and the Law* (2005) para 3.4.1.15.

[6] In this regard, see the comments of Lord Hoffmann in *Lonsdale*.

principal's interests, and that accordingly, in certain circumstances, he should be allowed to act for competing principals where such action did not jeopardise the joint interests of both parties.

A further issue can be seen from the following example. Consider the position of an agent who acts as agent for more than one principal in the same geographical market. It is likely to be selling complementary ranges of products. How does the agent resolve its conflicting duties to the various principals, in particular the duty to look after their respective interests? This problem has always existed, but the agent now has a statutory duty in addition to any common law duty.

## 7.3 THE PRINCIPAL'S DUTIES

Unlike Regulation 3, Regulation 4 represents a marked change from the status quo ante. It will be recalled that English law has traditionally viewed the principal as the person requiring protection and the common law therefore developed very few rules for the protection of the agent and correspondingly very few obligations on the principal.[7]

The position has now changed, as a result of the Regulations. As has been made clear in a number of judgments from the ECJ, one of the aims of the Directive is to ensure the protection of commercial agents:[8]

> [I]t is common ground that the Directive aims to coordinate the laws of the Member States as regards the legal relationship between the parties to a commercial agency contract. Accordingly, the Directive seeks in particular to protect commercial agents in their relations with their principals.

This perceived need to protect commercial agents, who were likened by Staughton LJ to a 'downtrodden race',[9] clearly required the imposition of obligations on principals, which is the effect of Regulation 4.

Examination of the key obligations on principals in relation to acting dutifully and in good faith reveals that they are similar to those imposed on agents. It is therefore not surprising that in the case of *Poseidon*, the ECJ held that

> It should be noted in this connection that, as is clear from Article 1(2) of the Directive, a commercial agency contract is characterized in particular by the fact that the agent, defined as a self-employed intermediary, is invested by the principal with continuing authority to negotiate. That is clear from several provisions of the Directive especially Articles 3 and 4 on the obligations upon the parties to act dutifully and in good faith towards each other.[10]

---

[7] See Bowstead and Reynolds, *Agency*, 18th edn, para 11-023.

[8] See most recently, Case C-348/07: *Semen* 26 March 2009 (not yet reported), para 14.

[9] See *Page v Combined Shipping and Transport Co Ltd* [1997] 3 All ER 656 at 660.

[10] See Case C-3/04: *Poseidon Chartering NV v Marianne Zeeschip VOF and Others* [2006] ECR I-2505 at para 24.

The Court here appears to be indicating that these obligations on the agent and principal contained in Regulations 3 and 4 are in fact a mirror image of each other.

However, that is not totally accurate. Although the substantive content of the respective obligations is the same or very similar, there is a distinction insofar as concerns the scope of the respective obligations. Regulation 3 provides that '[i]n performing his activities a commercial agent must' comply with the various obligations set out. Regulation 4, on the other hand, provides that '[i]n his relations with his commercial agent a principal must' comply with its various obligations set out.

It has to be presumed that the difference in wording was deliberate, which presumption is reinforced by the earlier drafts of the Directive, which contain the same distinction. If the difference is deliberate, then what is its effect?

The Directive is not overly helpful in this regard. Article 1(1) thereof provides that the 'harmonising measures prescribed in this Directive shall apply to the laws, regulations and administrative provisions of the Member States governing the relations between commercial agents and their principals'. That provision has, however, to be read in the light of the second recital to the Directive, which states that the differences in national laws concerning commercial representation substantially affect the conditions of competition and the carrying-on of that activity within the Community. Thus, the terms 'activities' and 'relations with' are both employed.

In so far as the Regulations are concerned, it can be noted that, as in the Directive, the provision dealing with the entitlement to post-termination compensation states: '[T]he commercial agent shall be entitled to compensation for the damage he suffers as a result of the termination of his relations with his principal.'[11]

Whatever the reason for the difference in wording, the effect could be quite dramatic. It could be argued that in keeping with the perceived need to protect commercial agents, the duties to act dutifully and in good faith placed on principals should be construed as being more onerous than those imposed on agents, at least in terms of their temporal extent. The basis for this argument would be that the words 'relations with' are wider than the performance of 'activities'. The latter is clearly restricted to matters taking place during the agency agreement between the parties. The former could include pre- and/or post-contractual matters.

The logic of this argument would lead to a principal being fixed with a duty to act dutifully and in good faith in, say, pre-contractual negotiations, whilst the agent was not so fixed. Whilst some commentators suggest that such a conclusion might well infringe common law principles,[12] we do not share that perception. First, there is no general duty of good faith on a principal in English

---

[11] Reg 17(6).
[12] See Saintier and Scholes, above n 5, para 3.4.10.

law. Secondly, fiduciary duties imposed on agents are specific in nature and do not necessarily cover this issue, although it is correct to recognise that agents are fixed with a good faith duty in their dealings with and on behalf of their principals.[13]

This approach—of imposing greater duties on the principal than on the agent—could also chime with the one of the key aims of the Directive, which is to protect commercial agents, as noted above.

### 7.4 SPECIFIC DUTIES

Both Regulation 3 and 4 give particular examples of the type of action to be taken by the respective parties to ensure compliance with the general duties set out in Regulation 3(1) and 4(1). Clearly, these are merely non-exhaustive examples rather than a complete list. Some of the examples merit discussion.

Regulation 3(2)(b) provides that a commercial agent must communicate to his principal all the necessary information available to him. Regulation 4(2)(b) provides that a principal must obtain for his commercial agent the information necessary for the performance of his agency contract.

The principal's duty seemingly extends to securing information which the principal does not have available. In addition to the 'information necessary', to what could this duty extend? As a matter of principle why should it extend, for instance, to lists of potential customers or to details of potential new legislation in the territory which could affect the products, even if that information is deemed necessary for the performance of the contract? If the duty extends to this sort of information, is that not material which the principal could legitimately expect the agent to secure, rather than vice versa? Further, who is to decide what is necessary? Is that a matter for the agent, the principal or for both parties acting in agreement?

Regulation 4(2)(a) provides that a principal must provide his commercial agent with the necessary documentation relating to the goods concerned. What does this mean? Is this a reference to technical specifications, promotional material, price lists or otherwise? The answer is likely to vary on a case-by-case basis, but remains uncertain.

Regulation 4(3) provides that a principal shall inform his agent within a reasonable time of his acceptance or refusal of, and any non-execution by him of, a commercial transaction which the agent has procured for him. There is some overlap here with Regulation 12 which requires the principal to supply the agent with a statement of commission due and the main components used in calculating the amount of commission. It is difficult to see how the principal could comply with the latter obligation if it did not tell the agent which transactions had gone forward and which would not be proceeding.

---

[13] See eg *Bristol and West Building Society v Mothew* [1998] Ch 1.

## 7.5 REGULATION 5

Regulation 5(1) makes clear that Regulations 3 and 4 are mandatory. Any attempt by a party to a commercial agency agreement to weaken or exclude its obligations under those Regulations will therefore be bound to fail.

Regulation 5(2) provides that the applicable law of the contract shall govern the consequence of any breach of the Regulations in question. In so far as that law is English law, the consequences of any such breach will depend on the manner in which the duties contained in the Regulation are treated in English law. In essence, the choice will be between their classification as terms which are to be implied into every contract, or as part of a statutory scheme which overlies the contractual position.

To illustrate this point, consider the difference between the Sale of Goods Act 1979 as amended and employment protection legislation—in particular the Employment Protection (Consolidation) Act 1978.

The 1979 Act states that certain provisions will be implied into every contract for the sale of goods. The Act states that those terms will be conditions (ie major terms) of the contract and it is accordingly clear that a breach of those terms gives rise to contractual remedies and that these include a right in favour of the innocent party to terminate the contract as a result of that breach.

In contrast, the 1978 Act overlies the contractual position. So, therefore, an employee who is dismissed wrongfully and without notice has two claims:

— one claim is a claim for breach of contract and is remedied by the award of damages; and
— the other remedy (which is provided by an employment tribunal) is for non-contractual compensation based upon the terms of the 1978 Act.

This may seem like an academic question, but it has some serious consequences for the operation and enforcement of the terms of the Regulations.

If the Regulations are intended to imply terms into contracts (as in the 1979 Act):

— they do not state this and do not state whether those terms will be conditions of the contract (allowing the innocent party to terminate) or will be lesser terms (giving rise to a right in damages, but not to a right of termination);
— there would be little need to spell out the basis upon which damages are to be calculated since there is a wealth of material at common law on this subject.

If, however, the Regulations are to operate in a non-contractual manner (as with the 1978 Act):

— none of the necessary mechanics are included in the Regulations (with some exceptions—see below) to enable the Court to operate those provisions effectively. If, for instance, Regulations 3 and 4 are statutory obligations, is there a remedy in damages for their breach?

— are damages to be calculated on a contractual or a tortious basis, or on some other basis?
— without specific provision, if the Regulations provide statutory non-contractual remedies, then there is presumably no question of an ability to terminate the contract for breach of them.

The position has been somewhat clarified by some recent decisions in the English courts, which will be analysed in more detail below. Suffice it to say at this juncture that the English courts do not rule out the possibility that Regulations 3 and 4 provide statutory non-contractual remedies which overlay the particular contractual provisions in any given contract.

The position can further be clarified by comparing the position of Regulations 3 and 4 with Regulation 17.

It is clear from the Regulations that the rights set out in Regulation 17 are statutory non-contractual remedies—or at least this is clear as a result of Regulation 17(5) in the case of the indemnity. The authors suggest that the same is true of the compensatory option. Any remedies under Regulation 17 are in addition to, and not in substitution for, contractual remedies.[14] Indeed, many of the circumstances in which compensation or an indemnity is payable are not circumstances which amount to a breach of contract by either party. This mirrors to a great extent the position regarding wrongful and unfair dismissal at common law and in the 1978 Act.

It would be even more strange, therefore, if other elements of the Regulations were intended to operate on a contractual basis, since there is no provision in the Regulations which enables the reader to make the distinction between the 'contractual' obligations and the 'statutory' obligations.

The conclusion, therefore, is that the Regulations do not operate by way of implying terms into contracts but rather form part of a statutory scheme overlying the contractual position. It is important, however, to recognise that this view is not universally adopted. In Saintier and Scholes, the opposite view is taken.[15] This view is based on three points. The first is that the contractual nature of good faith fits with the ability of the agent to claim compensation if that party terminates for reasons attributable to the principal. With respect, we suggest that this begs the key question. The fact that an agent is able in effect to repudiate its

---

[14] This view of the Regulations as creating extra-contractual remedies seems to be reinforced by the case-law to date, such as *Moore v Piretta PTA Limited*. The Court of Justice was asked to consider an associated issue in *Arcado SPRL v SA Haviland* [1988] ECR 1539. In that case, it was held that a claim for commission and compensation under national legislation implementing the Directive arose from 'matters relating to a contract' for the purposes of the Brussels Convention on Jurisdiction. This view, that rights under legislation implementing the Directive arise in contract rather than, for instance, in tort, does not disturb the reasoning in this paragraph. However, see the recent decision of the French Court de Cassation in *Figot v Leithauser GmbH and Co* [2000] ILPr 28 for a finding that a claim for an indemnity by a commercial agent on termination was a claim independent of the contract between the parties. See also more recently the judgment of Elias J in *Bell Electric Ltd v Aweco Appliance Systems Gmbh* [2002] EWHC 872 (QB): 8 May 2002.

[15] Saintier and Scholes, above n 5, para 3.4.16.

contract with its principal where such action is justified by circumstances attributable to the principal does not answer the question of whether a breach of the duty of good faith would constitute such a justified event. Further, it does not answer the question of the nature of the breach. We would suggest that in fact it points to the statutory overlay argument—Regulation 18(b) lays down statutory provisions pursuant to which an agent is entitled to terminate a contract whilst safeguarding its right to post-termination indemnity or compensation. This is accordingly a statutory provision setting out the right of a agent to terminate in certain circumstances without losing the ability to seek an indemnity or compensation. The second point relied on by Saintier and Scholes is the judgment in *Arcardo SPRL v Haviland SA*.[16] However, for the reasons set out in the footnote above, this point is not conclusive. Thirdly, reliance is placed on the judgment of Elias J in *Bell Electric*,[17] stating that the ECJ appeared to treat the claim for post-termination compensation as contractual. That, with respect, does not accord with our reading of the judgment, in which the Court notes that it was a claim which did not bring anything additional to the contractual claim. The Court did not conclude that the claim under the Regulations was contractual in nature.

In summary, we would argue that the better approach is that Regulations 3 and 4 comprise statutory duties imposed on the parties to a relevant commercial agency contract.[18] That approach may, however, give rise to some differences of treatment as between agent and principal, eg in relation to the effect of terminating an agreement for breach of the duty to act in good faith. If English law is the applicable law of the contract, it will govern the consequences of any breach of Regulations 3 or 4.[19] As noted by Her Honour Judge Alton in *Simpson v Grant & Bowman Limited*,[20] a breach of duty to act in good faith does not necessarily amount to a repudiatory breach as a matter of domestic English law. It will always be necessary to examine whether the breach in question was sufficiently serious to entitle the victim to treat the contract as repudiated. However, that exercise may well only be necessary where a principal is seeking to assert repudiatory conduct on behalf of the agent, pursuant to Regulation 18(a). If an agent is faced with a breach of good faith by a principal, reliance could be placed on Regulation 18(b) which simply requires the agent to demonstrate that the termination was justified by circumstances attributable to the principal, which is not the same as proving repudiatory conduct. This lopsided effect in relation to the parties' different remedies reflects one of the key aims of the Directive and thus the Regulations—ie to protect the commercial agent.

---

[16]   [1988] ECR 1539.

[17]   Above n 14.

[18]   This approach chimes with that of the Scottish Court of Session in *Gailey v Environmental Waste Controls* [2004] EuLR 424, which described the compensation rights under the Regulations as being 'special rights in addition to, or even despite, . . . contractual rights'.

[19]   Reg 5.

[20]   *Simpson v Grant & Bowman Limited* [2006] EuLR 934.

## 7.6 RECENT CASE-LAW

There has been little case-law, either from the ECJ or from the domestic courts, on agents' duties under the Directive or Regulations.

### The European Court of Justice

Aside from side references to Regulations 3 and 4 in passing,[21] there has been no substantial decision by the ECJ on the matter.

### UK Courts

In what was possibly the first reported decision applying the Regulations, the Court of Appeal had the opportunity to look at the duties of agent and principal in *Page v Combined Shipping and Trading Co Ltd*.[22] This is an interlocutory decision—Mr Page was appealing against refusal by the lower court to award him a freezing injunction (formerly a *Mareva* injunction)—but the Court had to decide as part of its consideration whether he had a good arguable case under the Regulations entitling him to substantial compensation.

Mr Page had entered into a four-year agency agreement with CST in January 1995. His role was to buy and sell commodities as agent for CST. However, by June, CST's parent company had decided to close the CST business. Mr Page claimed that this was a repudiation and started proceedings. However, his difficulty was that the agreement left a lot of latitude to CST—it could decide from day to day how much business it wanted to do through Mr Page. As a matter of common law,23 the Court would assume that a defendant such as CST would, where it had discretion, have acted so as to minimise its liability. If it had done so, its liability to him might be nil.

The Court decided, on the basis of CST's duty of good faith under Regulation 4, that CST could not rely on the common law rule. Combining the duty of good faith with the wording of Regulation 17 ('commission which proper performance of the agency contract would have procured for him'), and seemingly swayed by the fact that in other language versions of the Directive, the word 'normal' appeared in place of the word 'proper', Millett LJ concluded that compensation should be calculated on the basis of normal future performance and not abnormal (even if lawful) performance.

The Court seems here to be stretching the phrase 'good faith' to its limits. By logical extension, had the contract continued in force but CST had reduced

---

[21] See eg *Poseidon*, above n 10; Case C-19/07: *Chevassus-Marche v Groupe Danone* [2007] ECR I-159; and Case C-485/01: *Caprini* [2003] ECR I-2371.

[22] [1997] 3 All ER 656.

[23] *Laverack v Woods* [1967] 1 QB 278.

trade to zero, the Court of Appeal would presumably have upheld a claim by Mr Page for damages based on the good faith principle!

'Good faith' here seems to comprehend something more than merely fair and honest dealing and extends to a positive obligation to consider the agent's business interests ahead of one's own. It is suggested that this is broader than the common law duty on agents and is tantamount to imposing fiduciary obligations on the principal in favour of the agent.[24]

*Page* makes an interesting contrast with the traditional English approach taken in *Airconsult Ltd v British Aerospace Regional Aircraft Ltd*,[25] a case in which, bafflingly, the Regulations were not referred to or applied. In that case, A was entitled to commission on a sale or lease of aircraft by British Aerospace Regional Aircraft Ltd (BARA) to certain nominated third parties. A procured a lessee and started to earn commission. BARA then sold the aircraft, subject to the leases, to a third party outside the nominated group of third parties. The judge in the Queen's Bench Division concluded that: 'Unless . . . there is an implied term that [BARA] . . . will not terminate the operating lease . . . [A] cannot be entitled to the fee.' The judge also said that: 'There is no question here of denying the defendants [BARA] freedom to deal with their property as they choose [or] . . . denying them freedom to [either] their business or not to continue it as they wish.'

In *Julian Smith v Reliance Water Controls Limited*[26] it was argued on behalf of the principal that there had been a breach of Regulation 3 in that the agent had failed to inform the principal of certain information. The Court found on the evidence that certain of the information had been communicated and the remainder was clearly not relevant. In the Court's words, 'the respondent's contention of lack of good faith does not reach first base'.[27]

In *Cooper and Others v Pure Fishing Limited*,[28] the Court found that the defendant principal, in forcing its agents to take a new range of products which competed with a range the agent was also selling on behalf of another principal, had acted in breach of its duty of good faith by creating a conflict of interest, thereby engineering a situation in which the agents had no choice but to refuse to take the new range and thereby permitting the principal not to renew its agents' agreements. The principal appealed the decision, but the Court of Appeal found in favour of the agents without the need to review the first instance court's finding on good faith.[29]

In *Turner v Steinhoff UK Furniture Limited*,[30] the principal gradually dis-

---

[24] It has even been suggested that to understand the Court of Appeal's judgment in *Page* necessitates a review of French law on the subject (S Saintier, *The Company Lawyer* 248, 249); *cf* the position taken by the High Court in *Simpson v Grant & Bowman*.

[25] *Airconsult Ltd v British Aerospace Regional Aircraft Ltd*, unreported; QBD 13 February 1998.

[26] *Julian Smith v Reliance Water Controls Limited* [2003] EuLR 874.

[27] See judgment at para 32.

[28] *Cooper and Others v Pure Fishing Limited* [2004] EuLR 664.

[29] [2004] 2 Lloyds Rep 514.

[30] *Turner v Steinhoff UK Furniture Limited* [2006] EuLR 50.

continued the ranges of products which its agent was contractually bound to sell on its behalf. The agent asserted that this course of conduct amounted to termination and claimed post-termination compensation from the principal. Surprisingly, although there is a substantial overlap on the facts with the case of *Page*, that case appears not to have been cited to the Court. In arriving at the decision that compensation was indeed due to the agent, the Court held as follows:

> A contract of agency of the kind with which this case is concerned, cannot be performed effectively without the co-operation of the parties, and in contracts requiring such co-operation it is generally implied (in the absence of appropriately drafted express provisions) that both parties will do all that is necessary on their part to enable the contract to be performed.

The Court came to this conclusion on the basis of the contract and not on the basis of Regulations 3 and 4. However, the conclusion demonstrates the similarity between the common law concepts of co-operation to be implied into such a contract and the statutory duties to act dutifully and in good faith

In the case of *Simpson v Grant & Bowman Limited*,[31] HHJ Alton sitting in the High Court made some important observations in relation to the principle of good faith under Regulation 4. She started by making it clear that it would neither be necessary nor appropriate to attempt some broad definition of the meaning or scope of the obligations under Regulation 4. Such obligations could not be assessed in a vacuum. However, she did feel able to arrive at the following broad conclusions:

— It was not necessary, in order to demonstrate a breach of the duty to act in good faith, to prove bad faith in the sense of dishonesty or some deliberate intent to damage.
— Given that the duty to act in good faith imports an obligation to act with commercial propriety towards the agent in the performance of the agency, sharp practice falling short of actual dishonesty or an intent to harm could well constitute a failure to act in good faith.
— That said, Regulation 4 did not import into the agency relationship some general and broad obligation on the part of the principal to treat the agent fairly, the assessment of which having to be made from the perspective of the agent and without regard, or significant regard to the need of the business and the entitlement of the principal to make what appears to be proper commercial decisions as to the effective management of that business. It was neither appropriate nor of assistance to draw parallels with the duties owed to an employee, and in particular to seek to equate the statutory regime applicable with unfair dismissal with the duties owed to a commercial agent under the Regulations.

---

[31] [2006] EuLR 933.

— The duty did not import some obligation to treat all agents in the same manner.
— A breach of the duty to act in good faith under Regulation 4 did not necessarily amount to a repudiatory breach of contract or justify the agent terminating the agency so as to give that person the right to claim a right to post-termination compensation. In order for it to do so, it would be necessary to consider on the facts of the case whether the breach amounted to a sufficiently serious breach of contract to enable the agent to treat the contract as repudiated.

In *NPower Direct Ltd v South of Scotland Power Limited*,[32] Cresswell J had to determine whether a request by the principal to its agent to reduce its sales by 70 per cent and the fact that the principal then increased its prices significantly were actions which were inter alia in breach of Regulation 4. In determining the issue against the agent, the Court held that both actions had to be seen in their context, which in effect demonstrated that they were justified. Further, the argument that Regulation 4 could give rise to a wider obligation on the part of the principal than that set out in the contract itself was rejected, the Court finding expressly there 'there is no scope for a duty to have some wider and uncertain effect at common law or in reliance on Regulation 4'. The authors would respectfully disagree with this conclusion. It is clear that Regulation 4 imposes additional duties on principals to those arising under the common law.

In *Michael Edwards v International Connection (UK) Limited*,[33] the Court held that the fact that an agent fell below the expectations of his principal did not give rise to a repudiatory breach of Regulation 3, which was pleaded on the basis that the agent had to make a proper effort to negotiate.

In the case of *Janet Mann v Flair Leisure Products plc*,[34] HHJ Alton sitting in the Birmingham Mercantile Court found that an agent was entitled to post-termination compensation in circumstances where action by the principal had the effect of depriving her of 95 per cent of her commission. It was argued on behalf of the principal that it had the right to do as it wished with its product ranges. In this particular case, the principal had sold all its right to sell a particular product range because one of its competitors had acquired the company that made the range of products in question. In determining the issue, the Court held that in the light of inter alia Regulation 4, it could not be right that a principal was entitled to remove, albeit for perfectly good commercial reasons, the whole foundation of the agency relationship.

In *Cureton v Mark Insulations Limited*,[35] an agency was terminated by the principal on the basis that the agent, whilst attending to the affairs of his principal, sought to solicit further non-competing business on behalf of another business owned and operated by the agent. The termination letter specifically

---

[32] *NPower Direct Ltd v South of Scotland Power Limited* [2005] EWHC 2123 (Comm).
[33] *Michael Edwards v International Connection (UK) Limited*, judgment of 25 November 2005 (unreported).
[34] Above n 2, judgment of 15 December 2005 (unreported).
[35] *Cureton v Mark Insulations Limited* [2006] EWHC 2279.

cited Regulation 3. The Court, finding in favour of the principal, held that there was no agreement at the start of the relationship between the parties that the agent would do no other work than that for the principal. In coming to that decision, the Court pointed out the difference between an employment contract, where it would generally be expected that the employee would only work for the employer, and a non-exclusive agency agreement. However, because the agent failed to disclose the material facts of his additional work to his principal, the Court held that there had been a breach of inter alia Regulation 3, which breach was sufficiently serious to give the principal the right to terminate under Regulation 16.

In *Vick v Vogle-Gapes*,[36] in a somewhat novel development, the contract between the principal and agent actually contained mutual obligations of good faith. Although the agent's case on this issue was pleaded both on the basis of the express terms of the contract and on the basis of Regulation 4, in the event, that latter case was not pursued. However, the Court's findings on the issue of good faith are still of interest. On the basis of the express contractual provisions, it was common ground between the parties[37] that any power of the principal to do some act which could have repercussions on the agent was only to be exercised dutifully and in good faith. The Court also accepted that the said obligation was at least as wide as the obligation on the part of both and employer and an employee in a contract of employment to act towards each other with mutual trust and confidence. However, as the judge pointed out, the applicable case-law in that area demonstrated that whatever had been done which was said to be in breach of that duty had to have been done without reasonable and proper cause. Further, what was required to make good a case for breach was deliberate rather than inadvertent conduct.

In the case of *Crane v Sky-in-Home Service Limited and Others*,[38] Briggs J held that the passing-off by an agent of his extended warranty service as that of his principal's was a continuing and serious breach of inter alia Regulation 3, described as a duty of fidelity. In doing so, the learned judge did not feel the need to explore the scope of such a duty, doubtless because, on the facts, the agent's actions self-evidently breached it.[39]

---

[36] *Vick v Vogle-Gapes* [2006] EWHC 1579 (QB).
[37] Although not necessarily with the judge—see para 84 of the judgment.
[38] *Crane v Sky-in-Home Service Limited and Others* [2007] EuLR 549.
[39] See in this regard the obiter comments of HHJ Alton in *Janet Mann*, above n 2, para 26.

# 8

# Regulations 6–12:
# Remuneration of the Agent

## 8.1 OUTLINE

THIS CHAPTER DEALS with the key issues relating to the remuneration of a commercial agent, including when commission is payable and the circumstances which can extinguish the agent's right to commission.

## 8.2 STRUCTURE

Regulation 6 deals with remuneration in the absence of agreement and states that Regulations 7–12 inclusive do not apply unless the agent is remunerated wholly or in part by commission. It should be noted that compensation or an indemnity payment is due on termination even when the agent is not remunerated by way of commission.

The Court of Appeal has held, unsurprisingly,[1] that the concept of 'remuneration' for the purposes of the Regulations does not extend to circumstances in which the representative earns a 'turn' on the difference between purchase and resale price, where the representative buys and later resells, the mark-up being determined by the representative. To conclude otherwise would have brought all distributorships within the scope of the Regulations.

Regulation 7 deals with entitlement to commission during the term of the contract, Regulation 8 deals with entitlement to commission on transactions concluded after termination and Regulation 9 deals with apportionment of commissions between an incoming and an outgoing agent following termination.

Regulation 10 deals with the circumstances in which commission becomes

---

[1] In *AMB Imballagi Plastici SRL v Pacflex Limited* (CA) [1999] 2 All ER (Comm) 249. However, see also in this connection the judgment of Andrew Smith J in the Commercial Court in *Mercantile Industrial Group plc v Chuan Soon Huat Industrial Group plc* [2002] 1 All ER (Comm) 788 in which the fact that the agent received a 'turn' between the purchase and resale prices did not mean that the Regulations were not applicable. It simply meant that the agent was not remunerated by way of commission. This decision has been upheld on appeal: see [2002] EWCA Civ 288. Generally, see ch 8.4 below.

due and the date upon which commission is payable, Regulation 11 deals with the extinction of the right to commission in certain circumstances and Regulation 12 deals with supply of information by the principal to the agent.

## 8.3 REMUNERATION IN THE ABSENCE OF AGREEMENT

Regulation 6(1) states that in the absence of agreement as to remuneration between the parties, the agent will be entitled to:

— the remuneration that agents appointed for the goods which are the subject of the agency contract are customarily allowed in the place where the agent carries on his activities;
— (if there is no such customary practice) reasonable remuneration taking into account all the aspects of the transaction.

This Regulation is likely to be of relevance only in a very few cases, since even in the briefest of oral agreements, commission is likely to be an issue on which there is express agreement.

It should be noted that there is nothing which requires the parties to agree an objectively reasonable level of commission, although given that the reason for the Directive was the perceived inequality of bargaining power, it might have been expected that the Directive would tackle this issue. Indeed, the fact that the commission rate agreed is lower than average or lower than some objective standard is not even stated to be a factor to be taken into account in calculating compensation or an indemnity payment.

### Customary Remuneration

The relevant custom is that of the place where the agent carried on his activities (compare earlier drafts of the Regulations which took a slightly different stance). It is conceivable, therefore, that agents in different territories performing the same obligations might receive differential rates of commission (or other remuneration) as a result of the operation of this provision. Rather than harmonising, therefore, in this respect the Directive perpetuates existing inequalities.

If there is no custom on which to rely, the agent is entitled to reasonable remuneration (presumably whether this reasonable remuneration takes the form of commission or not) taking into account 'all the aspects of the transaction': is this a reference to the agreement between principal and agent, or between principal and third party? If the latter, it would require a separate consideration of the issues in respect of each transaction on which the agent was entitled to commission. It is an almost inescapable conclusion of the wording used that the reference is to each individual transaction between principal and third party, particularly since the same word is used in Regulations 7 and 10 to refer to the contract between principal and third party, but if this is correct, then it engenders uncertainty in so far as the parties will find it difficult to determine whether the right amount of commission has been paid. Would it not have been more logical to have used the duties which the agent was expected to perform as the touchstone for this calculation?

Regulation 6(2) states that it is without prejudice to the application of any enactment or rule of law concerning the level of remuneration. There are no such enactments in England and Wales.

## 8.4 COMMERCIAL AGENTS AND 'MARK-UPS'

What is the status of a representative who, instead of receiving a commission from the principal, instead applies a mark-up to the goods and sells them on at the increased price, retaining the mark-up in lieu of commission? Is the answer affected by whether the mark-up is agreed by the representative or set by/agreed with the principal?

It is possible that part of the rationale of the ECJ's judgment in *Mavrona*[2] is that an agent remunerated in this way is not a commercial agent for the purposes of the Regulations, although the key focus of that decision, rendered without the benefit of a formal Advocate General's Opinion, is that agents for undisclosed principals are not within the scope of the Directive.

The English Courts have made heavy weather of this issue. The touchstone is authority, so the issue of mark-up should be irrelevant unless it bears on this issue. There is no reason in principle why a 'true' agent should not have authority to amend prices or other terms (although any such latitude is rare). As Waller LJ put it in *Pacflex*:[3]

> If a person buys or sells himself as principal he is outside the ambit of the Regulations. That is so because in negotiating that sale or purchase he is acting on his own behalf and not on behalf of another.

As the Court of Appeal noted in *Sagal v Bunz*,[4] 'Mark-up is not, however, conclusive against commercial agency.' In *Mercantile International* although the agent retained an undisclosed margin on sales, given that the documentation clearly constituted the representative as the principal's agent, unless the documentation was held to be a sham, the Court held that the relationship would be one of commercial agency. Conversely, in *Sagal v Bunz*, it was clear that the relationship was not one of commercial agency, and the mark-up issue was not determinative.

---

[2] Case C-85/03 [2004] ECR I-1573.
[3] *AMB Imballagi v Pacflex Limited* (CA) [1999] 2 All ER 249.
[4] See para 15 of the judgment.

## 8.5 ENTITLEMENT TO COMMISSION DURING THE TERM OF THE CONTRACT

Regulation 7 sets out three circumstances in which the agent is entitled to commission on transactions concluded during the term of the contract, as follows:

— where the transaction is concluded as a result of the agent's action;
— where the transaction is concluded with a third party whom the agent has previously acquired as a customer for transactions of the same kind; or
— where the agent has an exclusive right to a specified geographical area or to a specific group of customers and the transaction is entered into with a customer belonging to that area or group.

Each of these limbs is considered separately below. It should be noted that the preamble to Regulation 7 uses the word 'concluded', perhaps an unintentional echo of the words 'negotiate and conclude' as used in the definition of 'commercial agent' itself. The authors' view is that this word can only refer, in both contexts, to the conclusion of a binding contract between principal and third party. To this extent, it can be contrasted with the word 'executed' which is utilised in Regulation 10 and which refers to the performance by a party of its obligations under the contract that has been concluded.

## 8.6 THE FIRST LIMB

The first limb of Regulation 7 refers to transactions concluded as a result of the agent's action. At common law, the question was whether the agent was the effective cause of the transaction, and there is much case-law in this area, concerning in particular the role of estate agents. It is not sufficient for the agent's act to be the causa sine qua non of the transaction. In case of conflicting claims to commission, the courts at common law would determine which of the competing agents was the effective cause of the transaction (compare with the issue discussed below at chapter 8.7).

Could two agents both state that a single transaction had been entered into as a result of their respective actions? In this sense, it may be that the standard set by the Regulations is more lax and entails greater danger for the principal than the common law rule.

## 8.7 THE SECOND LIMB

The second limb of Regulation 7 refers to the conclusion of a contract with a third party whom the agent has previously acquired as a customer for transactions of the same kind. It should be noted that there is no reference to obtaining this customer as a customer for the same principal, nor is there a reference to goods of the same kind as the goods in question. Is it enough that, in a previous incarnation as agent (or perhaps distributor or employee) of the present principal's main competitor, the agent secured this customer as a customer for similar goods? If so, then the principal may be in a worse position (from the point of view of the Regulations, at least) in engaging an experienced agent known in the market than he would otherwise be.

Assuming, however, that the agent has received some compensation or indemnity upon termination of its relationship with the competitor (if that relationship was that of principal and agent), why should the agent effectively receive a second payment even though, by definition, it has not satisfied the first limb of Regulation 7 and the transaction has not resulted from its action? In fact, the perverse conclusion is that the customer concerned could have come direct to the present principal precisely because he or she was dissatisfied with the agent's former principal or even with the agent itself! It seems an odd conclusion that the principal should be obliged to pay commission in such circumstances.

## 8.8 THE THIRD LIMB

The third limb of Regulation 7 contemplates a degree of exclusivity, either in respect of a geographical area or group of customers. It should be noted that it is not necessary for this exclusivity to have been agreed on the face of the contract and there must be a danger for principals that the mere fact of having one agent for a particular area or group of customers will give rise to claims under this limb. Confusingly, both the Directive and the Regulations use the words 'concluded' and 'entered into' to refer to the same transaction, but the different wording is presumably not intended to import any difference of meaning.

What does 'exclusive' mean in this context? Does it mean strict exclusivity, with neither the principal nor any other party having the right to seek customers in the territory concerned, or does it cover 'sole' agencies where in effect the agent is in competition with the principal for orders? Particularly given the fact where the agent is only 'negotiating' (and not 'negotiating and concluding') that the principal will be involved in contract formation, it may be that the intention is that 'sole' agencies will be covered as well as 'exclusive' agencies.

It should be noted that both the second and third limbs of Regulation 7 operate where the agent has not been the cause of the transaction concerned.[5] It is a frequent complaint of principals with mature agency networks that, in fact, sales volumes stagnate as agents who originally worked hard for relatively modest remuneration at the outset rest on their laurels when earning significant commissions as a result of repeat orders from long-term customers. The Regulations do nothing to address this situation.

---

[5] As regards Reg 7(2), this was confirmed by the Court of Justice in Case C-104/95: *Kontogeorgas v Kartonpak AE* [1996] ECR I-6643.

In *Kontogeorgas v Kartonpak AE*[6] the Court of Justice stated that the expression 'customer belonging to that area' in Article 7(2) of the Directive (and therefore Regulation 7(2)) means that, where the agent is a legal person, one looks for the location of that person's commercial activities.

The Court recognised, however, that this alone could result in a single transaction being regarded as attaching to the territories of two different agents. Accordingly it stated that, where customer or agent operated in several places, one must consider other factors to determine the centre of gravity of the transaction, including where negotiations took place (or should have taken place in the normal course), the place of delivery and the location from which the order was placed.

The Court of Justice has, however, held[7] that the *principal* must be involved in the transaction with the customer if the agent is to be entitled to commission under Regulation 7(2): although this is not apparent from Article 7(2) itself, the Court held that it was apparent from the terms of Articles 10(1) and (2) as confirmed by Article 11.

## 8.9 DOUBLE AND TRIPLE TROUBLE—MULTIPLE CLAIMS

A particular difficulty may arise with a multi-location customer and competing claims to commission. Suppose that a principal is represented in territories A, B and C by agents X, Y and Z, respectively. Each of the agents has been appointed on an exclusive basis. Q plc places an order with the principal through its branch in territory A, but does not go through agent X. Agent X is nevertheless entitled to a commission under the third limb since he has an exclusive right to territory A. However, the order concerned resulted from work carried out by agent Y, who has persuaded the finance director of Q plc, at a trade fair recently held in territory B, to purchase the principal's products. Y is entitled to a commission under the first limb. Agent Z had nothing to do with the present order, but has previously acquired Q plc as a customer for this principal, perhaps at a time when he was the exclusive agent of the whole of the territory now divided up between X, Y and Z. Z seems to be entitled to commission under the second limb.

How are these competing claims to be handled? Although Regulations 8 and 9 are considered below, it will be noted that Regulation 9 provides a way of dealing with competing claims as between an incoming and outgoing agent. Why is there no such provision to deal with competing claims during the term of agency contracts?

This difficulty is compounded in practice since the principal may, at the time when the order referred to above is received, pay commission to agent X. It may be some months or years since agent Z acquired business for Q plc and

---

[6] Ibid.
[7] *Heirs of Chevassus-Marché v Groupe Danone* (ECJ) Case C-19/07, decided on 17 January 2008.

the principal may not even know at this stage that agent Y has attempted to sell the products to Q plc. This 'double' or 'triple' trouble ideally should be resolved by amendment to the Regulations. But what is the position in the meantime?

There are two answers to this question. First of all, it is to be hoped that the courts will take a sensible approach to this issue, allowing the principal to divide commission on an equitable basis between the three agents. This does not, however, obviate the risk that the basis of such division is subsequently challenged, even assuming that the principal is aware of all claims on deciding how to divide commission.

The reality is that agents are unlikely to litigate this point during the term of the contract and that this issue may therefore only arise once the agency contract has determined. Suppose that, at the time concerned, the principal merely paid the whole of the commission due to agent X. It is only on termination of agent Y's contract that, in addition to claiming compensation or indemnity under Part IV of the Regulations, agent Y also claims commissions on a large number of orders including that which we are considering. Would the court entitle the principal subsequently to set off any sums actually paid to agent Y against sums subsequently due to agent X? Even if the court would allow this, this set-off is only available to the principal if agent X is still in existence and if there is still an entitlement to commissions. If agent X has died or (if a company) has been liquidated, then this option is not available to the principal.

The second answer to this question is that the principal should take care in drafting agency contracts with a view to providing for the payment of differential commission rates in such circumstances. It should be noted that there is nothing in Regulation 6 or Regulation 7 to prevent the payment of differential commission rates depending upon the circumstances, and indeed Regulation 9, which is considered below, effectively sanctions the payment of a lower rate of commission in certain circumstances. In *Edwards v ICL*,[8] the county court judge decided that, where sales were invoiced within the agent's territory for delivery outside it, they did attract commission pursuant to Regulation 7(2).

Taking the drafting issue a stage further, is it possible to provide that the rate of commission will be zero, or that no commission will be due, on contracts concluded outside the given area? There seems no reason in principle why this should not be done unless the court would be prepared to state under Regulation 6 that there had been no agreement as to remuneration between the parties.

A broader issue here is the question of whether Regulations 7–9 are excludeable by express agreement in any event and that issue is considered below. The DTI's only comment on this issue in the 1994 Guidance Notes is the following rather delphic comment:

> The provisions of [7](2) include so-called 'House Accounts' held by the principal ie, where the principal deals directly with the third party although the agent has the rights to that area.

---

[8] *Edwards v International Connection (UK) Limited* [2005] WL 3804444, decided on 25 November 2005 (see para 30ff).

The assumption behind this provision is that exclusivity is an 'all or nothing' concept: either the agent has an exclusive right to a particular area, in which case the DTI is suggesting that the principal cannot carve out specific named customers from that exclusivity, or the area is not exclusive to the agent at all. In practice, the principal will frequently want to remove house accounts from the agent's entitlement to commission: where there is an agent of a large multi-national group in the territory and there are intra-group sales between the principal and an associated company in that territory, it could be disastrous for the principal if it were obliged to pay commissions on those intra-group sales as well as on sales to third parties. If this is the effect of the Regulations as the DTI suggests, why should this be the case? The agent is unlikely to have done any work to procure those intra-group sales and whether or not there is such a sale depends merely on the manner in which the principal has organised its business: if the local operation were merely a branch of the principal's business, then there would be no sale at all—just an intra-company transfer.

### 8.10 POSITION OF DEL CREDERE AGENTS

A del credere agent is an agent who accepts responsibility towards the principal in the event that customers fail to pay. As such, a del credere agent is an exception to the normal situation which is that following the formation of a contract between principal and customer, the agent has no liability on the contract. Are del credere agents in a different position as a result of the introduction of the Regulations?

In recognition of the extra liability which he takes on, the del credere agent receives an extra commission, known as the 'del credere commission' and one important question is whether these commissions will also be the subject of the rules set out in Part III of the Regulations. The del credere commission would seem to satisfy the definition of 'commission' in Regulation 2, but is the del credere agent not being remunerated for a separate service which he provides that is not of the type which the Directive intended to cover?

This point is not dealt with in the Directive or the Regulations but was addressed by the Court of Appeal in *Mercantile International Ltd v Chuan Soon Huat*,[9] the Court noting that the del credere guarantee does not stop the person concerned from being an agent. Del credere agency is, in any event, fairly rare and the point is unlikely to be a significant one in the context of the bulk of commercial agency relationships. In contrast, the draft of the Directive considered by the Law Commission Report contained specific provisions regarding del credere agents. The Law Commission asked the interesting question whether a del credere agent is due the normal commission in circumstances where he pays upon failure by the customer to pay. This question remains unanswered.

---

[9] *Mercantile International Ltd v Chuan Soon Huat* [2002] EWCA Civ 288 at para 41.

## 8.11 ENTITLEMENT TO COMMISSIONS ON
## TRANSACTIONS CONCLUDED AFTER TERMINATION

Regulation 8 states that the agent will be entitled to commission on transactions concluded after termination if:

— the transaction is 'mainly attributable' to the agent's efforts during the term of the contract and the transaction is entered into within a 'reasonable period' after termination;[10] or
— the third party's order reached the principal or the agent before termination.

Why have the words 'mainly attributable' been used in Regulation 8 when the words 'as a result of his action' are used in Regulation 7? With reference to the comments at chapter 8.6 above regarding Regulation 7(1)(a), it is presumably possible for only one agent to say that the transaction is 'mainly attributable' to his efforts. Was the test intended to be more severe under Regulation 8 than it is under Regulation 7? In the view of Fulford J in *PJ Pipe & Valve v Audco*,[11] there was little difference between the common law test and that set out in Regulation 8, at least on the facts of that case. According to the Court in *Simpson v Grant & Bowman*,[12] the effect of the requirement in Regulation 8(a) that the transaction be 'mainly attributable' to the agent's efforts means that an agent is not, post-termination, entitled to commissions simply because an order is received from a customer in its exclusive territory or customer group. There must be a causative element if Regulation 8(a) is to be engaged. Note that this may have a significant impact on the amount recoverable by an agent with an exclusive territory.

What is a 'reasonable period'? This will be determined by reference to the facts of each case, but the duration of the agency contract, and in particular the notice period to be given under it, are factors which should be taken into account. The nature of the principal's business should also be considered—for instance, if the goods are heavy plant, it may take many months to turn an enquiry into an order.[13]

In *Tigana v Decoro*,[14] the Court noted that the agency was 'front-loaded' (ie the agent's main efforts were at the outset) and in the circumstances found nine months to be a reasonable period notwithstanding the fact that the agency had lasted only one year. It was influenced by the considerable growth in turnover during that year and by the fact that orders continued to be received after termination even though no replacement agent had then been appointed.

---

[10] In *Tigana v Decoro* [2003] EWHC 23 at para 64, the High Court noted that these elements were 'cumulative and conjunctive'.

[11] *PJ Pipe & Valve v Audco* [2005] EWHC 1904 at paras 120 and 135.

[12] *Simpson v Grant & Bowman Limited* [2006] Eu LR 933 at para 86.

[13] This point was specifically examined in the High Court judgment of *Ingmar GB Limited v Eaton Leonard Inc* [2001] CLC 1825 decided on 31 July 2001.

[14] *Tigana v Decoro* [2003] EuLR 189.

## 8.12 SHARING COMMISSIONS: INCOMING AND OUTGOING AGENT

Under Regulation 9 the basic rule is that the incoming agent is not entitled to commission unless it is equitable for the commission to be shared. Regulation 9 does not contemplate any circumstances in which the outgoing agent would receive no commission—seemingly the outgoing agent gets everything or a share of the commission due. Will this always be appropriate?

Regulation 9 is likely to create further difficulties for the principal: by definition, the principal is parting company with one agent, who probably has a right to compensation or indemnity. The principal has to decide which of the incoming and outgoing agents is entitled to commission, or (if it would be 'equitable' to divide the commission) the ratio of sharing. Although Regulation 9(2) states that sums wrongfully paid by the principal to one of the parties shall be refunded, it is likely to be very difficult in practice for the principal to recover the sum due and the principal can presumably not set up the inability to gain recovery of commission from one of the agents as a reason to refuse to pay the other.

In effect, the principal has to make a judgment at the time as to the basis of division of the commission, even though he or she may not be in possession of all the facts. There is an effective 'right of appeal' from this decision to the court, which may decide that the principal's basis of division was completely wrong and require the principal to pay a further sum to the disgruntled agent. There is again the danger here of 'double trouble'. Although this is not likely to be a significant issue in most cases, if the order which gives rise to the dispute is a very substantial order with commission running to hundreds of thousands of pounds, this issue may for the principal be a question of commercial survival, not merely of the discomfort of paying twice. In such circumstances, principals would be well advised to ensure that both agents give a detailed summary of the circumstances surrounding the receipt of the order in support of their competing applications for commission: whether the court will allow the principal to plead that the agent is estopped from claiming a greater share of the commission on the basis that it is now presenting to the court information which it did not present to the principal is questionable.

Another possibility which has been considered by the authors in these circumstances is that the new agent could agree expressly as a term of his agency contract not to claim any commissions pursuant to Regulation 9 from the principal. This issue is considered in the following paragraph, as part of the general discussion of the ability to exclude Regulations 7–9.

## 8.13 ARE REGULATIONS 7–9 CAPABLE OF EXCLUSION?

Many of the provisions of the Directive state that they are not capable of exclusion, or are not to be varied to the detriment of the agent. These declarations are repeated in the Regulations. So, for instance, Regulation 19 states that Regulations 17 and 18 (relating to indemnity and compensation) are not capable of exclusion. Similarly, Regulation 10(4) states that any agreement to derogate from Regulation 10 (2) and 10(3) to the detriment of the agent shall be void.

There is no such statement in connection with Regulations 7–9. If these provisions are capable of exclusion, then this is of great importance to the principal who can hopefully avoid the prospect of 'double' or 'triple trouble' by providing:

— that the agent will not be entitled to commissions unless it has been the effective cause of the transaction (rather than the fact that it is a result of the agent's action or mainly attributable to its efforts—Regulations 7 and 8, respectively). Such a provision could be included even where the agent has an exclusive area;
— that the second limb of Regulation 7 would not apply at all;
— that the new agent would not be entitled to any commissions in respect of orders received before its contract commenced (even if it had carried out some work in ensuring that the contract was finally concluded) or on orders which are mainly attributable to the outgoing agent's efforts; and/or
— that the outgoing agent could agree that it would not be entitled to any commission save on transactions concluded during the term of the agency contract.

If exclusion is possible, then Regulations 7–9 are in reality only providing a framework to cover the situation where these issues are not addressed at all in the agency contract. This highlights the importance of concluding a suitable written agreement.

The DTI has not commented on this issue at all, save for the odd provision which appeared at paragraph 14 of the first draft. There is no clear pointer on this issue in the wording of the Directive or the Regulations and it seems that the DTI decided to sit on the fence on purpose. For instance, the parties are clearly entitled to derogate from Regulation 6 and this is reinforced by the opening words 'In the absence of any agreement as to remuneration between the parties . . .'. As mentioned above, areas where derogation is clearly not possible, or is not possible to the agent's disbenefit, are similarly highlighted in the Directive and the Regulations.

Conversely, the wording of Regulations 7–9 is not permissive but is absolute. Regulation 10 sets out some general rules, but then provides for a mandatory backstop although there are no such provisions in Regulations 7–9.

As mentioned above, the agent is unlikely to raise these issues during the term of the contract and the danger for principals is that, if they continue to operate upon the terms of their pre-1994 agreement and do not pay commission in the new circumstances contemplated by Regulations 7–9, the agent is unlikely to claim commission until he rolls all of these claims up with his claim for compensation and any claim for damages for breach of contract upon termination.

It should also be noted that, although the agent must notify the principal within one year from termination if it wishes to claim compensation or indemnity, there is no limitation period set out in the Regulations for any claim to commissions owed. Further, although Regulation 19 can be read so as to allow the parties to agree upon a settlement figure post-termination, if Regulations 7–9 are mandatory, then there is no express provision allowing the parties to agree a compromise.

The authors' view is that Regulations 7–9 are capable of exclusion and that it is therefore open to the parties to lay down their own rules as to the transactions upon which commission will be payable both during and after the termination of the agency contract. Given the uncertainty, however, the best advice which can be given to principals is to proceed on the basis that commission may be capable of exclusion in the circumstances set out in Regulations 7–9 but to be aware of the possibility of a successful claim in this regard in due course.[15]

Given the UK government's obvious dislike for the Directive, it is strange that (if the DTI shared this view) it did not set out in the Regulations a clear statement to this effect. This is another example of an area in which the government was perhaps worried by the prospect of *Francovich* actions, and chose merely to mirror the wording of the Directive. This indecision is damaging to business certainty, and in any event, if the English courts determine that Regulations 7–9 are not mandatory, but the ECJ takes the view that they are, then the government will be held to have improperly implemented the Directive and may be open to *Francovich* actions. Would it not have been preferable for the DTI to have clarified the position in this regard before making the Regulations with a view both to defending itself from *Francovich* actions and (more importantly) fostering legal certainty?

## 8.14 WHEN IS COMMISSION DUE AND WHEN IS IT PAYABLE?

Regulation 10 deals when the commission is due and when it is payable, and Regulation 11 deals with the extinction of the right to commission. It should be noted that the questions in the above heading are different questions: the first asks in what circumstances commission is due, and the second deals with the date upon which payment should be made.

Here, the question of ability to exclude is clearer: Regulation 10(1) sets out three tests as to the circumstances in which commission becomes due, but Reg-

---

[15] Such uncertainty is further evidenced by Reg 11—as to which see ch 8.16 below.

ulation 10(2) (which is expressly stated to be mandatory) sets out a 'backstop' last stage at which commission is due.

The three circumstances set out in Regulation 10(1) are that:

— the principal has 'executed' the transaction;
— the principal should have 'executed' the transaction according to the agreement with the customer; or
— the customer has 'executed' the transaction.

What does the word 'execute' mean? This word is taken from the French language version of the Directive. The Regulations lazily mirror the Directive in using a plethora of different expressions to describe the formation and carrying into effect of the contract between principal and customer. There was an attempt, particularly in the first draft, to clarify, but (no doubt on the *Francovich* ground once again) the DTI stepped back from the brink. This is unfortunate.

'Execute' must, however, mean something different from 'conclude', and in this context the normal meaning of the word 'execution' for English lawyers is something of a false friend. 'Execution' must mean performance, but does it mean 'starting to perform' or 'finishing performance'? The principal's obligations under the contract are most likely to involve delivery of goods and the customer's main (if not sole) obligation is to pay the price. But in a complex transaction, what if the principal carries out the design work agreed but the transaction proceeds no further? Or, what happens if the third party pays the first instalment of the price but not the remainder, or (even more confusing) pays for the goods element of the transaction but not the services element? The wording suggests that payment may be due only at the conclusion of all performance, but the courts may well take a different view. The DTI's view is that all commission is due upon delivery of the first instalment.

Although Regulation 10(1) is seemingly capable of exclusion, Regulation 10(2) is not. It states that commission becomes due at the latest when the customer has 'executed' his or her part of the transaction or should have done so if the principal had 'executed' its part of the transaction as it should have. This mandatory backstop will mean that in the majority of cases commission does not become due, seemingly, until the customer has paid. However, if the customer does not pay, or pays late, as a result of some failure or inability to perform on the part of the principal, then commission will become due when the customer would—if it had not been for that failure to perform—have paid. Thus, for instance, if the principal is in breach of its obligations to the customer or supplies defective goods and as a result the customer does not pay, then the principal still has to pay commission. Although this is logical and reasonable, it runs contrary to the provision generally found in agency contracts before implementation of the Regulations, stating that commission would only become due when the principal had received payment in cleared funds from the customer.

## 8.15 TIME FOR PAYMENT

Having established when the commission is due, Regulation 10(3) goes on to deal with the time for payment. Again, the provision operates as a 'backstop' since if the parties have agreed an earlier date for payment, that agreement will prevail.

The rule is that commission is to be paid not later than the last day of the month following the quarter in which it became due. Regulation 10(3) lays down a basis for determining the start date of quarters, in the absence of agreement. This is more favourable to the principal than the position generally laid down in agency contracts, which will typically require payment by the end of the month following that in which commission became due, or payment within 30 days. If the principal takes full advantage of the period allowed by Regulation10(3), then (if a quarter ends at the beginning of a calendar month) commission on an order received at the start of the quarter can be postponed for almost five months. The wording 'last day of the month following the quarter' is obscure, but presumably means the end of the calendar month following the calendar month in which the last day of the quarter falls.

## 8.16 EXTINCTION OF RIGHT TO COMMISSION

Regulation 11 is mandatory. The right to commission can be extinguished only if and to the extent that it is established that the contract between principal and the customer will not be 'executed' (see above) and that fact is 'due to a reason' for which the principal is 'not to blame'. Regulation 11(2) states that any commission which the agent has already received shall be refunded if the right to it is extinguished.

Several elements of Regulation11(1) merit further comment as follows:

— It could be argued that the 'right to commission' to which Regulation 11 refers is the right created by Regulations 7–10 (inclusive). If so, this would suggest that Regulations 7–9 are not capable of exclusion because of the prohibition on excluding Regulation 11(1) created by Regulation 11(5).
— '. . . It is established' that the contract will not be executed: who is to establish this? There could presumably be substantial periods during which principal and customer are arguing as to the responsibility for delays or problems and it is unclear what will happen. If the contract provides for the reference of a matter to an expert, for instance, and the resolution of that dispute takes several years, then seemingly the principal will have to pay commission and will only have a right to a refund of it at some time in the future if the matter is resolved in his favour. Thus, the principal could have paid substantial sums to the agent long before the principal receives any payment from the customer.
— 'The contract . . . will not be executed': the word 'executed' has been the subject of detailed comment above (chapter 8.14) and there is no reason to

believe that it will have a different meaning here. However, the word has previously always been related to performance by either the principal or the agent. Here the reference is merely to execution. Presumably this has to be read as a reference to performance by both parties. The first reaction might be to assume that, if the principal has not executed, this will always be for a reason for which the principal is to blame and that therefore the point is not an important one. However, as noted below in relation to *force majeure* and frustration this is not necessarily the case.

— The fact of non-execution is 'due to' a reason for which the principal is 'not to blame': why use the words 'due to' when the words 'as a result of' are used in Regulation 7 and are clearer? Is a different level of causation intended? It appears that this wording is merely a lazy use of inelegant language from the Directive. The more difficult question is what reasons are reasons for which the principal is 'not to blame'. Clearly this encompasses breach of contract by the customer, and customer insolvency. But does it apply to the full range of events or actions which could have caused the principal to fail to perform? In particular does it apply to all breaches of contract by the principal, *force majeure* situations, or frustration?

Taking each of these in turn, if goods are not delivered by the due date, then the principal may be in breach of contract. However, if this is the fault of a transport contractor, for instance, then (although the principal is in breach) is it appropriate to say that the principal is 'to blame'?

In cases of *force majeure* (such as strikes, power failures and acts of God) should the question of whether the principal is to blame or not depend upon whether its contract with the customer includes a *force majeure* provision excusing it from liability for breach of contract? Presumably, in the case of frustrated contracts, there is no question of the principal being 'to blame' at all.

These words do not sit happily with English law concepts of negligence or breach of contract, nor is there any attempt in the Regulations to clarify their meanings. The authors' view is that the words should properly be viewed as relating to breach of contract, and not 'blame' in a moral or causative sense. The underlying principle seems to be the idea that the principal should not be entitled to use its failure to perform as a ground upon which to refuse payment of commission.

The DTI's 1994 Guidance Notes suggest (following a comment in the Explanatory and Consultative Note) that the principal will still be liable to pay commission if (although not paid by the customer) he obtains payment in some other way, eg through an insurance policy. It is unclear where the DTI finds the basis for this statement within the Regulations. Should the principal be obliged to pay if he has borne the cost of an insurance policy?

## 8.17 FRUSTRATED CONTRACTS AND *FORCE MAJEURE*

If the above interpretation is correct, a suitably worded *force majeure* provision in the principal's contract with the customer should protect the principal and entitle the principal to reclaim commission paid in the event that the contract does not proceed by reason of a *force majeure* event. Comment has been made in several places above regarding the desirability of a suitably worded agency contract for the protection of the principal: on this point, it is the wording of the principal's contract with the customer that needs to be considered carefully.

## 8.18 FRUSTRATION

The Regulations do not consider frustration. When the Regulations talk of the principal executing his part of the transaction 'as he should have', what happens if the contract has been frustrated?

It would seem logical that in so far as the customer has paid the principal and commission has been paid, the principal will by definition not bear any 'blame' and that accordingly the commission should be recoverable under Regulation 11 (see section 8.16 above).

As an aside, at least where an agent is negotiating and concluding on behalf of the principal, it is ironic to note that the question of whether commission is repayable by the agent to the principal under Regulation 11 could depend upon whether the agent successfully ensured that the principal's conditions of trading became part of the contract between the principal and the customer. If the principal's conditions contain a *force majeure* clause, then the agent's failure to ensure that those conditions become part of the contract may perversely have the effect of ensuring that the commission is not repayable by the agent. If the agency contract is properly worded, however, then a sales agent who fails to contract on the principal's standard terms may be in breach of contract in any event and perhaps commission that is not recoverable from the agent could form part of a claim for damages against the agent. But in such circumstances would such a claim, and therefore the provision requiring the incorporation of the principal's terms in the first place, amount to a derogation of the type prohibited by Regulation 11(3)?

As a final point, can the principal set off sums recoverable under Regulation 11 against either commission due or any compensation or indemnity payment? There seems to be no reason why such a provision in an agency contract should not be effective.

## 8.19 SUPPLY OF INFORMATION AND RIGHT
## OF INSPECTION OF PRINCIPAL'S BOOKS

Regulation 12 requires the principal to supply the agent with a statement of commission due not later than the last day of the month following the quarter in which the commission became due (ie the date that is the latest date for payment of commission under Regulation10(3)). Such statement must set out the 'main components used' in calculating the amount of commission. The main components are, presumably, the commission rate and the value of the contract upon which commission is payable. Reading this with Regulation10(2), this will be a statement as to the relevant value of transactions which have been executed by the customer, or which the customer would have executed if the principal had executed its obligations on time.

Regulation 12(2) goes on to state that the agent is entitled to demand that it be provided with all information which is available to the principal and which the agent needs to check the amount of commission due. This is stated in particular to include an extract from the principal's books, although (unlike earlier drafts of the Regulations) there is no definition of 'books'.

Both of these provisions are mandatory. Regulation 12(4) preserves any rule of law that recognises the right of an agent to inspect the principal's books, although the only such circumstance in English law would be the obligation of disclosure as part of the litigation process.

## 8.20 LACK OF REMEDIES

No specific remedy is provided in the event of a failure by the principal to comply with either of the main obligations under Regulation 12. This issue relates to the question of whether the rights of the parties under the Regulations are contractual obligations or otherwise, a subject that was considered earlier.

There is a serious deficiency in so far as the Regulations do not lay down any penalties in the event of breach. Compare this with the position in employment law where there is a failure to provide a statement of the terms of the contract pursuant to section 1 of the Employment Protection (Consolidation) Act 1978, for which there is no sanction and the penalties for failure to consult unions in advance of redundancies. This may be an area in which the DTI's failure to clarify could lead to claims based on the *Francovich* principle.

Regulation 12 does not impose any obligation of confidentiality on the agent as regards information it obtains from the principal's books. Such an obligation may be implied by the common law and/or as part of the duties imposed upon the agent under Regulation 3 (see above). This point can be covered by the inclusion of an express confidentiality provision in the agency contract. Even if there is no such provision, it is probably the case that a stipulation by the principal as to the confidentiality of information so supplied at the time of supplying it would either impose an obligation of confidentiality at common law or would amount to a reasonable instruction given by the principal for the purposes of Regulation 3(2)(c).

# 9

# Regulations 13–20: Conclusion and Termination of the Agency Contract

## 9.1 OUTLINE

THIS CHAPTER INCLUDES an analysis of the rights of agents to compensation or indemnity payments on termination of their agreements even when such termination is lawfully effected. The seminal decision of the House of Lords in *Lonsdale v Howard & Hallam Ltd.*[1] on the manner in which compensation is to be calculated will be examined together with the judgments from the ECJ in *Honyvem*[2] and *Semen*,[3] which both deal with indemnity payments. This action by the courts throws welcome light on an area which for too long has been shrouded in uncertainty, much to the detriment of interested parties. However, as will become apparent, despite the clear hopes of Lord Hoffmann, who gave the leading speech in *Lonsdale*, the calculation of post-termination compensation still gives rise to problems. To that end, a separate chapter on valuation, written by a leading expert on such matters, has been included in this book to assist in the process and to try to resolve some of the ever-present difficulties which arise when such an exercise is carried out.

## 9.2 REGULATION 13: THE RIGHT TO A WRITTEN STATEMENT OF TERMS

Regulation 13 sets out almost verbatim what appears in the Directive at Article 13(1). The only change between the provision as it was originally proposed by the Commission and the final text from the Council are the words 'on request', which suggestion was put forward by the European Parliament in its opinion. This means that the agent or the principal must request the statement of terms.

---

[1] *Howard & Hallam Ltd* [2007] 1 WLR 2055.
[2] Case C-465/04 [2006] ECR I-2879.
[3] Case C-348/07 judgment of 26 March 2009 (not yet reported).

It should be noted that the Directive contains the following provision:

Notwithstanding paragraph 1 a Member State may provide that an agency contract shall not be valid unless evidenced in writing.[4]

The UK decided not to take up this option, which decision follows the practice under English law. It has been suggested—see the 1987 DTI Explanatory and Consultative Note—that it is sensible to retain flexibility, especially in cases where agreements cover minor transactions for which written contracts will not be worthwhile. Despite the obvious benefit for both parties of reducing an agency agreement to writing, it is the authors' experience that many such agencies still operate either by way of oral agreement or by way of very short form written agreement, which simply sets out the fact that one party is to act as the other's agent, the territory and the commission rate. Given the increased liability for the parties, and in particular for principals, brought about by the the introduction of the Regulations, we would suggest that all relevant agency agreements be set out in writing.

The Regulation is self-explanatory. The right to receive on request a signed written document setting out the terms of the contract is wide-ranging; it will apply even if the parties agreed originally that a written contract was not required—see the 1987 Explanatory and Consultative Note, paragraph 25. For the avoidance of any doubt, there is no duty on the parties to agree a written agreement. The only obligation is to produce a written statement of the terms agreed between the parties. It should be noted that apart from restraint of trade clauses (Regulation 20(1)(a)) there is no obligation that particular clauses must be in writing if they are to be enforced.

What is the sanction for non-compliance? Given that the UK has not taken up the possibility under Article 13(2) of the Directive to provide that an unwritten agency contract will not be valid, it is clear that invalidity will not arise on non-compliance. Indeed, in the original Explanatory Memorandum of the Commission[5] attached to its original proposal, it was made clear that the automatic nullity of a contract was one particular reason for not making this provision mandatory. One remedy which might be available if, for example, one party refuses a relevant request, is a mandatory injunction, since the English courts must as a matter of Community law provide an adequate remedy. However, it is not clear whether this should be the case given that, as the Law Commission Report suggests (p 25), the provision might be interpreted as being merely exhortatory.

It is often assumed by both principals and agents that if there is no written agreement, there is no contract; that is clearly incorrect as can be seen from

---

[4] Art 13(2) of the Directive. Note that national rules requiring any other formalities to be observed as a condition of validity of agency contacts are precluded by the Directive: see the judgment of the ECJ in Case C-215/97 *Barbara Bellone v Yokohama SpA* [1998] ECR I-2191. However, note also the recent judgment of the ECJ in Case C-485/01: *Caprini* [2003] ECR I-2371.

[5] COM(76)670 final of 14 December 1976.

what is set out above. However, particularly given Part III of the Regulations, principals should view the conclusion of a suitable written agreement with the agent as of paramount importance. This is always good practice, but is now more important because of the effects of the Regulations.

### 9.3 REGULATION 14: WHAT HAPPENS TO A FIXED-TERM CONTRACT ONCE THE FIXED TERM HAS EXPIRED?

This provision, like Regulation 13, follows almost verbatim the original Commission proposal. The only difference is that the original proposed version was preceded by the words 'unless otherwise agreed'. These were deleted in the amended Commission proposal and it is therefore clear that the parties cannot derogate from the provisions of this Regulation. Once this provision has come into operation in a given situation, and the contract has been converted into one for an indefinite period, the rules as to notice set out in Regulation 15 will apply. Needless to say, those contracts for a fixed or determinable period, which are not continued thereafter, will end on the expiration of the period for which they were made. This statement formed part of the original proposal for what became Regulation 14. However, it was removed by the Council in its adopted text. Its removal does not signify its non-application; merely that such matters did not need to be spelt out in the Directive. It should be noted, however, that where there is a fixed-term contract which expires and is replaced with another fixed-term contract, it may be argued that the parties would not be bound by the notice period laid down in Regulation 15. Compensation or indemnity will not, however, be calculated only by reference to the latest fixed term—the court will adopt a broad definition of the term 'agency contract' and take earlier fixed terms into account.[6]

### 9.4 REGULATION 15: THE MINIMUM PERIODS OF NOTICE FOR TERMINATION OF THE AGENCY CONTRACT

Unlike the two preceding Regulations, this Regulation has undergone a number of important changes since it was first proposed by the Commission. However, the Regulation mirrors the final version of the Directive almost exactly.

The initial proposal differed in three important respects from the final adopted Directive. First, it was proposed that only notice in writing would be valid; secondly, that the period of notice should be the same for both parties; and thirdly, that Member States were entitled to prescribe a maximum period of notice but that the period in question could not be less than 12 months.

---

[6] See *Moore v Piretta PTA Limited* [1999] 1 All ER 174, 180; see also the judgment of the Court of Appeal in *Stuart Light and Others v Ty Europe Limited* [2004] 1 Lloyds Rep 693. See also by analogy, Reg 15(5) which makes clear that previous periods should be taken into account.

The first proposal was deleted by the Council. It is to be assumed that the reason for this is that in some Member States valid notice can be given orally. The second proposal was also deleted by the Council.[7] There has been criticism of this provision,[8] stating that such a rigid rule would not always be appropriate and that confusion could arise where parties made different arrangements in breach of this paragraph. The third proposal changed as a result of amendments put forward by the European Parliament. However, when the Council moved away from the concept of variable periods, with long-stop minima towards mandatory notice periods, the minimum limits were no longer relevant.

The drafts of Regulation 15 followed the wording of the Directive on this point fairly closely. Up until the second draft, it had been stated that the provisions of the Regulation could not be excluded, varied or restricted to the detriment of the commercial agent. This statement does not appear in the Regulations as adopted. However, Regulation 15(2) provides that parties may not agree on any shorter periods of notice, which clearly has the aim, albeit unstated, of protecting the commercial agent.

Regulation 15 itself is clear. The minimum periods of notice are one month for the first year of the contract, two months for the second year commenced and three months for the third year commenced and for subsequent years. The end of the notice period must coincide with the end of a calendar month.

The UK did not take up the possibility given to it by the Directive to fix notice periods for the fourth, fifth and sixth years of the contract (Article 15(3) of the Directive). As the DTI stated in the 1987 Explanatory and Consultative Note, the Government felt that the three-month notice period was sufficient and that if the parties wished to fix longer notice periods, they were entitled to do so pursuant to Regulation 15(3). Regulation 15(3) also provides that in the event that the parties choose longer periods, the notice periods to be observed by the principal must not be shorter than those observed by the agent.

## 9.5 CRITICISMS OF THE REGULATION

Various criticisms have been raised against Regulation 15, largely on the ground that it is too restrictive. For example, there is no provision for parties to be able to terminate with immediate effect except as provided for by Regulation 16. Does this mean that even if parties agree to do so, they will not be entitled to rely upon such an agreement? There is also no provision for payment in lieu of notice, which is a well-known feature of agency law in the UK. Despite the lack of express provision in this regard, it is the authors' experience that payments in lieu are readily agreed between parties to a commercial agency dispute.

---

[7] However, see Reg 15(3), which explicitly refers to the need for the principal's notice period to be no shorter than that for the agent, in the event that the parties agree to longer periods than the minima laid down in Reg 15(2).

[8] See eg the Law Commission Report, 25.

There is also no provision for reasonable notice. However, it could be suggested that the Regulation simply codifies what was good practice and should thus be deemed to include the concept of reasonableness. It is also unclear what happens if the proper periods of notice are not observed. The better view would be that the notice would be ineffective. However, in the early drafts of the Directive, remedies for unlawful termination were set out and one of the examples given of unlawful termination was where the proper period of notice had not been observed—see, for example, Article 28(1) of the Commission's original proposal to the Council. It has also been suggested that the notice periods, which are more generous than those existing under the current UK employment legislation, will force principals to acknowledge that agents will become their quasi-employees.[9] However, in the light of the *dicta* by HHJ Alton in *Simpson v Grant & Bowman Limited*, this is to be doubted.[10]

## 9.6 REGULATION 16: THE RIGHT TO TERMINATE WITH IMMEDIATE EFFECT

Regulation 16 makes it clear that the Regulations as a whole do not affect the rights of parties to terminate with immediate effect either because of the failure by one of the parties to carry out all or part of his obligations under the contract or where exceptional circumstances arise.

Again this Regulation faithfully reproduces Article 16 of the Directive. However, the relevant provision has changed quite markedly from the early Commission drafts. It is not only instructive to see what was left in, but also what was left out.

In the original Commission proposal, the emphasis in the first limb was placed on the fault of one of the parties. The doctrine of fault in a contractual setting is known in certain continental law systems but not in the UK where the emphasis is on breach by the relevant party. The Law Commission Report predicted that difficulties would arise if the concept of fault were allowed to remain.

With regard to the second limb, the proposal spelt out what has since become 'exceptional circumstances'. Article 27(1)(b) of the Commission proposal provided that termination may take place 'where some circumstance arises which makes it impossible to perform the contract, or which seriously prejudices its performance, or which substantially undermines the commercial basis of the contract'. Such details may be helpful when seeking to interpret 'exceptional circumstances'.

One provision in the early drafts which has since been omitted from the Directive and thus from the Regulations is that where the contract was termi-

---

[9] R Lister, 'Time to Re-think UK Agency Agreements' [1992] *International Financial Law Review* July.
[10] [2006] EuLR 934.

nated in the relevant manner, the party 'at fault' was liable in damages to the other. The fact that it was omitted by the Council does not mean that damages are not capable of being awarded in such situations, rather that it was felt that this was something which should be dealt with by national law rather than harmonised by EC law.

The opinions from the Economic and Social Committee and from the European Parliament attempted to put a gloss on the provisions, especially with regard to the first limb. These attempts worked to the extent that in the Commission's amended proposal, it was provided that termination should only arise where a party to the contract had 'conducted himself in a manner which [was] seriously inconsistent with his obligations, or [has] in relation to the contract committed a serious fault'. Wisely, it is thought, these new emphases were not adopted by the Council.

The early drafts were almost identical to the Regulations, save for later drafts which stated that the rules of the common law relating to this issue should apply to the contract. The question could therefore be asked as to the position in equity, say for misrepresentation.

Regulation 16 preserves the rules in English law (and it is thought in other continental legal systems as well) whereby parties may terminate a contract without observing a notice period.

The first limb of Regulation 16 clearly covers rescission for failure to perform and should also cover termination in cases of anticipatory breach. It should be noted that in both cases, damages are available under English law. It should also be noted that despite the general rule in English law that rescission of a contract for failure to perform requires a minimum degree of default, because Regulation 16(a) includes failure to carry out part of the obligations due under the contract, a party may terminate and seek damages even though that party has suffered little or no prejudice. The DTI's 1993 Guidance Notes stated (paragraph 63) that the provisions of the Regulation have the effect of preventing disputes as to whether there has been a failure to perform such as to justify rescission.

As to the second limb, the first explanatory note from the DTI in 1987 states that it would include *force majeure* or unforeseeable, uncontrollable events[11]. It should be noted that as a general rule of English law, payments which are outstanding at the time when frustration (which may not have the same ambit as 'exceptional circumstances') occurs would cease to be payable except insofar as the court in its discretion sees fit, taking into account the facts of the situation. In the Commission's Explanatory Memorandum of its original proposal, the example of a commercial agent finding it impossible to continue in business for reasons of health, old age or serious and unforeseeable family circumstances is given as illustrating the type of situation to fall within the term of exceptional circumstances (p 49). It is interesting to note that this example does not differ markedly from Regulation 18(b)(ii), which sets out some of the circumstances

---

[11] See the DTI Explanatory and Consultative Note, para 29.

under which indemnity or compensation payments will be payable despite the fact that the agent terminated the agreement. It should also be noted that the example only mentions the circumstances of the commercial agent. It is to be assumed that the same rationale would arise if the position of the principal was the same.

## 9.7 REGULATION 17: AN AGENT'S RIGHT TO INDEMNITY OR COMPENSATION ON TERMINATION

The right to an indemnity or compensation is at the heart of the Regulations. The rights of agents to claim an indemnity or compensation at the end of a contractual agreement irrespective of whether a breach of contract has occurred, and thus imposing a form of strict liability on the principal, were, when introduced, entirely novel in the English law of agency and thus have been the subject of much comment. Regulation 17 also has the most potential effect on the finances of the parties involved and thus is of more immediate concern to individuals than certain other provisions. It is for this reason, and the fact that there is little certainty about the calculation of such payments, that many disputes are settled prior to trial, generally by way of mediation.

Such rights are, however, well known in continental legal systems where it is felt that the agent should be protected in its dealings with the principal.[12] It has been pointed out that the agent's entitlement to such indemnity under German law is

> intended to compensate him for the fact that as a rule the agent's work increases the goodwill of the principal and not that of the agent and that on termination of the agency the principal thus derives a benefit from this accrued goodwill, while the agent suffers a corresponding loss.[13]

Indeed, it is interesting to note that under German law, a commercial agent appears to be some sort of quasi-employee rather than the independent agent more familiar to English lawyers.

In terms of compensation, which is the default provision under Regulation 17, the initial approach of the courts in the UK was to follow the French law rationale for post-termination compensation, as being the representation of the cost of purchasing the agency to the agent's successor or being a representation of the time it would take to reconstitute the client base of which the agent had been forcibly deprived. However, recent judgments of the English courts

---

[12] It should be noted that this perceived need to protect commercial agents is not necessarily shared by the English judiciary. Lord Hoffmann, when commenting on Staughton LJ's now well-known description of commercial agents as being a 'down-trodden race', ventured to suggest that the learned judge had been employing 'more than a touch of irony'—see para 19 of his speech.

[13] EJ Cohn, An Introduction to the German Law on Agents and Sole Distributors, British Institute of International and Comparative Law: Special Publication No 3 (1964) 17.

have moved away from a rigid adherence to French law,[14] and following the House of Lords' decision in *Lonsdale*, it is clear that French law and practice per se will have little impact on the manner in which such matters are dealt with in the English courts.[15] As Lord Hoffmann made clear in his speech, the French system is based on a commercial practice—that of a premium being charged on the purchase of an agency, which premium is then recouped by way of payment of post-termination compensation—which simply does not exist in England. Accordingly, 'the difference between French and English practice exists not because their respective courts are applying different rules of law but because they are operating in different markets'.[16]

## 9.8 COMPLIANCE WITH THE DIRECTIVE

The question of compliance by Regulation 17 with the relevant provisions in the Directive arises because of a last-minute change by the UK government, based, it is said, on late advice from the European Commission.[17] Before this advice, the UK had taken the view that Article 17 of the Directive required Member States to choose between indemnity and compensation payments for agents. Article 17(1) of the Directive provides:

> Member States shall take the measures necessary to ensure that the commercial agent is, after termination of the agency contract, indemnified in accordance with paragraph 2 or compensated for damage in accordance with paragraph 3.

Most Member States have opted for the indemnity system. The UK authorities had originally chosen the compensation system, with which apparently they were more familiar, despite the fact that the concept was alien to the English common law. At the last moment, there was a radical change, allowing the parties to individual contracts to make the choice themselves as between compensation or indemnity. The question that arises is whether a Member State, in this case the UK, is entitled to do this. The DTI does not shirk from explaining what this might mean in practice. In its 1993 Guidance Note, the DTI states that the system as chosen by the UK will enable the parties to a particular contract to choose one provision for inclusion in one contract and the other in another contract. That in itself is not surprising, although such a course of action will no doubt lead to prolonged negotiations every time a new contract is entered into. However, in its more recent 1994 Guidance Note, the DTI goes further and states that the Regulation as it stands does not preclude the parties from using the compensation provisions in some cases and indemnity ones in others when

---

[14] See eg the judgments in *Frabo v Duffen*, *Barrett McKenzie v Escada*, *Ingmar v Eaton Leonard Inc* and *Tigana Ltd v Decoro*.

[15] However, that will not necessarily be the position in Scotland, where the courts may well wish to continue the approach taken in *King v Tunnock* [2000] SC 424.

[16] See para 18 of *Lonsdale*.

[17] See the DTI Explanatory and Consultative Note, para 29.

terminating a particular contract. This seems remarkable. The provisions with regard to indemnity or compensation relate to termination of an agency contract. It would seem that the DTI envisages partial termination of a contract giving rise to these rights, which is not at all the It could be argued that the UK has failed to implement the Directive correctly by failing to choose which system should operate within its jurisdiction.[18] Despite the fact that the UK's decision was apparently based on advice from the Commission, the ultimate arbiter will be the ECJ.[19] It is to be remembered that if the UK were found to have failed to implement the Directive correctly, then it could be liable in damages to disgruntled agents or principals.

### 9.9 DRAFTING HISTORY OF REGULATION 17

Aside from this difference, the regulation follows the relevant provisions of the Directive very closely. However, it is worth briefly examining the drafts of the Directive.

There are two main differences between the adopted text of the Directive and the previous drafts.[20] First, in the early drafts, there was only provision for payment of a goodwill indemnity; there was no provision made for compensation for damage suffered. It is assumed that this was because the German system upon which much of the original proposal was based only knew of the goodwill indemnity concept. Secondly, the amount of goodwill indemnity payable was limited to one-tenth of the annual remuneration calculated on the basis of the average remuneration during the previous five years. This would normally yield a rather low sum. However, the text as adopted increased the claimable amount so that it was not to exceed one year's remuneration based on the agent's average remuneration over the preceding five years, ie 10 times the former amount. It is interesting to note that this is similar to the measure of quantum set down in the original draft of the Directive for lump-sum indemnities payable when unlawful termination had taken place.

---

[18] For an example of a party challenging the UK's approach to the implementation of the Directive in the context of the adoption of the Schedule to the Regulations, see the judgment of Briggs J in *Crane v Sky In-Home Service Limited and Secretary of State for Trade and Industry* [2007] EuLR 549 at paras 24–44.

[19] However, in the light of the Court of Appeal's decision in *Oakley Inc v Animal Ltd* [2006] Ch 337, any such challenge faces very substantial obstacles.

[20] The importance of changes in draft legislation can be seen from the Opinion of Advocate General Geelhoed in Case C-3/04: *Poseidon Chartering BV v Marianne Zeeschip VOF and Others* [2006] ECR I-2505.

## 9.10 TERMINATION

It will be noted that indemnity or compensation payments are only available once a contract is terminated. The question thus arises as to what constitutes termination.

The DTI, in the 1987 Explanatory and Consultative Note, sets out the following as examples of termination under Regulation 17. It should be noted that the list is not exhaustive:

— the principal's breach of the agency agreement with the agent's acceptance of the repudiation; this might include service of a notice shorter than that provided for in Regulation 15;
— the frustration of the agency agreement, which would include the agent's death (Regulation 17(8)), or the agent's retirement or illness (Regulation 18(b) (ii)); it is not thought that this provision can be taken to include the liquidation of a company;
— the principal giving notice under Regulation 15 or under an express term for early termination of a fixed-term agency contract;
— the expiry by passage of time of a fixed-term agency contract.

As to the issue of expiry through passage of time, following a relatively long period of uncertainty, the English and Scottish courts have clarified that the term 'termination' includes the expiry of a fixed-term contract.[21] Interestingly, this approach goes contrary to the position under French law, which, as will be seen below, was the source for the provisions in the Directive relating to post-termination compensation. However, as will also be seen below, the position of French law, even where that law was the basis for a particular concept in the Directive, has been ruled by the House of Lords to be irrelevant to the manner in which the Regulations are to be interpreted in the English courts.[22]

Termination leading to the entitlement of the agent to indemnity or compensation will not arise in the following circumstances:

— where the principal has terminated because of a breach by the agent which justifies immediate termination (Regulation 18(a)); the DTI's view in the Note was that this wording in the Directive is a reference to repudiatory breach, but the authors would query whether this is correct; Regulation 18 refers back to Regulation 16, which talks of immediate termination because of the failure of one party to carry out all or part of his obligations under that contract which will encompass repudiatory breach but is not solely governed by it;
— where the agent has terminated the agency contract, unless the termination was justified by circumstances attributable to the principal or on grounds of

---

[21] See *Whitehead v Jenks & Cattell Engineering Limited* [1999] EuLR 827; *Frape v Emreco International Ltd* [2002] EuLR 10; *Tigana Ltd v Decoro* [2003] EuLR 189; *Stuart Light and Others v Ty Europe Limited* [2004] 1 Lloyds Rep 693; *Cooper and Others v Pure Fishing (UK) Ltd* ]2004] 2 Lloyds Rep 518.
[22] See Lord Hoffman's speech in *Lonsdale v. Howard & Hallam Ltd* [2007] 1 WLR 2055 at para 26.

age, infirmity or illness of the agent due to which it cannot reasonably be required to continue its activities (Regulation 18(b)); the DTI referred to termination by the agent on notice, but both the Directive and the Regulations are silent on this point;

— where the agent has assigned his rights and duties to another person (Regulation 18(c)).

Unfortunately, the DTI only sets out the uncontroversial occasions when termination leading to indemnity or compensation will occur. The following examples show the extent of the agent's new rights under the Regulations.

An agent will be entitled to be indemnified or compensated when:

— the agent retires[23] or dies;
— the principal assigns the contract, eg on the sale of the business;
— the agent has breached the contract but not so that it would justify the immediate termination of the contract;
— the contract is terminated on grounds of *force majeure*.

It should be noted that with regard to this last point, it has been said that the agent should not be entitled to indemnity or compensation because of the operation of Article 16 of the Directive. It will be recalled that Article 16 provides that nothing in the Directive shall affect the application of the law of the Member States where the latter provides for the immediate termination of the contract because, inter alia, exceptional circumstances arise. In the draft Regulations, it was provided that the agent was not entitled to payment where, inter alia, such exceptional circumstances arose. *Force majeure* will generally fall within the term 'exceptional circumstances' in so far as it will lead to the immediate termination of a contract. However, in the Regulations as they were adopted, if a principal is to avoid the payment of compensation or indemnity on termination by the principal, that termination must be due to a 'default attributable to the commercial agent'. It must follow that where a contract is terminated on grounds of *force majeure*, by definition not being the agent's default, such termination will entitle the agent to be indemnified or compensated.

Termination will also not arise within the meaning of the Regulations where a part but not the whole of the contractual arrangements between the parties were terminated.[24]

---

[23] As to the English courts' approach to the issue of age, see *Abbott v Condici* [2005] 2 Lloyds Rep 450.

[24] See the judgment of the Court of Session (Outer House) in *Scottish Power Energy Retail v Taskforce Contracts Ltd* [2009] EuLR 62.

## 9.11 DISTINCTION BETWEEN INDEMNITY
## AND COMPENSATION

An indemnity payment will only be due to an agent where there has been an agreement to that effect between the parties;[25] failing such an agreement, the default post-termination remuneration under Regulation 17 will be by way of compensation.

As has been seen above, indemnity payments under the Directive (and therefore under the Regulations) are modelled on German law. Chapter 10 sets out a detailed analysis of that law. A further analysis of that law in so far as it specifically applies to the question of indemnity payments is set out in the 1996 Commission Report on the application of Article 17 of the Directive, a copy of which can be found at Appendix 7. The Report not only sets out the law, but the steps taken by the German courts to calculate how an indemnity should be paid and in what amount. However, it should be noted that the position as set out therein has changed somewhat in the light of recent developments in Germany, which are examined in Chapter 10.

One critical distinction between indemnity and compensation payments is that an upper limit is set on indemnity payments whilst there is no limit on compensation payments. Regulation 17(4) makes it clear that the upper limit shall be an indemnity for one year based on the agent's average remuneration over the preceding five years. Despite this limit on the indemnity available, it should not be forgotten that the agent is entitled to make a further claim for damages (Regulation 17(5)). The 1993 DTI Guidance Notes give the following example of when such a situation might arise (p 35). If the principal dismisses the agent by giving one month's notice instead of three months, then the agent will be able to claim indemnity for the commission on orders obtained in the first month and will also be able to claim damages for being deprived of the opportunity to earn commission during the two other months. However, this example would appear to be problematic, given the fact that an indemnity claim in such circumstances should normally cover the claim for the whole notice period.

Why do the Regulations provide an alternative? As noted above, initially and indeed up until and including the final 1993 draft, the UK authorities took the view that only compensation would be available on termination. However, interested parties, especially those representing the interests of principals, were very unhappy about this because of the lack of a maximum limit. Because of this pressure and using the advice from the European Commission, the Regulations

---

[25] Reg 17(2). See the judgment of the Court of Session (Outer House) in *Hardie Polymers v Polymerland Ltd* [2002] SCLR 64 for a generous approach to the question of whether the parties had chosen an indemnity remedy, even though the word itself was not mentioned in the contractual clause in question, particularly given that the relevant section in the agreement was headed 'Compensation'.

were amended to allow parties to agency contracts to choose either indemnity or compensation.

## 9.12 INDEMNITY PROVISIONS UNDER THE REGULATIONS

An agent will only be entitled to an indemnity if the following conditions are met:

— new customers have been brought to the principal by the agent; or
— the volume of business with existing customers has been significantly increased by the agent; and
— the principal continues to derive substantial benefits from such business; and
— the payment of the indemnity is equitable having regard to all the circumstances and in particular the commission lost by the commercial agent on the business transacted with such customers.

Thus, if any or all of the criteria listed above are not met, the agent will have no right to an indemnity payment.

## 9.13 INDEMNITY: THE DTI GUIDANCE NOTES

The DTI usefully sets out in its 1993 Guidance Notes at pp 33 and 34 the background to the indemnity provisions in the Directive. It points out that under German law, which provided the model for the Directive generally and for the indemnity provisions in particular, three considerations arise with regard to the payment of indemnities to agents:

— that the termination of the agency contract involves an enrichment for the principal in that the latter will still be doing business with clients introduced by the agent, but without now having to pay commission to that agent;
— that the agent suffers a loss because it would have earned commission on the transactions had the agency agreement continued;
— that the indemnity payment has to be equitable in all the circumstances.

On the basis of the above, it is clear that as there has to be a benefit for the principal, the agent is less likely to get such a payment where the agency contract is terminated because the principal is unable to carry on the business.[26] It

---

[26] See by contrast the position in *Lonsdale*, where the principal ceased trading and yet compensation was still found to be payable, although Judge Harris QC, sitting at first instance, whose judgment Lord Hoffmann described as a model of clarity and common sense, held as follows on this point: 'This was an agency producing a modest and falling income in a steadily deteriorating environment. There is no evidence that anyone would have paid anything to buy it. . . . I am strongly tempted to find that no damage has been established. . . . But perhaps that conclusion, though I regard it as logical, is a little over-rigorous given that the defendant has already made a payment. Doing the best I can, I find that the appropriate figure for compensation is one of £5,000.'

is also clear that it is for the agent to prove its loss. If, therefore, the agent soon after termination, secures a comparable position selling into the same market, then there may be no loss and therefore no indemnity to be paid. Finally, the issue of equity will take into account, according to the DTI, such circumstances as the parties' respective financial situations and how actively the agent worked.

## 9.14 INDEMNITY: THE COMMISSION REPORT

The Commission Report, referred to above, makes clear that the indemnity provisions in the Directive, which have been carried through intact into UK law by operation of the Regulations, were modelled on Article 89b of the German Commercial Code, which has provided for the payment of a goodwill indemnity since 1953. Chapter 10 of this book provides an overview of the relevant German legislation and case-law, in so far as they relate to the operation and availability of post-termination indemnities. The authors are of the view that in contrast to the position relating to post-termination compensation, knowledge of the applicable German law will be of use in calculating indemnities before the English courts as the mechanisms for such calculation will be the same[27]. As the Commission Report itself states, the German case-law and practice 'should provide invaluable assistance to the Courts of other Member States when seeking to interpret the provisions of Article 17(2) of the Directive'. This approach has been confirmed by the ECJ in *Honyvem*,[28] which held that the Commission Report 'provides detailed information as regards the actual calculation of the indemnity and is intended to facilitate a more uniform interpretation of Article 17'.[29] However, the Court went on to record that although the system established by Article 17 of the Directive was mandatory and prescribed a framework, it did not give any detailed indications as to the method of calculation of the indemnity, and that, accordingly, Member States enjoy a margin of discretion which they may exercise, particularly in relation to the criterion of equality.[30]

The following points of interest arise from the Commission Report:

— An agent is only entitled to an indemnity payment if and to the extent that it has brought new customers to the principal or has significantly increased the volume of business with existing customers and the principal continues to derive substantial benefits from such customers after the cessation of the agreement. This is in contrast to the compensation payment system, which, as will be seen below, requires no such prerequisite facts.

---

[27] Although the English courts are plainly not obliged to follow the principles of German law in this regard, for as pointed out by Elias J in *Bell Electric Ltd v Aweco Appliance Systems GmbH & Co* [2002] EuLR 444 at para 55, 'the Community legal order should not be assumed in general to have intended to define concepts by reference to the law of one or more national legal systems unless there is an express provision to that effect'.

[28] Case C-464/04: *Honyvem Informazioni Commerciali Srl v Mariella De Zotti* [2006] ECR I-2879.

[29] Ibid, para 35.

[30] Ibid, paras 34 and 36.

— The payment of an indemnity must be equitable having regard to all the circumstances and in particular the commission lost by the agent on the business transacted.
— There is a maximum level of indemnity, limited to one year's average annual remuneration.
— The indemnity represents the continuing benefits to the principal due to the agent's efforts.
— With regard to the criterion of the principal continuing to derive substantial benefits with its customers post-termination, it will be met even if the principal sells its business or client list, if it can be shown that the purchaser would use the client base.

As to the actual calculation of any indemnity due, the Commission Report sets out three stages.

The first stage is to ascertain the number of new customers and/or the increased volume of business with existing customers. The gross commission related to such customers over the last 12 months of the agreement can then be calculated. It is then necessary to estimate the likely length of time the business with these customers will last. In order to make such an estimate, it will be necessary to consider the market situation at the time of termination. A level of migration then has to be determined, as it will be natural that some customers will naturally move away. This figure comprising the above is then reduced to take into account the accelerated receipt of income.

The second stage investigates the issue of equity and its impact on the indemnity calculation. The following points are taken into account when making this investigation:

— whether the agent is retained by other principals;
— any fault of the agent;
— the level of remuneration of the agent;
— any decrease in the principal's turnover;
— the extent of any advantage to the principal;
— any payment of pension contributions by the principal;
— the existence of any restraint-of-trade clause; if such a clause exists, then the indemnity will be higher.

The third stage takes the figures calculated above and compares them with the maximum remuneration permitted. On this latter point, it is interesting to note that the Report states that it is rare for the maximum to be reached unless the agent has procured all or most of the customers.

However, the courts will no doubt be made aware of the philosophy behind the Regulations—the protection of the agent—and therefore it is likely that this provision will be widely interpreted with this aim in mind. The decision in the High Court in the case of *Moore v Piretta*[31] supports this analysis. It should

---

[31] *Moore v Piretta PTA Ltd* [1999] 1 All ER 174.

nonetheless be noted that in so far as the equity of the indemnity payment was concerned, one factor taken into account led to a reduction in the indemnity— that factor was that the agent would receive the monies more quickly overall than would have been the case had the contract between the parties continued. The court reduced the award by 8 per cent because of the accelerated payment factor.

## 9.15 INDEMNITY: THE CASE-LAW

There have been some recent developments in case-law from the ECJ. However, there still remains only one reported case in the UK courts on the calculation of indemnity payments.

In so far as concerns the ECJ, there have been two judgments which deal with the manner in which indemnities under the Directive are to be treated and calculated.

The first is the decision in *Honyvem*. The case arose out of the fact that a principal paid a terminated agent a post-termination indemnity pursuant to a national agreement, which indemnity was less than an indemnity which would have applied under the Directive. The critical question was whether such an approach breached the provisions of Article 19 which prohibits the derogation from the right to, inter alia, an indemnity to the detriment of the commercial agent before the agency contract expires.

Having analysed the purpose of an indemnity payment under the Directive and its source, the Advocate General makes the useful point in his Opinion that Article 17(2) effectively does away with the risk of the principal behaving in an opportunistic manner in putting an end to the contract and thereafter enjoying the fruits of the agent's labours without compensating the latter properly.[32]

He then goes on to tackle the issue of whether it can be said that the national agreement is more disadvantageous to the commercial agent than the statutory rules contained in the Directive. If the national agreement were judged to be disadvantageous, then it would clearly be unlawful and devoid of effect. The Advocate General found that the exercise of deciding which system was better could only be carried out after the agreement had been terminated, as the result would depend on a multiplicity of factors which would only come to light at that point. Although it would be possible to compare the two systems in the light of the amount of indemnity achieved, that was not what was required by Article 19. Rather, it was necessary to compare the substantive nature of the different schemes. It would only be proper to compare 'final figures' if the sole and exclusive aim of the Directive was the economic protection of the agent. That was not the position. The aims of the Directive included other matters such

---

[32] Para 19 of the Opinion.

as the elimination of restrictions of the carrying on of activities by commercial agents and the increasing of the security of commercial transactions.

In an apparent self-contradiction, the Advocate General admitted that it was correct to compare the schemes in advance, having said earlier that the assessment should take place post-termination. On that 'advance' examination basis, the Advocate General found that it could not be said that the national agreement was no more disadvantageous than the provisions of Article 17 of the Directive. This was because the Directive was based on a meritocratic approach, benefiting agents who had produced an increase in the clientele.

The Advocate General then went on to look at how an indemnity should be calculated and found that the Directive laid down the methodology to be used for that calculation. He sets these out, basing himself firmly on the Commission 1996 Report.[33]

Based on his findings, the Advocate General concluded that the national indemnity scheme was to be seen as a derogating scheme to the detriment of the agent, contrary to Article 19 of the Directive. He also went on to find that Article 17(2) specified not only the conditions for recognising the commercial agent's entitlement to an indemnity but also the actual items for calculating that indemnity, so that the fairness (or equity) principle will only come into play if it is necessary to adjust the amount of the indemnity as initially quantified.

The ECJ then delivered its judgment on 23 March 2006. It made the following points:

1.  The interpretation of Articles 17 and 19 of the Directive had to be considered in the light of the aims of the Directive and the system it established.
2.  The Directive aims to co-ordinate the laws of the Member States as regards the legal relationship between the parties to a commercial agency contract.
3.  The Directive seeks to protect commercial agents in their relations with their principals, to promote the security of commercial transactions and to facilitate trade between Member States by harmonising their legal systems within the area of commercial representation.
4.  As regards Article 19, the terms used to establish exceptions to general principles laid down by Community law are to be interpreted strictly.
5.  Article 19 provides the opportunity to parties to derogate from Article 17 before the contract expires, providing that derogation is not unfavourable to the agent. The issue of derogation must therefore be addressed at the time the parties contemplate it.
6.  Accordingly, a derogation from the provisions of Article 17 is only acceptable if *ex ante* there is no possibility that at the end of the contract the derogation will prove to be detrimental to the agent—that will be a matter for the national court.
7.  It would only be if the national agreement allowed for cumulation, 'even partial', of the indemnity available under the Directive, that the agreement

---

[33] See footnote 20 to his Opinion.

could be treated as favourable to the commercial agent—in other words, the derogating measure to be legal must be equal or greater than the results of the application of Regulation 17.

8.　As to the actual method of calculation, the ECJ held that the provisions of the Directive do not give any detailed indications as regards the method of calculation, although the 1996 Commission Report does—its aim being to facilitate a more uniform interpretation of Article 17.

9.　Accordingly, the Member States enjoyed a margin of discretion which they may exercise particularly with regard to the concept of 'equity'.

The second is the decision in *Semen*.[34] The case concerned the methodology used in German law to calculate post-termination indemnities and whether such methodology was in conformity with the Directive. Essentially, the critical question was whether the limit placed by German law on indemnities to the extent that they could not exceed the losses incurred by the agent on termination was compatible with Article 17 of the Directive.

The Advocate General found that it was, as long as the German law was sufficiently flexible to take into account the benefits derived by the principal from the activity of the agent. In so far as concerning whether the group which included the principal could be taken into account for the calculation of the indemnity, the Advocate General found that the Directive did not require the calculation of an indemnity to take into account the advantages accruing to companies other than the principal.

The ECJ did not agree with the Advocate General on the first issue, but did agree on the second.

Regarding the first issue, the Court pointed out that the aims of the Directive had to be investigated when determining the matter, in particular the protection of commercial agents. Any discretion given to Member States in relation to post-termination methodologies had to be exercised within the strict framework established by Articles 17 and 19. The Court then went through the three stages set out in Article 17(2). The position under German law could only be compatible with the Directive if its effect was not detrimental to the agent—see Article 19. The ECJ then referred to the 1996 Commission Report, which it found listed various factors to be taken into consideration, which factors the Court found would militate in favour of an indemnity higher than lost commissions. Accordingly the Member State's discretion to adjust the amount could not only be exercised, as in the German approach, in a downwards fashion.

In agreeing with the Advocate General on the second point, the ECJ stressed the importance of legal certainty, which principle precluded the taking into consideration of benefits accruing to third parties—here members of the same corporate group—unless that was contractually agreed between the principal and the agent.

---

[34] Case C-348/07: *Turgay Semen v Deutsche Tamoil GmbH*, judgment of the ECJ of 26 March 2009 (not yet reported).

The Court's approach shows that the mere fact that the indemnity provisions in the Directive were derived from German law does not mean that German law or practice is to be followed.

At the time of writing, there is still only one UK decided case on how an indemnity claim should be calculated.[35] This is unsurprising because of the non-default nature of the right to an indemnity—if such a claim is to arise, the parties must have expressly chosen it in their agreement. That case is *Moore v Piretta*,[36] which was somewhat unsatisfactory for the following reasons:

— The judge decided to look to German law for help in ascertaining how the Directive should be construed,[37] but seems completely to have misapplied German law, in particular by using as the base for the calculation of indemnity, not the commissions earned on business with customers obtained by the agent, but the total value of the business done by the principal with those customers.[38] Unsurprisingly, the resulting figure (even after various deductions) exceeded the capped figure of one year's commission and the agent was accordingly awarded the maximum indemnity allowed by the Regulations. This error would have been avoided had the court applied the principles set out in the Commission's 1996 Report, which is all the more mystifying given that the judgment was given in 1998.

— Having purported to follow German law, the court then departed from it in deducting from the potential award the agent's costs in performing his agency duties. The authors believe that such a deduction is not made under German law. The court declined to apply the principle of mitigation because it interpreted the indemnity payment as a payment in respect of goodwill.[39]

— The judge did not assume any 'migration', ie gradual loss by the principal of the new customers won by the agent, although the Commission's 1996 Report states that this is part of the calculation under German law.

— Although the German system envisages consideration of the period for which the principal will continue to derive benefit from agency customers introduced by the agent and the Commission's 1996 Report suggests[40] that a period of two to three years is usual, the judge gave no reason for choosing a period of 2.75 years—it appears he did so simply for convenience, this being the period elapsed between termination and trial and accordingly the period for

---

[35] In *Scottish Power Energy Retail Ltd v Taskforce Contracts Ltd* [2009] EuLR 62, although the parties had contractually agreed that post-termination relief should be by way of an indemnity, the Court of Session held that the requisite termination had not occurred so as to trigger the right to an indemnity.

[36] [1999] 1 All ER 174.

[37] As to the appropriateness of and consequences of doing this, see above.

[38] Although the Commission's 1996 Report is admittedly vague, it is clear from the illustrative example set out on p 4 of the Report that the appropriate base is commission not total turnover. The authors believe that the approach adopted by the 1996 Report accords with German law, which the judge said he was seeking to follow.

[39] P 182 at c.

[40] P 3, para (b).

which counsel supplied figures.[41] Would an earlier or later trial have resulted in a different figure?

— Although we do not know the agent's age or other business or many other facts, it must be highly doubtful whether a case involving an agency which had subsisted for less than 7.5 years merited the maximum award. Even after the calculation error referred to above, the court should have carried out a common-sense check on the resulting award and revisited its conclusion.

Lessons for principals from *Moore v Piretta* are as follows:

— Beware of the indemnity route until it is clear the courts have a settled approach to calculating indemnities.
— If the court is to refer to 'foreign' law, ensure clear expert evidence is used and applied in any dispute.
— Consider whether delays to the trial date will work for or against you.
— Do not assume that future awards will be net of costs or will apply common law principles of accelerated receipt or mitigation.
— If mitigation cannot be argued, even an agent who has immediately gained a new agency or employment, or compensated for the loss of one agency by devoting more energy to his other agencies, will receive a full award.

## 9.16 COMPENSATION PROVISIONS UNDER THE REGULATIONS

In order to be entitled to compensation, an agent must show damage suffered as a result of termination of relations with the principal. The Regulations give three non-exhaustive [42] examples of when such damage will arise:

— when the termination of relations with the principal has deprived the agent of commission which would have arisen with the proper performance of the contract whilst providing the principal with substantial benefits due to the agent's activities;
— when the termination of relations with the principal has meant that the agent has been unable to amortise costs and expenses incurred in the performance of the agency contract on the principal's 'advice';
— when the termination of relations with the principal has arisen because of the agent's death.

As to the word 'damage', it is interesting to note that in the first draft of the Regulations, it was substituted by 'losses, liabilities, costs and expenses'. Particu-

---

[41] The judge was probably not assisted by the fact that the figures were supplied to him at 'the 59th minute of the 11th hour of the case' (p 184).

[42] The fact that they are non-exhaustive was confirmed in *King v Tunnock* [2000] EuLR 531 at paras 41 and 42 of the judgment.

larly because of the inclusion of the latter, it is clear that something other than merely contractual loss is covered.

As has been noted above, the compensation provisions of the Directive are taken from French law. Prior to the House of Lords' decision in *Lonsdale*, the position of the case-law in the UK was split between two schools of thought as to the impact that French law should have on the calculation of compensation by courts in the UK. On the one hand, cases such as *King v Tunnock* took the view that UK law should imitate French law. On the other hand, cases such as *Frabo v Duffen*, *Barrett McKenzie v Escada* and *Ingmar* showed a willingness of English courts to move away from second guessing what French law might or might not do in a given situation, and instead seek to use common law principles, such as the duty to mitigate one's loss and the need to avoid windfall payments, to justify departing from the strict French law approach. A good example of that less hidebound approach could be seen in the High Court judgment in *Ingmar*, in which the Court stated that two years' gross average commission (the norm under French law) would have given a windfall to the claimant and therefore three years' net average commission should be used instead as the measure for compensation.

However, the position has now been made clear, at least in so far as concerns the courts in England and Wales, following the decision of the House of Lords in *Lonsdale*, which endorsed the stand-alone approach and rejected the use of French law and practice when calculating compensation due under Regulation 17(6).

It will be noted that compensation is payable for damage suffered as result of the termination of relations with the principal. It has been argued by certain commentators[43] that this phrase encompasses more than simply the terms of the agency contract, ie that it is different from termination of the contract. However, although it is true that different words are used, it is clear from both the Regulations and the Directive that compensation will be paid on termination of the agency contract—Regulation 17(1) and Article 17(1), respectively. These provisions govern generally the granting of compensation, inter alia, to agents and thus all subsequent subordinate provisions should be read in the light of these general provisions. It is thus thought that the better view is that the phrase 'relations with the principal' should be read as comprising the terms of the agency contract.[44]

As to the first of the examples given above, it is clear that difficulties may arise with the quantification of the phrase 'substantial benefits'. The following decisions

---

[43] See eg Scholes and Blane, 'Agency Agreements—New Protection for Commercial Agents', *PLC Magazine* November 1993, 43.

[44] In support of this approach, see the analogous position taken by the High Court in *Moore v Piretta* [1999] 1 All ER 174 at 180a–c; however, see a contrary finding to this effect by McGonigal J in *Light v Ty Europe Ltd* [2003] EuLR 268 at para 49, though that decision was overturned by the Court of Appeal: *Stuart Light and Others v Ty Europe Ltd* [2004] 1 Lloyds Rep 693 and at para 57 thereof, Ward LJ specifically rejects the argument that 'relations with his principal' is wider than 'agency contract'.

may, however, be of assistance in that regard. In the case of *Duffen v Frabo*,[45] HHJ Hallgarten QC, sitting in the Central London County Court, held that Regulation 17(7)(a) only came into play to the extent that the principal could be said to have benefited from the agent's efforts prior to termination, and that in relation to any customer procured by the agent for the principal, there would probably be two benefits: (i) the very existence of that customer for future business; and (ii) the principal's ability to deal with that customer without any longer having to bear the burden of paying a retainer or commission to the agent.[46] In the Scottish case of *Gailey v Environmental Waste Controls*,[47] the Court of Session (Outer House) held that the notion of goodwill was central to the framework of the Schedule to the Regulations, and thereby to their applicability. It might well be that the term 'substantial benefits' should be defined with a view to the goodwill engendered by the agent continuing post-termination with the principal. In *Tigana Ltd v Decoro Ltd*,[48] Davis J opined that one of the factors which could be taken into account when deciding on the amount of post-termination compensation was the extent to which the principal retained, after termination, the benefit of the agency, eg by way of enhanced trade connections or goodwill.[49] The judge went on to find that one important element in the concept of the right to compensation is 'to avoid a principal being unjustly enriched by retaining for itself without payment the entirety of the benefit of goodwill to which the activities of the agent during the agency have contributed'.[50] In *PJ Pipe & Valve Co Limited v Audco India Limited*,[51] Fulford J held that 'the reference in Regulation 17(7)(a) to the agent 'providing his principal with substantial benefits' may have a prospective or retrospective focus (or both), depending on the circumstances'.[52] In the Court of Appeal's judgment in *Lonsdale*,[53] Moore-Bick LJ stated that if a court is seeking to put a value on the agency business itself, it was difficult to see what relevance was to be attached to the benefits obtained by the principal prior to the termination of the agency.[54] In *Vick v Vogle-Gapes Ltd*,[55] HHJ Richard Seymour QC, sitting as a High Court judge, found that the terms of Regulation 17(7), and in particular the reference therein to 'substantial benefits' for the principal, to be 'very alien and not to possess any obvious logical foundation'. The judge based this conclusion on the assumption that if there were no substantial benefits, then there could be no compensation, whilst if there were substantial benefits, no matter how large or small, then full com-

---

[45] *Duffen v Frabo* [2000] 1 Lloyds Rep 180.
[46] Ibid, 198.
[47] *Gailey v Environmental Waste Controls* [2004] EuLR 424.
[48] *Tigana Ltd v Decoro Ltd* [2003] EuLR 189.
[49] Ibid, para 89.
[50] Ibid, para 90.
[51] *PJP Pipe & Valve Co Limited v Audco India Limited* [2006] EuLR 368.
[52] *Ibid*, para 164.
[53] [2006] 1 WLR 1281.
[54] Ibid, para 38.
[55] *Vick v Vogle-Gapes Ltd* [2006] EWHC 1579(QB).

pensation would be payable.[56] However, in arriving at this position, the learned judge appeared to have not had regard to the fact that the word 'particularly' precedes the key provisions in Regulation 17(7), thereby signifying that its contents were non-exhaustive and therefore non-compulsory. Secondly, the word 'substantial' must be taken to mean that insubstantial benefits will not trigger any right to compensation. In the House of Lords' decision in *Lonsdale*,[57] Lord Hoffmann specifically agreed with the first instance judge in *King v Tunnock*, who found that the agent in that case was not entitled to compensation because the principal, having closed the business, would not enjoy any benefits from the goodwill generated by the agent.[58] As Lord Hoffmann put it: 'The goodwill disappeared when the business closed.'[59]

### 9.17 COMPENSATION: THE DTI GUIDANCE NOTES

Surprisingly, given that compensation is the default option under the Regulations, the DTI Guidance Notes are silent on the manner in which compensation is to be calculated.

### 9.18 COMPENSATION: THE COMMISSION REPORT

The Report makes it clear that the compensation provisions in the Directive, which, as with their indemnity counterparts, have been carried through intact into the Regulations, were based on a 1958 French law, the aim of which was to compensate an agent for loss suffered as a result of the termination of the agency contract. According to the Report, the French case-law arising out of the operation of this law seeks to justify the payment of compensation on the ground either that it represents the cost to the agent's successor of purchasing the agency or that it represented the time it took for the agent to reconstitute the client base which has been removed through termination.

In contrast to indemnity and the German law on which it was modelled, the principle of compensation is not dependent on future developments. Indeed, French law pays no regard to the future, and therefore issues familiar to an English lawyer, such as mitigation of loss, play no part in the calculation of compensation under French law. Although as has been already noted, the approach post-*Lonsdale* has been to exclude considerations of French law, nonetheless the general approach taken by the courts to date has been to continue with the position of ignoring the concept of mitigation of loss. This is explicable on the basis that the language of the Directive and the Regulations militates in favour

---

[56] Ibid, para 125.
[57] [2007] 1 WLR 2055.
[58] *Ibid*, para 22.
[59] *Ibid*, para 23.

of excluding concepts such as mitigation of loss because the goodwill in question can be regarded as a species of property; accordingly, one is not concerned with what an agent could have done to obtain alternative employment.[60] However, in the earlier case of *Janet Mann v Flair Leisure Products plc*,[61] the High Court came close to using the concept of mitigation, when finding that it might be appropriate in a particular case to take into account future earnings which the agent made as a direct consequence of the termination of its agency.[62] Although the Court specifically stated that this did not amount to an attempt to introduce the concept of mitigation in the compensation calculation, it passes the 'duck test'.[63] To be fair to HHJ Alton, Lord Hoffmann opened the door to a similar argument being made by stating in terms that he did not think that 'the court was required to shut its eyes to what actually happened [post-termination]. It may provide evidence as to what the parties were likely to have expected to happen'.[64] According to the Report, judicial custom in France has fixed a benchmark of two years' annual gross remuneration for the calculation of post-termination compensation, although this benchmark may move depending on the factual circumstances of the case.

As with indemnity payments, the 1996 Commission Report mentioned above usefully sets out the French law background to this provision. Chapter 11 of this book contains a detailed analysis of the relevant French law provisions and the manner in which they have been interpreted by the domestic courts in France.

## 9.19 COMPENSATION: THE CASE-LAW

In contrast to the position on indemnity, there are a large number of cases in which a judgment has been given for compensation. Even this is the tip of the iceberg—the authors' experience is that most cases settle before trial. Despite the increased number of reported cases and despite the fact that the House of Lords has opined on the matter, there is still uncertainty, particularly in so far as concerns the actual calculation of post-termination compensation. That said, the House of Lords' decision in *Lonsdale* has answered many of the questions that had previously exercised practitioners. With that in mind, the following section will briefly summarise the case-law prior to *Lonsdale*, then examine that case in some detail and finally examine the few reported decisions which have arisen since then. It is to a large extent because of the continued uncertainty in this area that early settlement of disputes is still common.

Aside from *Ingmar*,[65] in which the ECJ held that a principal could not rely

---

[60] See to this effect the judgment of Moore-Bick LJ in *Lonsdale*.
[61] *Janet Mann v Flair Leisure Products plc*, judgment of HHJ Alton, sitting as a High Court judge, dated 15 December 2005.
[62] Ibid, para 37.
[63] If it looks like a duck and sounds like a duck, it probably is a duck.
[64] See above n 61, para 39.
[65] Case C-83/00: *Ingmar GB Ltd v Eaton Leonard Technologies Inc* [2000] ECR I-9305.

on a choice-of-law clause to avoid the obligation imposed by the Directive to pay compensation, there has been no case-law from the ECJ on the subject of compensation. This is perhaps unsurprising given that it held in the case of *Honyvem*[66] that Article 17 of the Directive does not give any detailed indications as to the method of calculation. Although in that case, the Court was examining the issue of an indemnity, there is no reason to suppose that the same is not true for compensation. Indeed, as pointed out by Lord Hoffmann in *Lonsdale*, the method by which compensation is to be determined is a discretionary matter for the domestic laws of the Member States: 'It is the way in which our domestic law should implement that discretion which has been uncertain and the resolution of that uncertainty is the task of this House and not the European Court of Justice.'[67]

In so far as concerns the decisions of the UK courts on the calculation of compensation, these have been growing in size, if not in clarity. Prior to *Lonsdale*, the position can be described in summary as follows:

1. The unreported case of *Skingsley v KJC Carpets*[68] should, the authors believe, be ignored by anyone reviewing the case-law. The court looked to German rather than French law for assistance even though this was a compensation case, and some commentators have suggested that the judge was motivated by pity for the claimant. The amount awarded for post-termination compensation was £45,000 on the basis of a four-year multiplier. An appeal was started but discontinued.

2. *Page v Combined Shipping and Trading*[69]—in this case judgment arose out of an interlocutory application in which the Court of Appeal concluded that the claimant 'has a good arguable case to recover a substantial sum'.[70] Millett LJ went on to opine that in the circumstances, he did not think that the amount of US$300,000 was excessive (in so far as concerned the terms of the interlocutory injunction) on the grounds that the contract had been terminated after one year of a four-year agreement, and that the agent had earned nearly US$400,000. Millett LJ also stated that it was plainly arguable that Regulation 17(7) provided for compensation in the amount of commission which the agent would have earned had the agency agreement been performed throughout its further life in the manner in which the parties intended it to be performed.[71] These remarks were made in light of the facts of the case, which involved the principal deliberately running down the business of the agency.

3. *King v Tunnock*[72]—at first instance, the Sheriff found that no compensation

---

[66] See above n 28.
[67] Ibid, para 40.
[68] Unreported, Bristol County Court, 4 June 1996.
[69] *Page v Combined Shipping and Trading* [1997] 3 All ER 656.
[70] Ibid, 660j.
[71] Ibid, 661h–j.
[72] *King v Tunnock* [1996] SCLR 742.

should be paid because the principal had closed down its business, which act led to the termination of the agency. Given that, the Sheriff found that the principal was not continuing to benefit from the actions of its erstwhile agent and therefore no compensation was due. Interestingly, in a later decision in the same case by the Sheriff Principal, it can be seen that the Sheriff was asked after his original decision to provide figures for compensation on the hypothesis that such a claim could be made out. The learned Sheriff took the French practice of two years' gross commission as a starting point and then deducted a third, seemingly to take into account the fact that the agent had received certain state sickness and invalidity benefits after termination and that thereafter he was employed in a part-time job.

4.  *Cybermedia Incorporated v Roderick Manhattan Group Ltd*[73]—in determining the amount of compensation due, the court took into account the fact that (i) the agency agreement had lasted a bare two years; (ii) it was inevitable that the agency agreement would in any event have come to an end very soon after it did because of the intention of the agent to set up its own European-based operation. Based on those factors, the judge calculated the compensation on the basis of an 18-month period and awarded the sum of £458,751.

5.  *Roy v MR Pearlman Limited*[74]—in this case, the Scottish Court of Session concluded that the national court was entitled to have regard to French law in determining the quantum of the compensation sought. The amount was not determined as the agent was ordered to further particularise its claim.

6.  *Duffen v Frabo*[75]—the court held as follows on the issue of Regulation 17 compensation:

    • it was not meant to duplicate what otherwise may be recoverable at common law;

    • a better understanding of the Regulations may be gained from having some idea of the principles applicable within the legal system or systems from which those Regulations may have been derived;

    • English courts would be ill-equipped to perform the task of attempting to mimic what a French court would actually do in relation to the calculation of compensation;

    • compensation should be payable at least in relation to the earliest date when the agency agreement could have expired;

    • further to Regulation 17(7)(a), the Court had to ask itself what commission might have accrued to the agent in the normal course of events—it then had to ask to what extent depriving the agent of that commission nonetheless gave substantial benefits to the principal linked to the agent's activities;

    • it would be offensive to look at gross, as opposed to net, earnings;

---

[73] Unreported—decision of Judge Perrett QC of 12 February 1999.
[74] *Roy v MR Pearlman Limited* [1999] 2 CMLR 1155.
[75] *Duffen v Frabo* [2000] 1 Lloyds Rep 180.

- Regulation 17 was framed so as to provide compensation and not a windfall. The judge concluded that on the facts, the agent had failed to show that he had suffered damage as a result of the termination of his agency and accordingly awarded no compensation.

7.  *King v Tunnock*[76]—this decision of the Extra Division of the Inner House of the Scottish Court of Session was the leading UK authority on the calculation of post-termination compensation until the House of Lords' decision in *Lonsdale*. In it, the Court overturned the decision at first instance in relation to the payment of compensation and held that the agent was entitled to compensation calculated on the basis of French practice. At first instance, as noted above, the Court had relied strongly on the fact that the termination of the agency arose directly from the closure of the principal's business and that accordingly, there could be no compensation payable as the principal did not continue to enjoy the benefits derived from the agency. On appeal to the Extra Division, the Court held that it was not necessary to demonstrate a continuing benefit to the principal post-termination; the only condition for the right to compensation being damage done to the agency relationship by the termination. This position was, the Court said, to be contrasted with the indemnity provisions, which made clear that continuing benefits for the principal were prerequisites for the payment of an indemnity. The Court, in so finding, made it clear that it was not concerned with what happened after the termination of the agency. Having determined that the agent was entitled to post-termination compensation pursuant to the Regulations, the Court based its calculation thereof firmly on the basis of French practice of two years' gross commission. The award made was in the sum of £27,144 together with interest.

8.  *Barrett McKenzie v Escada (UK) Ltd*[77]—in this case, the High Court disagreed with the approach taken in *King v Tunnock*. Although agreeing with that Court in terms of the 'nature of the beast'—compensation was to remedy the loss of the value of the agency—it did not accept the need or obligation to follow French practices in the area. This was because (i) that approach was not spelled out in the Directive, (ii) the deeming provisions at Regulation 17(7) would be otiose if the broad-brush French practice simply had to be followed and (iii) the general difficulty for an English court to second-guess what a French court would do in the circumstances. Rather, the High Court suggested that the following factors would be of relevance: the duration of the agency and its history, the precise terms of the agency agreement, and whether the agent was dealing with a regular, repeating base or whether it was simply dealing with one-off transactions with different persons. Finally, the Court held that it would be offensive to take gross, rather than net, earnings when calculating the amount of compensation due. As the Court was dealing with preliminary issues rather than the

---

[76] *King v Tunnock* [2000] EuLR 531.
[77] *Barrett McKenzie v Escada (UK) Ltd* [2001] ECC 50.

actual substance of the case, no calculation of the compensation due in the case was made.

9.   *Ingmar GB Limited v Eaton Leonard Inc*[78]—following the referral of this case to the ECJ and the subsequent judgment in favour of the agent, the matter was remitted back to the High Court for the determination of the compensation due. Morland J first held that he considered he was bound by the decision of the Scottish court in *King v Tunnock* on matters of law. In arriving at this conclusion he relied by way of analogy on certain Inland Revenue cases. Although the Scottish court laid down guidelines in the case, rather than rules of law, those guidelines should, the Court argued, be followed unless they were inappropriate for the facts and circumstances of the particular case. The Court then decided to follow the Commission Report in which the French practice was described as allowing courts there a discretion to depart from the benchmark of two years' gross commission. The Court in the present case held that on the facts, an injustice to the principal would result if compensation were to be calculated on the basis of the traditional benchmark and that therefore the amount should be based on three years' deemed net commission, comprising the salary paid to the agent's sales director together with his pension and a charge to the principal, which was in effect the commission levied by the agent. The multiplier was three years and the amount awarded was £183,600.

10.  *Cooper & Others v Pure Fishing (UK) Ltd*[79]—in this case, upheld on appeal, HHJ Kershaw QC, sitting in the Manchester Mercantile Court, awarded compensation on the basis of the average of three years' commission multiplied by two, thereby following the French law approach. The total amount awarded for the three agents was £ 219,061.99

11.  *Tigana Ltd v Decoro Ltd*[80]—in this case, the High Court pointed out forcefully (and in contrast to the position taken in *Ingmar*) that it was not aware of any practice or precedent in which English courts were bound by the decisions of Scottish courts, other than the fact that there was a general practice to do so in revenue and taxation cases. The Court then respectfully disagreed with the judgment in *King v Tunnock* in so far as concerned the deference it gave to French law, and in particular the imposition of a benchmark tariff. The Court found on the facts that the requisite damage to the agent had occurred and that the principal retained for itself the substantial benefits derived from the agent's activities, and that therefore the agent would be entitled to significant compensation. The Court held that in some cases, reliance could be placed on the gross amount of commission—in other words, it would not always be 'offensive' to do so. However, in the present case, it would be appropriate to calculate the compensation due based on net commission for the period of the agency, which amounted

---

[78] *Ingmar GB Limited v Eaton Leonard Inc* [2001] CLC 1825.
[79] *Cooper & Others v Pure Fishing (UK) Ltd* [2004] EuLR 664.
[80] *Tigana Ltd v Decoro Ltd* [2003] EuLR 189.

to US$452,346. It should be noted that this was in addition to a finding that post-termination commission in the sum of US$606,836.64 pursuant to Regulation 8 should be paid. In arriving at his decision, Davis J suggested that the following factors would generally be of relevance when calculating compensation under the Regulations:

- the period of the agency as provided in the contract;
- the actual period of the agency up to termination;
- the terms and conditions in the agency contract;
- the nature and history of the agency and the particular market involved;
- the matters specified in Regulations 17(7)(a) and (b);
- the nature of the client base and of the kind of contracts anticipated to be placed;
- whether the agency was exclusive or non-exclusive both from the perspective of the principal and the agent;
- whether the principal retained the benefit of the agent's activities post-termination;
- the existence and extent of any post-termination restraint-of-trade clause;
- whether any payments under Regulation 8 were made and which ought to be taken into account;
- the manner in which the agency contract was ended;
- the extent to which the parties to the agreement contributed financially to the goodwill accruing during the period of the agency;
- the extent to which there may have been loss caused by any relevant breach of contract or duty.

12. *Turner v Steinhoff UK Furniture Ltd*[81]—the Taunton County Court in this case agreed with the High Court in *Tigana* that it was inappropriate to follow French practice; it also followed the checklist set out in *Tigana*. However, that did not mean that a court should lose sight of the importance of the value which would have been attached to the agency as at the time of termination. It was therefore necessary, the Court held, to examine what a purchaser would have been prepared to pay for an assignment of the agency. In carrying out this examination, the Court declined to have regard to matters arising post-termination. Taking all relevant matters into consideration, the Court held that the appropriate amount of compensation was that equivalent to the agent's average gross commission over a period of 15 months, which amounted to £14,055.

13. *PJ Pipe & Valve Co Limited v Audco India Limited*[82]—the High Court once again refused to follow the position of the Scottish courts as set out in *King v. Tunnock*. As Fulford J said:

For my part, I consider the court in a given case should not be subject to the straight-jacket [*sic*] of one particular test or approach. . . . The relevant approach to

---

[81] *Turner v Steinhoff UK Furniture Ltd* [2006] EuLR 2006.
[82] [2006] EuLR 368.

be applied when assessing compensation will be largely fact-dependent, and judges should be free to identify those matters that are relevant to the circumstances of a particular case. This is not to absolve the judge from the need to make a decision on a principled, logical and just basis—to the contrary, it is to ensure that there there is an appropriate and fair result, bearing in mind the particular circumstances of the case.[83]

The Court then endorsed the approach taken in *Duffen v Frabo* that the right approach was simply to look at the earnings which might have accrued to the claimant during the relevant period had he remained as the principal's agent. The authors note in passing that this approach would appear to go contrary to the established view that the calculation of compensation should be based on the position as at the date of termination. As we shall see, the House of Lords in *Lonsdale* has left the position slightly open. Based on the above approach, the Court held that compensation was to be calculated on the basis of a 12-month period post termination on the assumption that there would have been one successful introduction involving the various projects. As that approach was rather conservative from the agent's perspective, given that introductions occurred historically at a rate of well over one per year, the Court determined that the commission used should be gross rather than net. The sum in question amounted to US$118,518.60.

14.  *Smith, Bailey, Palmer v Howard & Hallam Ltd*[84]—this case was brought after Mr Lonsdale sued the same company for post-termination compensation, in a claim which eventually led to the leading House of Lords decision, which will be analysed further below. This case was, however, the subject of one judgment from the High Court. HHJ Overend preferred the previously described flexible approach to the benchmark tariff position preferred by the Scottish courts. Contrary to the position in the *Lonsdale* case, the agents in the present case were offered and accepted new agencies from the purchaser of their old principal's business. Notwithstanding that fact, the Court held that they were entitled to compensation, which it calculated on the basis of the price the new principal paid for the principal's business reduced by an amount equal to the appropriate percentage of the value of that business. That reduction was based on the amount of commission payments when compared with the sale price. The figure reached amounted to the equivalent of a multiplier of 1.9 years of gross commission. The Court then reduced that multiplier to one year's gross commission to reflect the fact, inter alia, that the agents had been able to continue their agencies with the new principal. The figures awarded were between £20,497.33 and £33,724.80.

15.  *Janet Mann v Flair Leisure Products plc*[85]—in this case, HHJ Alton, sitting as a High Court judge, endorsed the position taken in the previous decisions by the High Court in the cases of *Tigana* and *PJ Pipe and Valve Co.*

---

[83] Ibid, para 162.

[84] *Smith, Bailey, Palmer v Howard & Hallam Ltd* [2006] EuLR 578.

[85] See above n 61, judgment of 15 December 2005.

In addition, she made clear that there might be situations in which it would be appropriate to have regard to the future potential of the lost agency. Based on the length of the agency (some 2.5 years), the extent of the agent's contribution in the course of the agency, the fact that the agency was non-exclusive and did not require any form of capital or other investment from the agent, and the fact that the agent was free post-termination to take on an alternative agency in respect of the same products and did in fact do so, the Court calculated the compensation on the basis of net monthly commission adjusted by a multiplier of 6. The amount consequently awarded was £8,800. In this case, with the Claimant seeking compensation in excess of £170,000, the Defendant paid £18,000 into Court when filing its Defence. Accordingly, the Claimant was bound to pay the costs of the claim.

16. *Michael Edwards v International Connection (UK) Limited*[86]—the judge in this case was very concise when dealing with the quantification of compensation. This is perhaps unsurprising given that it was common ground between the parties that the criteria listed by Davis J in *Tigana* should be applied. It would appear that the Court used a quasi net monthly commission figure—it accepted in principle the principal's argument that the commission figure should be net but then stated that it could not net the figure down any further. A multiplier of 18 was used, giving a total figure of £16,617. This was for an exclusive agency which had lasted 10.5 years. The case was appealed by the principal, but not with regard to the quantification of compensation. In any event, the appeal was unsuccessful.[87]

## The *Lonsdale* Case

The case arose out of the sale of the principal's business due to long-term decline in the British shoe manufacturing industry. That led to the termination of its agency agreement with Mr Lonsdale, on six months notice after some 13 years. Mr Lonsdale sought compensation from the principal pursuant to Regulation 17 in the sum of £27,000.

At first instance, Judge Charles Harris QC, sitting in the Oxford County Court,[88] held that the agent was entitled to the sum of £5,000 which equated to approximately six months' net commission. In arriving at that figure, he made the following comments/findings:

1. The calculation of an indemnity (as opposed to compensation) would not be difficult—the provisions were tolerably straightforward, logical, just and there was a cap of one year's remuneration.

2. The 'damage' sought to be repaired by compensation was, it was agreed by

---

[86] *Michael Edwards v International Connection (UK) Limited*, judgment of 25 November 2005 in the Central London County Court.

[87] [2006] EWCA judgment of 27 April 2006.

[88] Judgment of 13 May 2005, unreported.

the parties, a form of statutory compensation for the loss of the value of the goodwill of the agency.

3.   As a matter of fact, Mr Lonsdale's commission had been falling for some time, from a high point of nearly £17,000 in 1997/98 to some £9,600 in 2002/03.

4.   Mr Lonsdale was a non-exclusive agent and worked for another shoe-manufacturing principal, with whom he continued to work after the termination of the Howard & Hallam agency.

5.   The calculation of compensation could not depend on future earnings, as the Regulations provided for the payment of compensation even when the agent died.

6.   An agent seeking compensation needed to prove that, after termination, he had lost the value of an agency asset which had existed prior to termination; if it was kept in mind that the damage for which the agent is to be compensated consisted in the loss of the value or goodwill he could be said to have possessed in the agency, then it could be seen that valuation should be reasonably straightforward.[89]

7.   The commercial value of the agency would be the amount that someone would be willing to pay for the agency; in the present case therefore, it was necessary to calculate what someone would be willing to pay for an agency with a net annual income of £8,000.

8.   The Claimant had provided no evidence as to the commercial value of the agency—however, a broad-brush approach was appropriate in such cases.

9.   The approach taken by the Scottish court in *King v Tunnock* with regard to the link between the damage suffered and the use of the French two-year benchmark tariff was unclear: 'What the French do is a matter for the French. Their system is not our system and there is no more reason in European Law for English courts to follow French reasoning than for the French to follow English reasoning.'

10.  Accordingly, the Court agreed with Davis J in *Tigana* that there was no binding two-year tariff or guideline.

The matter was appealed to the Court of Appeal. In the leading judgment,[90] Moore-Bick LJ upheld the first instance decision, making the following findings/comments en route:

1.   The question at the heart of the case was whether there was, or should be, a general rule that in the ordinary case compensation should be assessed at two years' gross commission, or, if not, on what basis it should be assessed.

2.   The 1996 Commission Report noted that the French courts justified the payment of compensation either on the ground that it represented the cost to a successor of purchasing the agency business or on the ground that it

---

[89] This earnest hope has not, however, been fulfilled in practice.
[90] [2006] 1 WLR 1281.

represented the time it took for the agent to reconstitute the client base of which he has been deprived.

3.  In most of the previous cases on compensation, the courts had had regard primarily to the nature and duration of the agency and the commission the agent was able to generate from it as providing the basis for the assessment.

4.  It was also generally accepted (although the basis for such a position was not entirely clear) that the concept of mitigation of loss had no part to play in the calculation of compensation.[91]

5.  In general, judges had approached the matter on the basis of what was just and equitable in all the circumstances, rather than attempting to calculate compensation for any specific loss suffered by the agent.

6.  There was little or no assistance to be gained from the language of the Directive itself when approaching the construction of the Regulations.

7.  The Commission's 1996 Report may have been given too much importance—the summary of French practice was helpful and informative, but it did not mean that the manner in which the Directive was applied in France should be transposed to the English domestic courts.

8.  The provisions in relation to compensation were to be distinguished from those relating to indemnity in that the latter specifically provided that the payment of an indemnity should be equitable. No comparable provision existed in relation to compensation and accordingly, that payment was to be made for any damage the agent suffered as a result of the termination of the agency, without regard to whether such payment was fair and reasonable having regard to all the circumstances of the case.

9.  The damage that the agent could be said to have suffered on termination could relate to the loss of the goodwill attaching to the agency business which the agent would have enjoyed if the relationship with the principal had not come to an end.

10.  However, loss of goodwill was not the only damage which an agent could suffer on termination—where, for example, there had been an inability to amortise expenses incurred at termination, then the value attaching to the business might or might not provide sufficient compensation.[92]

11.  Accordingly, the agent was entitled to recover whatever loss that could be demonstrated to have been suffered.

12.  There were strong reasons for doubting the approach taken by the High Court in *PJ Pipe & Valve v. Audco India*, in which the damage in respect of which compensation was available extended to losses arising from the principal's wrongful repudiation of the agreement.

---

[91] One reason must be that pursuant to the Regulations, an agent who dies is entitled to compensation—by definition there can be no mitigation in such circumstances.

[92] As will be seen, this point was not examined by the House of Lords on appeal from this decision and could be seen to go contrary to a central theme of Lord Hoffmann's speech, that compensation was to be measured in terms of loss of the agent's goodwill.

13. The compensation to which the agent is entitled should reflect the value of the business as at the date of termination;

14. Although the Court in *Tigana* made a valiant attempt to list the factors which should be taken into consideration by a court when determining compensation, many of those factors would have little or no relevance to the task of assessing the value of the business at the date of termination;

15. However, one factor not mentioned by Davis J which would be relevant was the state of the principal's business; it was obvious that the amount that a potential purchaser of an agency would pay to acquire it would depend to a considerable extent on the amount of commission that it could be expected to produce, which in turn would depend in part on the strength of the principal's business.

16. Neither the Directive nor the Regulations required a person to shut his eyes to what was likely to happen in the future; accordingly the Court could not agree with the approach taken in *King v Tunnock*, which was to disregard, for the purpose of the calculation of compensation, the fact that the principal's business had closed down.

17. The fact was that the perception of the way in which an agency business was likely to develop in the future was bound to affect its value.

18. However, where a contract expired through the passage of time, it was necessary to adopt a purposive approach which took into account the fact that the agent had built up a business to which goodwill attached and which, if the agreement had continued, would have continued to produce benefits in the form of commission.

19. The argument that a court should have regard to the one-year cap for indemnity payments when calculating compensation payments was not accepted; the Directive clearly offered a choice of remedy which gave rise to different results; accordingly the degree of harmonisation sought by the Directive was limited.

20. The judge at first instance was correct in the manner in which he had approached the calculation of the compensation due; nothing could alter the fact that the principal's business was in decline and, with it, the prospects for the agency.

21. In most cases involving the quantification of compensation, courts would be likely to benefit from having the assistance of an expert witness (preferably a single joint expert) who could give evidence as to the appropriate manner in which to value the particular business in question.

The matter was then appealed to the House of Lords. After two days of argument, judgment was reserved and handed down on 4 July 2007.[93] The leading speech was that of Lord Hoffmann, who made the following findings/comments in dismissing the appeal:

---

[93] [2007] 1 WLR 2055.

1.  The two systems of recompense under the Directive—indemnity and compensation—could plainly lead to different results and therefore, to that extent, the degree of co-ordination achieved by the Directive was modest.

2.  The right to be compensated under the Directive was for the damage suffered as a result of termination; in other words, the concept of compensation was predicated on the notion that the agent had lost something of value as a result of the termination and was entitled to be compensated for that loss.

3.  As the compensation provisions in the Directive were based on French law, one was entitled to look at that law for guidance or confirmation as to what it means.

4.  The French jurisprudence appeared to regard the agent as having a share in the goodwill of the principal's business which he had helped to create; the relationship between the parties was treated as having existed for their common benefit; the agent had acquired a share in the goodwill, an asset which was retained by the principal after termination and accordingly, the agent was entitled to compensation.

5.  Instead of trying to attribute an appropriate portion of goodwill to the agent in order to determine the compensation due, the French courts sought to compensate the agent for the damage suffered, which involved placing a value on the right to be an agent, which primarily meant the right to future commissions; it was this right for which the Directive required agents to be compensated;

6.  The value of the agency relationship lay in the prospect of earning commission and the agent's expectation that proper performance of the contract would provide him with a future income stream; it was that income stream which was to be valued.

7.  That valuation exercise required one to say what could reasonably have been obtained, as at the date of termination, for the rights which the agent had been enjoying.

8.  For that purpose, it was obviously necessary to assume that the agency would have continued and that the hypothetical purchaser would have been able properly to perform the agency contract.

9.  Given that the exercise would place a present value on future income, it was necessary to discount future earnings by an appropriate rate of interest; it would also be necessary to take into account whether the market in which the agent operated was rising or falling as that would impact on what the hypothetical purchaser would be willing to pay; if the agent had to incur expenses in generating commission, then that too would have to be taken into account.

10. The argument that the above approach would produce less than that awarded by a French court, with its benchmark of two years' gross commission, and that as such was contrary to the 1996 Commission Report which endorsed the French approach, was not accepted. That Report, on which the Appellant placed great reliance, did not endorse any method of calculation as a

true reflection of Community law; further the ECJ case of *Honyvem* made clear that the Member States enjoyed a margin of discretion in terms of the method of calculation of the post-termination relief available to the agent on the termination of contract; finally, on this point, commercial agencies in France operated under different market conditions to those prevailing in England—there was no market in England for the premiums charged in France on the transfer of agencies, because no such premiums were charged.

11. The fact that the valuation of the income stream would not be as favourable as the French approach did not mean that the income stream approach was contrary to the aims of the Directive; a useful cross-check for this conclusion could be garnered from considering the position under the indemnity scheme: under such a scheme, payments were capped at one year's remuneration—it could therefore not be argued that the Directive's policy required the payment of twice gross annual commission, which was the French practice.

12. In *King v Tunnock*, the agency was worth nothing following the closure of the principal's business; no one would have given anything for the right to earn future commission on the sales of cakes and biscuits (the ex principal's business), because there would be none to be sold; nor had the principal retained any goodwill in the business.

13. When valuing the future income stream, it was necessary to determine what the agency would fetch based on real factors—what the earnings prospects of the agency were and what people would have been willing to pay for similar business at the same time.

14. Prima facie, the value of an agency should be fixed by reference to net earnings.

15. In the case of an agent who had more than one agency, it was necessary to attribute costs fairly to each one.

16. The approach taken by Judge Overend in *Smith, Bailey and Palmer v Howard & Hallam* was flawed in so far as the judge sought to attribute 42 per cent of the value of the brand to the agent, the percentage figure being derived from the relationship between the agent's commission and the total of sales and distribution expenses; it was flawed because it attributed the entire value of the brand to sales and marketing, because no allowance was made for the fact that the agent was actually paid the commission and because the calculation was based on cost rather than what anyone would have paid for the agency.

17. It should not be difficult for parties to such disputes to agree on an appropriate valuation, with the benefit of advice as to the going rate for relevant businesses; however, if the matter did go to court, the judge would need some information as to the standard methodology for the valuation of the relevant businesses.[94]

---

[94] As will be noted in the valuation chapter (ch 12), this supposed ease of valuation is not borne out in practice.

18. In the case of an agent transferring the goodwill created with one principal to another, possibly competing, principal, that fact would be reflected in the process of valuation; if it appeared that all the customers were likely to defect to the former agent, then that would be reflected in the price payable for the agency.
19. Although what mattered was what would have appeared likely as at the date of termination, nonetheless a court was not required to shut its eyes to what actually happened—that might provide evidence of what the parties were likely to have expected to happen.
20. It was not necessary to refer the matter to the ECJ as the issue before the House was how a particular discretion should be exercised and the resolution of that question was not a matter for the ECJ.

There are a number of comments that can be made about this judgment. First, practice since the ruling has shown that the hope that the calculation of compensation would be relatively straightforward has not been fulfilled. It is the authors' experience that it has become a battle of expert valuers, with different concepts of valuation being favoured by different experts. There is no particular consensus appearing, not least because most disputes end up being resolved in mediations, which will normally impose confidentiality as to the result and how it was achieved. Secondly, the relatively severe attack on Lord Caplan in *King v Tunnock* overlooked the point clearly raised in that latter case that it was not necessary in order for compensation to be paid for the principal to continue to benefit from the agent's activities. It would appear strongly arguable that the fact that a principal goes out of business should not lead to a negative decision on the payment of compensation. However, as this was a decision of the House of Lords, it is most unlikely that this matter will be revisited in the foreseeable future, unless a party manages to convince a court of the need for a reference to the ECJ. This leads to the third point: the almost throw-away remark that a court was not required to shut its eyes to what actually happened post-termination. Lord Hoffmann did not explain how this approach sat with the generally recognised acceptance of the position that compensation is to be measured as at the date of termination, because it is the damage which occurs at termination which is the subject of the compensation. If it is to be the case that a court can peek into what happened post-termination, then there could be advantages to delaying the determination of a dispute when the market was rising and conversely seeking speedy resolution if it were falling. Also, there is no indication of how long a peek is permissible or acceptable. Finally, it is not clear why it was felt necessary to cross-refer to the position under the indemnity system when it was made clear earlier in the judgment that it was completely different, with different results pertaining.

There have been few reported cases since the House of Lords handed down its decision in *Lonsdale*. What few there are do not inspire confidence as to how courts will determine such matters in the future.

In *Nigel Fryer Joinery Services Ltd. and Another v Ian Firth Hardware Ltd*,[95] the Manchester County Court dealt with the issue of the calculation of compensation by way of obiter remarks, given that it had found that the principal had been entitled to terminate the agency so as to exclude the payment of compensation. However, the remarks are of interest:

1.  One of the difficulties of the approach taken by the House of Lords in *Lonsdale* was that there was no actual market in agencies because they were not assignable; accordingly any valuation reports would be based on hypotheses as to what a willing purchaser would be willing to pay on the assumption that the agency was in fact assignable.
2.  In the case before the Court, the agent's expert had valued the income stream at between £80,000 and £100,000. That calculation assumed a future maintainable pre-tax profit of between £20,000 and £25,000 per annum, which netted back post-tax and expenses, amounted to between £16,000 and £20,000. To that figure was added a profit/earnings ratio of 5. However, after cross-examination, it appeared that the net income figure would have been £14,100. That figure took no account of the time worked in order to earn the commission.
3.  The figure of £14,100 was modest and very much less than the 2005 New Earnings Survey figure for sales representatives; the Court found that almost anyone could obtain an income at that level in an unskilled job without paying a premium for it; the Court opined that no hypothetical purchaser would be willing to pay a substantial sum for the opportunity of earning that amount through his own labour and that therefore no compensation would have been ordered.

It is not clear why Patten J came to the obiter conclusion he did—it would appear to amount to a conclusion that no compensation should be due where the amount of the income stream is low. There is no basis for this approach in either the Directive or the Regulations and it appears to go clearly against one of the stated aims of the Directive—that of protecting the commercial agent.

In *John Francis Camm and Another v Seac Diving Pro srl*,[96] the agent sought payment of compensation in the sum of between £165,000 and £228,000. The following findings/comments were made:

1.  The agent earned a total of £284,549.87 in commission over the 5.5 years of the agreement.
2.  Over the last four years of the agreement, the average annual maintainable gross commission amounted to £51,000.
3.  Following termination of the agreement, the agent negotiated a new agreement with a rival principal.

---

[95] *Nigel Fryer Joinery Services Ltd. and Another v Ian Firth Hardware Ltd* [2008] 2 Lloyd's Rep 108.
[96] *John Francis Camm and Another v Seac Diving Pro srl*, judgment of HHJ Behrens in the Chancery Division of the Leeds District Registry, unreported.

4.  Because of the inability of a hypothetical purchaser to sell competing goods, the decline in the market as at termination and the high costs incurred by the agent, it was likely that there would be someone willing to pay for the income stream represented by the agency but the sum would not be large.
5.  In the circumstances, the compensation would be set at £35,000.

Although this case is instructive in that it sets out in detail the views expressed in the competing expert reports, there is no reasoning given for the final figure reached save for the fact that it approximates to the agent's own estimate of its net annual average commission. The Court does not explain why it appears to have relied on the agent's costs figures when it had previously dismissed them as too low, nor does it explain why one year was deemed sufficient, aside from saying that because of the uncertainty over costs, the traditional multiplicand/multiplier approach could not be adopted.

In *Alex Berry v Laytons and Another*,[97] the question of compensation arose in the context of a claim for professional negligence. The High Court found that the solicitor advising the agent had been negligent in its advice in relation to the impact of, inter alia, Regulation 17. The question then arose as to the loss suffered by the agent. In determining that matter, the Court had to consider what would have been the likely outcome had the agent pursued a claim under Regulation 17 against the principal in the year 2000. The Court made the following findings/comments in this regard:

1.  The case would have taken about two years to settle.
2.  During that period, no English case-law would have provided the principal with any comfort as to whether or not the agent would be entitled to substantial compensation.
3.  It was common ground that had the matter gone to trial, it would have done so before the judgment of the House of Lords in *Lonsdale*.
4.  The agent's original valuation was based on the past pattern of commission and costs incurred, giving a figure of between £576,000 and £648,000, based on a net multiplicand of £144,000 and a multiplier of 4–4.5.
5.  The Defendant's original valuation ranged from about £75,000 to £269,000, based on a net multiplicand of £31,000–59,000.
6.  The key difference between the experts was how they attributed costs: the agent's expert worked on the basis of apportioning costs equally between the three agencies for which it operated, only one being the principal in the present case; the solicitor's expert preferred to base the cost allocation on the turnover and customer numbers of the different agencies. The agent's approach was accepted on the basis of evidence tendered to the Court by the agent.
7.  The Court also accepted the agent's submissions in relation to the amount

---

[97] *Alex Berry v Laytons and Another* [2009] EWHC 1591 (QB) judgment of Mrs Justice Sharp.

of management salaries which should have been taken into account in the valuation process.

8.    In the circumstances of the case, it was not reasonable to reduce the multiplier to take into account the possibility that the agent would compete with the hypothetical purchaser's customers, not least because of the probability that the agent would in all likelihood have agreed a non-compete clause on sale, and also because of the very specialised nature of the agency.

9.    Based on the above, the Court was of the view that a sum of £500,000 could have been ordered by way of compensation had the matter gone to court and been determined on the basis of the ruling in *Lonsdale*; even accepting some of the Defendant's submissions, the figure would still have been of the order of £372,000.

This case is instructive as it sets out how a court will approach expert valuations post *Lonsdale*. As is clear, the matter is detailed and technical and it is more likely than not that the hope expressed by Lord Hoffmann in *Lonsdale* of a joint expert witness may not be achieved, particularly where there is a substantial sum at stake and there are marked differences between the parties. Accordingly, it is difficult to see how Lord Hoffmann's hope of a straightforward process, particularly in terms of costs, can come to fruition in the near future.

It should be noted that the DTI produced a compliance cost estimate with regard to the provisions relating to, inter alia, compensation. The low range was put at £5,000 and the high range at £80,000. Interestingly, under a more recent cost compliance estimate dated December 1993, this low range stayed the same but the high range has dropped to £40,000. As already noted, many cases settle prior to trial and therefore the actual sums paid out under the Regulations are not known. However, it is thought that the DTI figures are a serious underestimate of sums actually received by agents for post-termination compensation.

Finally, the issue of liquidated damages arises. Can the parties to an agency agreement agree in advance a limit on the monies to be paid to the agent in the event of termination? As mentioned below, Regulation 19 prevents derogation to the agent's detriment before termination, so that in so far as any such agreement limited the agent's rights, it would be unenforceable. The discussion above regarding the nature of the rights created by the Regulations is also relevant. At least if the Regulations create contractual rights, the ordinary rules of English law would apply, so that in order to be effective, where the sum was payable on breach, it would have to be a genuine pre-estimate of the monies to be paid. This generally arises in the context when the sum has been fixed at such a level as to act as a deterrent to ensure that the contract in question is performed. In the situation of a principal and an agent, it is much more likely that the sum of money agreed will be below any estimated losses. In this case, regard will have to be paid to Regulation 19.

**Precedent Clause**

If the indemnity route is chosen, the following precedent clause is suggested:

C If the Commercial Agents (Council Directive) Regulations 1993 (as amended) apply to this Agreement, then upon determination of this Agreement (howsoever effected), the Agent shall be entitled to be indemnified and not compensated.

## 9.20 INDEMNITY OR COMPENSATION?

As to which is the preferred option, the authors remain agnostic. It will depend on the particular circumstances of each case as to which option may be preferable. The fact that indemnity payments have a fixed limit will appeal to many principals. However, it is not to be forgotten that the agent may claim damages as well under the indemnity provisions.

In so far as compensation is concerned, although there is no limit fixed it must be based on actual damage and a sizeable part of it may be attributed to unamortised costs and expenses, in which case potential liability can be reduced by not advising that such costs and expenses be incurred. In addition, the recent English case-law shows that the courts are much less willing to give what they describe as windfall payments in the form of compensation to agents.

## 9.21 IN WHAT CIRCUMSTANCES ARE THE RIGHTS TO INDEMNITY OR COMPENSATION UNDER REGULATION 17 INAPPLICABLE?

Regulation 18 provides that the agent does not have a right to indemnity or compensation where:

— the principal has terminated the agency contract due to breach by the agent, such breach justifying immediate termination; or
— the agent has terminated the contract himself, unless such termination is justified by circumstances attributable to the principal or is justified on grounds of age, infirmity or illness of the agent due to which he cannot reasonably be expected to carry out his activities;
— the agent assigns his rights and duties under the contract, with the consent of the principal, to another person.

This Regulation has been dealt with above when examining the scope of Regulation 17. It is, in refreshing contrast to many of the other Regulations, very clear. The Regulation is important in that it sets limits to the rights of agents to claim an indemnity payment or compensation. Only one point need be made. Under English law, a default justifying immediate termination would include a serious breach or a breach of a fundamental term in the contract.

## 9.22 CAN THE PARTIES DEROGATE FROM REGULATIONS 17 AND 18?

Regulation 19 provides that neither the principal nor the commercial agent may derogate from the terms of Regulations 17 and 18 to the detriment of the commercial agent before the agency contract expires.[98] This Regulation follows verbatim the relevant provision in the Directive. As mentioned above, this may impact on the opportunity to use liquidated damages clauses in agency contracts in order to try to limit the amount of compensation which could be payable to an agent.

## 9.23 BRINGING A CLAIM

Regulation 17(9) states that an agent's entitlement to indemnity or compensation will be lost if the agent has not 'notified his principal that he intends pursuing his entitlement' within one year following termination.

The required notice was considered in the unreported High Court case of *Hackett v Advanced Medical Computer Systems Limited.*[99] The court apparently stated that notice was sufficient if it gave notice of an intention to pursue claims even if it was not stated whether compensation or indemnity was being claimed.[100] The question has been the subject of a recent determination of a preliminary issue in the case of *Claramoda Limited v Zoomphase Limited.*[101]

## 9.24 TO WHAT EXTENT ARE RESTRAINT-OF-TRADE CLAUSES VALID UNDER THE REGULATIONS?

Regulation 20 provides that restraint-of-trade clauses are only valid if they are concluded in writing and they relate to the geographical area or group of customers and geographical area entrusted to the commercial agents and to the kind of goods covered by their agencies. It also provides that such clauses will not be valid for more than two years after termination. The Regulation implements Article 20 of the Directive almost verbatim.

However, it is interesting to examine the previous drafts of the Directive on this issue as certain changes have taken place which may affect parties to an agency agreement.

In all of the drafts of the Directive up to and including the amended Commission proposal, there were provisions for the payment of a suitable indemnity

---

[98] The fact that Reg 17 is mandatory was confirmed by the ECJ in Case C-381/98: *Ingmar GB v Eaton Leonard Technologies* [2001] 1 CMLR 9.

[99] 24 September 1998: see *PLC Magazine*, Jan/Feb 1999, 57.

[100] See also the more recent decision in *Devers v Electricity Direct (UK) Ltd*, Leeds District Registry, 7 November 2008 (unreported), in which it was held that sufficient notice had not been given.

[101] *Claramoda Limited v Zoomphase Limited*, judgment of Simon J on 13 November 2009.

by the principal to the agent during the time when the restraint of trade was in force. The only exception to this entitlement was when the principal had terminated the contract because of default attributable to the agent which justified immediate termination. This provision was not carried through to the Directive as adopted by the Council, but there would appear to be nothing in the Directive or the Regulations to prohibit the agent from forcing the principal to take into account in the calculation of the indemnity or compensation the time during which a restraint-of-trade clause was operational.

In terms of English law, it is worth noting that prior to the implementation of the Directive, unwritten restraints of trade were valid. Thus this is a change of which principals should be aware. Also under English law, restraints of trade for periods of less than two years have been held to be invalid. It is the DTI's view that the restraint-of-trade doctrine does not apply to the extent that it is overridden by Regulation 20. It remains to be seen whether this is a correct interpretation of Regulation 20(2). It is thought that if a restraint of trade clause is set at say four years, the last two years could be severed leaving the clause valid for two years: the first draft of the Regulations stipulated that a restraint-of-trade clause would be valid only if it was limited to a period of not more than two years after termination. The Directive and the Regulations both state that a restraint-of-trade clause 'shall be valid for not more than two years after termination'.

Finally, if such clauses are to be valid, they will still have to be reasonable as between the parties as well as not being against the public interest in keeping with the English common law doctrine.

The High Court considered the application of Regulation 20 in *BCM Group PLC v Visualmark Ltd*,[102] holding that a restrictive covenant which was broad enough to apply to customers dealt with by employees of the principal in addition to those dealt with by the agent encompassed customers who could not be said to have been 'entrusted' to the agent and that, accordingly, the restrictive covenant was too broad.[103]

There are a few other interesting issues arise from the court's judgment in this case as follows:

— the court seems to have assumed that the 'blue pencil rule', which is part of the common law doctrine of restraint of trade and allows deletion of words from a restrictive covenant, leaving the remainder enforceable, would also apply where Regulation 20 was applicable;
— the court considered that the position of agents in the context of restrictive covenants could be analogised with the position of employees;
— the court did not consider the duration of the restrictive covenant in this case (two years) to be excessive.

---

[102] *BCM Group PLC v Visualmark Ltd* [2006] EWHC 1831 (QB).
[103] Although the court would have found the clause to be too broad and accordingly unenforceable on common law principles in any event (see para 52 of the judgment).

# 10

# Commercial Agency
# Law in Germany

Dr Michael Reiling
*Rechtsanwalt, Noerr LLP*

I
N GERMANY, THE Commercial Code of 1900, the first such codification
in the world, introduced special provisions regarding commercial agents. In
a first revision in 1953, the original nine sections were modified. The purpose was to integrate, in addition, non-merchants as possible principals and to
introduce a more precise differentiation between commercial agents and simple
merchant's clerks (section 84(2) German Commercial Code). The law on the
implementation of Council Directive 86/653 amended sections 84ff quite significantly, though without changing the wording of many provisions. As—from a
German perspective—the Directive was so heavily oriented on the then already
applicable German legal framework, a major part of the implementation consisted merely of the interpretation of the already applicable provisions in the
light of the new European parameters. It is therefore not just pure coincidence
that the most important ruling of the ECJ since *Ingmar*[1]—*Semen*[2]—was initiated by a reference for a preliminary ruling from a German court.[3] The ruling
in *Semen* led to the most recent revision of the German Commercial Code in
August 2009,[4] amending section 89b German Commercial Code.

## 10.1 GENERAL REMARKS ON COMMERCIAL
AGENCY AGREEMENTS

German law on commercial agency is regulated by both voluntary and compulsory provisions pursuant to sections 84ff German Commercial Code.

When no mandatory provision applies, it is possible to deviate from any

---

[1] Judgment of the ECJ in Case C-381/98: *Ingmar* 9 November 2000, [2000] ECR I-9305.

[2] Judgment of the ECJ in Case C-348/07: *Semen* 26 March 2009, [2009] ECR (not yet published).

[3] Decision of the Regional Court (*Landgericht*) Hamburg, in case 415 O 138/06 of 18 June 2007.

[4] The new s 89b German Commercial Code entered into force on 5 August 2009, approximately
four months after the ECJ judgement.

voluntary provisions which could otherwise apply, by virtue of section 84 German Commercial Code, when entering into a commercial agency agreement. Commercial agency agreements may be concluded orally, except for del credere agreements (section 86b(1) German Commercial Code) and for non-competition agreements (section 90a(1) sentence 1 German Commercial Code). Section 85 German Commercial Code contains an exception regarding the form of the agreement, which states that either party may demand that the terms of the agreement be set out in a document signed by the other party. When using a standard form for commercial agency agreements, the German provisions regarding 'standard terms and conditions' (section 305ff German Civil Code) are applicable. In those circumstances, section 307 German Civil Code will apply, pursuant to which provisions in business terms are invalid if—contrary to the requirement of good faith—they place the contractual partner of the user at an unreasonable disadvantage. Such unreasonable disadvantage may also result from the fact that the provision is not clear and not comprehensible. Further, an unreasonable disadvantage must be assumed if a provision is not compatible with the essential principles of the statutory regulation from which it deviates. The jurisprudence holds, for example, that reducing the limitation period for claims of the commercial agent from the statutory period to six months would be regarded as an unreasonable disadvantage.[5]

The commercial agent may be a natural person or a legal entity (limited liability company, stock corporation, registered association, registered co-operative, limited partnership, general commercial partnership or a civil law partnership). The commercial agent is considered to be a merchant pursuant to sections 1 and 2 German Commercial Code, as long as the person or entity is a commercially organised or registered business operation or as long as it is a merchant by mandatory law (eg pursuant to section 3 German Stock Corporation Act). The commercial agent is also required to have a commercial firm name according to section 17 German Commercial Code.

A commercial agent is subject to the general legal requirements of registration in the commercial register (section 1 German Commercial Code) and must hold a trading licence. The commercial agent must comply with these obligations; the principal carries no responsibility in this context.

## 10.2 CONSTITUENT ELEMENTS OF A COMMERCIAL AGENT

A person soliciting business on behalf of another is a commercial agent if all of the constituent elements contained in section 84 German Commercial Code are met. The person must be:

---

[5] Judgment of the Federal Court of Justice (*Bundesgerichtshof*) in case I ZR 166/78 of 12 October 1979, BGHZ 75, 218 regarding the then applicable four-year period pursuant to s 88 German Commercial Code.

— an independent person engaged in business;
— regularly entrusted with soliciting business for another (the 'principal') or
  with entering into business agreements in the principal's name.

The person is an independent person engaged in business if he is essentially
free to structure his activities and to determine his hours of work. Where these
conditions are not met, the person is considered to be an employee according
to section 84(2) German Commercial Code. However, the boundaries here are
flexible rather than fixed. According to the prevailing view of the courts and
of the literature, the matter has to be determined by an assessment of the contractual arrangement and the work of the person involved. Formal criteria of
self-employment include, for example, membership of a Chamber of Industry
and Commerce (Industrie- und Handelskammern (IHK)), the making of commission payments to sub-agents or the operation of several agencies. Substantive
indications for self-employment include, for example, the ability to structure
one's own activities and whether instructions are given by another on how to
operate the business in question.[6]

According to section 84(1) German Commercial Code, a commercial agent
has to solicit business or actually enter into business transactions on behalf of
another. 'Soliciting' means that the commercial agent will directly or indirectly,
eg through sub-agents, assist the business transactions through negotiations with
third parties. Commercial agents who are authorised to enter into transactions
are in practice quite rare. Section 91a German Commercial Code deals with the
particular situation of an agent acting without authority, when the third party
in question did not know about that lack of authority. However, section 91a
German Commercial Code is not applicable in cases when the authority is
misused or in cases of authority by estoppel (*Anscheinsvollmacht*). The general
provisions of the sections regarding the liability for acting without contractual
authority (sections 177–79 of the German Civil Code) remain unaffected: in
the UK, where an agent fails to disclose the fact that it is acting as agent for a
principal, the agent will be liable to the customer who (if it has a legal claim)
can choose to sue either the agent or the principal if it discovers the agency;
under German law, a party who does not disclose that it acts as an agent and
who acts in its own name binds only itself. This applies also in a situation where
the intention of acting for the principal does not become apparent to the third
party. There is no dual liability of both principal and agent in such a case. A
person who acts in his own name, but for the account of another, is not, under
German law, a commercial agent, but rather a commission agent to whom the
German law on commercial agents also applies to a large extent (ie to the relationship between the agent and the principal).

France, Italy and Germany have developed the concept of the 'commissionaire'
(*Kommissionär*). The relationship between a commissionaire and his principal is

---

[6] Decision of the Federal Court of Justice (*Bundesgerichtshof*) in case VIII ZB 12/98: *Eismann*
4 November 1998, [1999] NJW 218.

similar to that between an agent and an undisclosed principal. A commissionaire acts in his own name and on behalf of the principal. The principal is contractually bound to the commissionaire to deliver (through the commissionaire) the products sold to the customer, and the commissionaire is bound to the principal to remit the price received from the customer. No relationship is created between the principal and the customer; the customer does not have any claim against the principal, nor can the principal sue the customer for the price.

Acting within the scope of his regular authorisation to solicit business for the principal, the commercial agent solicits business in the name of and on behalf of the principal. The so-called *ständige Betrauung* (the permanent authority to solicit business for the principal) refers to a certain time period during which the commercial agent's relationship is in force and during which the commercial agent tries to procure a number of business transactions for its principal.

## 10.3 TYPES OF COMMERCIAL AGENT

There are several types of commercial agents defined in section 87(2) German Commercial Code:

— the commercial agent who has been assigned to a specific district (*Bezirksvertreter*), who has the right to commission for business transactions entered into in this specific district;
— the commercial agent who is exclusively assigned to a particular group of customers within a specific district (*Alleinvertreter*) and who, in addition, has the claim of protection against the principal for this assigned group of customers.

Furthermore, the main commercial agent may entrust third persons, sub-agents (*Untervertreter*), with the power of representation. Sub-agents, however, as auxiliary staff, do not take over the obligation owed by the commercial agent to the principal. It is not necessary to seek the principal's permission to work with sub-agents; however, such permission requirements are widely used in agency agreements.

Special forms of commercial agents are the insurance, building and loan association agents pursuant to section 92 German Commercial Code. Given that an insurance agent generally solicits long-term contracts which, in principle, do not lead to additional orders, the general provisions of section 84ff German Commercial Code are only narrowly applicable.

Pursuant to section 92b German Commercial Code, various provisions (especially section 89b German Commercial Code) are not applicable for a part-time commercial agent whose business time is not totally occupied by his commercial agency activities. This will not apply to a commercial agent working for several principals at the same time or when working as a commercial agent alongside his full-time employment for another company. The special provisions pursuant to section 92b German Commercial Code are only applicable if the commercial agent was explicitly employed part-time when entering into the agreement.

## 10.4 DUTIES OF THE COMMERCIAL AGENT

The duties of the commercial agent are regulated by section 86 German Commercial Code. Where an agent operates in the EU and the Directive applies, the agent is under an obligation to look after its principal's interests and act dutifully and in good faith. In particular, it must:

— make proper efforts to negotiate and, where appropriate, conclude the transactions it is instructed to take care of;
— communicate to its principal all the necessary information available to it; and
— comply with reasonable instructions given by its principal.

While these duties are mandatory and may not be contracted out (Article 5 of the Directive), it is, of course, always possible in an agreement with an agent to include obligations which go further than a general duty of good faith, eg an obligation to use best endeavours. Where the Directive does not apply, national law (section 86 German Commercial Code) will in any case impose similar obligations.

Principally, the commercial agent must fulfil its duties with the care of a prudent merchant (sections 86(2), 347(1) German Commercial Code). The commercial agent is obliged to make efforts towards the solicitation or conclusion of business transactions (*Vermittlungs- und Abschlusspflicht*). Further duties are to be regulated by individual agreement; principally, the commercial agent is not obliged to fulfil functions that are not directly connected to its business, eg collecting sums due or performing customer services.

In generating business, the commercial agent has to be guided by contractual standards or—when in doubt—its duty to solicit business shall pertain to all of the goods of the principal.

Furthermore, the commercial agent has to act in the interests of the principal (sections 86(1) sentence 2 German Commercial Code), and has to subordinate its own interests to those of its principal, eg its prospect of commission.

As long as it is possible without further costs and difficulties, the commercial agent is obliged to check the credit status of its clients. Should it become necessary to obtain further expensive information or should the commercial agent have doubts concerning the credit status, it always has to involve the principal.

Furthermore, the commercial agent has to comply with the obligation not to work for competing principals (*Wettbewerbsverbot*), which originates from the obligation to safeguard the principal's interests. In judging competitive activity, court rulings focus on the mere possibility of influencing the interests of the principal. In such circumstances, the commercial agent has to inform the principal and obtain its approval. The prohibition not only covers the obligation not to work directly for competing principals, but also every activity which could influence the interests of the principal, eg activities as a shareholder of a competing company.

The duties listed in sections 86(1) and (2) German Commercial Code are general concepts of law which are to be fulfilled by the parties. Section 86(4) German Commercial Code has to be interpreted accordingly. The parties may determine the way in which the commercial agent has to safeguard the rights of the principal, and, therefore, may in this context contractually exclude the prohibition on non-competition. Where the prohibition is infringed, the contractual relationship may be terminated and/or compensatory damage may be claimed (section 89a German Commercial Code).

Pursuant to the duty to act in the principal's interests, the commercial agent is bound by instructions from the principal. The instructions, however, should not impair the legal self-employment status of the agent and should only focus on the sales policies and the business transactions of the principal.

The commercial agent is obliged pursuant to its fiduciary duties to treat business and trade matters in a confidential manner, especially during, but also after, the conclusion of the agency agreement, pursuant to section 90 German Commercial Code.

The commercial agent is obliged to keep and to return all objects given to it for the purpose of representing the principal and may be obliged to insure valuable objects. Pursuant to section 86(2) German Commercial Code, the commercial agent shall give the principal all necessary information of every solicitation and of every transaction concluded. This duty also includes all detailed information which the principal needs to know of in order to further promote its business, eg the relevant market situation or competitive offers. Again, the requirement to give all necessary information shall not be detrimental to the legal self-employment status of the commercial agent.

Where the commercial agent guarantees in writing the fulfilment of (payment) obligations arising from the transaction towards the principal, it assumes a del credere liability for this transaction (section 86 b I German Commercial Code). This liability has features of a guarantee, so that the commercial agent and the customer are jointly and severally liable. The commercial agent formally does not have the defence that the creditor must first unsuccessfully try to execute its claim on the debtor (*Einrede der Vorausklage*) according to section 349 German Commercial Code; it is disputed whether section 349 German Commercial Code can be contracted out.

The high risk involved with a del credere liability is compensated by a special del credere commission (section 86(2) German Commercial Code).

## 10.5 PRINCIPAL'S DUTIES

Aside from the duties the principal owes to the commercial agent, the principal is free to arrange its field of business. However, the principal may not act arbitrarily or seek to cause damage to the commercial agent. All of the principal's obligations under section 86a German Commercial Code are mandatory and any deviating agreements are void.

The principal has the duty to support the commercial agent in providing it with necessary materials pursuant to section 86a(1) German Commercial Code. This duty must be executed at the agent's business seat (*Bringschuld*), meaning that the material has to be delivered by the principal without further costs of delivery to the place where the commercial agent needs it. The 'material' includes samples, drawings, price lists, advertising material, and terms and conditions of business.

According to section 86a(2) sentence 1 German Commercial Code, the principal shall keep the commercial agent generally informed prior to and during the contractual relationship with all information necessary for the agent's business activities. In evaluating necessity in this context, the interests of the commercial agent have to be considered. Pursuant to sections 86a(2) sentences 2 and 3 German Commercial Code, the principal shall inform the commercial agent promptly of any acceptance or rejection of a transaction solicited or concluded by the commercial agent. Further, if the principal wishes to—or is likely to—conclude business on a significantly reduced scale in comparison with what the agent could have expected under normal circumstances, the agent must be informed. The principal is generally obliged to support the commercial agent. The commercial agent must have the opportunity to discharge its duties. In this sense, the principal shall not in any way compete with the commercial agent, either directly or indirectly, eg by way of using another representative.

The German Commercial Code also includes an obligation to pay commission (section 87). There are also provisions on when the commission is due (section 87a German Commercial Code) and the rate of commission (section 87b(1) German Commercial Code). Agreements deviating from these legal provisions are possible, although conclusive evidence of such agreement will be required in each case.

The commercial agent's expenses will be reimbursed only if this has been specifically agreed. In order to avoid the classification of the agency as an employment agreement, the reimbursement of expenses to the agent must not relieve the agent of all investment risk.

## 10.6 REMUNERATION OF THE COMMERCIAL AGENT ('COMMISSION')

Sections 87ff German Commercial Code set out the transactions for which commission is due. Commission is to be paid if a transaction is concluded through the activities of an agent (section 87(1) first alternative) or even if the commercial agent is only indirectly involved therein (section 87(2)). It is also possible to agree on a commission guaranteed at a certain level in the agreement.

Section 87 German Commercial Code sets out the general rights to commission, whereas section 87a determines specifically when the commission is due and under what conditions the right to commission is enforceable. This division protects the commission claim from termination of the agreement or from changes to contractual conditions, which may occur in the period after the claim arose but before the claim became due. A valid commercial agency agreement must be in force at the time when the commercial agent acts in accordance with the terms of those transactions for which commission is due. After the commission becomes due under to section 87a German Commercial Code, the claim for commission is assignable. According to section 87 German Commercial Code, for the right to commission to arise, a transaction having legal effect must be concluded between the principal and the customer. As to the issue of causation, the commercial agent has to be the contributing factor in promoting the transaction. There are two exceptions:

1.  Pursuant to section 87(1), second alternative, German Commercial Code, commission is due for transactions concluded with customers whom the agent has previously acquired for transactions of the same kind; in cases of repeat orders, it is not necessary that the repeat order can be attributed to the actions of the commercial agent.
2.  Where the commercial agent has been assigned to a specific district or a particular group of customers, it also has a right to commission for transactions whether or not the transactions in question were attributable to the agent.

Furthermore, the commercial agent has a right to administration commission, eg collection commission, for amounts collected by it pursuant to instructions given by the principal, pursuant to section 87(4) German Commercial Code and—when agreed in writing—a del credere commission.

## 10.7 'OVERLAPPING' COMMISSION

An important provision regarding commission is contained in section 87(3) German Commercial Code, which deals with two exceptions to the principle that commission is only to be paid if the transaction was concluded during the term of the contractual relationship. These exceptional commissions are called 'overlapping commissions' (*Überhangprovision*). According to section 87(3) sentence 1 German Commercial Code, the agent shall have the right to commission for transactions concluded after termination of the contractual agency relationship if it solicited or was instrumental in obtaining the transactions. The transaction has to be concluded within a reasonable time after termination of the agency agreement.[7] According to the second sentence thereof, the agent shall have a right to commission if, prior to the termination of the agency agreement, the offer of a third party has been received by the principal. This is to prevent the

---

[7] Depending on the circumstances of the contractual relationship and the duration this could be between six weeks and—for sophisticated and complicated goods such as special machines— two years.

principal from holding back contract offers from customers until the agency agreement has been terminated in order to reduce commission due to the agent.

## 10.8 CLAIMS FOR COMMISSION

According to section 87a German Commercial Code, the commercial agent has a right to commission as soon as and in so far as the principal has completed the transaction. Thus, the right to commission arises immediately and unconditionally when the customer performs or when it is contractually agreed that the customer will subsequently perform. Even outside of such circumstances, the commercial agent has a right to a reasonable advance payment according to section 87a (1) sentence 2 German Commercial Code. 'Reasonable' is what both parties consider to be reasonable pursuant to the circumstances. The right to receive payment ceases to exist when it is clear that the customer will not pay. Advances that have already been paid have to be returned if the underlying business transaction is cancelled. The commercial agent is entitled to partial commission payment if the customer only pays in part (section 87(1) sentence 1, (3) German Commercial Code).

If performance of an obligation under the contract is adversely affected, it will have the following influence on the right to commission:

— where it has been determined that the customer does not perform because, for example, its performance has become impossible, there is no right to commission (section 87a(2) German Commercial Code);
— If the principal does not demand performance from its customer, the commercial agent maintains the right to commission.

A customer's non-performance has to be judged by objective criteria. The right to commission will continue to exist if substituted performance is made. On the other hand, it is possible for the principal to interfere with the performance: in such situations the right to commission will broadly speaking continue to exist, and the risk is hence shifted to the principal. According to section 87a(3) sentence 2 German Commercial Code, no right to commission shall exist in the event of non-performance where this is due to reasons beyond the control of the principal, ie because of *force majeure* or when the law has been changed.

## 10.9 FORMAL CRITERIA FOR COMMISSION ACCOUNTING

The commission due shall be accounted for by the last day of the month following the business transaction in question, unless the parties have agreed upon an extension to a maximum of three months, pursuant to section 87c(1) German Commercial Code. Most often, the amount of the commission is set out in the agreement. Where the amount of commission is not specified, the customary rate is deemed to be agreed upon according to section 87b sentence 1 German Commercial Code. The amount of commission may also be implicitly agreed upon, eg constant payments of a certain amount. The amount of commission shall furthermore not be reduced by way of partial contract termination, which generally is not admissible under the relevant provisions of German law, unless otherwise provided for in the contract. It is, however, possible to terminate an agreement combined with the option of a new agreement on altered conditions (*Änderungskündigung*).

When judging the customary rate of commission, the practice in the line of business of each agent's district shall be decisive. When calculating the commission itself, the remuneration which the client or the principal has to pay for the business conducted by the agent is decisive. However, the allowance of price reductions for cash payments or incidental expenses such as freight, package or insurance costs are not taken into account. Contractually negotiated rebates, however, may be deducted. According to section 87b (2) sentence 3 German Commercial Code, the commission shall be calculated from the gross amount of the invoice; in practice, however, most often it is agreed upon using the net value of the goods. The commission of the agent is subject to VAT at a rate of 19 per cent pursuant to section 12(1) of the German Turnover Tax Code. In long-term contractual relationships with customers, where the remuneration of the principal is determined by reference to a certain time period, the commercial agent is entitled either to a one-off commission which is calculated for the whole contractual period, or to a sum calculated until the time the customer is entitled to terminate the contract. In cases where the commercial agency agreement is terminated during the period of a long-term contract, such termination has no effect on the right to commission fixed with respect to that long-term contract.

## 10.10 CHECKING OF THE COMMISSION PAYMENTS BY THE AGENT

According to section 87c German Commercial Code the agent has several ways of checking the commission payments: it may demand a monthly account from the principal (paragraph 1); it may demand an excerpt from the books concerning all transactions in respect of which it has a claim for commission (paragraph 2); it may demand to be provided with corresponding information (paragraph 3) or to inspect the business books (paragraph 4).

The principal's rights are to demand monthly accounting and an excerpt from the books. Where reasonable doubts exist as to the accuracy or completeness of the account or the excerpt, the commercial agent may request permission to inspect the business books. The right to an excerpt from the books and the right to inspect the business books may only be pursued consecutively, not concurrently. The final possibility the commercial agent has is to demand an affidavit from the principal. The agent has to declare its intention unequivocally to accept the billing: then the billing is considered as recognising a debt according to section 781 German Civil Code.

The agent has a right to claim for an excerpt from the books according to section 87c(2) German Commercial Code until the parties have agreed upon the accounting relating to the commission. The excerpt has to be provided in written form by the principal and must be precise and complete in order to be understood by the agent.

In German legal practice this right to bookkeeping excerpts is a threat which is widely used by commercial agents after termination of the agreement. The German jurisprudence holds[8] that, inter alia, the following information must be itemised in such bookkeeping excerpt for the relevant time period for each customer:

— date of the order;
— order number;
— product according to order number;
— amount of product according to number;
— value of the order according to order number;
— acceptance and acceptance number (if any);
— deviation from the order in the acceptance and reason for the deviation (if any);
— date of the invoice;
— number of the invoice;
— amount of the invoice;
— customer with exact address;
— state of the fulfilment of the contract;
— cancellation (total quantity of ordered products cancelled, and the total price of the cancelled items);
— products which have not been shipped (total quantity of unshipped goods, and the single and total price for the quantity of unshipped goods);
— the exact reason for any cancellation and/or failure to ship products.

As the preparation of this information may in some cases be extremely expensive (and sometimes due to missing data, the duration of the agreement or technical difficulties, even impossible for the principal), the demand for such bookkeeping excerpts—in practice— forces the principal very often into a settlement agreement after expiry of the agency agreement, if only to avoid these costs.

The right to information according to section 87c(3) German Commercial Code makes it possible for the agent to receive all necessary information which it cannot obtain through the books or accounting.

The principal has the option to permit either the agent, an auditor or a certified accountant designated by it to inspect the books according to section 87c(4)

---

[8] Decision of the Federal Court of Justice (*Bundesgerichtshof*) in case I ZB 82/06 of 26 April 2007.

German Commercial Code. The costs have to be borne by the agent, but if it is proved that the accounting of the principal is incorrect to the agent's detriment, the agent then has the right to demand reimbursement of the costs arising from the breach of contract.

Furthermore, the agent is able to claim retention of tangible property of the principal that is in its possession (section 273 German Civil Code). In addition, the merchant's right of retention according to section 369 German Commercial Code gives the agent the right to satisfy its claim pursuant to section 371 German Commercial Code. However, the right of retention is restricted in section 369(3) German Commercial Code in so far as the retention of the item would conflict with instructions given by the debtor before or upon delivery thereof or would conflict with the creditor's duty to deal with the item in a specific way. After termination of the agency agreement, the agent has the right to retain materials placed at its disposal only by reason of unpaid commissions or reimbursement of expenses due to it.

## 10.11 STATUTORY LIMITATIONS FOR CLAIMS

An act of 9 December 2004 repealed section 88 German Commercial Code, which provided a four-year limitation period for claims arising in connection with agency agreements, with effect from 15 December 2005. As a result of the repeal of section 88, the usual limitation period now applies to these claims (three years, beginning with the end of the year in which they became due, as provided by section 195 German Civil Code).

Although, as a general rule, German law provides that the statute of limitation begins with the end of the year in which the claim has become due, section 202 German Civil Code allows this period to be shortened (except for claims resulting from intentional acts) if acknowledged interests exist.

## 10.12 REIMBURSEMENT OF EXPENSES

The commercial agent may only demand reimbursement of its regular business expenses if this is customary within the trade. The extent of the business shall be in accordance with the agency agreement. In contrast, if a commercial agent is paid a standard salary, works for a fixed number of hours at the principal's premises and/or has all his expenses reimbursed, he may be considered an employee. The result is the right to claim the usual and/or minimum salary and social security contributions. In Germany, the risk that a natural person may be regarded as a 'pretend independent trader' must be carefully considered when agreeing any reimbursements in agency agreements.

## 10.13 TERMINATION

Whether the contractual relationship is intended to be for a definite or indefinite duration, it may be terminated subject to a certain period of notice. Section 89 German Commercial Code, however, excludes the provisions dealing with termination of an employer/employee relationship.

German law provides for two possible types of termination in relation to commercial agents:

— Ordinary termination (section 89 German Commercial Code). Here, only the legal notice periods, which depend on the duration of the contract (in the first year: one month; in the second year: two months; in the third to fifth years: three months; and over five years: six months), must be observed. The notice periods can be extended. A commercial agency agreement may also be entered into for a definite limited period. No reasons need to be given for issuing a notice of ordinary termination.

— Extraordinary termination without notice (section 89a German Commercial Code). Either party may terminate the contract for good cause without notice. This right cannot be excluded or restricted by agreement. Examples of circumstances which would constitute good cause are:

1. significant breach of contract by the agent due, in particular, to intentional or gross negligence, eg prejudicing the interests of the principal for its own benefit;
2. unjustified and final refusal to carry out its duties;
3. significantly writing-up customer orders;[9]
4. non-compliance with justified instructions of the principal, eg in the processing of insurance applications;[10]
5. neglect of duty, which results in loss of turnover;
6. a continuing dispute between principal and agent, so that lasting co-operation could no longer be expected to continue;
7. insulting the principal or its management employees or other insulting degradation or behaviour or circumstances which could undermine the authority and standing of the principal with its employees or customers; and
8. competing activity of the agent on behalf of a third party.

For the sake of clarity, other circumstances which would be deemed to constitute grounds for extraordinary termination can be stated in the contract. The validity of the inclusion in a commercial agency agreement of grounds for extraordinary termination which do not constitute good cause within the meaning of section 89a(1) sentence 1 of the Commercial Code is unclear. Such grounds

---

[9] Decision of the Federal Court of Justice ('*Bundesgerichtshof*') in case I ZR 118/78 of 21 November 1980, [1981] DB 987.

[10] Decision of the Federal Court of Justice (*Bundesgerichtshof*) in case I ZR 161/84 of 4 June 1986, [1986] VersR 1072.

will be examined on a case-by-case basis. Termination without notice has to be defined as such; the time limit of two weeks according to section 626(2) German Civil Code is not applicable; rather, the party terminating the contract has a notice period which is appropriate for each situation. Where termination results from conduct of the other party, that party is obliged to compensate the terminating party for damage arising from the termination (section 89a German Commercial Code).

In order to claim damages, a good cause must theoretically be given—but there is no need to mention it expressly. Hence, a termination with a notice period may also establish a claim to compensatory damages if theoretically there is a good cause. If the party receiving the termination without prior notice could also have terminated the contractual relationship for cause, the claim for compensatory damages will fail.

Furthermore, the contractual relationship between the agent and principal may be terminated through rescission according to section 142(1) German Civil Code.

## 10.14 INDEMNITY CLAIM

After termination of the commercial agency agreement, the agent has the right, in addition to commission accrued and a possible claim for damages, to an indemnity payment (section 89b German Commercial Code). The claim to an indemnity payment is subject to the following conditions:

— the principal has terminated the agreement by ordinary termination;
— the commercial agent has terminated the agreement for age or health reasons (these grounds for termination do not apply to a commercial agent who is not a natural person);
— the commercial agent has terminated the agreement due to conduct on the part of the principal justifying such termination.
— the commercial agent and the principal terminate the contract by agreement.

No claim for indemnity under section 89b German Commercial Code arises if the principal terminates the contract for good cause arising from culpable conduct by the agent, or if the agent terminates the contract by ordinary termination without special reasons. German court decisions show a trend towards treating commercial agents very favourably on the issue of indemnity payments.

As a precondition for the commercial agent's indemnity claim, the principal must have gained substantial advantages from business relations with new customers solicited by the commercial agent or from intensified contacts with old customers after termination of the contractual relationship. The business relations with new customers must have a certain degree of intensity, with an expectation of further business transactions. There have to be substantial advantages regarding the theoretical profit expectations resulting from the new clientele. The advantages are substantial if the principal gains economic benefit from the new customer relationships, when transactions in general are in decline. There might also be financial advantages when selling the newly established clientele. The commercial agent has the burden to prove that the preconditions of an indemnity claim are met.

Calculation of the indemnity payment is based first on a basic amount, which is then compared to the highest possible amount.

1. The basic amount is calculated by first taking the amount of turnover achieved by the agent with customers similar to those procured by him for the principal during the currency of the agreement in the financial year immediately preceding the termination of the contract ('new customers'). Old customers (ie those with whom the principal had business dealings prior to the conclusion of the commercial agency agreement) are excluded from the calculation at this stage. However, if the turnover with any such old customer in the preceding year of the contract exceeded 100 per cent of that in the year prior to the commencement of the commercial agency agreement, such a customer is to be regarded as a new customer and the turnover with such customer included in the calculation of the basic indemnity amount. On the basis of the commission turnover for the previous financial year, future turnover will be projected. The period of projection depends on the lifespan of the goods which are the subject of the agency contract. Court rulings assume a time frame of three to five years. The projection itself will take into account the degree to which new customers are lost. In general, the loss of the commission for the years following the termination of the contractual relationship is based on the calculation of each commission quota per year minus the quota resulting from departing clientele. All commission losses for all these years together are added up and then added to the total commission loss. From this amount 10 per cent will be discounted, because the amount is paid in full at once and not in instalments. The discounted amount may then be adjusted due to equity.

   In the calculation of the basic amount, considerations of equity and the loss of future commissions as anticipated in the projection of the future development of turnover are also taken into account. The agent's indemnity claim shall not be reduced if the business turnover has declined as a result of fault on the part of the principal. Administration commissions are to be excluded therefrom. Unpaid 'overlapping commissions' from business transactions already performed may not be taken into consideration for the debit calculation.

2. The basic amount so calculated will be compared with the highest amount possible, which is the annual average of *all* commission income achieved by the agent in the preceding five years.

3. If the basic amount calculated is lower than the highest amount, then the agent receives the basic amount. On the other hand, if the basic amount is higher than the highest amount, the agent receives the highest amount.

In detail, German courts have established a very complicated, quasi-mathematical mechanism for calculating the indemnity.

This calculation procedure will change after the ECJ ruling in *Semen*[11] and the following amendment of the German Commercial Code in August 2009.[12] Section 89b(1) German Commercial Code previously read:

> (1) The commercial agent may, after expiration of the contractual relationship, demand from the principal reasonable indemnity if and in so far as:
>
> 1.    the principal retains substantial advantages, after expiration of the contractual period, from business relations with new customers solicited by the commercial agent,
>
> 2.    the commercial agent, by reason of termination of the contractual relationship, loses rights to commissions relating to concluded business or business to be concluded in the future with those customers it had solicited, and which rights it would have had if the contractual relationship had been continued, and
>
> 3.    the payment of indemnity is equitable after consideration of all the circumstances.

It was constant jurisprudence that these conditions are cumulative. As the ECJ ruled clearly in *Semen*[13] that

> Article 17(2)(a) of [Council Directive 86/653] is to be interpreted to the effect that it is not possible automatically to limit the indemnity to which a commercial agent is entitled by the amount of commission lost as a result of the termination of the agency contract

an amendment of section 89b(1) no 2 German Commercial Code was inevitable. As a result, the new section 89b(1) German Commercial Code reads as follows:

> (1) The commercial agent may, after expiration of the contractual relationship, demand from the principal reasonable indemnity if and insofar as:
>
> 1.    the principal retains substantial advantages, after expiration of the contractual period, from business relations with new customers solicited by the commercial agent, and
>
> 2.    the payment of indemnity is equitable after consideration of all the circumstances, especially after consideration of the rights to commission the agent might lose regarding these customers.

The German point of view that losing future commission payments is a necessary element of the indemnity calculation has, therefore, been changed into one element—albeit an important element—of equity. It can be expected that the total amounts awarded to commercial agents will rise in the future as the element of equity gives the courts more flexibility in the assessment of whether or not future losses of commission are considered when weighing the interests of the parties.

The agent must, within one year of the termination of the commercial agency, express its intention of claiming indemnity under section 89b(4) sentence 1 German Commercial Code.

---

[11] Judgment of the ECJ in *Semen*, above n 2.
[12] See above n 4.
[13] Judgment of the ECJ in *Semen*, above n 2.

It should be noted that in Germany, in accordance with the judgments of the Federal Supreme Court, any salesman (excluding employees) who is integrated in the principal's sales organisation in a manner comparable to a commercial agent (eg an authorised dealer) is entitled to demand indemnity under the same legal provisions as apply to commercial agents.

Pursuant to Article 17(1) Council Directive 86/653, as an alternative to an indemnity payment, Member States might also choose the option that the agent is entitled to be compensated for the damage it suffers as a result of the termination of its relations with its principal. Damage which will give rise to a right to compensation is deemed to occur particularly when the termination takes place in circumstances: (i) depriving the commercial agent of the commission which the proper performance of the agency contract would have earned him while providing the principal with substantial benefits linked to the commercial agent's activities; and/or (ii) which have not enabled the commercial agent to amortise the costs and expenses that it had incurred for the performance of the agency contract on the principal's advice (Article 17(3) Council Directive 86/653). This system was not implemented in German law.

## 10.15 INDEMNITY CLAIM AND CHOICE-OF-LAW CLAUSES

It is still strongly disputed how the rather complicated indemnity scheme of Germany can be avoided by choosing another governing law for the commercial agency agreement. As a general rule, the law of the country in which the agent's business seat is situated shall apply (Article 4(1) lit (f) Regulation 593/2008[14]). If the parties choose the law of another jurisdiction, the general position in Germany—at least since the ruling of the ECJ in *Ingmar*[15]—can be described as follows:

1. The commercial agent is based and acts outside the EEA: the parties may choose the law of another jurisdiction. If they choose German law, the parties may exclude the application of section 89b German Commercial Code pursuant to section 92c German Commercial Code.
2. The commercial agent is based inside and acts within the EEA: the parties may choose the law of another jurisdiction of an EEA country, provided that this jurisdiction correctly implemented Council Directive 86/653 as this directive safeguards a minimum standard and not necessarily the standards of section 89b German Commercial Code. If the parties choose German law, section 89b German Commercial Code shall apply as it is binding for the internal German legal order.
3. The commercial agent is based and acts in Germany; the principal is based

---

[14] Regulation (EC) 593/2008 of the European Parliament and the Council of 17 June 2008 on the law applicable to contractual obligations ('Rome I').

[15] Judgment of the ECJ in *Ingmar*, see above n 1.

abroad: the parties may choose the law of another governing law; however, section 89b German Commercial Code shall apply as it is internationally binding[16] for the internal German legal order.[17] If the parties choose German law, section 89b German Commercial Code shall also apply.

## 10.16 AGREEMENTS PROHIBITING COMPETITION

Non-compete obligations may be agreed with a commercial agent both during the term of the agreement and after its expiry.

### (a) During the Term of the Agreement

As a general rule, competition between the agent and principal is prohibited during the time of the contractual relationship. An agent will typically accept restrictions with respect to the customers to whom it may sell, the territory in which it may sell, the prices and terms under which it may sell, and its ability to deal in competing products. A true agency agreement should not generally give rise to competition law concerns.

German competition law is divided into two parts: the competition law in the broader sense (anti-trust law) and competition law in the narrow sense (fair competition). Unfair trade law, the content of which is mainly provided by the German Law Against Unfair Competition, is directed in the first place at protecting consumers and competitors. Anti-trust law has the primary objective of protecting the functioning of competition in the market by means of the German Law Against Restraints on Competition and the applicable EC law. These two aspects overlap in many respects.

The German Law Against Restraints on Competition has implemented EC Regulation 1/2003, harmonising German anti-trust law with EU competition law. Section 1 German Law Against Restraints on Competition mirrors Article 101(1) TFEU—formerly Article 81 EC Treaty. Section 2 German Law Against Restraints on Competition mirrors in turn Article 101(3) TFEU and declares Commission Regulation 2709/1999[18] applicable. As these provisions apply mainly to the legal relations between a seller and a buyer or reseller, they are not applicable, in general, to the legal relationship between the principal and the commercial agent.

[16] Last decision in this respect: judgment of the Higher Regional Court Munich (*Oberlandesgericht München*) in case 7 U 1781/06 of 17 May 2006, [2006] IHR 166.

[17] It should be noted in this respect that many authors hold the position that 'the minimum guarantee' of Council Directive 86/653 is respected also in such cases when the parties choose the law of another EEA country (eg a US principal could choose English law for its agent acting in Germany including the Arts 17–19 Council Directive 86/653 as implemented in the UK) and thus avoid the indemnity payments under s 89b German Commercial Code. This position is—from an EU law perspective—legally correct, but is not the prevailing point of view in Germany.

[18] Commission Regulation (EC) 2709/1999 of 22 December 1999 on the application of Art 81(3) of the EC Treaty to categories of vertical agreements and consorted practices.

This follows from the fact that the commercial agent does not sell or resell the goods of its principal, but rather solicits business transactions for its principal and can conclude business transactions with customers in the name of its principal. However, in certain cases, transactions which deviate from this principle are possible, where the commercial agent may be regarded as an independent seller or buyer of the goods or services offered. The European Commission Guidelines on Vertical Restraints[19] outline various criteria by which 'true' and 'false' agency agreements are distinguished,[20] with the result that the true commercial agent (to which the prohibition found in Article 101 TFEU does not apply) must not have made any significant investment to enable him to carry out its occupation. The application of these restrictive criteria to a commercial agent who has made such an investment and who can bring about or even conclude business transactions for a principal has been sharply criticised. Future developments in this area will have to be followed closely.[21] Where an agent bears such financial or commercial risks, it is to be regarded as an independent dealer. An agreement that falls within Article 101(1) TFEU may nonetheless be exempted under Commission Regulation 2709/1999.

It should be noted, however, that even in a genuine agency relationship non-compete provisions, including post-term non-compete obligations, may infringe Article 101(1) TFEU if they lead to foreclosure on the relevant market where the goods/services which form the subject of the agency agreement are sold or purchased. Furthermore, an agency agreement may fall within the scope of Article 101(1) TFEU if it facilitates collusion—eg where a number of principals use the same agents while excluding others from using them, or when they use the agents to collaborate as regards marketing strategy or as a means of exchanging confidential market information between principals.

On the subject of tied selling, under cartel law, linked transactions brought about or concluded through a commercial agent do not give rise to any reservations from a competition law point of view. However, the German Law

---

[19] [2000] OJ C291/1.

[20] An agency agreement is considered a genuine agency agreement, falling outside Art 101(1) TFEU if the agent bears no, or only insignificant, financial or commercial risks in relation to the contracts concluded and/or negotiated on behalf of the principal. Two types of financial or commercial risks are relevant: those which are directly related to the contracts negotiated or concluded by the agent on behalf of the principal, for example, financing of stocks; and those which relate to investments specifically required for the type of activity for which the agent has been appointed by the principal. The question of risk is assessed on a case-by-case basis. Art 101(1) TFEU will generally not apply to sales or purchases made on behalf of a principal if property in the goods sold or bought does not vest in the agent or the agent does not act on his own account, and the agent does not undertake any of the following activities: contribution to the costs relating to the agency or purchase of the contract goods or services, including transport costs; investment in sales promotion; maintenance at his own cost or risk of stocks of the contract goods; creation or operation of an after-sales service, repair services or a warranty service, unless it is fully reimbursed by the principal; investment in equipment, premises or training of personnel; acceptance of liability to third parties for harm caused by the products sold and acceptance of liability for customers' non-performance of the contract (except for the loss of the agent's commission), unless the agent is himself liable.

[21] *Cf* judgment of the CFI in Case T-325/01: *DaimlerChrysler/Commission* of 15 September 2005, [2005] ECR II-3319.

Against Unfair Competition must be observed. While the law on discounts and the regulations on gifts was repealed in 2001, a breach of section 1 of the Law Against Unfair Competition will be presumed if the price for each item in the linked service or goods transaction cannot—from the point of view of the customer—be understood or compared. This problem arises in German law not only in respect of sales by commercial agents but also in the case of every sale of goods, rights or other services.

### (b) After Expiry of the Agreement

After termination, the parties are free to negotiate an agreement prohibiting competition. This agreement must be within the limits set forth in section 90a German Commercial Code. According to section 90a(1) sentence 2 German Commercial Code, the agreement may run for no longer than two years following termination and may only cover the geographical area or group of customers assigned to the agent. The principal is obliged to pay reasonable compensation to the commercial agent for the duration of the prohibition on competition.

In determining the amount of the compensation, the advantages and the disadvantages on both sides have to be considered taking into account the commissions last received by the agent. The indemnity of the agent should not be taken into account (section 89b German Commercial Code). If the parties are unable to agree on the amount, the reasonable amount can be fixed by the competent court.

The non-compete agreement (but not the obligation of the principal to pay reasonable compensation for the non-compete obligation) must be in writing.

During the contractual relationship, the principal may at any time waive the non-compete obligation (section 90a(2) sentence 1 German Commercial Code). However, compensation must be paid to the agent for six months starting from the date of that declaration—even if this time goes beyond the end of the contractual relationship.

# 11

# Commercial Agency
# Law in France

Dr Séverine Saintier
*Sheffield University*

## 11.1 INTRODUCTION

FRENCH COMMERCIAL AGENTS have been protected since 1958.[1] The 1958 decree was the first text to recognise formally the specificity, needs and requirements of the profession by providing commercial agents with their own status and a special protection in the form of compensation on termination of their relationship with their principals. The statute implementing[2] the Directive[3] is now incorporated in the commercial code.[4] The French implementing text does not follow the Directive to the letter, as it was drafted in a manner to ensure continuity with the French legal tradition in this field.[5] This continuity is at its most obvious in three specific respects: (i) the definition of commercial agents, (ii) the notion of common interest mandate and (iii) the compensation methodology. Whilst it is relevant for the purpose of this chapter to review in detail the first two points, the same cannot be said of the latter. Following the ECJ decision of *Honyvem Informazioni Commerciali Srl v De Zotti*[6] and the House of Lords' ruling in *Lonsdale v Howard & Hallam Ltd*,[7] the compensation methodology is a matter for the courts of each Member State

---

[1] Decree 58/1345 of 23 December 1958, D 1959, L 132 ('the 1958 Decree').

[2] Statute 91-593 of 25 June 1991 [1991] OJ 27 June, 8271 is complemented by Decree 92-506 of 10 June 1992, D 1992, L 320 ('the 1992 Decree').

[3] Council Directive 86/653 on the co-ordination of the laws of the Member States relating to self-employed commercial agents, [1986] OJ L 382/17 of 31 December.

[4] Arts L 134-1 to L 134-17 codify the text of the 1991 statute and Arts R 134-1 to R 134-5 codify the text of the 1992 decree.

[5] There are nevertheless some areas where the implementing text follows the Directive closely as the 1958 Decree was silent. This is especially true in relation to the provisions on remuneration and post-contractual non-competition clause.

[6] Case C-464/04: [2006] ECR I-2879

[7] [2007] UKHL 32, [2007] 1 WLR 2055. For comment, see S Saintier (2008) 124 *LQR* 31–37.

and the manner in which the French courts approach it will consequently not be considered.

In spite of the clear determination of the French legislature to implement the Directive in as close as possible a manner to the French legal tradition, there is nevertheless one area where implementation has brought about a substantial change: that of the exclusion from the ambit of the implementing text of commercial agents whose activity is secondary (Article L 134-15 Commercial Code). This will be the third area of study of this chapter.

## 11.2 WHO ARE COMMERCIAL AGENTS AND WHAT IS THEIR COMMERCIAL ROLE?

Only those commercial intermediaries who are regarded as 'commercial agents'[8] pursuant to the conditions defined by Article L 134-1 Commercial Code can claim the legal protection of the commercial code.

Article L 134-1 of the French Commercial Code[9] defines commercial agents as:

> Agents who, as independent professionals not linked by contracts for services, shall be permanently entrusted with negotiating and possibly concluding sale, purchase, rental or service provision contracts for and on behalf of producers, industrialists, traders or other commercial agents. Commercial agents may be natural or legal persons.

> Agents whose representation tasks are carried out in the context of economic activities which are covered, with regard to these tasks, by special acts shall not come under the provisions of this chapter.

At first glance, it is clear that the definition in the Commercial Code is wider than that of the Directive since commercial agents can sell services as well as goods for their principals. Moreover, since commercial agents are expressly allowed to use other commercial agents, commercial sub-agents are therefore covered by the Commercial Code and its protection.

The first part of Article L 134-1 is the most important one since, aside from providing the necessary conditions to be regarded, by law, as commercial agents, hereby delineating the scope of application of the implementing text, it also indicates who commercial agents are and what their commercial role is. Such an understanding is crucial not only to differentiate them from other commercial intermediaries but also to explain why they are considered to be the weaker party within the relationship and as such in need of protection.

---

[8] Considering that the Commercial Code confers protection on commercial agents as defined, the title of 'commercial agent' is therefore specific to such a profession and can only be used by members of that profession. In *TGI Paris 2-12-1997 Fédération Nationale des Agents Commerciaux v SNCF*, the French national railway was barred from calling some of their controllers 'commercial agents': case unreported but cited in JM Leloup, 'Agents commerciaux, statuts juridique, strategies professionnelles', *Delmas*, 6th edn, 1.

[9] Note that the translation of all the Articles quoted in this chapter is taken from the official French government website: www.legifrance.gouv.fr.

Anyone claiming to be a commercial agent bears the burden of proof[10] and French courts have the power to check compliance with this part of the Code.[11] The courts will do so by considering the manner in which the activity is exercised and the role that each party plays[12] by sole and express reference to Article L 134-1 Commercial Code without any regard to what has been expressed in this matter by either the parties or the contract, since the Article was held to be of a mandatory nature (*ordre public*) by the Court of Appeal of Paris in the case of *SAS Glaxo Smith Kline v SARL Interpharm*.[13] Given the protective stance of the Commercial Code towards commercial agents, the mandatory nature of Article L 134-1 is logical.

Let us now turn to the conditions relating to the commercial agent's status in order to see how the French courts apply them.

## (a) The Conditions Providing Commercial Agents with their Own Status

Article L 134-1 Commercial Code provides three conditions to be satisfied: (i) the commercial agent, as a mandated agent, must act on behalf of the principal for the negotiation and/or conclusion of contracts. However, it must do so (ii) independently and (iii) on a permanent basis.

Due to the mandatory nature of Article L 134-1, these are the only conditions necessary to obtain the status of commercial agent. The situation is therefore considerably improved compared to the 1958 Decree which required the contract to be entered into in writing and the commercial agent to be registered in a special registry before commercial agents could be protected.[14] Following the implementation of the Directive, the commercial agent must still be registered in the registry of commercial agents,[15] but this is only required for administrative purposes.[16] Failure to do so will consequently not deny the commercial agent its status and does not amount to a serious fault preventing it from claiming compensation on termination of the relationship.[17] Similarly, the Commercial

---

[10] *Cass Com 24-9-2003*, Lettre Distribution 2003, 2. See also *CA Metz 30-1-2007, SARL AGCE SACA v SA Valentin Charcut 88*, Juris-Data 2007-335460, where the court held that in the absence of a registration in the commercial agency register or a written contract, the party who claims that it is a commercial agent must prove so in accordance with Art L 134-1 Commercial Code. It is therefore not enough to show that it received commissions from the principal.

[11] *Cass Com 14-6-2005*, D 2006, Pan 514.

[12] *Cass Com 10-12-2003*, D 2005, Pan 150.

[13] *CA Paris 5ème ch, B, 2-5-2002*, Juris-Data 2002-181440.

[14] Art 1 of the 1958 Decree.

[15] The conditions are defined by the arrête of 1993. For details, see Leloup, above n 8, 70–72.

[16] Case C-215/97 *Barbara Bellone v Yokohama SpA* [1998] ECR I-2191 and Case C-454/98 *Centrosteel Srl v Adipol GmbH* [2000] ECR I-6007.

[17] *Cass Com 15-10-2002 Sté Lenne v M Haudebault*, JCP, cahiers de droit de l'entreprise (2003), no 8, 24.

Code does not require the contract to be entered into in writing.[18] It is, however, advisable to the parties to do so for evidential purposes.[19]

### (i) A Mandated Agent

The commercial agent does not act for itself but for the principal; it is therefore a mandated agent and the rules of the Civil Code apply to it. However, as its mandate is a *mandat d'intérêt commun*, a common interest mandate,[20] the commercial agent is a special kind of mandated agent and the rules of the Civil Code only apply to the relationship it has with its principal provided that they do not contradict the rules defined by the Commercial Code.[21]

The fact that the commercial agent does not act for itself but for the principal is one of the reasons behind the civil law rationale that it needs protection[22] and therefore is a crucial part of its status.

In order to determine whether or not the commercial agent does indeed act on behalf of the principal, the courts will consider all the circumstances surrounding the case and will pay close attention to the way the parties behave in practice. The courts will, for instance, look at how the intermediary behaves towards the clients. In *Sté Bacchus Wine and Spirits Merchants Ltd v SA Champagne F Bonnet P et fils*,[23] the court had to decide whether the claimant was a distributor, as the contract stipulated it was, or a commercial agent as the claimant was arguing it was. In this case, the court held that the claimant was a distributor, not only because that is what the contract stipulated, but more importantly because the claimant behaved as a distributor and not as a commercial agent towards the clients. This was shown by the fact that although the invoices to the clients were in the name of the defendant, those clients were in reality those of the claimant who behaved towards them as a distributor by considering itself to be contractually bound to the clients as soon as the order was sent; in an agency context, the order is not usually binding until it has been

---

[18] Art L 134-2 Commercial Code simply gives the right for the parties to request that the agreement, and any subsequent covenant, be entered into in writing and such a right cannot be contracted out (Art L 134-16 Commercial Code).

[19] Two clauses will only be valid if entered into in writing: the renunciation to the protection (Art L 134-15 Commercial Code) and the post-contractual non-competition clause (Art L 134-14 al 2 Commercial Code).

[20] It is accepted that the main purpose of the mandate the principal gives the commercial agent, ie its mission, is to create and/or develop a customer base for the principal's goods. During the relationship, both parties benefit financially from this mission: the commercial agent through the commissions it receives and the principal through increased sales. The mandate is therefore regarded as having been entered into for the common interest of the parties, hence the term 'common interest mandate'. This notion, which is one of the reasons behind the civil rationale that commercial agents are in need of protection, will be developed in more detail below (section 11.4).

[21] FJ Pansier, 'Agents commerciaux' [2004] *Jurisclasseur Contrats-Distribution* para 10.

[22] The clientele does not belong to the commercial agent but to the principal. Civil law therefore recognises the risk that once the commercial agent has fulfilled his role, the principal will terminate the contract in order to deal directly with the customers and therefore benefit alone from the common interest that the commercial agent has helped to create.

[23] *Cass Com 10-7-2007*, Juris-Data 2007-040136.

confirmed by the principal. The Cour de Cassation also stated that it was clear from the written correspondence between the clients and the claimant, that they considered the latter as a distributor and not as the defendant's agent. The claimant was therefore a distributor and not a mandated agent.

The courts will also look at the way the principal behaves towards the intermediary. In *Sté MCX Co Ltd v SA Sagem*,[24] the principal did not allow its 'agent' to negotiate or take orders from clients and did everything itself directly with the clients. Since there was no representation, there was no agency relationship let alone any commercial agency relationship.

When checking whether a party is a commercial agent for the purpose of the Commercial Code, the French courts have the power, if necessary, to ignore the title that the parties have given to their contract and requalify the contract according to its true nature.[25] An example of this is the case of *SAS Glaxo Smith Kline v SARL Interpharm*.[26] In this instance, the parties had entered into a promotional contract—a *contrat de promotion*. Although the defendant's activities were clearly those of a commercial agent since it was selling the claimant's goods on the claimant's behalf, the contract nevertheless prevented it from introducing itself to the clients as acting for and on behalf of the claimant. When the contract was terminated, the defendant claimed compensation under Article L 134-12 Commercial Code. The lower court accepted its claim and the claimant appealed, arguing that the terms of the contract were such that the defendant could not be a commercial agent.

The Paris Appeal Court rejected this claim; relying on the fact that the contentious clauses were contradicting other terms of the contract, the Court stated that such clauses had the effect of artificially avoiding the application of the provision relating to the status of the commercial agent, ie Article L 134-1 Commercial Code and the contentious clauses were therefore void. The defendant was a commercial agent for the purpose of the Commercial Code and could therefore claim the protection accorded by such a status.

### (ii) An Independent Professional . . .

Although the commercial agent acts on behalf of the principal, it is nevertheless a separate legal entity from that of its principal and is as such an independent contractor. This characteristic is important to differentiate commercial agents from employed sales representatives and is emphasised by the Commercial Code which stipulates that commercial agents are 'independent professionals not linked by contracts for services'.[27] This independence manifests itself in two

---

[24] *CA Paris, 5ème ch B, 27-11-2003*, Juris-Data 2003-232143.

[25] Art 12 of the New Code of Civil Procedure stipulates that 'the judge must give or requalify the facts and litigious acts, without paying attention to the denomination proposed by the parties'.

[26] *CA Paris 5ème ch, B, 2-5-2002*, Juris-Data 2002-181440.

[27] The need to differentiate the two professions is important because the employed sales representatives have their own status.

ways: the freedom for the commercial agent to conduct its agency activities as it wishes and the freedom to have other commercial interests, besides its commercial agency activities.[28]

### 1. Freedom over the Way an Agent Conducts Agency Activities

As previously mentioned, a commercial agent will be appointed, primarily because it has the necessary skills to create and/or expand the customer base of the principal. The commercial agent is, in essence, a marketing tool for the principal. As an independent contractor, the way the commercial agent conducts its mission is therefore up to it alone and is not to be dictated by the principal as is the case for self-employed intermediaries. Case-law shows that in order to differentiate between the two professions, the courts will consider whether there is a subordination link between the parties. In *Eclimont v Guibout*,[29] it was held that the intermediary was not a commercial agent, even though he was registered as such, but an employed sales representative since he had no independence from his employer: he had no office, no personal telephone line, no letterheaded paper in his name and he was required to go to weekly meetings organised by the employer. Similarly, in *Fouque v Dutot*,[30] the company required the agent to visit clients according to a predetermined timetable and imposed sanctions upon him should he fail to comply. The Montpellier Appeal Court held that this clearly showed a subordination link between the two parties.

As an independent contractor, the commercial agent is also free to decide which resources are necessary to meet the demands of the mission. It can therefore choose its own workforce, ie whether to use employees or even other commercial agents, as is expressly allowed by the definition.

As an independent contractor, a commercial agent is also free to select the status of the agency. Although Article L 134-1 Commercial Code expressly stipulates that 'commercial agents may be natural or legal persons', this aspect of the freedom still had to be reiterated in the case of *SA Golden Lady v Cotton*.[31] In this instance, the commercial agent modified the status of his agency by creating a limited company registered in Belgium. Even if the contract allowed him to do so by giving him complete freedom in the way he organised his business, the principal nevertheless terminated the contract arguing that such behaviour constituted a serious breach preventing the commercial agent from claiming compensation. This argument failed.

Although the principal cannot dictate the manner in which the commercial agent conducts its agency business, the latter, as a mandated agent, must nevertheless act in the principal's best interests and account to the principal for its actions. Its freedom is therefore not infinite. As a consequence, the principal can give the commercial agent some instructions, such as the price to charge cus-

---

[28] *Cass Com 22-5-1967*, Bull Civ 1967, III, no 199.
[29] *CA Angers, 3ème ch, 17-12-1995*, Juris-Data 1995-052379.
[30] *CA Montpellier 6-5-1988*, as cited in Juriscl Dalloz, fasc 1230, 1.
[31] *CA Lyon 3ème ch, 12-2-1999*, Juris-Data 1999-040445.

tomers, for instance, or any other relevant instructions that do not contravene the commercial agent's independence.

### 2. Freedom of the Commercial Agent to Conduct other Activities Apart from the Agency

The second aspect of the commercial agent's independence, which may appear a little more controversial, is his freedom to represent other, non-competing, principals (Article L 134-3 Commercial Code) or even to set up his own business, which again, must not be in competition with that of the principal.[32]

This freedom is not to be confused with the situation where the commercial agent acts for its principal in a secondary capacity as will be explored in more detail in the second part of this chapter.

### (ii) . . . Who Acts on a Permanent Basis

The permanence of the relationship is another characteristic of the status of commercial agents compared to traditional mandated agents, whose relationship with the principal usually ends when the mission they were appointed for is completed.[33] Such a characteristic is logical in the light of the agent's mission and the common interest since the commercial agent will need a certain amount of time to put in place the necessary means to fulfil its mission.

This criterion is also crucial to distinguish commercial agents from brokers or other intermediaries who only act for a principal sporadically or on an ad hoc basis as *Mega Assistance Services America v SA Inter Mutuelles Assistance*[34] illustrates. In this case, the claimant, a US company, had been appointed by the defendant, an insurance company, in order to deal with, on their behalf, the invoices that the principal's clients had paid in relation to some medical interventions carried out on these clients whilst in the United States.

The claimant was paid a proportion of the value of such invoices. The claimant, arguing that it was a commercial agent under the French implementing text, claimed compensation. The Poitiers Court of Appeal rejected such a claim on the ground that although the claimant was acting on behalf of the principal, it was not doing so on a permanent basis since it was only appointed as and when its services were required, ie as and when clients of the principal made a claim on their policies.

Finally, one must not confuse the permanence of the activity with exclusivity. As previously mentioned, the commercial agent is free, aside from its commercial agency activities, to pursue other commercial activities.[35]

---

[32] Leloup, above n 8, para 312 at p 46. See also *CA Paris 20-1-1995*, D 1995, SC 260, note Y Serra.
[33] PF Pansier, 'Agents commerciaux, contrat d'agence', jurisclasseur commercial, fasc 3500, para 20.
[34] *CA Poitiers 15-4-2007, 2ème ch*, Juris-Data 2007-342066.
[35] Pansier, above n 33, para 12.

## (b) The Main Function of the Commercial Agent: To Negotiate and/or Conclude Contracts for the Principal

The Commercial Code protects two categories of commercial agents: those who have a limited authority to negotiate contracts and those who have a wider authority to conclude contracts on behalf of their principal. Given that 'to negotiate' is the lowest threshold required for protection, to understand what 'negotiating' precisely entails is therefore of crucial importance. Following the silence of the Directive and the implementing text on that aspect, the task of defining such a role fell to the French courts. In carrying out such a task, the courts appear to have had regard to the main function of a commercial agent which, as is widely acknowledged,[36] is to create, expand or maintain a client base for the principal's goods or services, ie the common interest. Considering the importance of the notion, to have regard to it in order to decide whether the commercial agent is negotiating seems perfectly logical.

The French courts seem to consider that a commercial agent will be 'negotiating' when it is prospecting (in French, *démarcher*), ie actively looking for new customers, or looking for new ways to boost the existing ones. Anything less, it seems, will not amount to 'negotiating'.[37] In fact, in *Dispharm v Société Solvay Pharma*,[38] the claimant's role was simply to contact doctors, pharmacists, nurses and other medical practitioners to inform them of new products of the defendant and give them technical information about such products. The Cour de Cassation held that the agent's role was simply to pass information to potential clients and this did not amount to 'negotiating' for the purpose of this part of the Commercial Code.

A similar line of reasoning seems to have been adopted by the courts of appeal of Versailles and Paris, respectively, in three recent decisions. In *SARL Eurotech v Sté Eagle Picher Wolveruine Gmbh*,[39] the claimant and the defendant, a German company, entered into a 'contract of representation' for the commercialisation of specialised automobile parts manufactured by the defendant. The Versailles court held that the claimant was not a commercial agent for the purpose of the Commercial Code since its role was simply that of a 'technical intermediary' (in French, an *intermédiaire technique*) whose role consisted of informing potential clients of the products of the defendant manufacturer. It therefore did not 'prospect' or 'negotiate' since its actions did not generate new sales or lead to firm orders from clients.

In *SA TPG v Société Antalis Division Montevrain*,[40] the parties were linked

---

[36] Ibid, para 25.
[37] In *CA Paris 28-6-2002, Sté La Française des Jeux v Morel*, Juris Data 2002-188810, the court expressly referred to the fact that the claimant could not recruit new customers as an indication that he was not 'negotiating' for the purpose of the Commercial Code and therefore could not be a commercial agent.
[38] *Cass Com 3-10-2000*, unreported.
[39] *CA Versailles 8-2-2007, ch 12, sect 2*, Juris-Data 2007-338141.
[40] *CA Paris, 22-3-2007, 5ème ch, B*, Juris-Data 2007-335883.

by a contract called 'promotion of sales' whereby the claimant's role was to visit printing companies and other firms whose business involved the use of printing products or paper in order to show them the products of the defendant and explain how such products compared and contrasted with those of competing companies in the field and judge the reaction of such potential clients. The claimant was required to pass the information gathered to a distributor of the defendant company who then visited such potential clients and negotiated the contracts by taking orders. The Paris appeal court therefore held that the claimant was not 'negotiating' pursuant to Article L 134-1 Commercial Code and could therefore not be regarded as a commercial agent.

Finally, in *SA Société Etam International Sourcing v Société Tekstil Mumessilik Dis Ticaret Ktd Sirketi (TTM)*,[41] the Paris appeal court held that the only 'negotiating' that the agent was doing was when choosing which of the potential suppliers' names it would pass onto the defendant, which would then decide who to contract with. This did not amount to 'negotiating' for the purpose of the Commercial Code and the claimant was therefore not a commercial agent but a broker.

The underlying theme of these cases seems to be that an agent will not be seen as negotiating if, through its actions, it plays no active part in the creation or development of the clientele of the principal, if its actions are not at the root of the expanded clientele. In other words, if the agent is doing nothing more than giving potential clients the relevant information about the goods, the latter deciding themselves whether or not to buy the goods in question, this is not enough to amount to 'negotiating'. Similarly, an agent will not be negotiating if it has a very restricted mission to accomplish as the case of *SA Grand Café de Paris v GEI PMU*[42] illustrates. In this case, the claimant was an '*exploitant point-course*'. Although it worked for the principal, its role was merely to register the bets and give the money received for such bets to the principal. The claimant was not negotiating since the manner in which it could run its business was dictated by the principal.

If, however, through his actions, the commercial agent clearly contributes to the creation or development of the common interest, it will be negotiating for the purpose of the Commercial Code as *SARL SACED v SARL LMC*[43] illustrates. In this case, the defendant, a manufacturer, had fallen on hard times. Wishing to reinvigorate what was once a thriving business, the defendant asked the claimant to renew commercial links with a certain number of businesses, whose custom the defendant had lost following its financial difficulties.

The claimant duly complied and contacted the businesses in question. Using its marketing skills in various ways (by organising visits to the principal's manufacturing premises to show how the manufacturing process had been modernised and by organising meetings between the potential clients and the principal and

---

[41] *CA Paris, 27-9-2007*, Juris-Data 2007-348057.
[42] *CA Paris, 18-1-2001*, Juris-Data 2001-161533.
[43] *CA Rouen 12-4-2007, 2ème ch*, Juris-Data 2007-333442.

its board), the claimant successfully restored the former clients' confidence in the principal's business since they placed orders with the principal, which amounted to 'negotiating' for the purpose of Article L 134-1 Commercial Code.

Although in all these cases the various courts of appeal appear to be interpreting the meaning of 'negotiating' in a similar manner, in 2008, in the case of *SA Radio Communication Equipements (RCE) v SA Société Française du Radiotéléphone (SFR)*,[44] the Cour de Cassation appears to have adopted a much more restricted view as to what amounts to 'negotiation'. In January 1997, the claimant entered into a rather complex partnership contract (in French, a *contrat partenaire*) with the defendant, requiring the former to fulfil four different roles. The claimant was first in charge of the 'diffusion de services de radio téléphonie' by getting potential clients to subscribe to mobile telephone contracts with the defendant. The claimant was also buying telephones from the defendant and then reselling them at a profit. In addition, the claimant was providing after-sales services on the telephone contracts, and finally, it was participating to the promotion of the defendant's activities. The contract, initially entered into for a period of two years, was renewed once. In January 2002, following the defendant's notice of non-renewal, the claimant sought compensation pursuant to Article L 134-12 Commercial Code.

The Cour de Cassation rejected its claim, upholding the decision of the Court of Appeal of Paris[45] on the ground that the claimant was not 'negotiating' for the purpose of Article L 134-1 Commercial Code since it had contractually agreed that it could not vary the terms of the mobile telephone contracts proposed by the defendant to potential clients. For the Cour de Cassation, 'to negotiate' therefore necessarily included the power to have an input on the principal's contract terms with third parties. As has been remarked,[46] since the essence of the negotiating role of the commercial agent is that of enlarging the principal's client base by prospecting potential clients and getting them to buy the goods of the principal, such a definition appears very narrow.[47] Others, noting the very highly standardised nature of the contract linking the parties, have said that, given the increasing number of highly standardised contracts in the modern distribution of goods and services, commercial agency activities may not be adapted to this type of distribution.[48] One has to await further decisions to see whether or not this restrictive view will be confined to highly standardised contracts.

---

[44] *Cass Com 15-1-2008*, Juris-Data 2008-042333, D 2008, 350.

[45] *CA Paris 23-2-2006*, Juris-Data 2006-297425, JCP G 2006, II 10108, 1297–98.

[46] N Mathey. 'Nature juridique du contrat conclu par un distributeur d'abonnement de téléphonie mobile' [2008] CCC no 3, March, Comm 68. For a similar comment made in relation to the decision of the Paris Court of Appeal, see D Ferrier, D 2006, 2306.

[47] For a contrary view, see Stoffel-Munck who praised the Paris Court of Appeal's position on the ground that since the principal had contractually agreed that it would contract with all the names the claimant had passed onto them, the intermediary was merely a 'conduit pipe' (in French, a *tuyau*) when passing the names of clients on to the principal. Ph Stoffel-Munck 'Le distributeur d'abonnements de téléphonie mobile et la qualification d'agent commercial ou de mandataire d'intérêt commun' [2006] JCP G, II 10.108, 1297–1300, 1300.

[48] Mathey, above n 46.

In addition to looking at the provisions of Article L 134-1 Commercial Code, the courts may also consider other elements such as whether the commercial agent is registered in the special registry, and whether it is remunerated by commission, the preferred method of remuneration of commercial agents,[49] or through a set tariff.

*1. The Specific Case of Sub-agents:*

Article L 134-1 Commercial Code clearly covers sub-agents who are therefore commercial agents in their own right. They are therefore entitled to the full protection the status gives them, including the right to claim compensation from the principal[50] and the right to assign their *carte*, ie the part of the agency they are in charge of.[51] The sub-agent therefore has a clear right of direct action against the principal. However, this is not a perfect direct action (*action directe imparfaite*)[52] since the principal can use against the sub-agents, any payment already made to the main agent.[53] Indeed, although the commercial agent has a right to use sub-agents, the principal must not bear the burden of it. The sub-agency relationship is therefore accessory to the main agency relationship.

*2. Exclusions*

The second part of Article L 134-1 Commercial Code expressly excludes agents whose status is already defined by other statutes, ie travel agents, insurance agents, intermediaries in banking and financial dealing, estate agents, *administrateurs judiciaries*, and intermediaries who buy space in journals and publications for adverts.[54] Although this part of the Commercial Code is self-explanatory,[55] the question arose as to whether negotiating agents who represent estate agents (*négociateurs immobiliers*) could claim protection of the Commercial Code. Although the Cour de Cassation answered this question in the negative in 2004,[56] this was changed by legislation[57] in 2006: self-employed *négociateurs immobiliers* are now covered by this part of the Commercial Code.

Let us now turn to the other exclusion, that of commercial agents whose activities are regarded as secondary.

---

[49] Compare and contrast the following two cases: in *CA Versailles 8-2-2007, SARL Eurotech v Sté Eagle Picher Wolveruine GmbH*, Juris-Data 2007-338141, JCP G 2007, IV, 2908, the court considered that the fact that the intermediary was remunerated by a tariff and not through commission was additional evidence that he was not a commercial agent. In *Cass Com 3-10-2000 Dispharm v Société Solvay Pharma* (unreported), the intermediary argued that the fact that he was paid by commission was an element that he was a commercial agent. The court rejected such a claim, saying that, in this instance, paying the agent through commission made financial sense since it only reflected the quality of the marketing abilities.

[50] *Cass Com 3-12-2002*, D 2003, 786 note B Mallet-Bricout.

[51] *Cass Com 23-6-1998 Rossignol v Debono* as cited in Leloup, above n 8, 270.

[52] Expression of Professor Leloup. Leloup, above n 8, 270.

[53] *Cass Com 3-12-2002*, D 2003, 786.

[54] As per Art 26 of L 93-122 of 29 January 1993, 'Loi Sapin'.

[55] For more details about the other sectors, see Leloup, above n 8, 38–42.

[56] *Cass Com 7-7-2004*, Bull Civ IV No 147, D 2004, AJ 2230.

[57] Statute 2006-872 of 13-7-2006 amends Art 4 of the statute L 70-9 of 2-1-1970 (Loi Hoguet).

## 11.3 THE NOTION OF SECONDARY ACTIVITIES AND ITS APPRECIATION BY THE FRENCH COURTS

Following the choice left in the Directive,[58] France opted for the possibility to exclude from the scope of the implementing text commercial agents whose activities are deemed secondary.

Article L 134-15 of the French Commercial Code stipulates that:

> When the activity of commercial agent is carried out under a written contract, signed by the parties, which is principally for another purpose, the parties may decide in writing that the provisions of this chapter do not apply to the part corresponding to the commercial agency activity.
>
> This renunciation shall be invalid if the performance of the contract reveals that the commercial agency activity is actually being carried out as the principal or decisive element.

The way France has opted to apply this part of the Directive works in two steps: first, the parties themselves decide, by complying with certain conditions, that the commercial agent will not be protected by the Commercial Code for its commercial agency activity. This renunciation is then subject to a control by the French courts. Article L 134-15 therefore appears to serve two functions. In its first section, the Article defines the necessary conditions for the renunciation of the protection offered by the Commercial Code to be valid, namely (i) there must be a written contract between the commercial agent and its principal; (ii) the main object of the contract must be *principally* for a purpose other than commercial agency; and (iii) the contract must expressly stipulate that the commercial agency activities are not regulated by the relevant provisions of the Commercial Code. The second section of Article L 134-15 gives the courts a regulatory role since they can consider null and void the express exclusion, should the commercial agency activity be carried out, in reality, as the *principal or decisive element* of the relationship.[59]

As mentioned above, this exception represents a clear departure from the French legal tradition[60] since the 1958 Decree did not make the distinction between principal activity and secondary activity.[61] It seems that France opted for the possibility granted by the Directive in order to ensure that motor agents (*agents de marque automobile*) would not be covered by the implementing text. Such agents are garage-owners specialising in the maintenance and repair of automobiles of a certain make. Under a contract with a car dealer of the same make, the garage owner offers his services to the clients of the car dealer. In

---

[58] Art 2(2).

[59] In French, the expression is '*déterminant*'.

[60] S Rouquié, 'Agents commerciaux, renonciation par contrat au statut protecteur de l'agent commercial' [2004] JCP G (issue no 49), 1928, para 6.

[61] The main criterion for the 1958 decree to apply was whether the activity was permanent (*activité habituelle*) as opposed to temporary (*activité ponctuelle*) in order to make the distinction between commercial agents and brokers.

return, the car dealer asks the garage owner to act as his selling agent by selling a certain quota of cars of the make in question on his behalf. Car dealers
themselves do not have the status of commercial agents and therefore have no
protection when their dealership is terminated. As a consequence, it was felt that
to impose upon them an obligation to compensate their car agents upon termination of their relationship would not only be profoundly unjust[62] but would
also risk destabilising the entire industry.[63]

The fact that France has opted for this exclusion has been criticised on various grounds. First of all, considering that very few car agents have claimed to be
protected by the 1958 Decree[64] or that their relationship with their dealers was
a common interest mandate,[65] some have found it puzzling that France went to
such lengths solely to exclude them from the protection of the text.[66] Indeed,
it would have been simpler to create a special status for car agents,[67] who by
virtue of the second section of Article L 134-1 al 2 Commercial Code, would
have been automatically excluded.

Secondly, in view of the protective stance of the French legal tradition in
this matter, it appears strange that France opted for such a possibility at all.[68]
Moreover, given that Article L 134-15 is drafted in general terms, its impact
could be wider than anticipated since it does not appear to be solely restricted
to car agents. This interpretation was confirmed by the Cour de Cassation in
*Societé Domi Hospital Nutrition v Sté Laboratoires Gilbert*,[69] where the contract
between the two parties was for the sale of pharmaceutical goods.

Finally, the drafting of Article L 134-15 is somewhat obscure since it fails to
define what amounts to a 'principal' or 'decisive' activity or the criteria by which
it should be assessed. The task of interpretation fell to the French courts and
although one had to wait until 2004 for the first case to emerge, unsurprisingly,
most cases since have raised that very question.

In *Societé Domi Hospital Nutrition v Sté Laboratoires Gilbert*,[70] the first case
on this part of the Commercial Code, the claimant, a manufacturer of pharmaceutical products, and the defendant, a medical laboratory, entered into a
mutual contract (in French a *contrat de collaboration*) for the purpose of creating
a common commercial strategy. The contract nevertheless stipulated that each
party would keep their respective clients. Aside from this main contract, the

---

[62] Ph Grignon, note under *Cass Com 12-7 2005* in JCP E 2006, no 2064, 1213–14 at 1213.

[63] See debates in parliament on this very question in Rapp Sénat M Huchon, no 268 annexé au PV
de la séance du 11-4-1991. Séance Sénat 18-4-1991: JO Sénat CR avr 1991, 539–50 and séance Sénat
31-5-1991: JO Sénat CR, may 1991, 1212–15. For academic comments, see in particular D Ferrier,
'Commentaire de la loi du 25 juin 1991' [1991] *Cah dr entr*, issue 6, 32, no 16.

[64] M Hémard, 'Les agents commerciaux' [1959] RTD Com 584–85 as cited by Rouquié, above n
60, para 7. Professor Leloup only cites two recorded cases: see Leloup, above n 8, para 314 at p 47.

[65] J Lambert, D 1970, 173, as cited by Rouquié, above n 60, para 7.

[66] Rouquié, above n 60.

[67] Ibid.

[68] Ibid, para 2.

[69] *Cass Com 3-3-2004*, Juris-Data 2004-022751, JCP G 2004, issue no 49, 1928.

[70] Ibid.

claimant also acted as commercial agent for the defendant. The main contract, signed by both parties in 1994, stipulated that the commercial agency activities would not be regulated by the Commercial Code. Yet, when the defendant terminated the relationship, the claimant nevertheless sought compensation for the loss suffered pursuant to Article L 134-12 Commercial Code. The Paris Court of Appeal dismissed its claim on the ground that its activity as commercial agent was not a decisive activity within its relationship with the defendant; the conditions of Article L 134-15 Commercial Code were complied with; the renunciation was therefore valid. The claimant appealed to the Cour de Cassation on two grounds: (i) that the Court of Appeal had failed to examine the 'common intention of the two parties' by not accepting that the claimant was a commercial agent pursuant to Article L 134-1 Commercial Code; and that (ii) given the mandatory status of the right to claim compensation as defined by Article L 134-16 Commercial Code, any clause rejecting such a right was invalid.

The Cour de Cassation upheld the decision of the Court of Appeal. After agreeing that the claimant was a commercial agent pursuant to Article L 134-1 Commercial Code, the Cour de Cassation nevertheless stated that they were not protected by the Commercial Code since their commercial agency activity, within their relationship with the defendant, 'was not exercised primarily, in the execution of the contract'. To do so, the Cour de Cassation compared the sums the claimant earned for each activity. The turnover (*chiffre d'affaires*) of the claimant, under the main contract, was in the region of 20,000,000 FF but the commission it received for its commercial agency activities was 234,223.54 FF. Comparing the two sets of figures, the court held that it was clear that the claimant's commercial agency activities were not its primary activities since they accounted for only 2 per cent of their entire *chiffre d'affaires* under the main contract. The clause whereby the claimant renounced the protection of the Commercial Code was therefore valid since it complied with the conditions defined by Article L 134-15 Commercial Code.

The Cour de Cassation's objective *quantitative* approach in assessing the importance of the parties' activities has been praised as the only 'legalistic answer' that it could reach.[71] However, it has also been remarked that the Cour de Cassation could have assessed *qualitatively* the importance that the commercial agency activities played within the contract of collaboration in order to find out whether, although accessory, such activities were nevertheless decisive for the relationship as a whole.[72] Interestingly, the 'qualitative analysis' was adopted by the Court of Appeal of Nîmes in *SA Société Diffusion Automobiles v Beauquis*.[73] However, the very same point was argued by a car agent two years later, but was rejected by the Cour de Cassation in favour of a similarly quantitative

---

[71] Rouquié, above n 60, para 9. This comment was made even earlier when the implementing text was enacted. See J Thréard, 'Les concessionaires et les agents dans l'automobile après la loi du 25 juin 1991', [1991] Gaz Pal, I, doctr, 74.

[72] Rouquié, above n 60, para 9.

[73] *CA Nîmes 17-4-2003*, Juris-Data 2003-220277, unreported.

assessment in *Corgna v SA Renault France Automobile*.[74] The precedent value of the decision of the Court of Appeal of Nîmes therefore appears limited.

In the *Corgna* case, in 1992, the parties agreed that the claimant, a garage owner, would act as the defendant's car agent in addition to his car maintenance and repair activities for Renault cars. The contract, signed by both parties, expressly stipulated that the claimant's commercial agency activities would not be regulated by the Commercial Code. In 1996, following the termination of the contract by the defendant, the claimant nevertheless claimed compensation for the loss suffered pursuant to Article L 134-12 Commercial Code. The Court of Appeal, looking at the turnover of his two activities, rejected his claim on the ground that, quantitatively, his commercial agency activity was secondary to the main contract and he was consequently not covered by the implementing text. The claimant appealed to the Cour de Cassation on the ground that it was not sufficient for the court to compare the two activities on a quantitative basis and that the Appeal Court should have enquired, on a qualitative basis, whether his activity as commercial agent, although secondary to his garage activity, was nevertheless decisive for his latter activity, ie whether the fact that he was selling under the banner of Renault was 'decisive' pursuant to Article L 134-15 Commercial Code, for his garage activity. The Cour de Cassation rejected such a *qualitative analysis* and held, again, using a *quantitative basis*, by looking at the sums earned under the two activities, that since his commercial agency activity only accounted for 1 per cent of his entire turnover, *chiffre d'affaires*, such an activity was clearly secondary.

On a final note, in the interesting case of *CCI de Strasbourg et du Bas-Rhin v Mme Elkouby*,[75] the Cour de Cassation stated that the question of secondary activity is only relevant for the commercial agent and not for the principal. In this case, the principal, the Chamber of Commerce and Industry of Strasbourg ('the CCI') had appointed Mrs Elkouby as their exclusive commercial agent in order to find clients to place adverts in the CCI's periodical journal. When the contract was terminated, Mrs Elkouby claimed compensation under the Commercial Code. The CCI counter-argued that she was not protected by the Commercial Code and could therefore not claim compensation on two grounds: (i) the CCI, as a public body under French law, could not be regarded as a principal under the Commercial Code since this was incompatible with its other activities; and (ii) that in any case, the CCI's activity as a principal was accessory to its other activities as a chamber of commerce. The Cour de Cassation rejected both parts of their claim. On the first point, the court stated that the Commercial Code only defined the commercial agent; Article L 134-1 Commercial Code was drafted in sufficiently wide manner so as to include even a public body. The second part of the claim was rejected on the ground that Article L 134-1 Commercial Code

---

[74] *Cass Com 12-7-2005*, Juris-Data 2005-029483, for comments, see JCP G 2005, IV 3093; Ph Grignon, JCP E 2006, issue 27–28, no 2064, p. 1213.

[75] *Cass Com 5-4-2005*, Juris-Data 2005-027933, unreported, but for comments, see JCP E 2005, no 31-34 of 4-8-2005, 1329, note by JLR.

did not require the status of the activity of the principal to be determined, ie whether primary or secondary activity, before the commercial agent could claim protection. As the Court remarked,[76] it would have been easier for the principal to argue that, according to the *Loi Sapin*,[77] Mrs Elkouby is excluded from the Commercial Code.

Let us now turn to the common interest, the notion which highlights the area where the desire to follow the French legal tradition is at its highest.

## 11.4 THE NOTION OF COMMON INTEREST AND ITS IMPACT ON THE PARTIES' RECIPROCAL OBLIGATION OF GOOD FAITH AND LOYALTY

Article L 134-4 Commercial Code, which cannot be derogated from,[78] stipulates that:

> The contracts concluded between commercial agents and their principals shall be in the common interest of the parties.
>
> The relationships between commercial agents and principals shall be governed by an obligation of loyalty and a reciprocal duty of information.
>
> Commercial agents must perform their mandate in a professional manner. Principals shall make sure that the commercial agents are able to perform their mandate.

The way France implemented this part of the Directive is clearly intended to follow the French legal tradition: where the Directive requires the parties to behave in good faith towards one another,[79] the Commercial Code first stipulates that the relationship is entered into for the common interest of the parties. The notion therefore appears to govern the relationship as a whole. As such, it is much wider than at its inception and its origin must consequently be considered, albeit briefly, in order to understand its importance as one of the main reasons why commercial agents are perceived to be, economically at least, weaker than their principal and consequently in need of protection.

Although commercial agents have had their own status since 1958, the idea that they needed protection emerged a lot earlier. Commercial agents act as the principal's representatives, and the Civil Code rules on the mandate therefore applied to regulate their relationship. However, the underlying rationale of the Civil Code, whereby the mandate is a temporary and gratuitous service entered into for the sole benefit of the principal,[80] allowing the principal to terminate the mandate at any time and without incurring any liability,[81] is clearly ill suited

---

[76] JCP E 2005, No 31-34 of 4-8-2005, 1329.
[77] See n 54 above and associated text.
[78] Art L 134-16 Commercial Code.
[79] Arts 3(1) and 4(1) of the Directive.
[80] Art 1986 Civil Code.
[81] Art 2004 Civil Code.

to the needs of commercial agents who, as professionals, represent the principal on a permanent basis and in return for payment. In an attempt to protect them, the French Supreme Court created the notion of common interest mandate (*mandat d'intérêt commun*) in 1885,[82] and stated:

> [W]hen the contract is created in the common interest of the principal as well as that of the mandated agent, it cannot be unilaterally revoked by one or the other party but can only be revoked by mutual consent, for a justified cause recognised by the courts or following contractual specification.

As previously mentioned, it is now settled law that this common interest is the interest shared by the principal and the commercial agent in the development of their common enterprise by the creation and development of a clientele for the principal's goods and services.[83] As the creation of the clientele is the common interest, both parties must therefore work together to reach this aim. The commercial agent provides its marketing expertise and financial resources to set up the marketing campaign and the principal provides the goods or services for the commercial agent to market. During the relationship, both parties benefit from their joint efforts since the commercial agent receives commission on the sales and the principal receives the profits from such sales. However, because the commercial agent does not act for itself but for the principal, the customers are not attached to the agent but to the principal. So, when their relationship ends, whereas the principal can still benefit from the common interest and from the efforts of the commercial agent, the latter cannot.[84] Economically, the commercial agent is therefore weaker than the principal and the payment of compensation on termination aims to re-establish the balance, as far as money can, between the parties.

The place that the common interest has in the Commercial Code is clearly wider today than at its creation. The notion, originally created by the judiciary in order to protect commercial agents on termination, now governs the relationship as a whole and is therefore at the very core of the relationship, in the same way that the Directive places good faith at the core of the relationship. The fact that the Commercial Code places the notion before the obligations of the parties means that it will be relevant when assessing whether the commercial agent or the principal has committed a breach of one of his obligations, which will

---

[82] *Cass Civ 13-5-1885*, DP 1885, I 350; S 1888, I, 220.

[83] Definition given first in *Cass Com 8-10-1969*, D 1970, J, 143, note Lambert and reiterated in *Cass Com 17-5-1989*, JCP G 1989, IV, 267. It is therefore enshrined in French law as recently restated by Mouveau, 'Notion de mandat d'intérêt commun dans le contrat d'agent commercial' [2002] JCP G, II, 10123.

[84] Some have even said that the principal could be seen as having been unjustly enriched and therefore the compensation is not so different from the German-based indemnity: R Bradgate and S Saintier, '"Compensation" and "indemnity" under the Agency Regulations: How the Common Law System Copes with the Invasion of Civilian Concepts' in P Giliker (ed), *Re-examining Contract and Unjust Enrichment. Anglo-Canadian Perspective* (Martinus Nijhoff), 311–36, at 323–25. For the argument that the legal basis for the right of the commercial agent to claim compensation, see FJ Pansier, 'Agents Commerciaux, fin du contrat d'agence' [2004] *Jurisclasseur Contrats Distribution* para 43.

have an impact at the stage of termination. An appreciation of the role played by the common interest must therefore be seen in that context.

The commercial agent's right to claim compensation on termination (Article L 134-12 Commercial Code) is excluded in three specific circumstances (Article L 134-13 Commercial Code), including a serious breach by the commercial agent (Article L 134-13 al 1 Commercial Code). The burden of proof that the commercial agent is guilty of a serious breach lies with the principal.[85] However, the courts alone are competent to determine what amounts to a serious breach and it cannot be predetermined by the parties.[86] Given the mandatory nature of the right of the commercial agent to claim compensation (Article L 134-18 Commercial Code),[87] the courts do so in a very strict manner. In *Lenne v Haudebault*,[88] the Cour de Cassation defined a serious breach as 'a breach which jeopardises the common aim of the common interest mandate and which renders impossible the continuation of the contract'.[89] In this case, the principal claimed that the fact that the commercial agent had failed to register in the special registry amounted to a serious fault which would allow him to terminate the relationship and avoid having to pay compensation. The court rejected this intention.

### (a) The Common Interest and the Commercial Agent's Obligation of Loyalty to its Principal

Loyalty is central to the relationship and therefore central to the common interest, as the Cour de Cassation recently reiterated in *SAS France Distribution Importation v Société Neuf Cégétel*.[90] In this instance, the commercial agent was found guilty of a serious breach when it acted for a competitor of the principal, without informing the principal. This case is interesting because, after emphasising that the obligation of loyalty was 'essential to the common interest mandate', the Cour de Cassation held that the obligation of loyalty requiring the commercial agent not to act for a competitor of the principal applies even when it has no exclusivity. The Cour de Cassation added that should the commercial agent wish to enter into a contract with a competing principal, it must inform its principal of such a wish, on the basis of the obligation of loyalty. The commercial agent's obligation to seek consent from its principal before contracting with a competing third party is expressly stipulated in the Commercial Code (Article L 134-3). It is therefore not clear what the obligation of information

---

[85] *Cass Com 15-10-2002 Sté Lenne v M Haudebault*, JCP, cahiers de droit de l'entreprise (2003), no 8, at 24.

[86] *Cass Com 28-5-2002, Arkopharma v Mlle Gravier*, D 2003, Somm Comm 459; D 2002 SC 3004 and RTDCiv 2002, 833.

[87] Case C-381/98: *Ingmar Ltd v Eaton Leonard Technologies Inc* [2001] CMLR 9.

[88] *Cass Com 15-10-2002*, CCC 2002, no 19, 12.

[89] In French: 'la faute grave est celle qui porte atteinte à la finalité commune du mandat d'intérêt commun et rend impossible le maintien du lien contractuel'.

[90] *Cass Com 15-5-2007*, Juris-Data 2007-038951.

adds, since obtaining the consent of the principal necessarily implies informing the principal of its intention.[91]

It seems that what was important for the Cour de Cassation in this instance was the fact that the commercial agent, in spite of some opportunities to reveal to the principal that it was acting for a competing principal, had failed to do so. In fact, emphasising that the commercial agent had 'consciously hidden his actions from the principal', such an act was disloyal and therefore amounted to a serious breach. However, perhaps an even more important aspect of this case is the fact that court held that as soon as the commercial agent fails to comply with this obligation of information, it is guilty of a serious breach. As a consequence, it did not matter that, in this case, the principal discovered the commercial agent's disloyalty only after termination. This is a hard outcome for the commercial agent.

The obligation of loyalty also covers the activities that the commercial agent may have in addition to its commercial agency activities,[92] including setting up its own business as the case of *SARL Pujol v SA Interseed*[93] illustrates. In this instance, the commercial agent used confidential information to which it had access, ie the list of the biggest customers of the principal, to try to entice them to the business that it was setting up itself. This behaviour was held to be disloyal since it caused the principal to lose confidence in its commercial agent.

The commercial agent's obligation of loyalty not only applies during the performance of the contract but also extends after the contract has terminated as the case of *Fabian Dzipeff v Société Samputensili SARL*[94] illustrates. In this case, the court held that if the commercial agent is indeed guilty of a serious breach, it will not only lose the right to claim compensation, but will also be liable, in tort, on the basis of Article 1382 Civil Code, for any loss that his breach will have caused the principal. The Cour de Cassation held that if there is no post-contractual non-competition clause, the commercial agent can act freely towards the clientele of its former principal.

However, this is so on the condition of the commercial agent not being guilty of a breach amounting to a *concurrence déloyale*, ie unfair competition. Although this makes sense in the light of the common interest, it appears harsh on the commercial agent. The matter has, however, been sent back to the Court of Appeal of Aix en Provence in order to determine whether there was indeed in this instance such unfair competition.

The burden of proof that the commercial agent has been disloyal by acting in competition with the principal is on the latter. In *Schauber v SAS Etablissement Gueze*,[95] the Aix en Provence Court of Appeal reiterated that the commercial agent's behaviour will only amount to a serious fault if it is an 'attack on the

---

[91] M Malaurie-Vignal, 'Respect de l'obligation de loyauté' [2007] CCC no 8, August.
[92] Leloup, above n 8, para 312 at 46. See also *CA Paris 20-1-1995*, D 1995, SC 260, note Y Serra.
[93] *CA Montpellier 30-12-1998*, Juris-Data 1998-035198.
[94] *Cass Com 15-5-2007*, Juris-Data 2007-039100.
[95] *CA Aix en Provence 12-4-2007*, Juris-Data 2007-338810.

common aim of the contract which renders the continuation of the relationship impossible'. In this case, the principal argued that it had just cause to terminate the contract since the commercial agent was guilty of a serious breach on three grounds, one of which was that he had accepted a job as a salaried director for a company which was undertaking activity in competition with its own. The court rejected such allegations since the principal had failed to establish how such activities were competing with its own.

When assessing whether the commercial agent is guilty of a serious breach, the French courts will look at all the circumstances surrounding the case, including the principal's behaviour, which, must itself act in a loyal manner and in line with the common goal. The common interest therefore appears to create a symmetry between the parties. In fact, the obligation of the commercial agent to perform its mandate in a professional manner corresponds to the principal's obligation to allow the former to perform its mandate (Article L 134-4 al 3 Commercial Code). If the principal fails to do so, this will be relevant for the courts when assessing the seriousness of the breach of the commercial agent as the case of *SAS Europfil v Avisse*[96] illustrates. In this instance, the principal argued that by representing another principal selling competing products without its consent, the commercial agent had been disloyal. The court rejected this claim on the ground that when the principal became aware of the agent's conduct, it waited for 21 months before terminating the relationship. The Caen Court of Appeal added that although the commercial agent's breach of loyalty was a 'violation of an essential obligation in the contract which can amount to a serious breach', because the principal had tolerated such a breach for 21 months and had not even mentioned it as a reason for giving the agent notice, the breach was not serious and the commercial agent had consequently not lost its right to claim compensation.

### (b) The Common Interest and the Commercial Agent's Obligation to be a Good Professional

This obligation requires the commercial agent to use reasonable care and skill when performing its mandate. Although the common interest is less often quoted when assessing the seriousness of this breach, the way in which the courts assess it is nevertheless important. The commercial agent can still be guilty of a serious breach if it fails to comply with this obligation as the case of *SARL Sud Millésime v SA Eyguebelle*[97] illustrates. In this case, the principal claimed that it had grounds to terminate the relationship and withdraw compensation because the commercial agent was guilty of a serious breach because it had failed to: (i) prospect clients in three *départements* in which it had an exclusivity; (2) pros-

---

[96] *CA Caen, 15-12-2005*, Juris-Data 2005-293818.
[97] *Cass Com 10-7-2007*, Juris-Data 2007-040258.

pect the *grands magasins* and (3) address the fact that one of its employees was not available by failing to organise a replacement. Furthermore, (iv) the agent had itself acknowledged, in writing, that it was not in a position to prospect the clientele in a serious manner. The Cour de Cassation accepted that the latter was in fact due to the commercial policy of the principal, which favoured the commercialisation of wines over that of spirits. Yet, the Cour de Cassation nevertheless held that taking all the breaches into consideration, the commercial agent was guilty of a serious breach allowing the principal to terminate the contract without owing the agent compensation.

Similarly, if, through its actions, the commercial agent causes the principal to lose customers, this will be regarded as a serious breach as the Court of Appeal of Montpellier held in 2003.[98] In this case, although the commercial agent had taken orders from clients, he had failed, without a valid reason, to then pass all of these orders on to the principal, causing a loss of revenue for the principal.

Although the common interest was not expressly invoked in these cases, the analysis of the court nevertheless makes sense in the light of the common interest. By failing to do its utmost and act as a good professional, the commercial agent fails to act for the common goal and therefore is guilty of a serious breach. However, there must be a clear breach by the commercial agent. As the Cour de Cassation made clear in the case of *Arkopharma v Gravier*,[99] 'it is not possible for the parties to decide that a certain pre-determined behaviour will be a serious breach'. The principal cannot, as it attempted to do in this case, stipulate in the contract that the fact that the commercial agent does not reach a sales target will amount to a serious breach. The non-reaching of the sales target, is not sufficient, per se, to constitute a serious breach if it is not attributable to a serious failure of the commercial agent to use reasonable care and skill when performing the mandate.

Correspondingly to the manner in which the courts determine whether a breach of loyalty has occurred, in order to decide whether the agent has acted as a good professional or not, the courts also look at all the surrounding circumstances, including the obligation of the principal to 'make sure that the commercial agents are able to perform their mandate'. As a result, if the commercial agent's breach is caused by the principal's own breach, the former's breach will not be regarded as a serious breach as *SA VOA Verrerie d'Albi v SA Roland Chateau*[100] illustrates. In this case the defendant acted as the commercial agent of the appellant. When the appellant terminated their relationship, the defendant sued it for compensation for wrongful termination. The principal responded that it did not owe the commercial agent any compensation since the commercial agent was guilty of breach of loyalty for having broken its terms of exclusivity by obtaining goods from another principal. The Cour de Cassation held that the commercial agent was forced to obtain goods from a competitor in order to

---

[98] *CA Montpellier 4-2-2003*, JCP, cahiers de droit de l'entreprise (2003), no 7, 24.
[99] *Cass Com 28-5-2002*, D 2003, Somm Comm 459; D 2002 SC 3004 and RTDCiv 2002, 833.
[100] *Cass Com 25-9-2007*, Juris-Data 2006-14.019.

perform the contract with the clients since the principal had failed to supply the goods in question. The commercial agent's behaviour therefore did not amount to a serious breach.

## 11.4 CONCLUSION

This chapter has shown that, contrary to their English counterparts, French commercial agents have long had a specific status affording them a high level of protection. The way in which France has implemented the Directive very much reflects the legal tradition already in place. The work done by the French courts when interpreting the Commercial Code since the implementation of the Directive has also been very much in line with this legal tradition, thereby enhancing commercial agents' protection, especially in relation to the status of commercial agents. On that aspect, section 11.2 has shown how its definition, wider than that of the Directive, clearly sets out who commercial agents are and what they do, which is crucial to understanding the needs and requirements of the profession, and thereby showing why they are perceived to be the weaker party in the relationship. The case-law considered has shown that the French courts understand such needs by applying the definition restrictively so as not to expand it beyond its boundaries but nevertheless in the light of the protective stance of the legal tradition by, for instance, declaring the provision relating to agent's status to be of a mandatory nature in *SAS Glaxo Smith Kline v SARL Interpharm*.[101] We have, however, seen that in *RCE v SFR*,[102] the Cour de Cassation, in one of its most recent decisions on the meaning of 'to negotiate', appears to have a rather restrictive application of what this entails. By doing so, the Cour de Cassation appears to lower the 'negotiating' threshold quite considerably. Whether this is just a hiccup or a sign of something more worrying in the light of the protective stance of the Commercial Code, only time will tell.

In section 11.3, we have shown that the specificity of the French system is undoubtedly at its highest at the stage of performance, in relation to the notion of common interest. Where the Directive imposes a reciprocal and compulsory obligation of good faith, the Commercial Code stipulates that the commercial agency relationship is entered into for the common interest of both parties. We have shown how the common interest appears to play a similar regulatory role to good faith since it is used by the courts when assessing the performance of the parties' obligations. The role of the common interest appears most important in relation to the obligation of loyalty, for which the courts require a very high standard from the commercial agent who is bound not only during the contract but even after the relationship has ended. On that aspect, the French courts appear to have as strong a standard as their English counterparts in relation to the fiduciary obligations of the agent.

---

[101] *CA Paris 2-5-2002*, Juris-Data 2002-181440.
[102] *Cass Com 15-1-2008*, Juris-Data 2008-042333, D 2008, 350.

In section 11.4, we have considered the one area where implementation has brought significant change to the legal tradition: that of secondary activities. Following the choice left in the Directive, but perhaps contrary to expectation given the protective stance of the legal tradition, France opted for the possibility of excluding from the protection of the Commercial Code commercial agents whose agency activities are regarded as secondary. We have seen that the manner in which France has done so is peculiar to that tradition and certainly very different from what is happening in the UK. The scope of the relevant provision of the Commercial Code in that respect is clearly wider than what was anticipated at its inception, since it will apply to any commercial agent who works for his principal in two different capacities.

Moreover, the French courts have rejected the argument that the exclusion is against the mandatory nature of the right for the commercial agent to claim compensation. In spite of this, the French courts play an important regulatory role by checking whether the renunciation of the protection of the status is valid. The approach of the courts in that role appears not only methodical and logical but, most importantly, appears to ensure that principals cannot abuse their ability to resort to Article L 134-15 Commercial Code.

# 12

# Valuation

Dr Ruth Bender
*Cranfield School of Management*

## 12.1 OUTLINE

THIS CHAPTER EXPLAINS some of the main methods used in valuing businesses. An agent is entitled to compensation suffered as the result of termination of the relationship with the principal. During the period of the agency, the agent has helped to build up goodwill in the combined business: on its termination the agent should be compensated for the future value that would be generated from that goodwill. This can be determined through valuing the business.

Three methods of valuation are considered, with valuation using discounted cash flow (DCF) being the preferred alternative.

## 12.2 APPROACHING A BUSINESS VALUATION

A commercial valuation reflects the future earning power of the asset, ie the business. This could arise in two different ways: from continuing to run the business as a going concern, or, if it would achieve more, from selling off its assets to the highest bidder.

In order to determine which of these valuations will give the higher amount, a strategic analysis is necessary. Without doing such an analysis, it will be impossible to evaluate how much money can be generated from the business, and thus what its value should be. Past profitability may give an indication of where the future lies for the business, but changes to the industry or to the operations of the individual business (other than, obviously, the agency termination) could change that dramatically.

Once the strategic analysis has been done, a set of forecasts for the business can be prepared, on which a valuation can be based.

## 12.3 STRATEGIC ANALYSIS

A useful way to approach strategic analysis is to consider first the industry and secondly the business itself. For valuation of an agency that is being terminated, this almost certainly will mean an analysis of the principal's industry, ie that of the products or services being distributed, as well as analysing the agency's own industry and competitors. Furthemore, depending on the nature of the agency, several different industries may need to be considered.

A common tool for industry analysis is the Five Forces model developed by Michael Porter.[1] Porter considered that the profitability of firms within an industry would be a function of how attractive that industry was. His model identifies five different forces that affect industry attractiveness.

| | |
|---|---|
| Degree of rivalry | The number of rivals and the intensity of rivalry will affect profitability. A crowded industry, with many players fighting for market share, will generate less profit for its incumbents than will a monopoly situation. A mature industry with three or four equally matched players is likely to prove more profitable for most of the participants than one where one company has 80 per cent of the market and a few others are scrabbling for the remainder. Likewise, the way in which the rivals compete is important: an industry with regular price wars is never going to generate super-profits for its participants. |
| Supplier power | Powerful suppliers can ensure that they retain most of the profit along a supply chain. Indicators of supplier power include situations where there are few choices of inputs, or if there are few suppliers of those inputs. Inputs could include materials and key services, but specialised labour is also a valuable supply. Supplier power can be reduced if the business has alternative sources of supply, if the supplier is dependent on the business as its main outlet, or if the relevant goods or services can easily be replaced. |
| Buyer power | Buyers can exert significant power over their supply chains. For example, some of the larger supermarket chains can specify quality, price and credit terms, ensuring their own profit at the expense of their suppliers. Indicators of buyer power include the size and importance of the buyer. Buyer power can be reduced if the buyer has 'switching costs', ie it would be expensive and/or time-consuming to change from one supplier to another. |

---

[1] Porter, M. *Competitive Strategy* (The Free Press, 2004).

| Threat of new entrants | In a profitable industry where there are no barriers to entry, new entrants will be attracted to join the industry and the super-profits will be competed away. Thus profitable industries tend to have barriers to entry that prevent or deter these new entrants. Barriers to entry are many and varied. They can include, for example: patents; a recognised brand; an established distribution infrastructure; a skilled workforce; or a network of trade contacts. |
|---|---|
| Threat of substitutes | If the customer or consumer can fulfil their need by buying a substitute product, then the profitability of an industry is reduced. Substitutes need to be considered in their widest sense. For example, a substitute for a cheap car might be a motorcycle, or to do without. However, a substitute for an expensive car, bought as a status symbol, could be a variety of other sorts of ostentatious spending. |

Having examined the Five Forces and established how attractive an industry currently is, the valuation demands that its future attractiveness be considered. To do this, a PESTLE analysis can be done. In this, the following issues are considered to see how the industry might develop:

Political
Economic
Social
Technological
Legal
Environmental

Examples of how PESTLE factors could affect the profitability of an industry would include: possible changes in health and safety regulations that might make a product more expensive; or new technologies that might make it obsolete; a forthcoming recession that might make it too expensive; or societal changes that might make it socially unacceptable. From analysis of these, a currently profitable business could be seen to have limited potential, or an unsuccessful business could see its route to profits.

Once the structure and potential of the industry are understood, the business itself needs to be considered. In valuing an agency for termination, it seems likely that two businesses will be relevant here: the agency's business and also the principal's. The future profitability of the agent is dependent on both of these.

For both of these businesses, an analysis of the strengths and weaknesses will be useful, together with an understanding of the opportunities and threats that come from the external environment. Specific matters to consider as regards the principal's business include the positioning of its products against competitors, in terms of both price and quality.

A good analysis of strategic issues is an essential element of the valuation. If the agent is being compensated for damage arising from the termination of the agency relationship, it is important to understand exactly what has been lost.

## 12.4 MAIN TECHNIQUES FOR VALUATION

Three main techniques are used to value businesses: an assets basis, profit multiples, and DCF. Of these, the DCF method involves the most work, but probably gives the best picture of the business.

Because business valuation is quite subjective, it is common for valuers to use more than one technique in the valuation, to sense-check results. Generally this would be done by comparing results of the DCF and the profit multiples methods. Both of these methods rely on the business's profit and cash flow rather than just its assets.

## 12.5 VALUATION ON AN ASSETS BASIS

When we speak about the value of a business, we are referring to the value, for a company, of its equity, the ordinary shareholders' funds. This is what is left after all the other stakeholders' claims have been deducted from the value of the assets.

Valuing an agency based on its published balance sheet without alteration is unlikely to give a meaningful result. For most companies, the balance sheet values of assets will represent the historic prices paid for them, not their current values. Accordingly, a valuation based on the balance sheet should include property and other significant assets at their current realisable values (what they could fetch in a sale, less costs of selling them at that price).

Another problem is that accounting conventions are such that internally generated goodwill and intangibles are not included on the balance sheet, with the result that for most businesses the balance sheet undervalues the business. The exception to this is where the owners could obtain more for selling the separate assets than they could for selling the business as a going concern. Of course, in such a circumstance, it is difficult to see why terminating the agency should cause financial hardship to the agent.

It might be the case that the agency owns assets that are 'separable', ie they could be sold off without affecting its ongoing business. As an example, the business could be run, mostly over the telephone and internet, from a room in a stately home owned by the company. Clearly, a valuation of the whole company would have to include the value of that property, as it is a company asset. Equally clearly, the agent has not lost this asset when the agency relationship is terminated, and so any compensation valuation should not reflect this asset.

## 12.6 DEFINING PROFITS AND CASH FLOW

Values on profit multiples or DCF both reflect the business's profits and cash flow. In order to explain how these work, it is necessary to set out some relevant terminology.

The profit a company makes on its operating activities, before paying any interest on borrowings, is known as its *operating profit*. Another name for this is the *earnings before interest and tax (EBIT)*, or *profit before interest and tax (PBIT)*. The operating profit is the profit earned on the net assets of the business (fixed and current assets less non-financing liabilities).

The term we use for the value of these net assets of the business, however they have been financed, is the *enterprise value (EV)*. Deducting the borrowings from the enterprise value gives the value of equity.

From the operating profit are deducted first any interest payments and secondly the tax charge. What is left is the *profit after tax*, and this belongs to the ordinary shareholders, the value of whose investment is the *equity*.[2] Ordinary dividends are deducted as an appropriation from this profit after tax, but their level is not relevant to valuing a 100 per cent stake in a business.

As regards cash flows used for valuation, the key term is *free cash flow*. This is the cash flow generated or used in operations in a period, before allowing for interest, dividends, loan repayments or any other financing flows. The calculation of free cash flow is as follows:

Operating profit
+ depreciation charge (which has reduced profit but has no cash impact)
– tax
– expenditure on fixed assets
± changes in working capital (net increases or decreases in inventories, debtors and trade creditors)
= free cash flow

## 12.7 VALUATION ON MULTIPLES

The logic behind a valuation on multiples is to compare the target business, the value of which is unknown, with a listed company (or preferably companies) in a similar area of activity. As the businesses are in the same line of operations, the thinking is that the ratio of company value to profits should be broadly similar.

Immediately one can see flaws in this approach. There may not be a listed company that has truly comparable activities, particularly when conducting the valuation of an agency. Further, listed companies tend to be large, and so have a different balance of risks and returns, both of which affect valuation. Their

---

[2] Further deductions may arise due to appropriations for non-equity shareholders (eg preference dividends), but this is not common.

value also reflects market sentiment rather than just their own position, and so at any time could be artificially high or low.

Despite these flaws, valuation on multiples is the most commonly adopted valuation method for companies in general, probably because of its ease of use. It is worth discussing for that reason. The steps to complete such a valuation are as follows.

1.  Determine the *sustainable* operating profit of the target business. The sustainable profit reflects what the business can make in an average year on an ongoing basis, ignoring any extraordinary costs or gains in the year, or any unusually large or small remuneration or charges taken by the owner.

2.  From the sustainable operating profit, deduct interest and tax to arrive at a profit after tax.

3.  Find one or more listed companies whose businesses could be said to be comparable to the target company. Take the average of their *price/earnings ratios* (*P/E ratios*).

    The P/E is the ratio of the company's share price to its *earnings per share* (*eps*). The eps is the amount of profit after tax earned for each ordinary share. Hence, the higher the P/E ratio, the more expensive a share is compared to the current level of earnings, which probably reflects the market's anticipation of high growth in profits. P/E ratios of listed companies are readily available in newspapers or on the internet.

    The ratio of share price to eps reflects the situation for an individual share. On a whole-company base, this is the same as the value of all of the equity (known as the *market capitalisation*) to the profit after tax.

4.  At this stage, the valuer generally uses professional judgement to reduce (or very occasionally increase) the market P/E ratio by a factor, to make it more relevant to the target company. Such reductions reflect differences in the companies' risk profiles and growth potential. Often, the deduction is by a factor of between 25 and 50 per cent.

5.  The equity value of the target company is derived by multiplying the adjusted P/E ratio by the target's sustainable profit after tax.

Rather than use the P/E as the multiple for valuation, many professionals prefer to use an EBIT multiple or an EBITDA multiple. These reflect the ratio of enterprise value to EBIT or to EBITDA, respectively. (EBITDA is EBIT before charging any depreciation or amortisation. Many practitioners prefer it, as it is seen as a proxy for cash flow, and is not distorted by accounting policies on depreciation of assets.) The ratio of EV/EBIT(DA) is not readily available from published sources as is the P/E ratio, but can be calculated using the listed companies' accounts.

If an EV-based multiple is used, the value determined for the target company is its enterprise value. However, what is needed is its equity value. Thus, the final stage is to deduct the company's borrowings from the enterprise value, to arrive at the equity value.

A fundamental problem with any valuation on multiples is that they rely on the underlying market being 'correct'. However, if stock market prices are unrepresentative, so will be any value based on these. During the dotcom boom, technology and media companies were overvalued, and basic engineering companies often undervalued; any valuation based on comparisons with these could have produced misleading results.

One other use of multiples is worth noting in valuing a business. In many industries, custom and practice suggests that businesses will change hands on a multiple of turnover, or a multiple of a physical quantity such as the number of units sold in a year. It is worthwhile to be aware of these, but essential to understand the underlying logic before using them.

## 12.8 VALUATION USING DISCOUNTED CASH FLOW

DCF is likely to be the most appropriate method of valuation for an agency, as it reflects the strategic analysis of the profits and cash flows arising from the agency, and does not require knowledge of any comparable listed companies. Because it reflects forecasts of the performance of the target business, rather than comparable multiples, DCF is known as valuation on *fundamentals*.

The logic underlying a DCF valuation is as follows. The value of a business is the amount of cash that it will generate for its owners year after year into the future. Cash received now is worth more than cash received in the future. Therefore we project out the cash flow stream into the future, and discount it for the reduction in value of the more distant funds.

The steps in valuing a company using DCF are as follows:

1. Determine a suitable initial time period for the valuation. In theory, this is the period over which you expect the company to maintain a competitive advantage. In practice, ten years is often used, unless it is clear that the business would not run for that long.
2. Based on the strategic analysis, forecast the free cash flow of the company for each year over that initial period.
3. Estimate the terminal value—what you think the business will be worth at the end of that initial period. There are several ways to do this, for example by assuming that cash flows in the final year will remain constant forever, or will grow at the average rate of the economy forever. As each variant gives a different result, valuers tend to use several methods.
4. Determine a suitable *cost of capital* for the investment. This cost of capital reflects the average requirements of the company's debt and equity funders.
5. Discount the cash flows, using the cost of capital. This involves applying a reverse interest calculation to the money to be received in the future. For example, if the forecast cash flow for next year is £11,000 and the cost of capital is 10 per cent, then the value of those cash flows in today's terms is £10,000: putting £10,000 on deposit at 10 per cent today would give that

£11,000 next year. Tables and calculators are available to make discounting easier.

6.   Add in the cost of any separable, non-operating assets. As discussed above, these are assets that can be sold without affecting the business.
7.   At this point you have calculated the *enterprise value*—the value of the whole business, which has been financed in several ways.
8.   The equity value is the enterprise value less the amount of borrowing the business has.

Although DCF analysis contains a many assumptions, a great advantage of it is that it can easily support a sensitivity analysis, with the underlying figures being changed to reflect different potential scenarios. A good understanding of the value of the business can be built up in this way.

### 12.9 VALUING GOODWILL

The advantage of using profit multiples or DCF analysis as the valuation technique is that there is no need to carry out a separate valuation of the company's 'goodwill'. Any goodwill would be reflected in the stream of profits generated by the business. As both of these methods value that stream of profits, the goodwill is implicitly included in the valuation produced.

### 12.10 VALUING PART OF A BUSINESS

It might be that the agency to be terminated represents only one income stream in a larger agency business. Both multiples-based and DCF valuations can still be used to value such an income stream. It is, however, important to ensure that costs are allocated reasonably across the different parts of the business.

Any costs that will no longer be incurred once the agency is terminated (*direct costs*) clearly belong in the valuation of that business, as it is the net profit that is being lost, not the gross sales stream.

As regards shared costs, valuation techniques differ. If the agency being terminated represents only a small part of the whole business, then it may be unreasonable to assume that any central costs will be cut. In such an instance, only the direct costs would be an appropriate deduction against profits and cash flows.

If, however, the terminated business forms the major part of the whole, then it may be appropriate for the agent to restructure the cost base once this agency is terminated. This being so, a large proportion of the cost base may be associated with the terminated business.

## 12.11 CONCLUSION

Company valuation is a complex subject, and even professional valuers will often disagree over what is the 'correct' answer. This chapter has set out an overview of the key techniques and considerations, but expert advice should always be sought.

## 12.12 LIST OF DEFINITIONS

| | |
|---|---|
| Cost of capital | The average return expected by a company's debt and equity investors. |
| Direct costs | The direct costs of an operation are costs that would be avoided if that operation were closed down. |
| Discounted cash flow (DCF) | A technique for calculating the present-day value of a stream of income to be received in the future. |
| Earnings per share (eps) | The profit after tax earned for each individual share in the company. |
| Enterprise value (EV) | The value of assets net of trading liabilities. It reflects the total value of financing in the business, debt and equity. |
| Equity value | The value of the shareholders' stake in the company. |
| Free cash flow | The cash flow generated from operations after allowing for tax payments, purchases of fixed assets and investment in working capital. |
| Market capitalisation | The number of shares in a listed company multiplied by the current market price of its shares. |
| Operating profit/EBIT/PBIT | Profit before deducting interest or tax. |
| P/E ratio | The price/earnings ratio is the current share price (of a listed company) divided by the eps |
| Sustainable profit | Profits adjusted for one-off or unusual items and charges or gains that would not be relevant under different ownership. |

# Appendix 1

# The Commercial Agents (Council Directive) Regulations 1993

(SI 1993/3053)

*Made on 7 December 1993 by the Secretary of State in exercise of the powers conferred on him by s 2(2) of the European Communities Act 1972, operative from 1 January 1994.*

## ARRANGEMENT OF REGULATIONS

SCHEDULE


PART I—GENERAL


## Citation, Commencement and Applicable Law


1(1)   These Regulations may be cited as the Commercial Agents (Council Directive) Regulations 1993 and shall come into force on 1st January 1994.

1(2)   These Regulations govern the relations between commercial agents and their principals and, subject to paragraph (3), apply in relation to the activities of commercial agents in Great Britain.

1(3)   [A Court or tribunal shall:

(a)  apply the law of the other member State concerned in place of regulations 3 to 22 where the parties have agreed that the agency contract is to be governed by the law of that member State;

(b)  (whether or not it would otherwise be required to do so) apply these regulations where the law of another member State corresponding to these regulations enables the parties to agree that the agency contract is to be governed by the law of a different member State and the parties have agreed that it is to be governed by the law of England and Wales or Scotland.

## Interpretation, application and extent

2(1)  In these regulations:
'**commercial agent**' means a self-employed intermediary who has continuing authority to negotiate the sale or purchase of goods on behalf of another person (the 'principal'), or to negotiate and conclude the sale or purchase of goods on behalf of and in the name of that principal; but shall be understood as not including in particular:
  (i) a person who, in his capacity as an officer of a company or association, is empowered to enter into commitments binding on that company or association;
  (ii) a partner who is lawfully authorised to enter into commitments binding on his partners;
  (iii) a person who acts as an insolvency practitioner (as that expression is defined in section 388 of the Insolvency Act 1986, or the equivalent in any other jurisdiction;
'**commission**' means any part of the remuneration of a commercial agent which varies with the number or value of business transactions;
'**EEA Agreement**' means the Agreement on the European Economic Area signed at Oporto on 2 May 1992 as adjusted by the Protocol signed at Brussels on 17 March 1993;
'**Member State**' includes a State which is a contracting party to the EEA Agreement;
'**restraint of trade clause**' means an agreement restricting the business activities of a commercial agent following termination of the agency contract.
2(2)  These regulations do not apply to:
  (a)  commercial agents whose activities are unpaid;
  (b)  commercial agents when they operate on commodity exchanges or in the commodity market;
  (c)  the Crown Agents for Overseas Governments and Administrations as set up under the Crown Agents Act 1979, or its subsidiaries.
2(3)  The provisions of the Schedule to these Regulations have effect for the purpose of determining the persons whose activities as commercial agents are to be considered secondary.
2(4)  These regulations shall not apply to the persons referred to in paragraph (3) above.
2(5)  These regulations do not extend to Northern Ireland.

PART II—RIGHTS AND OBLIGATIONS

## Duties of a commercial agent to his principal

3(1)  In performing his activities a commercial agent must look after the interests of his principal and act dutifully and in good faith.

---

[1] The words in brackets were substituted by the Commercial Agents (Council Directive) (Amendment) Regulations 1998 (SI 1998/2868).

3(2)   In particular, a commercial agent must:
    (a) make proper efforts to negotiate and, where appropriate, conclude the trans-
        actions he is instructed to take care of;
    (b) communicate to his principal all the necessary information available to him;
    (c) comply with reasonable instructions given by his principal.

## Duties of a principal to his commercial agent

4(1)   In his relations with his commercial agent a principal must act dutifully and in good
    faith.
4(2)   In particular, a principal must:
    (a) provide his commercial agent with the necessary documentation relating to the
        goods concerned;
    (b) obtain for his commercial agent the information necessary for the performance
        of his agency contract, and in particular notify his commercial agent within a
        reasonable period once he anticipates that the volume of commercial trans-
        actions will be significantly lower than that which the commercial agent could
        normally have expected.
4(3)   A principal shall, in addition, inform his commercial agent within a reasonable
    period of his acceptance or refusal of, and of any non-execution by him of, a com-
    mercial transaction which the commercial agent has procured for him.

## Prohibition on derogation from regulations 3 and 4 and consequence of breach

5(1)   The parties may not derogate from regulations 3 and 4 above.
5(2)   The law applicable to the contract shall govern the consequence of breach of the
    rights and obligations under regulations 3 and 4 above.

PART III—REMUNERATION

## Form and amount of remuneration in absence of agreement

6(1)   In the absence of any agreement as to remuneration between the parties, a commer-
    cial agent shall be entitled to the remuneration that commercial agents appointed for
    the goods forming the subject of his agency contract are customarily allowed in the
    place where he carries on his activities and, if there is no such customary practice, a
    commercial agent shall be entitled to reasonable remuneration taking into account
    all aspects of the transaction.
6(2)   This regulation is without prejudice to the application of any enactment or rule of
    law concerning the level of remuneration.
6(3)   Where a commercial agent is not remunerated (wholly or in part) by commission,
    regulations 7 to 12 below shall not apply.

## Entitlement to commission on transactions concluded during agency contract

7(1)  A commercial agent shall be entitled to commission on commercial transactions concluded during the period covered by the agency contract:
   (a) where the transaction has been concluded as a result of his action; or
   (b) where the transaction is concluded with a third party whom he has previously acquired as a customer for transactions of the same kind.

7(2)  A commercial agent shall also be entitled to commission on transactions concluded during the period covered by the agency contract where he has an exclusive right to a specific geographical area or to a specific group of customers and where the transaction has been entered into with a customer belonging to that area or group.

## Entitlement to commission on transactions concluded after agency contract has terminated

8  Subject to regulation 9 below, a commercial agent shall be entitled to commission on commercial transactions concluded after the agency contract has terminated if:
   (a) the transaction is mainly attributable to his efforts during the period covered by the agency contract and if the transaction was entered into within a reasonable period after that contract terminated; or
   (b) in accordance with the conditions mentioned in regulation 7 above, the order of the third party reached the principal or the commercial agent before the agency contract terminated.

## Apportionment of commission between new and previous commercial agents

9(1)  A commercial agent shall not be entitled to the commission referred to in regulation 7 above if that commission is payable, by virtue of regulation 8 above, to the previous commercial agent, unless it is equitable because of the circumstances for the commission to be shared between the commercial agents.

9(2)  The principal shall be liable for any sum due under paragraph (1) above to the person entitled to it in accordance with that paragraph, and any sum which the other commercial agent receives to which he is not entitled shall be refunded to the principal.

## When commission due and date for payment

10(1)  Commission shall become due as soon as, and to the extent that, one of the following circumstances occurs:
   (a) the principal has executed the transaction; or
   (b) the principal should, according to his agreement with the third party, have executed the transaction; or
   (c) the third party has executed the transaction.

10(2)  Commission shall become due at the latest when the third party has executed his part of the transaction or should have done so if the principal had executed his part of the transaction, as he should have.

10(3)  The commission shall be paid not later than on the last day of the month following the quarter in which it became due, and, for the purposes of these regulations, unless otherwise agreed between the parties, the first quarter period shall run from the date the agency contract takes effect and subsequent periods shall run from that date in the third month thereafter or the beginning of the fourth month, whichever is the sooner.

10(4)  Any agreement to derogate from paragraphs (2) and (3) above to the detriment of the commercial agent shall be void.

## Extinction of right to commission

11(1)  The right to commission can be extinguished only if and to the extent that:
    (a)  it is established that the contract between the third party and the principal will not be executed; and
    (b)  that fact is due to a reason for which the principal is not to blame.

11(2)  Any commission which the commercial agent has already received shall be refunded if the right to it is extinguished.

11(3)  Any agreement to derogate from paragraph (1) above to the detriment of the commercial agent shall be void.

## Periodic supply of information as to commission due and right of inspection of principal's books

12(1)  The principal shall supply his commercial agent with a statement of the commission due, not later than the last day of the month following the quarter in which the commission has become due, and such statement shall set out the main components used in calculating the amount of the commission.

12(2)  A commercial agent shall be entitled to demand that he be provided with all the information (and in particular an extract from the books) which is available to his principal and which he needs in order to check the amount of the commission due to him.

12(3)  Any agreement to derogate from paragraphs (1) and (2) above shall be void.

12(4)  Nothing in this regulation shall remove or restrict the effect of, or prevent reliance upon, any enactment or rule of law which recognises the right of an agent to inspect the books of a principal.

PART IV—CONCLUSION AND TERMINATION OF THE AGENCY CONTRACT

## Right to signed written statement of terms of agency contract

13(1)  The commercial agent and principal shall each be entitled to receive from the other, on request, a signed written document setting out the terms of the agency contract including any terms subsequently agreed.

13(2)  Any purported waiver of the right referred to in paragraph (1) above shall be void.

## Conversion of agency contract after expiry of fixed period

14 An agency contract for a fixed period which continues to be performed by both parties after that period has expired shall be deemed to be converted into an agency contract for an indefinite period.

## Minimum periods of notice for termination of agency contract

15(1) Where an agency contract is concluded for an indefinite period either party may terminate it by notice.

15(2) The period of notice shall be—
(a) 1 month for the first year of the contract;
(b) 2 months for the second year commenced;
(c) 3 months for the third year commenced and for the subsequent years;
and the parties may not agree on any shorter periods of notice.

15(3) If the parties agree on longer periods than those laid down in paragraph (2) above, the period of notice to be observed by the principal must not be shorter than that to be observed by the commercial agent.

15(4) Unless otherwise agreed by the parties, the end of the period of notice must coincide with the end of a calendar month.

15(5) The provisions of this regulation shall also apply to an agency contract for a fixed period where it is converted under regulation 14 above into an agency contract for an indefinite period subject to the proviso that the earlier fixed period must be taken into account in the calculation of the period of notice.

## Savings with regard to immediate termination

16 These Regulations shall not affect the application of any enactment or rule of law which provides for the immediate termination of the agency contract—
(a) because of the failure of one party to carry out all or part of his obligations under that contract; or
(b) where exceptional circumstances arise.

## Entitlement of commercial agent to indemnity or compensation on termination of agency contract

17(1) This regulation has effect for the purpose of ensuring that the commercial agent is, after termination of the agency contract, indemnified in accordance with paragraphs (3) to (5) below or compensated for damage in accordance with paragraphs (6) and (7) below.

17(2) Except where the agency contract otherwise provides, the commercial agent shall be entitled to be compensated rather than indemnified.

17(3)   Subject to paragraph (9) and to regulation 18 below, the commercial agent shall be entitled to an indemnify if and to the extent that—

(a) he has brought the principal new customers or has significantly increased the volume of business with existing customers and the principal continues to derive substantial benefits from the business with such customers; and

(b) the payment of this indemnity is equitable having regard to all the circumstances and, in particular, the commission lost by the commercial agent on the business transacted with such customers.

17(4)   The amount of the indemnity shall not exceed a figure equivalent to an indemnity for one year calculated from the commercial agent's average annual remuneration over the preceding five years and if the contract goes back less than five years the indemnity shall be calculated on the average for the period in question.

17(5)   The grant of an indemnity as mentioned above shall not prevent the commercial agent from seeking damages.

17(6)   Subject to paragraph (9) and to regulation 18 below, the commercial agent shall be entitled to compensation for the damage he suffers as a result of the termination of his relations with his principal.

17(7)   For the purpose of these regulations such damage shall be deemed to occur particularly when the termination takes place in either or both of the following circumstances, namely circumstances which—

(a) deprive the commercial agent of the commission which proper performance of the agency contract would have procured for him whilst providing his principal with substantial benefits linked to the activities of the commercial agent; or

(b) have not enabled the commercial agent to amortize the costs and expenses that he had incurred in the performance of the agency contract on the advice of his principal.

17(8)   Entitlement to the indemnity or compensation for damage as provided for under paragraphs (2) to (7) above shall also arise where the agency contract is terminated as a result of the death of the commercial agent.

17(9)   The commercial agent shall lose his entitlement to the indemnity or compensation for damage in the instances provided for in paragraphs (2) to (8) above if within one year following termination of his agency contract he has not notified his principal that he intends pursuing his entitlement

## Grounds for excluding payment of indemnity or compensation under regulation 17

18   The [indemnity or]² compensation referred to in regulation 17 above shall not be payable to the commercial agent where—

(a) the principal has terminated the agency contract because of default attributable to the commercial agent which would justify immediate termination of the agency contract pursuant to regulation 16 above; or

(b) the commercial agent has himself terminated the agency contract, unless such termination is justified—

---

² The words in square brackets were added by the Commercial Agents (Council Directive) (Amendment) Regulations 1993 (SI 1993/3173).

      (i) by circumstances attributable to the principal, or

      (ii) on grounds of the age, infirmity or illness of the commercial agent in consequence of which he cannot reasonably be required to continue his activities; or

    (c) the commercial agent, with the agreement of his principal, assigns his rights and duties under the agency contract to another person.

## Prohibition on derogation under regulations 17 and 18

19    The parties may not derogate from regulations 17 and 18 to the detriment of the commercial agent before the agency contract expires.

## Restraint of trade clauses

20(1)  A restraint of trade clause shall be valid only if and to the extent that—

    (a) it is concluded in writing; and

    (b) it relates to the geographical area or the group of customers and the geographical area entrusted to the commercial agent and to the kind of goods covered by his agency under the contract.

20(2)  A restraint of trade clause shall be valid for not more than two years after termination of the agency contract.

20(3)  Nothing in this regulation shall affect any enactment of rule or law which imposes other restrictions on the validity or enforceability of restraint of trade clauses or which enables a court to reduce the obligations on the parties resulting from such clauses.

PART V—MISCELLANEOUS AND SUPPLEMENTAL

## Disclosure of information

21    Nothing in these Regulations shall require information to be given where such disclosure would be contrary to public policy.

## Service of notice etc.

22(1)  Any notice, statement or other document to be given or supplied to a commercial agent or to be given or supplied to the principal under these regulations may be so given or supplied:

    (a) by delivering it to him;

    (b) by leaving it at his proper address addressed to him by name;

    (c) by sending it by post to him addressed either to his registered address or to the address of his registered or principal office;

or by any other means provided for in the agency contract.

22(2) Any such notice, statement or document may—
  (a) in the case of a body corporate, be given or served on the secretary or clerk of that body;
  (b) in the case of a partnership, be given to or served on any partner or on any person having the control or management of the partnership business.

## Transitional provisions

23(1) Notwithstanding any provision in an agency contract made before 1 January 1994, these Regulations shall apply to that contract after that date and, accordingly any provision which is inconsistent with these regulations shall have effect subject to them.

23(2) Nothing in these regulations shall affect the rights and liabilities of a commercial agent or a principal which have accrued before 1 January 1994.

THE SCHEDULE

Regulation 2(3)

1    The activities of a person as a commercial agent are to be considered secondary where it may reasonably be taken that the primary purpose of the arrangement with his principal is other than as set out in paragraph 2 below.

2    An arrangement falls within this paragraph if—
  (a) the business of the principal is the sale, or as the case may be purchase, of goods of a particular kind; and
  (b) the goods concerned are such that—
    (i) transactions are normally individually negotiated and concluded on a commercial basis, and
    (ii) procuring a transaction on one occasion is likely to lead to further transactions in those goods with that customer on future occasions, or to transactions in those goods with other customers in the same geographical area or among the same group of customers, and
  that accordingly it is in the commercial interests of the principal in developing the market in those goods to appoint a representative to such customers with a view to the representative devoting effort, skill and expenditure from his own resources to that end.

3    The following are indications that an arrangement falls within paragraph 2 above, and the absence of any of them is an indication to the contrary—
  (a) the principal is the manufacturer, importer or distributor of the goods;
  (b) the goods are specifically identified with the principal in the market in question rather than, or to a greater extent than, with any other person;
  (c) the agent devotes substantially the whole of his time to representative activities (whether for one principal or for a number of principals whose interests are not conflicting);
  (d) the goods are not normally available in the market in question other than by means of the agent;

(e)  the arrangement is described as one of commercial agency.

4    The following are indications that an arrangement does not fall within para 2 above—

(a)  promotional material is supplied direct to potential customers;

(b)  persons are granted agencies without reference to existing agents in a particular area or in relation to a particular group;

(c)  customers normally select the goods for themselves and merely place their orders through the agent.

5    The activities of the following categories of persons are presumed, unless the contrary is established, not to fall within paragraph 2 above—

Mail order catalogue agents for consumer goods.

Consumer credit agents.

# Appendix 2

# Department of Trade and Industry: Implementation of the EC Directive on Self-Employed Commercial Agents

**An Explanatory and Consultative Note**

## CONTENTS

### INTRODUCTION

The EC Directive on self-employed commercial agents (Council Directive 86/653/EEC) was adopted on 18 December 1986 after some ten years of discussion. The purpose of the Directive is to harmonise the laws of the Member States on the relationship between commercial agents and their principals and to strengthen the position of the commercial agent. It does this by setting out basic rules regulating the main aspects of the agency contract between them. The United Kingdom and Ireland are required to adapt their laws to give effect to the Directive by 1 January 1994. The remaining Member States must implement the Directive by 1 January 1990 although Italy, exceptionally, has until 1 January 1993 to implement Article 17.

2     The present legal position in the United Kingdom is described at A of this Consultative Document. At B the main features of the individual Articles of the Directive are summarised and explanatory notes given where appropriate. Two Articles of the Directive require Member States to choose one of two specific alternatives. Also, in respect of certain other Articles the Directive allows Member States to take different positions on a few points. These options are discussed in C.

197

3    The Department would welcome views on the various issues described in this Consultative Document. They should be sent by Friday 30 October 1987 to:
>    Chemicals, Textiles, Paper, Timber,
>    Miscellaneous Manufacturing and Service
>    Industries Division (CTPS)
>    Department of Trade and Industry
>    Room 804A
>    Ashdown House
>    123 Victoria Street
>    London SW1E 6RB

4    Further copies of this Consultative Document can be obtained by telephoning (01) 212 0022 or by applying in writing to the address given in the previous paragraph.


A THE LEGAL POSITION

5    There is little United Kingdom statute law in this area: the rights and duties of the principal and commercial agent depend on the express or implied terms of the agency relationship between them. Common law rules exist which apply in the absence of, or may override, express stipulation by the parties. The rules which will apply when the Directive is implemented will be significantly different and will involve changes in the existing law to introduce detailed provisions governing certain aspects of the relationship between principal and agent. It is proposed to make the necessary changes through secondary legislation under Section 2(2) of the European Communities Act 1972. There are further comments in part B when individual Articles refer to the position under Member States national laws.


B SUMMARY OF THE DIRECTIVE

## Chapter 1: Scope

6    *Article 1* requires Member States to apply the harmonisation measures outlined in the Directive to their laws governing the relationship between commercial agents and their principals. It defines the term "commercial agent" for the purposes of the Directive as being a self-employed intermediary (individual, company or partnership) who has continuing authority to negotiate the purchase or sale of goods on behalf of another person (the principal) or to negotiate and conclude such transactions on behalf of and in the name of that principal. The Directive applies to both incorporated and unincorporated bodies as well as individuals.

7    Article 1 also lists certain categories of persons the term "commercial agent" is *not* regarded as including. These are:
>    —officers of a company or association (as agents of the company or association) and partners (as agents of the partnership);
>    —receivers, liquidators and trustees in bankruptcy.

8    The Directive does not apply to commercial agents or distributors who purchase on their own account and in their own name (as principals) for resale nor does it apply

to services. The wide range of service agencies such as travel agents, advertising agents and so on, are not covered.

9    *Article 2* lists categories of commercial agent specifically excluded from the scope of the Directive. These are:

—commercial agents whose activities are unpaid, ie not paid by monetary consideration or in kind;

—commercial agents when they operate on commodity exchanges or in the commodity market. A clearer definition will be required in the United Kingdom's implementing legislation and comments are invited from those with a particular interest or involvement in this area on a definition along the following lines:-

commercial agents operating on a commodity exchange in any part of the world or in the commodity market. For the purposes of this exclusion the term 'commodity market' is defined as a 'a market for any kind of tangible assets (other than assets of a financial nature) which is in fact traded on a commodity exchange in any part of the world'

—the Crown Agents for Overseas Governments.

10   Member States are also given the option of not applying the Directive to people whose activities as commercial agents are considered secondary by the law of that Member State. It is our intention that certain secondary activities be clearly excluded from the scope of the Directive. This is discussed further under C(ii) paragraphs 50 and 51.

11   Whether Member States' commercial agents operating *outside* the European Community would be subject to the Directive would depend on the proper law governing the agency contract, ie if the law governing the agency contract was that of a Member State then the Directive would apply.


## Chapter II: Rights and Obligations

12   *Article 3* lists the essential duties of the agent, notably his *general* duty to look after his principal's interests and to act "dutifully and in good faith" and his *specific* duty to make proper efforts to negotiate such business as his principal has entrusted to him to communicate with his principal and to comply with all reasonable instructions from his principal. Under United Kingdom common law the agent already has a number of fiduciary duties which broadly require him to act in good faith.

13   *Article 4* lists the essential duties of the principal. In particular it requires the principal to provide the necessary documentation and information to the agent for the performance of the agency contract to notify the agent as soon as he anticipates the volume of business will be significantly lower than the agent could normally have expected and to inform the agent of his acceptance, refusal and any non-execution of the business the agent has procured for him. In order to comply with the last requirement a principal would need to keep his agent informed of any omissions on his own part in completing his side of the transaction.

14   In addition to the mandatory requirement for the principal to inform the agent of his acceptance, refusal and any non-execution of the business the agent procured for him (Article 4(3)), it is open to Member States to include a provision requiring the

principal to inform the agent within a reasonable period of the *execution* of a commercial transaction the agent procured for the principal. This is discussed more fully at C(ii) paragraph 52.

15　*Article 5* states that the parties may not derogate from the provisions of Articles 3 and 4, ie these provisions are binding on the parties.

## Chapter III: Remuneration

16　*Article 6* records the commercial agent's right to remuneration according to customary practice in the place where he carries on his activities or, where there is no customary practice, to such remuneration as is reasonable, in the absence of prior agreement between the parties and without prejudice to Member States' compulsory provisions on the level of remuneration. There are no compulsory provisions in United Kingdom law covering the level of remuneration for commercial agents although there is generally in any event an implied term for reasonable remuneration. The "place" where the agent "carries on his activities" embraces his operating territory as well as his office base.

17　*Articles 7 to 12* only apply where the agreement or custom is that the agent is to be paid by commission (and not solely by a flat rate fee), or where the reasonable remuneration to which he is entitled in the absence of agreement or any custom is payment by commission.

18　*Article 7* specifies the circumstances under which the agent entitled to commission on commercial transactions concluded during the period of the agency contract. Commission is to be payable on repeat orders from customers *acquired* by the agent even if those orders were not placed through the agent (Article 7(1)).

Additionally, where an agent has an exclusive responsibility for a specific area or group of customers, he is again to be entitled to commission on transactions which were not negotiated by him if they were concluded with customers within that allocated area or clientele, even where those customers had *not* been acquired by him (Article 7(2)). Member States must decide whether to extend this automatic entitlement so that it applies also where the agent's field of responsibility has *not* been given to him to the exclusion of the rights of any other agent (or the principal himself) to operate within it. This is discussed further at C(i), paragraphs 40 and 41.

19　*Article 8* states that the agent is entitled to commission on commercial transactions concluded after the agency contract has come to an end if the transaction was mainly a result of the agents efforts during the period of the agency contract and the transaction was entered into within a reasonable period after the end of the agency contract and/or the order of the third party reached the principal or agent before the agency contract came to an end.

20　*Article 9* deals with the apportionment of commission between a new agent and his predecessor for the same transaction. The new agent is not entitled to commission in accordance with Article 7 if it is payable to the previous agent in accordance with Article 8, unless it is "equitable because of the circumstances" for the commission to be shared between them. The new agent therefore loses his right to commission where his predecessor was mainly responsible for the eventual transaction although this Article allows for apportionment where this would be equitable. However, no apportionment is available to the Predecessor agent who was partly but not mainly responsible for the transaction concluded by his successor.

21  *Article 10* prescribes

  (i)  the point at which commission becomes due, namely when the principal has or should have carried out the transaction or, if earlier, the third party has completed his part of the transaction. (Article 10 goes on to add that the latest date that the commission is due is when the third party has carried out his part of the transaction or should have done so if the principal had completed his part of the transaction as he should have; but it is difficult to see what this adds).

  (ii)  the time of payment of commission.

The parties are only permitted to agree on different provisions to those set out in Articles 10(2) and (3) if these are no less favourable to the agent.

22  *Article 11* outlines the circumstances when the agent's right to commission is forfeited. It is intended to *protect* the agent's right to commission by specifying that this right can only be extinguished in the strictly limited circumstance of establishing that the contract between third party and principal will not go ahead for a reason that is not the fault of the principal (ie circumstances outside the principal's control). However, this Article also provides for commission the agent has already received to be refunded if it is established that his right to it had been extinguished. The parties may only derogate from Article 11(1) if this is to the benefit of the agent.

23  In connection with Article 11(1) non-execution of the contract is not regarded as including cases where the principal is paid in another capacity in connection with the transaction. Thus where the principal is indemnified for the non-performance of the contract by receiving payments under an insurance policy, guarantee or contract of indemnity, commission remains payable by the principal.

24  *Article 12* specifies the principal's obligation to provide the agent with a statement of commission due requiring the principal to provide the agent with all necessary information, including extracts from his (the principal's) books, to check the commission due. (However see also the comments under Article 21 which precludes any disclosure from the principal's books which would be contrary to public policy). Article 12 also stipulates that the Directive shall not conflict with Member States' national provisions which recognise the right of the agent to inspect the principal's books. Under United Kingdom law the agent has the eight to inspect the principal's books only in cases of litigation. The parties may not agree on provisions different to Articles 12(1) and (2) if they are less favourable to the agent.

## Chapter IV: Conclusion and Termination of the Agency Contract

25  *Article 13* entitles each party to receive from the other on request a signed written contract setting out the terms of the agency contract. They are entitled to require this at any time even if they have previously agreed not to. Member States are also allowed to provide that the agency contract is not valid unless evidenced in writing. This option is discussed further under C(ii) paragraph 53.

26  *Article 14* provides that an agency contract for a fixed period which continues to be performed by both parties after that period has expired shall be deemed to be

converted into an agency contract for an indefinite period. This provision is relevant to the calculation of the periods of notice which must be given to terminate an open ended (not fixed term) agency contract which are laid down in Article 15.

27    *Article 15* prescribes the minimum periods of notice for open ended agency contracts of one month for the first year of the contract, two months for the second, three months for the third and subsequent years. This Article also gives Member States the option of fixing certain minimum periods of notice for the fourth and subsequent years of the agency contract (up to a maximum of six months). This is considered in more detail at C(ii) paragraph 54.

28    Article 15 also applies to collective contracts when, in Member States' legislation, such contracts have legal or contractual force. The term "collective contracts. ordinarily means agreements between organisations of employees and those of employers. The Government is not aware of any collective contracts covering commercial agents' transactions in the United Kingdom. Consequently it is not intended to deal with this in the implementing legislation.

29    *Article 16* provides that the Directive will not affect the laws of Member States relating to immediate termination of the agency contract where (a) one party fails to carry out his obligations and (b) exceptional circumstances arise. "Exceptional circumstances" means circumstances which under the law of the Member State give grounds for immediate termination of the contractual relationship, such as force majeure or unforeseeable, uncontrollable events. Under United Kingdom law, on breach of contract by one party the other party has a right to sue for damages and may also have the right to treat the agency contract as repudiated (and so cancel it). Where exceptional circumstances arise, a frustrating event freezes the agency contract and releases the parties from any further implementation of the contract. Any payments which remain to be made cease to be payable except in so far as the court, in its discretion, decides that payment should be made for benefits already conferred or expenses already incurred.

30    *Article 17* requires Member States to include in their implementing legislation a provision ensuring that the agent is entitled, in certain circumstances, to receive *either* a lump-sum "indemnity" in accordance with the provisions of Article 17(2) *or* compensation for "damage" in accordance with the provisions of Article 17(3), as a result of termination of the agency contract. Such a provision will be new in UK law and is discussed more fully in C(i) paragraphs 42–49. Article 17(2a) Indent 2 allows Member States to take any restraint of trade clause which is included in the agency contract into account when assessing the amount of "indemnity" that is equitable. This is discussed further under C(ii) paragraph 55. Article 17(6) stipulates that the Commission shall report to the Council by 1 January 1995 on the implementation of Article 17 and submit proposals for amendments as necessary. This provision relates to a *review* of the operation of Article 17.

31    *Article 18* specifies the circumstances where the "indemnity"/compensation is not payable. These are when:
      —the agent is guilty of a repudiatory breach of the agency contract (the entitlement is unaffected where it is the principal who is in breach);
      —the agent has given contractual notice for reasons other than age, infirmity or illness:
      —the agent has assigned the benefits and obligations of the agency contract to another person with the principal's consent.

32    *Article 19* renders both Articles 17 and 18 binding to the extent that the parties may not agree on different arrangements, if they are less favourable to the agent, before the agency contract expires.

33    *Article 20* deals with restraint of trade agreements (ie agreements which restrict the agent's business activities after termination of the agency contract). It specifies that such agreements are only valid if they are in writing and relate to the geographical area, or the group of customers as well as the area, entrusted to the agent and the kind of goods covered by the agency contract. The restraint can last for up to two years only of any period for which it is expressed to last as from termination of the agency contract.

34    *Article 20 (4)* states that Article 20 shall not affect national laws that impose other restrictions on the validity or enforceability of restraint of trade agreements or which enable the courts to reduce the obligations on the parties resulting from such an agreement. In the United Kingdom there is a general common law restriction on the enforceability of restraint of trade agreements in that they must be reasonable in ambit.

35    *Article 21* specifies that nothing in the Directive shall require a Member State to provide for the disclosure of information where this would be contrary to public policy. This provision limits the agent's right to have access to extracts from the principal's books (Article 12(2)) in cases where there is information relating to national security to protect.

36    *Article 22* lays down the transitional periods for implementing the Directive. For Member States *other than the United Kingdom and Ireland* the Directive is to be implemented before 1 January 1990. It will apply as from the date of implementation to new agency contracts. Contracts already in existence at the date of implementation must comply before 1 January 1994. Subject to those limits, the date of implementation is left to the choice of individual Member States. By way of exception, Italy has until 1 January 1993 to implement Article 17. The United Kingdom and Ireland must implement the Directive by 1 January 1994 in relation to both future and current agency contracts. The United Kingdom and Ireland have been granted this additional four year transitional period in recognition of the more fundamental changes that will be required to adapt their legal systems to implement the Directive compared to the position in other Member States.

37    The Government is committed to keeping to a minimum the burden placed on business by national and Community measures. An indication from interested parties of any additional costs or delays or other burdens they are likely to face when the Directive is implemented in the United Kingdom would therefore be welcome.

38    The full text of the Directive is provided in the Annex.

C  *OPTIONS*

39    The Directive requires Member States to select one of two specific alternatives in respect of two provisions (Articles 7(2) and 17). For certain other Articles the Directive allows Member States to take different positions on some points (Articles 2(2), 4(3), 13(2), 15(3) and 17(2a) Indent 2). These options are discussed below and comments on them are invited.

### *(i) Articles where choice of a specific alternative is required*

40    Article 7(2) deals with an agent's entitlement to commission on transactions other than those initiated by himself when the principal has placed such contracts during the period of the agency contract with third parties within the agent's allocated catchment area or pool of customers. Member States are required to choose whether their legislation should confer this entitlement where the agent is entrusted with a specific geographical area or group of customers (but not necessarily exclusively) (Indent 1), or only where he has an exclusive right (Indent 2) to an area or group of customers.

41    The Government's initial preference is for Indent 2. It finds it difficult to see the justification for the wider-ranging option that Indent 1 would give to the agent. However comments are invited from interested parties on their preferred choice with supporting arguments.

42    *Article 17* introduces a new concept into United Kingdom law. It sets out the agent's right, in certain circumstances on termination of the contract, to an "indemnity" by way of recompense for contribution to the principal's continuing goodwill (Article 17(2)) *or* compensation payment for "damage" (Article 17(3)). Member States are required to include one of these options in their implementing legislation.

43    The "indemnity" or compensation is due when the agency contract is terminated. The Government regards termination as including:

    (i)    the principal's breach of the agency contract (and the agent's acceptance of his repudiation), which might include service of a notice shorter than provided for in Article 15 (Article 18(b)). In the case of an "indemnity", entitlement is to be additional to any claim for damages at common law

    (ii)   the frustration of the agency contract, including the agent's death (Article 17(4)), retirement or illness (Article 18(b)).

    (iii)  the principal giving notice under Article 15 or under an express term for early termination of a fixed-term contract, ie a break-clause:

    (iv)   the expiry by passage of time of a fixed term agency contract.

However it is a matter of doubt whether either of the events in (iii) and (iv) could give rise to any deemed "damage" for which compensation under Article 17(3) could be claimed since the termination here would not be premature.

44    No payment arises where the agent:

    (i)    is guilty of a repudiatory breach of the agency contract;

    (ii)   has given contractual notice for reasons other than age, infirmity or illness

    (iii)  has assigned the benefits and obligations of the agency contract to another person.

"Indemnity" Payment

45    Article 17(2) lists three conditions for entitlement to an "indemnity" payment:

    (i)    contribution by the agent to the principal's goodwill by either:

        (a)   a significant increase to business with existing customers, or

        (b)   the introduction of new customers:

    (ii)   substantial continuing benefits to the principal; and

    (iii)  that it is equitable in all the circumstances and in view of the commission the agent has lost.

46    The method of calculation for the indemnity. payment is outlined in Article 17(2b). This sets a maximum size to the payment, namely one year's remuneration, calculated as the average annual remuneration over the preceding five years (total of preceding five years' remuneration divided by five) or the average for any shorter period that the agent has been engaged. It should be noted that this is an upper limit. Since the agent is only entitled to an "indemnity" "to the extent that . . . it is equitable" the amount would be whatever sum is fair and reasonable as determined by agreement (or in default of agreement, by the court), up to that limit.

**Compensation for "Damage"**

47    *Article 17(3)* specifies the one basic condition for entitlement to compensation, namely "damage" to the agent on termination of the agency contract. Two examples of such "damage" are given:

   (i)   (a)   deprivation of any commission which proper performance of the agency contract would have earned, and

         (b)   substantial benefit (in terms of goodwill) to the principal; or

   (ii)  unrecovered expenses incurred by the agent on the principal's encouragement.

48    If the agent intends to pursue his entitlement to indemnity or compensation for damages he must notify the principal of this intention within one year following termination of the agency contract (Article 17(5)).

49    The Government has an open mind on which option should be chosen and invites comments from interested parties on this important matter.

         (ii)   Articles where Member States may some points take different positions on

50    *Article 2(2)* allows Member States to exclude from the scope of the Directive persons whose activities as commercial agents are deemed by national law to be "secondary". No general definition of "secondary activities" exists under United Kingdom law. It is the Government's intention to define and exclude such activities under United Kingdom implementing legislation.

51    At present the Government has in mind to exclude the following categories of agent from the scope of the Directive:

   —all persons whose activity as a commercial agent is not their primary "business" occupation. Thus, for example, merchants whose primary occupation is the buying and selling of goods on their own behalf but who occasionally act as an agent for another person, would be excluded.

   —all persons for whom the selling of goods from mail order catalogues is a "secondary" activity (although often the sole "business" activity). Thus the many housewives who spend a few hours a week selling from such catalogues would be excluded.

      Comments on the above and suggestions of other categories of agent for exclusion under this Article are invited.

52    *Article 4(3)* Under this provision the principal is required to inform the agent within a reasonable period of his acceptance, refusal and any non-execution of a commercial transaction which the agent has brought his way. The Government does not, therefore, intend to stipulate in its implementing legislation that the principal must also inform the agent of his execution of the commercial transaction the agent procured for him. It does not regard this as a matter for legislation bearing in mind that commission becomes due when, under the agreement negotiated by the agent, the

principal ought to have carried out the transaction, even if he has not actually done so (Article 10(1b)). Also when the transaction falls through for reasons for which the principal is not to blame so that the agent is deprived of his commission (Article 11(1)), the principal is obliged to inform the agent that the contract has not been performed (Article 4(3)).

53    *Article 13(2)* allows Member States to provide that the agency contract is not valid unless evidenced in writing. Current United Kingdom law does not require commercial contracts to be evidenced in writing. It may be sensible to retain the degree of flexibility provided by Article 13(1) to cover exceptional cases where the agent prefers not to have a written contract and those minor transactions where written contracts are not worthwhile. In any event Article 13(1), from which the parties to the agency contract may not derogate, clearly stipulates that the renunciation of the right to a signed written document setting out the terms of the agency contract will not be effective. Written agency contracts would be expected to be the normal practice following implementation of the Directive. Comments from interested parties on this matter are invited.

54    *Article 15(3)* gives Member States the option of fixing minimum periods of notice (stipulated in this provision) for the fourth and subsequent years for indefinite period agency contracts. The Government does not propose to take up this option. It feels the three months notice provided for in Article 15(2) is sufficient. If the parties want to fix longer periods of notice this is a matter for agreement between them.

55    *Article 17(2a) Indent* 2 An earlier draft of the Directive included a provision by which, except on the agent's death, the maximum amount of "indemnity" under Article 17(2b) was to be halved if the agency contract did not include any restraint of trade clause. This provision has now been deleted from the Directive. However Member States now have the option of legislating to the effect that the inclusion of a restraint of trade clause in the agency contract should be taken into account in assessing the amount of "indemnity" that is equitable. Views on whether such a provision should be included in the United Kingdom's implementing legislation are invited.

# Appendix 3

# Department of Trade and Industry Guidance Notes on the Commercial Agents (Council Directive) Regulations 1993

CONTENTS

**PART I**

(a) *Historical background to the Directive*

The main purposes of the Directive were to harmonise the laws of member states, which the Council of Ministers considered detrimental to the functioning of the Single Market, and to strengthen the position of the commercial agent in relation to his principal.

Independent commercial agents can be in a weak position when dealing with their principals, although it is acknowledged that this is not always the case. Agents have found difficulty obtaining written contracts and access to all the information they need to verify

### (b)  *Preamble to the Directive*

The preamble to the Directive includes the following recitals which are at the heart of the thinking behind the need for the Directive:

> 'Whereas the differences in national laws concerning commercial representation substantially affect the conditions of competition and the carrying-on of that activity within the Community and are detrimental both to the protection available to commercial agents vis-a-vis their principals and to the security of commercial transactions; whereas moreover those differences are such as to inhibit substantially the conclusion and operation of commercial representation contracts where principal and commercial agent are established in different member states.

> Whereas trade in goods between member states should be carried on under conditions which are similar to those of a single market, and this necessitates approximation of the legal systems of the member states to the extent required for the proper functioning of the common market; whereas in this regard the rules concerning conflict of laws do not, in the matter of commercial representation, remove the inconsistencies referred to above, nor would they even if they were made uniform, and accordingly the proposed harmonisation is necessary notwithstanding the existence of those rules.'

### (c)  *Implementation of the Directive*

The Directive has been implemented as regards the law of England and Wales, and Scotland by Statutory Instrument No. 1993/3053 as amended by Statutory Instrument No. 1993/3173. Separate implementing provision is made in relation to Northern Ireland by the Commercial Agents (Council Directive) Regulations (Northern Ireland) 1993 (Statutory Rules for Northern Ireland No. 1993/483).

### (d)  *Purpose of the guidance notes*

The purpose of these notes is to assist commercial agents, principals, and their legal advisers to understand the effect of the Commercial Agents (Council Directive) Regulations 1993 by explaining why particular options for implementing the Directive were chosen and by setting out the Department's view on a number of points of difficulty. It must be emphasised that the Department's view is no more than that. As with other Community legislation, the Directive has to be interpreted uniformly throughout the Community and ultimately only the European Court can do that.

The guidance notes are in two parts. Part I continues by setting out, by regulation, the Department's general interpretation of the intention behind the Directive and hence the Regulations. Part II deals with other more specific and general points which arose during the consultation.

The notes deal only with those provisions which are novel or about which, during consultation, specific queries were raised. IN THAT CONNECTION IT SHOULD BE NOTED THAT THE TEXT OF REGULATIONS 5, 13, 14, 15, 18, 19, 21, 22 AND 23 IS NOT PRINTED, NOR DO THESE NOTES CONTAIN ANY SPECIFIC COMMENT ON THEM. Further issues on particular provisions may arise in the future, and the contact point is:

Christopher Farthing
Consumer Affairs Division 2a
Room 325
10–18 Victoria Street
London SW1H 0NN
Tel: 071 215 3302
Fax: 071 215 3396

The Department has taken the view that, for the most part, the substantive provisions of the Directive leave the member states with little or no discretion as to implementation of the Directive in national law and therefore, the wording of the Regulations follows that of the Directive very closely.

*(e)  Details of the Regulations and the Department's Interpretation*

REGULATION 1

1(1)  These Regulations may be cited as the Commercial Agents (Council Directive) Regulations 1993 and shall come into force on 1 January 1994.

1(2)  These Regulations govern the relations between commercial agents and their principals and, subject to paragraph (3), apply in relation to the activities of commercial agents in Great Britain.

1(3)  Regulations 3–22 do not apply where the parties have agreed that the agency contract is to be governed by the law of another member state.

INTERPRETATION

This Regulation sets out the circumstances in which the Regulations will apply to an agency contract. If the agent carries out his activities as a commercial agent in Great Britain, then the Regulations will apply *unless* the parties expressly choose the law of another member state as the law which is to apply to the agency contract. If the law of a non-EU country is chosen then the provisions of the Regulations are intended to override that choice of law in so far as any of the activities of the commercial agent are carried out in Great Britain.

Regulation 1(2) provides that the Regulations govern relations between commercial agents and their principals and apply in relation to the activities of commercial agents in *Great Britain* (whether or not the agent is physically based in Great Britain).

The provisions of the Regulations, where the agent carries on his activities outside Great Britain, do not, however, prevent the parties from choosing the law of a part of Great Britain (for example the law of England and Wales) and incorporating in the agency agreement some or all of the provisions of the Regulations which the parties might wish to agree should apply as though the agents' activities were, in fact, to be carried on in Great Britain. However, in such a case, if litigation arises, the court hearing the action may or may not:

(i)  uphold the choice of law, and

(ii)  accept the validity of such incorporation.

The state of the law of the other member states relating to commercial agents will depend, in part, on the manner in which the Directive has been implemented in those States, and advice as to the relevant foreign law (both within the EU and outside) should be sought in appropriate cases.

Some examples appear in the Annex to these notes which are intended to show the application (or otherwise) of the Regulations where the principal is based in one country and his agent performs his activities in another.

The Regulations apply to *Great Britain* (Regulation 2(5)). The Directive has been implemented separately in relation to Northern Ireland by the Commercial Agents (Council Directive) Regulations (Northern Ireland) 1993 (Statutory Rules for Northern Ireland No. 1993/483).

REGULATION 2

(*Articles 1 & 2 of the Directive*)

2(1)  In these Regulations—

'commercial agent' means a self-employed intermediary who has continuing authority to negotiate the sale or purchase of goods on behalf of another person (the 'principal'), or to negotiate and conclude the sale or purchase of goods on behalf of and in the name of that principal; but shall be understood as not including in particular:

(i) a person who, in his capacity as an officer of a company or association, is empowered to enter into commitments binding on that company or association;

(ii) a partner who is lawfully authorised to enter into commitments binding on his partners;

(iii) a person who acts as an insolvency practitioner (as that expression is defined in section 388 of the *Insolvency Act* 1986) or the equivalent in any other jurisdiction;

'commission' means any part of the remuneration of a commercial agent which varies with the number or value of business transactions;

'restraint of trade clause' means an agreement restricting the business activities of a commercial agent following termination of the agency contract.

2(2) These Regulations do not apply to—

(a) commercial agents whose activities are unpaid;

(b) commercial agents when they operate on commodity exchanges or in the commodity market;

(c) the Crown Agents for Overseas Governments and Administrations, as set up under the *Crown Agents Act* 1979, or its subsidiaries.

2(3) The provisions of the Schedule to these Regulations have effect for the purposes of determining the persons whose activities as commercial agents are to be considered secondary.

2(4) These Regulations shall not apply to the persons referred to in paragraph (3) above.

2(5) These Regulations do not extend to Northern Ireland.

INTERPRETATION

The Regulation sets out the definitions of the terms used within the Regulations and also excludes those agents where the activities are considered secondary.

The expression 'self-employed' is derived from Articles 52 and 57 of the Treaty of Rome (which deal with freedom of establishment and freedom to provide services) and is consistent with Community law, to be understood as including, for example, companies as well as self-employed individuals.

If an agent is appointed for a specified number of transactions, then he would be excluded from the scope of the Regulations, owing to his lack of continuing authority.

'Goods' clearly has to be interpreted in accordance with the EC Treaty and, for that reason, the Regulations do not define the word. However, it is considered that the definition of 'goods' in section 61(1) of the *Sale of Goods Act* 1979 as including, inter alia, all personal chattels other than things in action (eg shares) and money, may offer a reasonable guide, without necessarily being absolutely co-extensive with the Directive meaning.

Interpretation of the term 'secondary activities' and the provisions of the Schedule to the Regulations are dealt with later in these notes.

Some agents only effect introductions between their principals and third parties. The question arises as to whether such agents are commercial agents for the purposes of the Regulations. Such agents are sometimes known as 'canvassing' or 'introducing' agents. As such, they generally lack the power to bind their principals and are not really agents in the true sense of the word. However, to the extent that such an agent 'has continuing authority to negotiate the sale or purchase of goods' on behalf of his principal, even though, as a matter of fact, he merely effects introductions, it seems that he would fall within the definition of 'commercial agent' in Regulation 2(1). It is clear that an 'introducing' agent who lacks such authority falls outside the scope of the definition of 'commercial agent'. It may be that the courts would give a wide interpretation to the word 'negotiate' and that, as a result, 'introducing' agents will, in general have the benefit of the Regulations.

It is thought that the Regulations do apply to *del credere* agents who exhibit the characteristics set out in the definition of 'commercial agent'. The Department does not consider that the additional features of a del credere agency cause the agent to fall outside the definition. Questions can, however, arise as to whether a person is an agent at all who, in consideration of extra remuneration, guarantees to his principal that third parties with whom he enters into contracts on behalf of the principal will duly pay any sums becoming due under those contracts (and thus appears to be a del credere agent), or, whether that person is really acting on his own account.

Regulation 2(2)(b) provides that the Regulations do not apply to commercial agents when they operate on commodity exchanges or in the commodity market. A 'commodity' is any tangible good. So called 'commodity exchanges' deal in such goods and, to a large extent, in commodity 'futures' ie the right to buy or sell a particular commodity at a particular price at a particular time in the future, hence eg 'coffee futures'.

## REGULATION 3
(*Article 3 of the Directive*)
3(1) In performing his activities a commercial agent must look after the interests of his principal and act dutifully and in good faith.
3(2) In particular, a commercial agent must—

(a) make proper efforts to negotiate and, where appropriate, conclude the transactions he is instructed to take care of;
(b) communicate to his principal all the necessary information available to him;
(c) comply with reasonable instructions given by his principal.

INTERPRETATION
This Regulation sets out the duties which the agent owes to the principal and, in effect, restates the duties owed at common law by an agent to his principal.

It is not certain how an agent's duty to 'communicate to his principal all the necessary information available to him' is to be fulfilled where an agent is acting for several principals. However, parties to contracts of commercial agency will doubtless wish to explore the possibility of agreeing on express terms to cover that situation.

## REGULATION 4
(*Article 4 of the Directive*)
4(1) In his relations with his commercial agent a principal must act dutifully and in good faith.
4(2) In particular, a principal must—

(a) provide his commercial agent with the necessary documentation relating to the goods concerned;
(b) obtain for his commercial agent the information necessary for the performance of the agency contract, and in particular notify his commercial agent within a reasonable period once he anticipates that the volume of commercial transactions will be significantly lower than that which the commercial agent could normally have expected.

4(3) A principal shall, in addition, inform his commercial agent within a reasonable period of his acceptance or refusal of, and of any non-execution by him of, a commercial transaction which the commercial agent has procured for him.

## INTERPRETATION
This Regulation deals with the principal's duties to the commercial agent. It is thought that these duties merely amplify the position at common law.

A principal is required to inform his commercial agent accordingly once the principal knows that business will decrease significantly or where an order will not be concluded.

## REGULATION 6
(*Article 6 of the Directive*)
6(1) In the absence of any agreement as to remuneration between the parties, a commercial agent shall be entitled to the remuneration that commercial agents appointed for the goods forming the subject of his agency contract are customarily allowed in the place where he carries on his activities and, if there is no such customary practice, a commercial agent shall be entitled to reasonable remuneration taking into account all the aspects of the transaction.
6(2) This Regulation is without prejudice to the application of any enactment or rule of law concerning the level of remuneration.
6(3) Where a commercial agent is not remunerated (wholly or in part) by commission, Regulations 7–12 shall not apply.

## INTERPRETATION
This Regulation is applicable only where the parties have not agreed on the remuneration payable by the principal to the agent. In the event of a dispute as to the remuneration payable, the court would be likely to have regard to custom in the commercial area concerned.

Should there be no identifiable custom in the area concerned, then it is considered that the agent would be entitled to a reason-able amount of remuneration. The position under the Regulations is thought to be similar to the position at common law.

It should be noted that where the commercial agent is not remunerated (wholly or in part) by commission, Regulations 7–12 do not apply.

## REGULATION 7
(*Article 7 of the Directive*)
7(1) A commercial agent shall be entitled to commission on transactions concluded during the period covered by the agency contract—
  (a) where the transaction has been concluded as a result of his action; or
  (b) where the transaction is concluded with a third party whom he has previously acquired as a customer for transactions of the same kind.
7(2) A commercial agent shall also be entitled to commission on transactions concluded during the period covered by the agency contract where he has an exclusive right to a specific geographical area or to a specific group of customers and where the transaction has been entered into with a customer belonging to that area or group.

## INTERPRETATION
This Regulation sets out the circumstances in which the agent may be considered to have earned his commission, and in that connection the view is taken that a transaction is 'concluded' when the principal and the third party have entered into a contract. The provisions of (2) include so called 'House Accounts' held by the principal ie where the principal deals directly with the third party although the agent has the rights to that area.

## REGULATION 8
(*Article 8 of the Directive*)
Subject to Regulation 9 below, a commercial agent shall be entitled to commission on

commercial transactions concluded after the agency contract has terminated if—

(a) the transaction is mainly attributable to his efforts during the period covered by the agency contract and if the transaction was entered into within a reasonable period after the contract terminated; or

(b) in accordance with the conditions mentioned in paragraph 7 above, the order of the third party reached the principal or commercial agent before the agency contract terminated.

INTERPRETATION

This Regulation sets out when the agent is entitled to commission on commercial transactions concluded after the agency contract has come to an end. In particular where the transaction was mainly a result of the agents' efforts during the contract and the transaction was entered into within a reasonable period after the end of the agency contract.

The principal and agent may attempt to define 'reasonable period' in their agreement. However, in the event of a dispute, despite any such definition, the matter would be ultimately for the decision of the Court.

If the order was placed with the principal or agent before the termination of the agency contract, but the contract was not concluded until afterwards, then the principal would still be liable to pay commission.

REGULATION 9

(*Article 9 of the Directive*)

9(1) A commercial agent shall not be entitled to the commission referred to in Regulation 7 above if that commission is payable, by virtue of Regulation 8 above, to the previous commercial agent, unless it is equitable because of the circumstances for

the commission to be shared between the commercial agents.

9(2) The principal shall be liable for any sum due under paragraph (1) above to the person entitled to it in accordance with that paragraph, and any sum which the other commercial agent receives to which he is not entitled shall be refunded to the principal.

INTERPRETATION

This Regulation deals with the apportionment of commission between a new agent and his predecessor for the same transaction.

The new agent is not entitled to commission if it is payable to the previous agent unless it is 'equitable because of the circumstances' for the commission to be shared between them.

It is the principal's duty to pay commission owing to agents and where commission is paid inadvertently to one agent which was in fact owed to the other, the agent must repay it or the principal reclaim it. In either circumstance the agent entitled to the commission should receive it.

REGULATION 10

(*Article 10 of the Directive*)

10(1) Commission shall become due as soon as, and to the extent that, one of the following circumstances occurs:

(a) the principal has executed the transaction; or

(b) the principal should, according to his agreement with the third party, have executed the transaction; or

(c) the third party has executed the transaction.

10(2) Commission shall become due at the latest when the third party has executed his part of the transaction or should have done so if the principal had executed his part of the transaction, as he should have.

10(3) The commission shall be paid not later than on the last day of the month following the quarter in which it became due, and, for the purposes of these Regulations, unless otherwise agreed between the parties, the first quarter period shall run from the date the agency contract takes effect, and subsequent periods shall run from that date in the third month thereafter or the beginning of the fourth month, whichever is the sooner.

10(4) Any agreement to derogate from paragraph (2) and (3) above to the detriment of the commercial agent shall be void.

INTERPRETATION

This Regulation sets out when the commission to be paid to an agent becomes due and when it should be paid.

A transaction may be considered to be 'executed' in any of the following circumstances:

  (i) when the principal has accepted or delivered the goods;
 (ii) when the principal should have accepted or delivered the goods;
(iii) when the third party accepts or delivers the goods; or
 (iv) when the third party pays for the goods.

It is for the two parties to agree within the terms of the contract which of these circumstances will make the commission become due. Paragraph 2 of the Regulation provides for the latest date that the commission can become due.

It is not unusual for goods to be delivered by instalments. If the agency contract does not make specific provision for the matter, the question as to when commission is due would seem to depend upon the precise nature of the sale or purchase transaction. Where each instalment delivery is the subject of a separate contract, it seems likely that a separate commission payment will be due as each separate delivery is made, or should have been made. Where a single contract applies to a number of instalment deliveries, the position is somewhat less clear. However, in view of the words 'to the

extent that' in Regulation 10(1) the agent may be entitled to the commission which is attributable to each particular instalment delivery.

It should be noted that paragraph (4) of Regulation 10 renders void any agreement to derogate to the detriment of the commercial agent from paragraphs (2) and (3) of the Regulation.

REGULATION 11
(*Article 11 of the Directive*)

11(1) The right to commission can be extinguished only if and to the extent that—

  (a) it is established that the contract between the third party and the principal will not be executed; and
  (b) that fact is due to a reason for which the principal is not to blame.

11(2) Any commission which the commercial agent has already received shall be refunded if the right to it is extinguished.

11(3) Any agreement to derogate from paragraph (1) above to the detriment of the commercial agent shall be void.

INTERPRETATION

The Regulation outlines the circumstances when the agent's right to commission is forfeited. Should a contract not be executed the principal must not be at fault for the entitlement to commission to be extinguished. Any commission already paid by the principal under these circumstances would be refunded.

REGULATION 12
(*Article 12 of the Directive*)

12(1) The principal shall supply his commercial agent with a statement of the commission due, not later than the last day of the month following the quarter in which the commission has become due, and such statement shall set out the main components used in calculating the amount of commission.

12(2) A commercial agent shall be entitled to demand that he be provided with the information (and in particular an extract from the books) which is available to his principal and which he needs in order to check the amount of commission due to him.

12(3) Any agreement to derogate from paragraphs (1) and (2) above shall be void.

12(4) Nothing in this Regulation shall remove or restrict the effect of, or prevent reliance upon, any enactment or rule of law which recognises the right of an agent to inspect the books of the principal.

INTERPRETATION

The Regulation sets out the principal's obligation to provide the agent with a statement of commission due and must set out the main components in calculating the commission. It also requires the principal to provide the agent with all *necessary* information, including extracts from his (the principal's) books, to check the commission due, should the agent request such information.

*N.B.* the principal is only required to provide relevant extracts and *not* his full books.

REGULATION 16

(*Article 16 of the Directive*)

16 These Regulations shall not affect the application of any enactment or rule of law which provides for the immediate termination of the agency contract—

(a) because of the failure of one party to carry out all or part of his obligations under that contract; or

(b) where exceptional circumstances arise.

INTERPRETATION

This Regulation preserves the common law and statutory rules of jurisdictions within Great Britain which provide for the immediate termination of an agency contract on the basis of the two matters set out in sub-paragraphs (a) and (b) of the Regulation. It is thought that the expression 'exceptional circumstances' in paragraph (b) would include matters falling within the doctrine of frustration.

REGULATION 17

(*Article 27 of the Directive*)

17(1) This Regulation has effect for the purpose of ensuring that the commercial agent is, after termination of the agency contract, indemnified in accordance with paragraphs (3) to (5) below or compensated for damage in accordance with paragraphs (6) and (7) below.

17(2) Except where the agency contract otherwise provides, the commercial agent shall be entitled to be compensated rather than indemnified.

17(3) Subject to paragraph (9) below and to Regulation 18 below, the commercial agent shall be entitled to an indemnity if and to the extent that—

(a) he has brought the principal new customers or has significantly increased the volume of business from existing customers and the principal continues to derive substantial benefits from the business with such customers; and

(b) the payment of this indemnity is equitable having regard to all the circumstances and, in particular, the commission lost by the commercial agent on the business transacted with such customers.

17(4) The amount of the indemnity shall not exceed a figure equivalent to an indemnity for one year calculated from the commercial agent's average annual remuneration over the preceding five years and if the contract goes back less than five years the indemnity shall be calculated on the average for the period in question.

17(5) The granting of an indemnity as mentioned above shall not prevent the commercial agent from seeking damages.

17(6) Subject to paragraph (9) and Regulation 18 below, the commercial agent shall be entitled to compensation for the damage he suffers as a result of the termination of his relations with his principal.

17(7) For the purposes of these Regulations such damage shall be deemed to occur particularly when the termination takes place in either or both of the following circumstances, namely circumstances which—

(a) deprive the commercial agent of the commission which proper performance of the agency contract would have procured for him whilst providing his principal with substantial benefits linked to the activities of the commercial agent; or

(b) have not enabled the commercial agent to amortise the costs and expenses that he had incurred in the performance of the agency contract on the advice of his principal.

17(8) Entitlement to the indemnity or compensation for damage as provided for under paragraphs (2) to (7) above shall also arise where the agency contract is terminated as a result of the death of the commercial agent.

17(9) The commercial agent shall lose his entitlement to the indemnity or compensation for damage in the instances provided for in paragraphs (2) to (8) above if within one year following termination of his agency contract he has not notified his principal that he intends pursuing his entitlement.

INTERPRETATION

The Regulation deals with entitlement to indemnity/compensation upon termination of the agency contract. It is for the two parties to choose which of these options

they would wish to include in their contract with the backstop of compensation should no choice be indicated. There is however, nothing to preclude the two parties from agreeing to use the compensation provisions in some cases and indemnity ones in others when terminating a particular contract. The indemnity/compensation is only payable where the principal will continue to benefit from the business that the agent has brought to the principal.

It should be noted that although having fixed term contracts or giving correct periods of notice (see Regulation 15) could potentially reduce the level of indemnity compensation it would not necessarily exclude it. The issue of whether compensation is payable on the expiry of a fixed term contract or where the contractual notice period in an indefinite term contract has been given is a matter for the courts to decide.

It is thought that in view of the terms of Regulation 19 it would be possible for the two parties to derogate from this provision *after* the termination of the agency contract.

The word 'indemnity' has a rather more limited meaning than that which it normally bears in English law in that it:

(i) appears to fall short of a complete making good of the loss suffered by the principal; and

(ii) does not necessarily arise in relation to loss caused by the principal.

Its more limited nature may be inferred from Regulation 17(5) which contemplates the possibility of the agent wishing to seek damages. The amount of the indemnity is, in any event, limited by Regulation 17(4). The indemnity might appropriately be reviewed as approximating to a form of liquidated damages.

It remains to be seen how courts in Great Britain would assess amounts of indemnity, and the Department feels unable, at this stage, to offer any guidance as to the approach likely to be adopted.

Article 17.6 of the Directive requires the Commission to submit to the Council, by the end of 1994, a report on the implementation of Article 17 (indemnity/compensation) and, if necessary to submit to the Council proposals for amendments.

As to the meaning of 'substantial' in Regulation 17(3)(a), it is thought that word would be interpreted as meaning 'material 'or 'not insignificant' having regard to the history of dealings between the principal and the agents and other relevant circumstances.

'Equitable' in Regulation 17(3)(b) probably means 'just' or 'fair' rather than necessarily based on the doctrines or principles of equity—the latter, if they exist at all in the law of every member state, being bound to vary from State to State.

## REGULATION 20
(*Article 20 of the Directive*)

20(1) A restraint of trade clause shall be valid only if and to the extent that—

(a) it is concluded in writing; and

(b) it relates to the geographical area or the group of customers and the geographical area entrusted to the commercial agent and to the kind of goods covered by his agency under the contract.

20(2) A restraint of trade clause shall be valid for not more than two years after the termination of the agency contract.

20(3) Nothing in this Regulation shall effect any enactment or rule of law which imposes other restrictions on the validity or enforceability of restraint of trade clauses or which enables a court to reduce the obligations on the parties resulting from such clauses.

## INTERPRETATION

A 'restraint of trade clause' is any agreement which restricts the business activities of a commercial agent following termination of the agency contract (see the definition in Regulation 2).

The restraint of trade provisions only extend to the kind of goods that were cov-

ered in his contract. It is thought that the provisions would not extend to goods of a similar nature aimed at different types of purchasers.

## THE SCHEDULE

1. The activities of a person as a commercial agent are to be considered secondary where it may reasonably be taken that the primary purpose of the arrangement with his principal is other than as set out in paragraph 2 below.

2. An arrangement falls within this paragraph if—

(a) the business of the principal is the sale, or as the case may be purchase, of goods of a particular kind; and

(b) the goods concerned are such that—

(i) transactions are normally individually negotiated and concluded on a commercial basis, and

(ii) procuring a transaction on one occasion is likely to lead to further transactions in those goods with that customer on future occasions, or to transactions in those goods with other customers in the same geographical area or among the same group of customers, and that accordingly it is in the commercial interests of the principal in developing the market in those goods to appoint a representative to such customers with a view to the representative devoting effort, skill and expenditure from its own resources to that end.

3. The following are indications that an arrangement falls within paragraph 2 above, and the absence of any of them is an indication to the contrary—

(a) the principal is the manufacturer, importer or distributor of the goods;

(b) the goods are specifically identified with the principal in the market in question rather than, or to a greater extent than, with any other person;

(c) the agent devotes substantially the whole of his time to representative activities (whether for one principal or a number of principals whose interests are not conflicting);

(d) the goods are not normally available in the market in question other than by means of the agent;

(e) the arrangement is described as one of commercial agency.

4. The following are indications that an arrangement does not fall within paragraph 2 above—

(a) promotional material is supplied direct to potential customers;

(b) persons are granted agencies without reference to existing agents in a particular area or in relation to a particular group;

(c) customers normally select the goods for themselves and merely place their orders through the agent.

5. The activities of the following categories of persons are presumed, unless the contrary is established, not to fall within paragraph 2 above—

Mail order catalogue agents for consumer goods.

Consumer credit agents.

## INTERPRETATION

The Schedule sets out the criteria for determining the persons whose activities as commercial agents are considered secondary under UK law and are excluded from the provisions of the Regulations by virtue of Regulation 2(3).

The first test is to determine whether or not a contract comes under the provisions of the Regulations. The determining factor is whether the agent is required to keep, as his own property, a considerable stock of the product.

The comparison to be made is between the agent's activities as a commercial agent and his other activities and not the relationship with the principal.

It is not possible to say which of the provisions in paragraphs 3 and 4 take priority and this will have to be determined on a case by case basis taking into account the exact nature of the agency contract.

## PART II

(a) *Answers to specific questions raised during the consultation exercise*

Q. *Can the principle of set-off continue to apply?*

A. The Regulations do not mention set-off. It is thought that set-off will remain available to the principal, his agent and third parties in accordance with the rules of common law.

Q. *If a principal employs an agent to act for him in a number of different member states, could there be one agency contract governing the relationship?*

A. This would be possible subject to the comments made on page [109] concerning the applicability of English law to contracts outside the UK.

Q. *Regulation 17(8) expressly allows indemnity or compensation where the agency contract is terminated as a result of the commercial agent's death. Is the position the same if the commercial agent (being a company) goes into liquidation?*

A. Where the principal or agent is a company, at common law the actual authority of the principal or agent will be determined by its winding up or dissolution. It should be noted that where the authority is irrevocable it will not be determined by such events.

Q. *Can an age limit be fixed for a commercial agent?*

A. It is thought it can. Fixed contracts are permitted and if, for example, a 40 year old agent is appointed 'until he is 60' this is equivalent to a fixed contract for 20 years or until death.

Q. *To what extent can the Regulations be derogated from?*

A. There are three different types of Regulation within the Regulations: those which cannot be derogated from; those which cannot be derogated from to the detriment of the agent; and those which make no mention of derogation.

It can be argued that where Regulations mean there to be no derogation, they say so. It can also be said that if nothing is said it is to be inferred that it can be derogated from. If this is so then, for example, the agency contract could express the agent's entitlement to commission as arising where the transaction is 'wholly' as a result of his action.

The Department's conclusion on this, although not a firm one, is that the terms of the agency contract can vary the events upon which the agent becomes entitled to commission, although they could not do so to an extent that it excludes the right altogether since this would conflict with Regulation 11(1).

Q. *Are sub-agency agreements covered by the Regulations?*

A. Whilst the position is not clear, the Regulations are, in principle, capable of covering sub-agency agreements.

Q. *Is it possible to include a liquidated damages provision within the contract?*

A. Liquidated damages is a provision within a contract where one party agrees to pay to the other a specified sum of money in the event of a breach of contract.

Such clauses may be permissible provided that they represent a genuine pre-estimate of damage.

The Department's conclusion on this, although not a firm one, is that the terms of the agency contract can vary the events upon which the agent becomes entitled to commission, although they could not do so to an extent that it excludes the right altogether since this would conflict with Regulation 11(1).

Q. *Are sub-agency agreements covered by the Regulations?*

A. Whilst the position is not clear, the Regulations are, in principle, capable of covering sub-agency agreements.

Q. *Is it possible to include a liquidated damages provision within the contract?*

A. Liquidated damages is a provision within a contract where one party agrees to pay to the other a specified sum of money in the event of a breach of contract.

Such clauses may be permissible provided that they represent a genuine pre-estimate of damage.

Although one object of the clause will be to limit the principal's liability, it may not be a pure limitation clause in that it forms a compromise between the parties and is intended to be enforceable whether the actual loss is greater or less than the sum agreed. Nevertheless, as against the principal, such provisions risk attack by the agent as void by virtue of Regulation 19.

Q. *Are the Regulations retrospective?*

A. Only in the sense that they apply to all contracts as from 1 January 1994 and it is inevitable that in some respects account will have to be taken of what occurred before 1994. The Regulations do not, however, apply so as to affect the rights and liabilities of either the principal or agent if they have accrued before 1994.

Q. *Do the Regulations apply to agents who sell Christmas hampers?*

A. It is believed that the activities of such agents would be likely to be held as secondary, thus rendering the agents (by virtue of Regulation 2(4)) outside the scope of the Regulations.

ANNEX

(a) *Examples on the application of Regulation 1*

1 *Principal in Great Britain, agent in France (EU member state)*

The Regulations do *not* apply, since the agent's activities are in France and therefore are not in Great Britain (see Regulation 1(2)). However, if the parties choose English law to govern the contract between them, it is suggested that the contract could provide for the provisions of the Regulations to apply to the relations between them as though the agent's activities were in Great Britain. Although the agent is in France, if the parties choose English law to govern the agency contract, the provisions of French law implementing the Directive would not apply (unless those provisions are held to be 'mandatory rules' (see Article 3 of the Rome Convention on the law applicable to contractual obligations)).

2 *Principal in Great Britain, agent in Australia (non-EU member state)*

The Regulations do not apply, given that the agent's activities are in Australia and therefore not in Great Britain. However, again, it is thought that, as in the first example above, the parties could specifically adopt the provisions of the Regulations by contractual provision to that effect. Any 'mandatory rules' of the relevant Australian State(s) would need to be considered in case they were capable of over-riding any provisions of the contract.

3 *Principal in France, agent in Great Britain*

In the absence of an express choice of French law, the Regulations would apply, given that the agent's activities are in Great Britain. If the parties choose French law, the Regulations would not apply (see Regulation 1(3)), and the agent would have the protection of the Directive as implemented in French law.

4 *Principal in USA, agent in Great Britain*

If the law of a part of Great Britain is chosen by the parties to govern the agency contract, it is concluded that the Regulations will apply.

However, if the law of a state of the US is chosen, no doubt an exclusive jurisdiction clause in favour of the courts of that state would also be included in the agency contract, on the basis of which a Court in Great Britain may well decline jurisdiction. In the absence of such a clause, or if a Court in Great Britain nevertheless accepts jurisdiction, the Court may take the view (perhaps after making an Article 177 reference to the European Court) that the Regulations constitute mandatory rules of the law of a part of Great Britain and that the Regulations should, accordingly, apply, the intention of the Directive being to afford certain protections to commercial agents operating within the European Union (but possibly only where the principal is also established within the European Union (see the recitals to the Directive referred to on page 1 of the notes under the heading 'Preamble to the Directive')). Thus an agent in such circumstances would be unwise to assume that, despite operating in Great Britain, the Regulations would apply.

# Appendix 4

# The Law Commission

(LAW COM. No. 84)
Law of Contract
Report on the Proposed E.E.C. Directive on The Law Relating to Commercial Agents
Advice to the Lord Chancellor Under Section 3(1)(e) of the Law Commissions Act
(1965) (Footnotes omitted)

*The proposed EEC directive on the law relating to commercial agents*

CONTENTS

## THE PROPOSED EEC DIRECTIVE ON
## THE LAW RELATING TO COMMERCIAL AGENTS

### Advice to the Lord Chancellor under section 3(1)(e) of the Law Commissions Act 1965

*To the Right Honourable the Lord Elwyn-Jones, C.H.,*
*Lord High Chancellor of Great Britain*

PART I—INTRODUCTION

1. In April 1973 the Directorate for Social Affairs and the Directorate for the Internal market of the EEC prepared a document for consultation with Denmark, Ireland and the United Kingdom. This document consisted merely of a draft directive together with an explanatory memorandum. The Commission of the European Communities proposed that the draft directive be discussed by representatives of the Commission and representatives of Denmark, Ireland and the United Kingdom at a Conference on 21 and 22 June 1973 and that after this Conference a proposed directive taking into account the views of the new members would be sent by the Commission to the Council of Ministers. The draft directive had been prepared by the Commission after detailed discussions with the Six over a period of some years. The Commission considered it to be in virtually final form, so that the proposed directive could be sent to the Council of Ministers shortly after the Conference.

2. The Solicitor of the Department of Trade and Industry asked the Law Commission whether they could assist the Department in handling the draft directive. The legal staff of the Law Commission gave the Department assistance between May 1973 and May 1975. A member of the legal staff of the Law Commission was made available for the meeting on 21 and 22 June 1973 (where the draft directive was discussed by representatives of the Commission of the European Communities and representatives of Denmark, Ireland and the United Kingdom) and further assistance was given to the Department at meetings with members of the staff of the EEC and in discussion of the detailed provisions of the directive. The Department was also assisted in dealing with the consultation which they conducted on the draft directive and at meetings with representatives of the Manufacturers' Agents' Association, the Confederation of British Industry, the Bar Council, the Law Society and other bodies.

3. At that stage the Law Commission's function was confined to assisting and advising the Department on the first draft of the directive, and between May 1975 and the end of 1976 no further assistance was requested of them. On 14 December 1976, the Commission of the European Communities sent to the Council of Ministers a proposed directive which differs in some respects from the previous draft. A copy of the directive and the explanatory memorandum under cover of a letter from the Commission of the European Communities to the Council of Ministers dated 5 January 1977 is attached as Annex A. The Law Commission had played no part in the new draft. By letter dated 1 March 1977 we were asked to tender you our advice in accordance with section 3(1)(e) of the Law Commissions Act 1965 on the attitude which we would recommend the United Kingdom to adopt towards the proposed

directive. You will appreciate that our advice was asked for as a matter of some urgency and we have not therefore been able to follow our usual practice of extensive consultation through the publication of a working paper.

PART II—OUR GENERAL APPROACH

4. Before we consider the content of the directive as such, we should say something about its vires in terms of the Treaty of Rome and its status as an instrument of community law. The Commission of the European Communities have indicated that the directive is based on Articles 57 and 100 of that Treaty. Article 57 imposes on the Council of Ministers a duty to issue directives for the co-ordination of laws in Member States concerning the taking up and pursuit of activities as self-employed persons. Since Article 2 of the directive declares a defining characteristic of a commercial agent to be that he must be self-employed, it seems that the directive is intra vires Article 57 of the Treaty. Article 100 of the Treaty lays upon the Council of Ministers the duty to issue directives for the approximation of such laws in Member States as "directly affect the establishment or functioning of the Common Market". It is, we think, possible to contend with some justification that the differences in the laws of Member States relating to commercial agents do affect the functioning of the Common Market in that they inhibit the commercial agent's freedom of establishment in the EEC and may interfere with the freedom of movement of goods and services between Member States. Our conclusion is that the directive as a whole is almost certainly intra vires the Treaty of Rome.

5. A directive is, by Article 189(3) of the Treaty of Rome, "binding as to the result to be achieved, upon each Member State to which it is addressed, but shall leave to the national authorities the choice of form and method". Our view is that the directive, as presently drafted, contains provisions of such a detailed and complex nature as would in effect deprive the national authorities of the choice as to the method by which they should be implemented. We think that the contents of the directive are thus to some extent inconsistent with the status of a directive as an instrument of community law, and that the directive is an inappropriate vehicle for the creation of this kind of detailed set of rules of private law.

6. The proposed directive contains detailed rules regulating the legal relationship between "commercial agents", as defined by Article 2, and their principals. These rules relate to the rights and duties of the parties, remuneration and reimbursement of expenses, *del credere* commercial agents, bankruptcy of the principal and the making and cessation of the contract. It constitutes a fairly comprehensive codification of the law relating to the legal relationship between the commercial agent and his principal. Some of the rules are declaratory of terms of a general character that are implicit in the relationship of principal and agent, for example, the mutual obligations of good faith; others deal in detail with matters, such as the entitlement to remuneration, which one would expect to find provided for expressly in the agency contract, probably after negotiation. Many of the rules are made mandatory by Article 35; this article provides that any stipulation whereby the parties derogate, to the detriment of the agent, from a provision incorporating a mandatory rule is rendered void.

7. The proposed directive thus has three main features:—

(a)  it contains provisions, out of which the parties cannot contract, for the protection of the commercial agent;

(b)  it contains provisions which, in the absence of contrary agreement, will form the basis of the legal relationship between the principal and the commercial agent: it thus provides what might be described as a "model contract" for commercial agents;

(c)  it provides a codification of that part of the law of agency which deals with the relationship between the commercial agent and the principal.

8.  Before we discuss any of these three features of the directive it is obviously necessary to determine precisely the category of persons who are called "commercial agents" and who thus fall within the scope of the directive.

### The scope of the directive and its rationale

9.  "The word 'agency', to a common lawyer, refers in general to a branch of the law under which one person, the agent, may affect the legal relations of another person, the principal, as regards other persons, called third parties, by acts which the agent is said to have the principal's authority to perform, and which are often regarded as the principal's acts and not as those of the agent". "The mature law recognises that a person need not always do things that change his legal relations in person: he may utilise the services of another to change them, or to do something during the course of which they may be changed".

10.  Under the directive a commercial agent is an intermediary who has authority to negotiate and/or to conclude commercial transactions in the name or for the account of his principal. Under Article 9(1) he only has authority to conclude agreements when the principal empowers him to do so. To the extent that the power to affect the legal relations of the principal appears to be the exceptional situation rather than the normal one, the typical commercial agent differs from the typical agent of the English common law.

11.  It is also necessary to comment on the categories of the business intermediaries who are *not* within the definition in Article 2. Under the article the intermediary must be self-employed and this serves to exclude a large number of representatives and commercial travellers who are employees and who are paid partly by wage or salary and partly by commission. Under the article the intermediary must negotiate or transact in the name of and for the account of another person. This will exclude distributors who carry out sales and services in their own name.

12.  The term "commercial agent" has no precise connotation in English law. It does not represent a category of persons who have a common identifiable legal characteristic. Indeed, we are not convinced that the term has any precise connotation. Article 2 refers to the commercial agent's authority to negotiate or conclude "commercial transactions". Again, the English lawyer can attach no precise meaning to the term "commercial transaction".

### The directive and the German law

13.  The "commercial agent" of the directive is clearly based on the German *Handelsvertreter* and the provisions of the directive are based on sections 84–92c of the German Commercial Code, which were introduced in 1953. "The concept of '*Handelsvertreter*' or '*Handelsvertreter*' is of an entirely different nature from either that of *Vertretung* or that of agency (in the English sense). A *Vertreter* or an agent (in the

English sense) is a person who performs a certain function, no matter for whom and no matter whether he does so permanently or temporarily and in commerce or privately. A *Handelsagent*, too, is one who performs certain functions, but he must do so permanently in commerce and for a principal who must be his standing client. The law on *Handelsagenten* is thus a specialised branch of commercial law dealing with the affairs of a certain type of businessman, not one dealing with a technical legal function. It is the law of a social group, framed with due regard to the special social and economic needs and requirements of this group and of those who come into contact with it. The closeness of the definition (on which more will have to be said soon) has enabled the legislature to be definite in regard to the provisions which it could enact".

14. It is important to recognise that in German law the commercial agent is identifiable as a member of a particular social group with special social and economic needs. He appears to be a sort of quasi-employee, who, although he nevertheless retains some independence, is substantially dependent on his principal and so needs to be protected. "Commercial agents in the view of most contemporary continental laws, including German and Swiss law, are a group of men who deserve and require the special protection of the law in regard to their contractual relations. They are, or tend to be, it is thought, an exploited class so that the law must step in, in order to prevent or at least restrict their exploitation. The provisions intended to afford this protection are rules of strict law and in consequence incapable of being derogated from by these parties". The directive contains provisions similar to the mandatory provisions of sections 84–92c of the German Commercial Code and in addition contains further far-reaching mandatory provisions for the protection of the commercial agent.

15. All the rules in sections 84–92c of the German Commercial Code, the mandatory provisions and the other provisions, are, of course, understood by german lawyers and applied by the German courts in the context of the remainder of the German Commercial Code and the general provisions of German civil law. german lawyers and German courts will have this context to assist them in applying these sections, and in particular, they will be able to draw upon rules of German law in regard to interpretation of the rules, the ambit of the rules and the remedies available for the enforcement of the rules. However, an English lawyer in applying the directive will have no such body of law upon which to draw. The equivalent rules of English law will be inappropriate and may indeed be distorted by being so used.

16. There are two particularly striking mandatory provisions in the German law which we will mention at this stage:—

    (i) Section 89b of the German Commercial Code entitles the commercial agent to a special adjustment claim on termination, a type of redundancy or severance payment. A similar, although more elaborate and less flexible, provision appears in the directive (Articles 30 and 31). This payment is called by the directive "a goodwill indemnity".

    (ii) Section 90a of the German Commercial Code provides that the principal must pay reasonable compensation, not provided for by his contract, to the agent, during the currency of a restraint clause by which he is bound after the termination of his contract. Again, a similar, although more elaborate and less flexible, provision appears in the directive (Article 32). This payment we will call an "Article 32 payment".

17. Professor Cohn points out that the agent's entitlement to the goodwill indemnity under section 89b of the German Commercial Code is "intended to compensate him for the fact that as a rule the agent's work increases the goodwill of the principal and

not that of the agent and that on termination of the agency the principal thus derives a benefit from this accrued goodwill, while the agent suffers a corresponding loss". Presumably the rationale of section 90a of the German Commercial Code is the assumed inferior bargaining position of the agent.

18. Section 84(1) of the German Commercial Code defines a commercial agent in much the same way as Article 2 of the directive. It seems that commercial agents comprise a social group, with particular social and economic needs, that can be identified in Germany.

### The directive and English law

19. We are unable to identify such a social group in England. We are aware that there exists a class of persons who may be described as manufacturers' selling agents. We are also aware that the Manufacturers' Agents' Association is a body in this country which represents the interests of a number of such agents. We are also aware that this Association has been making representations to the relevant Department for many years for legislation to be enacted to protect its members' interests and that it has been making strenuous representations to the relevant Department in support of the proposed directive. We assume that the majority of its members fall within the scope of Article 2, although we do not know whether it is exceptional for such agents to be authorised to conclude transactions on behalf of their principals.

20. We do not know whether the present law sufficiently protects the social and economic needs of manufacturers' agents. It may be that they often have unequal bargaining power as compared with their principals, although it must be remembered that in English commerce and industry not all manufacturers are large corporations of great bargaining power and not all manufacturers' agents are one-man businesses of poor financial standing. It may of course be that there is a mischief and that manufacturers' agents do, as they contend, require special protection from English law. Such limited consultation as we have been able to engage in leaves us in doubt as to whether this is so. But manufacturers' agents do not comprise the whole, nor even a great proportion, of the persons who appear to be covered by Article 2. In the next paragraph we point out that wide categories of other intermediaries appear to be caught within the definition in Article 2. It is by no means clear that their social and economic needs are the same as those of manufacturers' agents and it seems highly improbable that they are in need of the extensive protection provided by the mandatory provisions of the directive.

21. It seems to us that, as drafted, Article 2 may very well catch persons such as travel agents, literary and theatrical agents, advertising agents, stockbrokers, loading brokers and forwarding agents to the extent that they act for particular principals over a period of time. Of course, to fall within Article 2 they must be self-employed and they must act in the name of and for the account of their principal, but it is suggested that this would not be an unusual relationship for many members of these classes of person. Indeed, solicitors, accountants and patent agents instructed on a retainer basis may also fall within Article 2. These examples are given by way of illustration only: in Germany it has even been held that a man employed to win customers for a dancing master fell within section 84 of the German Commercial Code, upon which Article 2 of the directive is based.

22. It is clear therefore that Article 2 extends to cover a large and amorphous body of very different persons. It is our view that although such persons have a continuing relationship with their principals, it would be wrong to assume that they have similar economic and social needs. [. . .] With regard to many of them it would be misleading

to assume a mischief arising from an interior bargaining position It is inconceivable to us that all the detailed mandatory provisions of the directive would be appropriate to all, or even to many, of them. It is also inconceivable to us that the provisions of the directive would constitute a desirable or an appropriate model contract for all, or perhaps for any, of them. Our reading of the decided cases on the present rules of the English law of agency has not suggested to us that these rules need amending to do justice to all, many, or indeed any, of these persons.

23. Before turning to the detailed provisions of the directive it will be convenient to make some general remarks about the mandatory provisions. We start with the two provisions which we have mentioned above, because they are the most important and will lead to most practical difficulties, and we then turn to a few of the difficulties to which the mandatory nature of some of the other provisions of the directive may give rise.

*Goodwill indemnity*

24. It is stated in the explanatory memorandum that "The indemnity is, of course, payable inter alia to the agent because on his side he provides a consideration which is not fully paid for by the normal remuneration". The equivalent claim granted to the agent by section 89b of the German Commercial Code is intended to compensate him for the fact that his work increased the goodwill of his principal. Articles 30 and 31 of the directive "zig-zag" between the two bases of entitlement; between remunerating the agent for his work and the principal paying for benefits which he has received. Thus Article 30(1) indicates that the entitlement is based on the benefit accruing to the principal as a result of the commercial agent's activities, while Articles 30(2) and (3) indicate that the computation of the amount of the indemnity is based on the effort expended by the commercial agent measured by the time over which this effort was expended.

25. When a principal and an agent enter into an agency contract in England the terms of the contract reflect the principal's assessment of the benefits accruing to him as a result of the agent's activities and the agent's assessment of the value of the efforts to be expended by him. It is difficult to see why in general the agent should receive a payment, for which he has not bargained, when the contract terminates. This is particularly so where the agency contract is for a fixed period and makes no provision for such a payment. Surely in such a case the commercial agent takes the risk that the particular source of income will dry up at the end of the period, and this risk will no doubt be reflected in his rate of commission. The argument is even stronger when the agency contract is for a relatively short period (and no qualifying period is included in Article 30(1)). It seems even more difficult to justify such a payment where the agent terminates the contract of his own free will, perhaps to retire or to take up more remunerative work. On what commercial or moral grounds is the right to such a payment based? The general position in England is that self-employed persons themselves have to make provision for their own retirement. No convincing case has been made for any special favourable treatment for commercial agents.

26. In some ways the directive treats the agent's connection with his principal as his property. Thus it provides that if the agent dies during the period of the contract, his "heirs" are entitled to the goodwill indemnity. The explanatory memorandum, commenting on Article 31(b) explains that "there is the situation where the principal continues to contract with the agent's successor by agreement either of the agent or of his heirs, the new agent succeeding to all the rights and duties of the old. One would, no doubt, be

justified in supposing that in these circumstances the old agent will receive a lump sum payment from his successor which will include the goodwill indemnity". Accordingly, Article 31(b) provides that there shall be no claim where the principal maintains the contract on foot with the agent's successor who was introduced by the agent or by his "heirs". Another surprising feature of the claim is that there is no entitlement where the principal closes down his business, even though substantial benefits would have continued to accrue to him had he remained in business.

27. It is interesting to compare the commercial agent's entitlement to his goodwill indemnity with the employee's entitlement to redundancy pay under English law. For the commercial agent there is no qualifying period; the commercial agent gets his goodwill indemnity if he dies or retires; the commercial agent is not entitled to his goodwill indemnity if the principal closes his business down. In the first and second respects the commercial agent is better off than the employee and in the third respect he is worse off.

28. Section 89b of the German Commercial Code is simpler and more flexible than Articles 30 and 31. The German Commercial Code provides for payment which is "fair and reasonable in all the circumstances". As will appear from our detailed discussion of Articles 30 and 31 below, the rules relating to entitlement under the directive are complex and give rise to much difficulty. We believe that it would be quite inappropriate to incorporate the provisions of Articles 30 and 31 into English law, and that no case has been made out for granting such compensation to *all* the persons who fall within the scope of Article 2, although it might be argued that some or all manufacturers' agents should be entitled to some compensation in certain circumstances on the termination of their contract. It is suggested, however, that the normal and acceptable way to provide for such compensation would be to ascertain the extent of the mischief; that is to say, to ascertain the class of persons who suffer hardship in this country, the precise circumstances in which this hardship arises and the type of compensation to which they should be entitled to alleviate this hardship. Apart from the detailed criticisms of Articles 30 and 31 which we make in the next Part of this paper, we consider these provisions to be wholly unacceptable

"Article 32 payment"

29. The explanatory memorandum to the directive refers to this payment in the following manner: "After termination of the contract the principal must pay to the agent a suitable indemnity throughout the whole period of currency of the agreement restricting competition". It is difficult to see the need for this type of payment. When the commercial agent and the principal are negotiating the terms of their contract, the restraint clause will be bargained for in the normal way and its inclusion will thus be reflected in the other provisions of the contract and in particular in the agreed rate of commission. Why should the commercial agent get an extra payment for observing it? Article 32 extends to restraint clauses entered into as part of an agreement made on the termination of the agency contract, and in these circumstances it seems particularly objectionable for the agent to receive such a payment. It also seems inappropriate for the agent to receive payment if he voluntarily terminates the contract in order, for example, to retire altogether or to take up more remunerative work in another area, or by selling other goods.

30. Section 90a of the German Commercial Code merely provides for the payment of "reasonable compensation in respect of the period of the restriction on competition".

Cohn comments: "Perhaps the best advice that a draftsman can give to his clients in view of the existing provisions may well be not to provide for a non-competition clause in respect of the period following upon the termination of the agreement, though this is in some cases not a very fortunate solution from the point of view of the principal".

31. Article 32 of the directive is more complicated than section 90a and gives rise to many difficulties, as appears from our detailed discussion of Article 32 below.

32. Article 32 would put the commercial agent in a better position than the employee who is, of course, entitled to no such payment during the currency of a period of a valid restraint clause. As a matter of policy we see no basis for such a payment and, in any event, Article 32 as drafted would be quite unjustified, even if there were a basis for some such payment to some agents in some circumstances.

*Mandatory nature of the provisions*

33. Although the rules regarding the goodwill indemnity and the Article 32 payment are the most striking of the mandatory provisions there are many others. Most of the others concern topics (such as the circumstances in which commission is payable) which would in the ordinary way be dealt with in the contract by express provision. Such express terms would be overridden by the directive with the result that the parties would find themselves bound by terms quite different from those that they had agreed. The directive thus represents a substantial, and, we believe, unwarranted interference with freedom of contract. This general point is most easily illustrated by supposing the following set of facts:—

> A UK company wishes to promote the sale of certain drinks on the Italian Riviera. An Italian company, with a paid up capital of 1 000 000 EUA or less, is engaged to canvass for orders, over a 12-month period, from customers on the Italian Riviera and, in particular, from hoteliers and bar proprietors. An agreement is negotiated and reduced into writing which requires the Italian company to organise and pay for a poster campaign (promoting the drinks in question) and to collect, and guarantee, payment in respect of orders placed during the 12-month period by customers introduced by them. The UK company agrees to pay a substantial monthly retainer together with 25% of the value of the first order (only) placed and paid for by each customer introduced by the Italian company during the 12-month period. The agreement provides that no commission will be payable in any other circumstances and that there will be no reimbursement for expenses. The agreement provides that the Italian company may deduct the agreed commission from monies collected and remit the balance at the end of each month, and that they are not entitled to a lien over goods or samples entrusted to them by the UK company. Finally the agreement provides that there is a possibility of "passing off" proceedings in Italy in respect of a new vermouth that the UK company is marketing; the canvassing of orders for this product is to be at the Italian company's own risk; there is to be no right of indemnity by the UK company if the promotion of this product by the Italian company results in proceedings.

34. An agreement along the lines indicated above would fall foul of the directive in a number of respects:
    (a) The Italian company would be entitled to *extra* payments (notwithstanding the terms expressly agreed):—

     (i)  for the cost of the poster campaign (Article 20(2));

    (ii)  for collecting money (Article 14);

    (iii)  for guaranteeing payment (Article 21(3));

    (iv)  for repeat orders from customers introduced by the Italian company (Article 12(1)(*b*));

    (v)  for orders from customers in the area introduced by persons other than the Italian company (Article 12(1)(*c*))'

    (vi)  for repeat orders from old customers (Article 12(1)(*c*));

    (vii)  for orders executed but not paid for (Article 15(2)(*a*)).

(b) On the other hand the Italian company would be in breach of Article 5(2)(*b*) in deducting commission from money received and in not paying over the balance until the end of the month.

(c) The guarantee would be invalidated by Articles 21(2)(*a*) *and* 21(2)(*b*) and 21(2)(*c*).

(d) The Italian company *would* be entitled to a lien (Article 29(2)).

(e) If the Italian company were involved in court proceedings over the new vermouth there *would* be a right of indemnity (Article 8(1)).

There are thus many respects in which the directive prevents the principal and the commercial agent from making a binding agreement which is acceptable to them both. However sensible, reasonable and fair it may be in its effect, it is liable to be converted by the directive into something which is intrinsically unfair and which makes a nonsense of the bargain that was made.

## Uncertainty created by the directive

35.  The explanatory memorandum states that the directive is intended to remove the uncertainties that may at present exist as to what the rights of commercial agents are. So far from removing uncertainties the mandatory provisions, just considered, are likely to create them wherever there is a conflict between what the directive provides and what the parties have in fact agreed. This might be acceptable if the mandatory provisions were themselves simple and clear, but they are intricate, confusing and inconsistent one with another. Our detailed analysis of the provisions in the directive follows, in Part III; a recurring theme is that even if the policy behind the directive is sound, which we doubt, its provisions are likely to produce great uncertainty across a very wide area.

PART III—THE DETAILED PROVISIONS OF THE DIRECTIVE

36.  In this Part we consider the detailed provisions of the directive article by article. We draw attention, in particular, to—

(a) the policy considerations on which the mandatory provisions appear to be based and the relevance of these policy considerations to the various different groups of people who come within the Article 2 description of "commercial agents";

(b) the policy considerations on which the non-mandatory provisions appear to be based and the extent to which the model contract thus produced is appropriate to the needs of the various different kinds of "commercial agent" (see (È), above);

    (c)  the consequences of superimposing the provisions of the directive upon the English law of contract;

    (d)  the obscure, complex and unsatisfactory nature of the directive's provisions.

37.  There are, however, some general observations to be made about the preparation and drafting of the directive and about the legal concepts incorporated into it which it is convenient to deal with first.

*General points on the drafting of the directive*

38.  We realise that directives are not prepared by utilising the same drafting techniques which are used by Parliamentary Counsel when drafting English statutes. We also realise that the style of drafting is that of states whose legal system is based on civil law rather than on common law. We think, however, that the points we are going to make are nevertheless valid and that their validity can be appreciated when a detailed comparison is made between the articles of the directive and the corresponding provisions of the German Commercial Code (sections 84–92c). Many of the criticisms which we make below cannot, or cannot to any great extent, we levelled at the German text. There are many faults in the directive which may merely be faults of translation or be minor drafting errors, but only part of our criticism is directed to these faults. The German provisions have been extensively adapted, changed and elaborated and many of our comments relate to these alterations. This does not mean that as a matter of content we would welcome any or all of the German rules, but at least we understand, or think we do, the meaning and ambit of most of the German rules, whereas we have found the directive much harder to follow and in places completely incomprehensible.

39.  There are three major drafting defects which run through the directive:—

    (a)  it lays down rules without specifying what consequences flow from their breach (see, for example, Articles 21(1), 23, 24, 26(1) and 27(2));

    (b)  it uses a number of different words to express the same idea (a list of examples is included in an Annex, identified as Annex C);

    (c)  it uses the same word to express a number of different ideas (a list of examples is included in the Annex referred to above).

40.  There are other points to be made about the draftsmanship which merit general comment not just because they make this particular directive hard to construe but because unless exception is taken to them they are likely to occur in other instruments within the Commission of the European Communities:—

    (a)  there is a tendency to make the same point twice, once positively and once negatively (compare, for example, Article 3 (first 7 lines) with Article 2; also Article 7(1) and Article 7(2));

    (b)  statements of general principle are followed by non-exhaustive, ill-chosen and misleading lists of illustrations (Articles 5 and 10);

    (c)  particular instances are given of a general principle which is nowhere stated (Article 8);

    (d)  a technique of descriptive drafting is used which does not exhaust all the possibilities (see, for example, articles 9(2) and 11(1)).

41.  We draw attention, in our article by article analysis, to provisions in the directive which we consider are badly drafted, unclear, ambiguous, internally inconsistent or which contain lacunae or are otherwise objectionable. We recognise that some of these points, taken in isolation, are of minor importance. But we suggest that the cumulative effect

is that, irrespective of the objections that there are to the policies in the directive and the content of its rules, the directive in its present form is quite unworkable.

*Problems for the common law*

42. There are a number of legal concepts and techniques which underlie or are found in the provisions of the directive which have no counterpart in English law. This does not, of course, in itself render them objectionable. Indeed, they should be considered as possible reforms of the law and evaluated as such. They do need to be examined, however, in the light of the wide scope of the directive which would make major changes in a broad, but quite ill-defined, area of the law of agency. Any uncertainty so engendered has to be balanced against the advantages, if any, that these new concepts might bring to English law. Three examples may be given:—
    (a) extraordinary termination;
    (b) secondary activities; and
    (c) the effect of failure to comply with the requirement of writing in the formation of the contract.

*(a) Extraordinary termination*

43. Article 27(1)(b) provides that either party may terminate a contract at any time—
    "where some circumstance arises which makes it impossible to perform the contract, or which seriously prejudices its performance, or which substantially undermines the commercial basis of the contract, so that the party who terminates cannot be required to keep it in being until the end of the period of notice or until the end of its agreed period of duration."
    This provision is mandatory. Section 89a of the German Commercial Code provides that
    "(i) the contractual relationship may be put to an end by either party without notice for important reasons. This provision may not be excluded or limited."
    Professor Cohn comments thus: "No doubt this rule introduces some measure of uncertainty into the relationship between principal and agent. German lawyers do not mind this so very much; they are accustomed to the principle embodied in section 89a from numerous other instances in which it applies. The rule that a contract may be terminated for 'important reasons' is, in fact, a fundamental principle of German law applicable to all contracts concluded for a period of any length. It finds its explanation in part in the desire not to tie parties for too long to obligations undertaken at a time when the future turn of events could not well be appreciated. No doubt, the turbulent history of the country during its last fifty years has contributed to rendering such a rule commendable". Perhaps English lawyers would be surprised at this measure of uncertainty. The concept of "extraordinary termination" is very much wider than the English doctrine of frustration, and "the colourful variety of grounds of termination" to be found in German decisions and in German legal writings would be new to the common law. In addition, whereas in English law the frustrating event brings the contract to an end without more, Article 27(2) requires that there should be an act of termination as such. These differences are likely to cause problems if Article 27 is superimposed upon the English law of contract. We are not convinced that the innovation is necessary or desirable.

*(b) Secondary activities*

44. An important distinction is drawn in the directive between the main category of commercial agents and those who act as commercial agents by way of "secondary activity" only (Article 4(1)).

45. Unfortunately, the directive does not way what is to constitute a "secondary activity". Apparently, (from what is said in the explanatory memorandum) a person may be an agent as a secondary activity although he has no other form of commercial activity that may be described as "primary". He may, it seems, carry on secondary activities with more than one principal. The explanatory memorandum fairly concedes that it is impossible to lay down suitable criteria which apply in every case, and yet the directive provides, in Article 4, that the question whether the activity is carried on by way of secondary activity is to be determined "in accordance with commercial usage in the State whose law governs the relations between principal and agent". Since there is, so far as we know, no established commercial usage in England regarding persons who act as commercial agents by way of secondary activity, any legislation introducing such a classification would, in order to comply with the directive, have to be cast in very general terms. This might well give rise to considerable litigation in a wide variety of agency relationships.

*(c) The function of writing in the formation of the contract*

46. Article 23 of the directive provides that either party shall be entitled to receive from the other a signed written document setting out the terms of the contract and any terms subsequently agreed, and that any purported waiver of this right shall be invalid. Section 85 of the German Commercial Code provides:

> "Either party is entitled to demand that the terms of the contract together with any subsequent additional agreements thereto shall be set out in writing and signed by the other party thereto. This provision may not be excluded by agreement."

As Professor Cohn points out, "the German legislator's desire to protect the agent begins literally with the moment of the conclusion of the agency agreement". He continues: "the right to demand written fixation is not merely academic: it can be enforced by proceedings in court which will lead to a judgment in which the court will lay down authoritatively the terms which the parties have been found to have agreed. Although little use has been made of these sweeping and beneficent powers of the court, the rule may well serve to illustrate the wide powers entrusted by the legislature to the judiciary. That the court will not make the contract for the parties is not a proposition with which a modern civilian will be able to find himself in agreement". Whilst a procedure could no doubt be devised in this country for compelling the principal to deliver a written agency agreement to the agent and for the agent to deliver one to the principal, we doubt whether such a procedure would be appropriate in the present broad but uncertain context.

*Article by article analysis*

47. In the rest of this Part we analyse the directive article by article.

## Article 1

We make no comment on this article at this stage although its terms are relevant to what we say about the directive's provisions in relation to third party rights (Articles 5(1) and 9) and rights on bankruptcy (Article 22).

## Article 2

(a) The main thrust of the directive seems to be to provide protection for commercial agents who are engaged to canvass orders for their principals' goods. Although the directive does not distinguish between buying agents and selling agents it seems that selling agents are the ones that the directive aims to protect: Article 17 (which provides that the commission should be geared to the gross amount of the invoice) and Article 30(1)(a) (which mentions "new customers") would produce some strange results if applied to buying agents. Similarly, although the directive covers the supply of services as well as goods it is clear from Articles 10(2)(a) and (b) that goods are the directive's prime concern.

(b) Article 2 is far too wide to be acceptable to English law and wider, it seems, than is necessary to serve the policies on which the directive is based. There is, we believe, no ground for extending its scope beyond selling agents dealing in goods. In particular no case is made out for the inclusion of buying agents and agents for services and we think they should be omitted.

(c) The policy of protection may be justified in regard to those individuals who rely for their livelihood on the sale of their principals' products (quasi-employees) but we can see no justification for extending the protection to

   (i) legal persons other than private individuals (for example, limited companies) or to

   (ii) intermediaries such as travel agents, advertising agents, literary and theatrical agents, stockbrokers, loading brokers, forwarding agents, solicitors, accountants, patent agents, etc.

(d) The policy of providing protection may be appropriate where the agent's income is derived wholly or partly from commission, but it is clearly inappropriate where his services are paid for by a fixed retainer. We think that Article 2 ought to limit the directive to commercial agents who are remunerated either wholly or in part by commission.

(e) The requirement that the agent should have a "continuing authority for a fixed or indeterminate period" would seem to be satisfied in the case of an agent appointed for the duration of a motor show; we would have expected the definition to include a requirement of "permanence" as a characteristic of the agent's appointment.

(f) The requirement that the agent's authority must extend to "an unlimited number of commercial transactions" is likely to lead to confusion. Presumably a manufacturer who limited his agent's sales by a quota system of so many sales a year would be outside the scope of Article 2.

## Article 3

(a) The first and third exclusions seem to be otiose as they add nothing to what is already excluded by Article 2 itself.

(b) The second exclusion causes difficulties where the agent has authority to act in his own name but doesn't use it and also where the agent has no such authority but acts as if he had.

(c) The exclusion of "those who carry on their activities in the insurance or credit fields" seems to be wider than the exclusion of those who act for insurance or financial institutions. The looser terminology of the directive is likely to lead to uncertainty.

(d) We should, perhaps, add that the very wide definition of commercial agents given by Article 2 would not be made acceptable by adding further specific exclusions, such as travel agents, stockbrokers etc. This would not be a satisfactory way of identifying the social group to whom the directive's provisions should apply.

## Article 4

(a) The term "by way of secondary activity" corresponds with the term "*Nebenberuf*" in section 92b of the German Commercial Code. The Code does not contain a definition of "*Nebenberuf*". In German law the test seems to be whether there is another, not necessarily commercial, activity which may be treated as primary. For these purposes students, pensioners and housewives who do agency work in their spare time are doing it by way of secondary activity. Presumably the full-time employee who does agency work on the side (whether during or out of his ordinary hours of employment) is acting "by way of secondary activity" whatever relation his income from one activity bears to his income from the other. Plainly there will be much uncertainty as to what constitutes a secondary activity; the entitlement to a goodwill indemnity may depend on which side of the line the particular agency falls.

(b) Assuming that those who act as commercial agents by way of secondary activity can be identified as a group (the housewife with a mail-order agency seems to be regarded as typical) the group should be excluded altogether from the scope of the directive, on the ground that its members are not quasi-employees and do not need special protection.

## Article 5

(a) This article purports to set out the subsidiary duties of the agent (to keep proper accounts, etc.) and to say how he should conduct himself (fairly and carefully) without saying what his main duty is. What seems to be missing is a general duty that the agent should obtain business for his principal.

(b) Article 5(1) requires the agent to act fairly vis-à-vis third parties. The rights of third parties vis-à-vis agents are a matter for national law and there is no justification for legislating for third parties in this directive.

(c) The references to the standard of care exercised by a sound businessman (Articles 5(1) and 5(2)(d)) derive from section 86(3) of the German Commercial Code. We are not altogether clear how English courts would fit this novel duty into the English law of agency.

(d) Articles 5(2)(a) to (e) pose various difficulties of construction, for example:—
  - (i) under (a) is it sufficient for the principal to supply such information as he has?
  - (ii) under (b) does "without delay" mean "the same day" "at the end of each month" or what?
  - (iii) under (e) what kind of instructions "basically affect the agent's independence"? What if the principal were to require the agent to visit certain named principals at certain stated intervals?

## Article 6

(a) "The principles of a sound businessman" is a novelty for English lawyers and it is doubtful whether it is apt here; a standard of "fair dealing" rather than "sound business" might be more appropriate.

(b) The directive precludes the agent from making disclosures to third parties even where this is justified by the public interest, or so it seems. How are the English courts to apply this article to facts such as occurred in *Initial Services Ltd. v Putterill*?

## Article 7

(a) The drafting of Articles 7(1) and 7(2) is cumbersome and apparently self-contradictory whereas, presumably, all the directive means to say is that the agent may not compete with the principal in relation to the goods (or services) in question without the principal's consent.

(b) We doubt whether this article is appropriate for inclusion in a model contract. It runs contrary to the English law approach which is, broadly, that if the principal wants to restrict the agent from working for other principals at the same time he must say so. Why should not a housewife who runs an agency for one mail order firm be allowed to run one for another firm as well, unless of course the contract expressly provides that she should not?

(c) There is a more general objection to Article 7 and, more particularly Article 7(3), that it would appear to make covenants in restraint of trade binding which would otherwise be invalid in English law. The conflict between this article and the existing state of English law is likely to lead to much confusion and uncertainty.

[Analysis of Articles 8–12 omitted]

## Article 13

(a) No doubt difficulties arise when one agent takes over from another. However, instead of allowing the principal and his agents to work out transitional provisions by agreement Article 13 lays down a set of circumstances in which the predecessor is to have the commission and his successor accordingly gets none. There seems no good reason why this crude all-or-nothing solution should be made mandatory.

(b) The rules that entitle the predecessor to his commission depend on fine distinctions (for example between "negotiation" and "preparatory work") and difficult questions of fact (like who is "mainly" responsible and what period after the change-over would be "reasonable" having regard to the type and volume of the transaction in question). The rules are singularly inappropriate for a model agency contract and would cause problems if superimposed on English law.

## Article 14

(a) The requirement that a commercial agent must be paid a special commission for collecting payment has no justification that we can see and is likely to lead to great difficulty in cases where the parties treat the remuneration from collecting payment as a factor in calculating the overall rate of commission or retainer.

(b) The "special commission" is not defined. No guidance is given as to when it becomes payable or on what basis or at what rate the commission is to be calculated.

(c) It is not clear whether the *del credere* agent is entitled to Article 14 commission when he makes the payment out of his own pocket.

## Article 15

(a) The provision that the right to commission should arise at the moment when the principal and third party enter into a commercial transaction is presumably intended to link up with the bankruptcy provision in Article 22, which provides that natural persons whose income is mainly derived from a commercial agency shall, as regards sums owing to them for remuneration and reimbursement of expenses, be treated as employees on the principal's bankruptcy. The policy, according to a somewhat bland statement in the explanatory memorandum, is to allow the commercial agent to prove in the bankruptcy for commission that has not yet become available, as if it were already due. We believe that this is inconsistent with the principles of bankruptcy law and with honest dealing, and as such should find no place in a directive on agency.

(b) There appears to be a conflict both in the explanatory memorandum and in Article 15 of the directive as to the policy on which the entitlement to receive the commission is based. The explanatory memorandum asserts that payment of the commission is generally dependent on payment by the third party and states that "The general rule is that the principal is not bound to pay commission unless the third party performs his part of the transaction". This seems inconsistent with a later statement that "The agent knows that where the third party has not performed his part of the contract, and however long that state of affairs continues, commission will be paid *as a general rule* at the end of the third month following that in which the principal performs his part. The exceptions to this are set out in Article 16". Article 15(2)(a), however, starts with a proposition that conflicts with the "general rules" in the explanatory memorandum, namely, that the commission is to be payable as soon as and to the extent that the principal has performed his part of the transaction, even if he fails to carry out his obligations fully in the manner agreed or satisfies some of them only partially. This provision is mandatory and yet Article 15(4) (which is also mandatory in some cases) allows the parties to agree that commission shall be payable at a later time so long as the third party has not performed his obligations! Article 15(4) provides a back stop of three months from performance by the principal as the date beyond which payment of the commission may not be postponed by agreement, but this depends on complete performance by the principal whereas Article 15(2) does not. The principal might postpone the payment of commission beyond three months by holding back say the last 5 of 100 articles that were due for delivery. This article is riddled with gaps and inconsistencies.

(c) It seems that although the agent has a "right to commission" when the principal and the third party first enter into the commercial transaction, no commission is ever payable if neither party performs the contract at all or if the contract is cancelled by mutual agreement. It is all very puzzling.

(d) Article 15(3) is badly drafted, complex in its structure and would be very difficult to apply in practice. Likewise with Article 15(5) it seems ridiculous, having regard to the wide variety of persons to whom Article 2 is likely to apply, to restrict them to monthly or quarterly accounting periods.


## Article 16

(a) Article 16(1)(a) extinguishes the agent's right to commission for breach of his duty under Article 5(2)(a). However Article 5(2)(a) describes a general duty to supply the principal with information that he needs and also a special duty as regards information on the solvency of third parties. Is the right to commission extinguished for breach of the general duty (which seems too wide) or only for breach of the special duty to keep the principal informed about the solvency of customers? The explanatory memorandum suggests the latter which is obviously too narrow.

(b) Article 16(1)(c) envisages that the principal has reasonable grounds for supposing that the third party will not perform but that the contract has not been frustrated and the third party is not actually in breach and has not repudiated. In English law this gives the principal no legal excuse for not performing the contract with the third party. There is thus likely to be a difficulty if Article 16 (which is mandatory) is superimposed on English law. Moreover, under Article 16(1)(c) the principal is absolved from having to pay commission as soon as "serious grounds for non-performance" exist even though the third party later defies expectations and performs after all. The explanatory memorandum points out that it is impossible to spell out in the directive the precise meaning of "serious grounds", the scope and significance of which has been "settled by the law or by the case law or in the juristic writings in the Member States". However, this is a novel concept in English law where its introduction is likely to cause considerable confusion and uncertainty.

## Article 17

(a) It is doubtful whether this provision (that commission should as a general rule be cal-
    culated on the gross amount of the invoice) is appropriate for a model contract.
    Sometimes the cost of transit may represent a large part of the amount of the invoice.
(b) The reference to "invoiced separately" is confusing. It is not clear whether it means
    "stated as separate items on the same invoice" or "stated in a separate invoice".

## Article 18

(a) Article 18 is mandatory and gives the commercial agent a right to see copies of extracts
    from the principal's books and, in certain circumstances, access to the books them-
    selves. It is not clear whether this is necessary (having regard to the principal's duties
    under Article 10(1)) or desirable.
(b) If the requirement in Article 18(1) is necessary and desirable (which we doubt) surely
    the procedure for its enforcement should be left to the laws of Member States. Article
    18(2) is an absurdly over-elaborate rule. Its implementation (and it is of course manda-
    tory) would entail the creation of a new category of auditors, "auditors-on-oath" and
    the making of special rules of procedure.
(c) The option allowed by Article 18(2) enables the principal to compel the agent *not* to
    employ a professional adviser. We find this objectionable.

## Article 19

(a) The policy underlying this article is unclear. It seems to go beyond the requirement that
    the principal should act in good faith (Article 10). Why should the agent be entitled to
    "fall-back" pay when he has merely "taken steps" towards performing his obligations
    or has fulfilled them by doing nothing more strenuous than caring for the samples? It
    will be remembered that he has no general obligation under Article 5 to promote his
    principal's business.
(b) The circumstances in which the principal is *not* required to make payments under
    Article 19 are likely to cause confusion in English law since they depend on a concept
    of "circumstances beyond his control" and this is not the same as the legal doctrine of
    frustration.
(c) Assuming that money is payable under Article 19 it is by no means clear when the right
    to payment arises. As for the basis of the computation, Article 19(2), which is geared to
    the loss of expected earnings, seems to be in conflict with Article 19(3) which is geared
    to the amount of money expended by the agent in setting up the agency.

## Article 20

(a) We can see no justification for including Article 20(2) in the directive. Why should
    the parties not be allowed to agree that "special activities" should be at the agent's

expense or that they should be taken into account in fixing the level of commission or retainer?

(b) Article 20(2) is extremely loosely drafted. How is the court to decide what are "*special activities?*"

## Article 21

(a) The entitlement to a "separate commission" in respect of certain *del credere* transactions is in some circumstances mandatory. It is likely to cause confusion when it runs contrary to what the parties have expressly agreed.

(b) Nowhere in the article is it provided when the agent becomes entitled to be paid his separate commission. Payment cannot be governed by Article 15 as that article depends on performance by (principal or third party) and a *del credere* agent is paid his commission for his promise.

(c) Article 21(1) requires that *del credere* agreements be evidenced in writing. Such agreements are not within the provisions of our Statute of Frauds and accordingly are not required by English law to be evidenced by writing. Confusion is likely to arise where some of the activities of an English *del credere* agent are affected by the directive and some are not.

(d) The effect of non-compliance with the requirement of written evidence (Article 21(1)) is not clear. Presumably the agent is not liable to the principal if the third party does not pay, but suppose the third party does pay. Can the agent get his *del credere* commission under Article 21(3) or is he barred by want of written evidence?

(e) Article 21(4) allows the parties to derogate from the earlier provisions as regards transactions "which the agent has been given full power to agree and to carry out". It is hard to see what situations are described by this provision; it seems to allow "contracting out" in every case.

(f) There are various obscurities in the text that are likely to cause difficulty:—,

    (i) Who are "particular parties . . . specified" (Article 21(b))? Do they have to be named or will a class description suffice? If the latter, can the class be "any customer introduced by the commercial agent"?

    (ii) Does "unlimited" (Article 21(2)(c)) mean "without financial limit"? If so, the provision is useless unless a financial limit is specified. Will 99% pass muster?

    (iii) What is "the place of business" (Article 21(4)(a)) where the principal (or the third party) has several?

## Article 22

(a) This article goes beyond the relations between self-employed commercial agents and their principals (Article 1). It seeks to change the laws on insolvency so as to give commercial agents preferential rights against the general body of creditors. We can see no justification for such provisions in this directive and doubt whether they have a sound jurisdictional basis.

(b) Remarkably this article is not mandatory. This is particularly odd because Article 15(1), which *is* mandatory, provides that a right to commission arises at the moment when the principal and the third party enter into the commercial transaction and so gives the agent improved rights on bankruptcy.

(c) It is by no means clear how Articles 15(1) and 22 are meant to work when the principal becomes insolvent. Article 15(1) is intended to allow the agent to prove for commission although neither the principal nor the third party have performed at all; but for what sum does he, in fact, prove?

(d) The broad aim of Article 22 is to make the agent a preferred creditor in respect of his commission as if he were an employee claiming for wages. However the agent may only so prove where his income is "mainly derived from a commercial agency" (Article 22(1)). The relevance of the agent's other income (for example from investments) is not clear. Moreover, the line may often be hard to draw in practice and is not effective to exclude stockbrokers, forwarding agents and so on, nor even to exclude those who act as agents as a secondary activity. It is unsatisfactory in every possible way.

(e) Employees are preferred creditors in English law for some of the wages that are payable but unpaid at the date of bankruptcy. Articles 15(1) and 22 do not merely put self-employed commercial agents on a par with wage-earners—although this would be hard enough to justify—but they purport to give the agent a preferential right to prove for commission that is not even payable at the date of the bankruptcy.

## Article 23

The explanatory memorandum makes it clear that the entitlement by the principal and the agent to receive a signed written document from each other arises on the request of the other party. What is the effect of failure to comply with the request? Under Article 23 no consequences appear to flow. It would be absurd if the result was that the contract was void. Does it impose a duty, the breach of which might justify termination and could give rise to damages, if it should lead to loss? Is it mere exhortation?

## Article 24

(a) Presumably failure to comply with Article 24 has no more effect than failure to comply with Article 23. This being so it is hard to see why the parties should bother to comply with Article 24.

(b) It is odd that the provision in Article 24 is not mandatory whereas Article 23 is. Presumably the invalidation of any waiver of rights given by the article is imported from Article 23, so that the parties, in order to release each other from the right to receive a written document upon request setting out the terms of the mutual termination, would have expressly to provide in their contract that Article 24 was not to apply. This is a good example of a wholly inappropriate provision for insertion into a model contract.

## Article 25

No comment.

## Article 26

(a) Article 26(1) is mandatory and provides, amongst other things, that the period of notice must be the same for both sides. This is not always appropriate and confusion will arise where the parties make more sensible arrangements in breach of the article.

(b) No sanction is specified where the notice of termination is not given in writing. The contract presumably continues (?)

(c) It is not clear what happens when the proper period of notice is not observed. One would have expected the notice to be ineffective but Article 28(1) seems to contemplate that an agreement may be "terminated" by a defective notice.

## Article 27

(a) This article provides that the agreement may be terminated on grounds that are not recognised in the English law of contract. Difficulties are likely to follow from the superimposition of this article upon English law. One of the novel grounds of termination is the other party's "fault"; an idea that may be well-established in civilian systems but is not part of the English law of contract.

(b) Another novel ground is the happening of "events which justify termination". It is clear that this goes beyond the English doctrine of frustration since the example given in the explanatory memorandum is of an agent who finds it impossible to continue in business for reasons of health, old age or serious and unforeseeable family circumstances. We can only guess at the other kinds of "events" that might justify termination. What about Japanese competition which undermines the financial prospects of the agency after it has run for two years? What is the principal (as opposed to the agent) becomes old or ill or has family problems? Or where it has become unprofitable for him to sell a particular line of goods? The inter-relation between the grounds for termination under this article and the grounds for non-payment of commission under Article 16(1)(c) remains unclear.

(c) Article 27(1)(b) differs from frustration in another respect which is likely to cause difficulties in English law, namely that the events justifying termination do not by themselves end the agreement: one party or the other has to "terminate" as well.

(d) The relation between this article and Article 13 should be noted. It seems that the agent may still be entitled to commission on a transaction negotiated by him, even though "at fault" in relation to the very transaction justifying his dismissal. Is this a desirable rule?

(e) Article 27(1)(a) uses the phrase "cannot be required", whereas in Article 16(1)(c) the phrase is "cannot reasonably be required". A similar point occurs in Article 27(1)(b). Is the difference intended to have a significance or is it just sloppy drafting?

(f) Article 27(2) refers to "termination vis-à-vis the other party". Presumably the communication would have to be in writing; otherwise the provision that the reasons for termination have to be given in writing is anomalous. But the point is not dealt with expressly.

## Article 28

(a) Article 28(1) seems to draw a distinction between "termination" and "declaring the contract to be at an end" although it is not clear what it is; it is unknown to English law. It is likely to cause uncertainty.

(b) Article 28 tells us nothing about the effects of failure to give *written* notice under Article 26(1) or to give *written* reasons under Article 27(2). In other words, it does not tell us what happens where the notice is good in substance but bad in form. Does the notice terminate the contract or does the contract nevertheless continue?

(c) Article 28(2) introduces the concept of the "lump sum indemnity" which is a novelty in our law of agency. It seems that the agent gets his average monthly earnings for the unexpired contract period, subject to the two year limit. Why should he get the whole "average remuneration" without allowing for the fact that he does not have to incur the expense of earning it? Why are the factors, relevant under Article 19(3)(b), not also relevant here? The English law requires that employees who have been wrongfully dismissed should only recover their real loss, after taking into account the extent to which the loss was or should have been mitigated. The directive aims to put the commercial agent in a better position, in this regard, than the ordinary employee.

## Article 29

There seems no reason why the agent's right of lien should be mandatory and in full force in all cases. There may be circumstances in which it would be fair and reasonable for the agent to contract for a qualified right of lien, or, perhaps, no such right at all. Furthermore Article 29(2) seems to allow a general lien covering, for example, goods entrusted to the agent for use only; this is in conflict with the existing English law and must result in uncertainty.

## Articles 30 and 31

Policy considerations relevant to whether there should be any payment at all

(a) We have already pointed out that we are not satisfied that any case has been made out that a goodwill indemnity should ever be payable unless the principal and the agent, in their contract, have bargained for such a payment.

(b) However, even if a case were made out for such a mandatory entitlement it should only be payable where the agency is for an indeterminate period and it certainly could never be justified where the agency is for a fixed term.

(c) Whatever justification there might be for giving the "quasi-employee" a goodwill indemnity there certainly can be none for giving it to:—

   (i) persons such as advertising agents, theatrical agents, stockbrokers, etc., who are caught by Article 2;

  (ii) persons acting as commercial agents as a secondary activity;

 (iii) companies or corporations; although Article 33(1) permits large companies to contract out of Article 30 we are of the view that not only is the mandatory rule inappropriate for small companies, but the entitlement is also inappropriate as a term of a model contract for large companies.

(d) We can see no justification for allowing the agent to claim the indemnity when he retires and terminates the contract by notice under Article 30(4). The agency is treated by the directive as alienable. If it is worth something then presumably the agent should be able to recover its value by selling it; if it is not worth anything then presumably he should not be entitled to anything. Furthermore, a principal may be prejudiced by having to pay out a lump sum at a time not of his own choosing. The right of indemnity on resignation could be abused by the agent if, after an interval (so that 30(1)(b) is satisfied) he begins to negotiate transactions between the customers he introduced to his former principal and a new principal with whom he subsequently has taken up work.

(e) Even if the goodwill indemnity ought sometimes to be payable to the agent whose services are dispensed with—so as to provide him with something comparable to redundancy money—it does not follow that the right to the indemnity should automatically pass to his estate if he dies while the contract is still on foot (as Article 30(1) appears to contemplate).

(f) On the other hand if the policy behind the goodwill indemnity provisions is that the agent should get a reward for effort it is hard to see why he should be deprived of it just because he receives something by virtue of Article 13. If under Article 13 the commercial agent receives commission on one or two transactions entered into after the contract has come to an end with two customers introduced by him, it seems that his right to goodwill indemnity is excluded. Can this be right? The position seems to be different if he gets Article 13 commission in respect of one customer and not in respect of the other: that is, he is then entitled to the *full* goodwill indemnity. Is this distinction defensible? The general policy of Article 30(1)(c) seems to be that the commercial agent is not to get goodwill indemnity in respect of a source of income that is in fact continuing. But the attempt to express this policy has been unsuccessful.

(g) Assuming, as in (f), that the basis of the goodwill indemnity is to provide a reward for effort it is remarkable that the agent who puts in many years of work gets no recompense if the principal does not as a result receive "substantial benefits [that] will continue to accrue", for example, where the principal decides to close down his business because it is no longer profitable.

*Policy considerations relevant to the calculation of the amount payable*

(h) Articles 30 and 31 "zig-zag" between two different principles for calculating the remuneration, one that it should be a reward to the agent for the work he has done, the other that the principal should account for the benefit that he is left with when the agent has left. The result is confusing and must create difficulties for the courts.

(i) There is no direct relationship between the conditions in which the right arises (Article 30(1)) and the amount to which the agent is entitled (Article 30(2)). Suppose the principal gets a slight benefit by introducing two new customers while also negotiating transactions with 98 old customers (with whom the volume of business is not "appreciably increased"). The minimum amount of the goodwill indemnity under Article 30(2) is based on the *whole* of his average annual remuneration—not on the *extra* amount attributable to the new customers. This might be adjusted under Article 30(3). But this confused position shows that sensible rules for computation have not been formulated: and, because of the conflicting bases of the entitlement (benefit/efforts), certainly cannot be formulated.

(j)  The first sentence of Article 30(4) envisages payment to the agent who terminates by notice without justification of an indemnity not exceeding the amount payable under Article 30(2), whereas the second sentence of Article 30(4) provides that the agent who terminates without justification might be entitled to the maximum indemnity in Article 30(3). It is quite possible, if the agent has worked for 20 years, for his minimum entitlement under Article 30(2) to be equal to his maximum entitlement under Article 30(3): the effect or providing a different way of calculating the indemnity is not clear. In any event, where the agent's termination was justified by the principal's conduct, the agent would presumably have his remedy in damages for breach.

(k)  Article 30(4) provides for a very unsatisfactory mixture of goodwill indemnity and some form of punitive damages. The principal becomes liable to the maximum amount (whether it is otherwise available or not) simply because he is in breach, even though the loss to the agent is much less.

*Points which are likely to give rise to difficulties in practice*

(l)  The question whether a right to goodwill indemnity exists may be very hard to answer in view of the words "appreciably" in Article 30(1)(a) and "substantial" in Article 30(1)(b). The latter provision also prompts the question for how long must the benefit continue to accrue? Is one month long enough after ten years of agency?

(m) In Article 30(2) it is not clear what "the preceding five years" precedes. If it is intended to denote the five years preceding the cessation of the contract, then it appears to be inconsistent with the provision that the basis for the calculation for the indemnity should include Article 13 commission in respect of transactions concluded *after* the cessation of the contract. If the words are not intended to mean that period, it is hard to see what they do mean.

(n)  Article 30(4), second sentence, seems to create some anomalies. It only applies (so as to give the commercial agent the right to the "maximum amount"—that is, two years' average pay) if the commercial agent gives due notice *and* the termination is justified; at least this seems to follow from the phrase "*such* termination". Why, if termination is "justified" must the notice periods be observed for this purpose? What, moreover, is meant by "justified"? Is the reference to "the principal's conduct" one to "fault" within Article 27(1)(a)? If so, why is this not stated? If not, what *does* "the principal's conduct" mean? Is the reference to a kind of constructive dismissal but without breach by the principal? What are "reasons which are particular to the agent"? Is the reference to circumstances listed in Article 27(1)(b) or is it to something wider? Do the words cover the case where the commercial agent is simply too old to carry on and wants to retire? What, finally, is supposed to be the effect of the last four words? Do they once again leave the assessment completely at large? Although Article 30(4) is concerned with quantification rather than entitlement, it contains many obscurities and badly needs clarification.

(o)  Article 31(c) provides that the commercial agent loses his right to goodwill indemnity if he miscalculates the period of notice by so much as one day. Should not the test rather be whether his failure to give proper notice causes serious prejudice to the principal? A somewhat similar point can be made about a commercial agent who terminates (or purports to do so) believing in good faith, and reasonably, that he has grounds under Article 27(1), but who then finds that he cannot substantiate those grounds. In view of the obscurity of Article 27(1)(b), this is no improbable contingency.

(p) Article 31(b) exempt the principal from having to pay the goodwill indemnity where one agent is replaced by another whom he has introduced. In English law there would, in such circumstances, either be an assignment of the agency by one agent to the other or (more likely) a new contract with the new agent. The directive contemplates that the old contract may be "maintained on foot" with the new agent being "substituted entirely". It is not clear whether this would apply to an assignment and very doubtful whether it would apply where there was a new contract. The article is likely to cause confusion and uncertainty in this country.

## Article 32

(a) It is extraordinary that this is not one of the articles which, under Article 4(1), Member States need not apply to persons who act as commercial agents by way of secondary activity.

(b) The weakness of Article 32(2) is that it will often be impossible to tell, when the agreement restricting competition is drafted, whether it is going to be valid. The agency agreement may last for many years; but in the last few months the agent may cease to be "entrusted" with a small part of his original territory. The result is that the restrictive agreement no longer satisfies the test of Article 32(2), though when made it did satisfy the test. What is the effect? Is the agreement wholly void? Can it be severed? Article 32(1) says nothing about failure to comply with substantive requirements,

(c) It should be noted that the restraint clause may be void by English law even if it is for a period of less than two years and this possibility does not seem to have been envisaged in Article 32.

(d) The meaning of Article 32(3) is unclear. Does it mean that only restrictive covenants of two years' duration are valid? If a restrictive covenant is for more than two years, would it be void *in toto*, or could the court sever the covenant, holding the first two years to be valid and the rest to be void?

(e) Is the payment provided for in Article 32(4) only available if the restrictive covenant is valid, or also, if it is invalid, but nevertheless observed?

(f) It is not clear what happens if the contract of agency is terminated by principal and agent, by mutual consent. Does the restriction run on under Article 32(3)? Can it not be ended by agreement of the parties? Presumably not since Article 32(3) is mandatory.There is a related problem under Article 32(5)(b). What happens if the agent terminates the contract under Article 32(5) but does not terminate the restriction in writing? Apparently it continues in force.

(g) In Article 32(6), line 1, why only "before the contract has come to an end" and not after?

(h) What, for instance, if after giving notice, the principal goes out of business? Why must he pay the indemnity for six months even though during those six months the agent is free to compete, does so, and suffers no loss of earnings at all?

(i) Article 32(6) provides that if the agent gives notice of termination in accordance with Article 26, then the principal during the currency of the notice can terminate the restrictive covenant, but only to release himself of the obligation to pay indemnity after a period of six months has elapsed. There seems no good reason why the principal should still have to pay the indemnity to the agent during the part of this period falling after the termination of the contract.

(j) Why should the agent who voluntarily resigns to work for another principal either in another area or selling other goods, be paid goodwill indemnity under Article 30, plus (possible) Article 13 commission, plus an Article 32 payment equivalent to a maximum two years' remuneration.

## Article 33

Article 33 attempts to distinguish between small companies which require protection granted by all the mandatory provisions of the directive and large companies which, presumably because of their financial standing, only require the protection of some of the mandatory provisions. The distinction is turned on the paid-up capital of the company. In our view, the paid-up capital of the company is not a reliable index of its financial strength and to turn the distinction on it is totally unrealistic.

## Article 34

No comment.

## Article 35

Article 35(2) permits the parties to derogate from the mandatory provisions in the directive in relation to activities which the agent carries on outside the EEC. If would obviously be cumbersome to have an agreement which was partly valid and partly invalid.

PART IV—OUR CONCLUSIONS

**48.** As we have seen, the directive attempts:—
   (a) to isolate a social group, "commercial agents", with special economic and social needs;
   (b) to lay down mandatory rules to give these agents protection commensurate with these needs;
   (c) to provide a model contract incorporating terms that ought to be implied between these agents and their principals unless the contract provides to the contrary;
   (d) to produce a clear and rational statement in the form of a code covering the relationship between these agents and their principals, in particular the rules governing the formation, performance and termination of their contracts.

**49.** With regard to (a) we are satisfied that the social group has not been identified and no case seems to have been made out for the alleged social and economic needs of all the persons falling within the ambit of the directive.

50. With regard to (b) we consider the directive to be one-sided and the mandatory rules to consist of an elaborate advancement of a sectional interest for which no case has been made out. The rules, as drafted, appear to us to be cumbersome and unworkable. Moreover, parties who devise clearer or more sensible rules to suit themselves do so at their peril.

51. With regard to (c) we do not consider that the provisions of the directive would constitute in English law appropriate terms to be incorporated in a model contract between any agent and any principal. With regard to many of them it seems inconceivable that the parties to such a contract would wish them to govern their mutual relationship. Yet this is what they will do, unless the parties expressly provide that they should not.

52. With regard to (d) we do not consider that the attempted codification has done anything to clarify the existing law. On the contrary, the rules which the directive purports to declare are full of uncertainties, gaps and inconsistencies and, in many respects, offend against basic principles of the English law of agency. Furthermore, they depend for their operation upon a corpus of law which is not stated in the directive. Their introduction would necessitate the distortion of the common law of agency and of other areas of commercial law. In our opinion, no justification, social or legal, has been made out for such a step.

53. Our conclusion is, therefore, that the directive's defects of substance, presentation and drafting are such that it fails even to provide a basis for negotiation.

## ANNEX A

**EUROPEAN COMMUNITIES**          Brussels, 5 January 1977
**The Council**                   R/3/77 (ES 1)

*Translation*

| | |
|---|---|
| *Letter from:* | The Commission of the European Communities, signed by Mr F. GUNDELACH, Member. |
| *Dated:* | 17 December 1976. |
| *To:* | Mr VAN DER STOEL, President of the Council of the European Communities. |
| *Subject:* | Proposal for a Council Directive to coordinate the laws of the Member States relating to (self-employed) commercial agents. |

Sir,

I enclose a proposal for a Council Directive to coordinate the laws of the Member States relating to (self-employed) commercial agents.

As the proposal is based in particular on Articles 57 and 100 of the Treaty establishing the European Economic Communities, consultation of the European Parliament and the Economic and Social Committee is mandatory.

The Commission believes that it should be possible for the Council to act on the proposal before the end of 1978. Given this time-scale, the European Parliament and the Economic and Social Committee should deliver their Opinions during the first half of 1977.

(Complimentary close).

*(Signed)* Finn GUNDELACH
Member of the Commission.

*Encl.*: COM(76) 670 final

---

R/3 e/77 (ES 1) ard/JM/jn
EEC

*EEC Directive*

COMMISSION OF THE EUROPEAN COMMUNITIES
COM(76) 670 final
Brussels, 14 December 1976

**Proposal for a Council Directive
to coordinate the Laws of the Member States relating to
(self-employed) Commercial Agents**

---

*(submitted to the Council by the Commission)*

EXPLANATORY MEMORANDUM

The object of this proposal for a Directive which is now presented to the Council is to harmonise the laws of the Member States relating to commercial agents, that is, commercial agents who carry on business as self-employed persons, as distinct from salaried or wage-earning commercial travellers.

Coordination of the law relating to commercial travellers will be dealt with in a subsequent proposal. Harmonisation in that field raises problems of a different type which arise in the context of labour law.

After examining the laws which are currently in force and consulting the various trade and professional organisations, it was clear that the first subject which should be dealt with was coordination of the laws relating to commercial agents. Such agents play a very important part in interpenetration of markets and, for that reason, in the growth of intracommunity trade. The need to coordinate national laws in the field of commercial representation in its widest sense became apparent when the restrictions on freedom of establishment and freedom to provide services in respect of activities of intermediaries in commerce, industry and small craft industries were abolished by Council Directive 64/224/EEC of 25 February 1964[56].

The differences which exist between one legal system and another in relation to commercial representation make for a continuing and quite definite inequality in conditions of competition. Moreover, those differences act as a barrier to the carrying on of the business of commercial representation in the Community.

This can be seen particularly in the differing degree of protection which is accorded to commercial agents from one State to another. The proposal for a Directive therefore provides in general for minimum rules establishing a common level of protection which the Member States must accord, those States that wish to provide more protection being at liberty to do so.

In the interests of the common market the said differences between legal systems must not be allowed to impede to any significant extent the making and operation of contracts between a principal who is established in one Member State and a commercial agent who is established in another. In point of fact the coordination here proposed applies not only to cases involving two or more Member States but also to cases arising in one Member State only, since trade in goods and the provision of services should always be effected in

---

[56] No. 56, 4/4/1964, p. 869.

*Explanatory Memorandum*

the Community under conditions which are similar to those of a single market. It would, moreover, be inconsistent with this objective to superimpose on the existing laws of Member States relating to commercial agents Community legislation applicable solely to transactions which involve a foreign element. Furthermore it would create unequal conditions of competition within one and the same State if commercial agents who carry on business in one Member State were subject to substantially different legal systems depending upon whether their activities were governed by the law of the Member State in which they carry them on or by some other system of law.

Lastly, it is not possible to solve these problems by means of uniform rules of conflict of laws. For one thing unification of the conflicts rules would not remove the differences which exist in substantive law. For another thing any such unification would not have the effect that the same substantive law would become applicable to all commercial agents who carry on business within one Member State.

Moreover the unification of the conflicts rules, which is currently being undertaken by the Community, will not remove the element of uncertainty as to which law actually applies to any specific agency contract. Even if the connecting factors were made uniform they would leave some degree of latitude in interpretation and would not make it possible to forecast with absolute certainty which substantive laws were applicable. One of the objects of the Directive is to make it possible to do so.

Thus, with the object of establishing certainty as to the law, renvoi to the internal law of Member States takes place solely in relation to matters for which it has not been possible to create uniform rules for the Member States of the Community, or in which no element of competition is involved, or which do not affect the degree of protection by the law which has already been achieved.

The provisions contained in the proposal make up a balanced set of rules covering the most important aspects of the relationship between commercial agent and principal. Some of the provisions are unknown in the laws of Member States, although similar results have sometimes been arrived at in legal writings, in case-law or by usage, the consequences varying according to the circumstances.

Other provisions deal with topics which are already covered in a wide variety of ways by national law, some of them less favourable to the agent than the proposed Community law would be, and some of them more favourable. In some cases the relationship between principal and agent is governed by collective agreements made between trade or professional organisations. It will be seen that this proposal is in effect a codification of the law.

Basically the proposal has two objectives. The first is to remove the differences in law which are detrimental to the proper functioning of the common market. They affect the conditions of competition and create considerable legal un-certainty. This applies, for example, in relation to the goodwill indemnity, which is known in some Member States but not in others. It is more expensive for the principal to have an agent in those countries in which the goodwill

*EEC Directive*

indemnity is already compulsory by law, and this operates very much to the economic advantage of principals who are not under an obligation to pay any indemnity after the contract has terminated. The second objective is to safeguard or improve the protection that already exists for commercial agents. Although they are self-employed, most commercial agents are economically in a weak position *vis-à-vis* their principals. In so far as the proposal envisages minimum rules it does not affect those provisions of national law which are more favourable to the commercial agent and does not stand in the way of progress. From a more general point of view the proposal is aligned on the principles set out in Article 117 of the EEC Treaty and, in harmonising the law, endeavours to achieve a levelling-up.

This Directive governs the relationship between commercial agent and principal. It sets out the law concerning in particular:

— the legal definition of commercial agent,
— the rights and duties of the parties,
— remuneration of the commercial agent, and especially his right to commission,
— agreements restricting competition,
— *del credere* agreements,
— protection of agents whose income is mainly derived from their agency, where the principal is declared bankrupt, is in liquidation, makes an arrangement or composition or is the subject of similar proceedings, or where an order for execution is granted to a third party affecting moneys owed to the agent by the principal, or where the agent makes an assignment of such moneys,
— termination of contract, goodwill indemnity,
— limitation periods,
— those rules from which the parties are not permitted to derogate.

*Explanatory Memorandum*

## CHAPTER I—SCOPE OF APPLICATION

*Article* 1

This Article specifies the subject-matter and scope of the proposal for a Directive.

Council Directive 64/224/EEC of 25 February 1964, which has already been referred to, was very wide in scope, whereas this proposal is concerned only with self-employed commercial agents as defined in Article 2. Agents of this kind and salaried or wage-earning commercial travellers resemble each other in that the continuing task of both is to represent their principal. Due consideration will have to be given to this similarity in their roles when the future Directive harmonising the law relating to salaried or wage-earning commercial travellers is being prepared. Article 3 specifies which types of commercial agent are not covered by the definition contained in Article 2 or are expressly excluded from it.

The legal relations between commercial agent and principal form the subject-matter of this Directive irrespective of whether they contain any foreign element. Where there is a foreign element the rules of private international law will determine which national system of law applies. Where the relevant national law happens to be that of a Member State the law relating to commercial agents as set out in this proposal will apply.

Paragraph 2 provides that national law and current trade usage continue to apply provided they are not inconsistent with the mandatory provisions hereof.

*Article* 2

It is essential to have a definition of "commercial agent". In some Member States the concept of "commercial agent" is unknown, whilst in others it remains undefined or is defined only partially. What is required is a line of demarcation between the activities of commercial agents and the activities of other intermediaries. The commercial agent is self-employed, that is, he arranges his activities as he thinks fit and uses his time as he pleases (see Article 5(*e*) of this Directive). It is in this respect that he differs from the salaried or wage-earning commercial traveller. Another distinguishing feature of the commercial agent is that he acts not in his own name but in the name and for account of his principal. This is the difference between the commercial agent and the commission agent (*commissionaire, Kommissionär*), the latter acting for account of another but in his own name. The third important distinguishing feature of the commercial agent is the continuing nature of his contractual tie with the principal. Where a person is appointed to act temporarily as intermediary to negotiate or conclude agreements for a specific number of transactions in the name of the principal, he is not on that ground alone to be taken to be the commercial agent of that principal.

Companies or legal persons may be commercial agents. Where the paid-up capital exceeds 100 000 U.A. Article 33 permits the parties to derogate from some of the mandatory provisions contained in the Directive. Commercial agents in this category are economically powerful enough not to require any special protection.

*Article* 3

For the sake of clarity this Article sets out the most important classes of persons who do not fall within the definition in Article 2. Also it excludes from the scope of application of the Directive agents who act for insurance or financial institutions; unless expressly excluded these agents would be covered by the definition. The reason for excluding them is that in a number of States there exist special laws which apply to agents of this kind or else they are expressly exempted from the ambit of particular laws which apply to commercial agents. A proposal for a Directive will be presented at a later date to coordinate the laws of Member States in this field.

*Article 4*

It is left to the Member States to decide whether the Directive is to apply in whole or in part to persons who carry on business as commercial agents but by way of secondary activity only, and to certain other trades or professions. There are, for example, persons who carry on some other trade or profession and who have a standing arrangement to sell goods which they have bought from the other party to that arrangement and it may be that from the economic point of view the relationship between those two persons is found upon a proper construction of the contract to be one of principal and agent. Indeed, some independent or sole trader businesses may well be merely a device to circumvent certain mandatory provisions of law. In such cases as these it may be necessary to apply the legal provisions relating to commercial agents. But it does not appear to be necessary to lay down rules to cover these special cases in this Directive the object of which is to provide uniform regulation of the law relating to commercial agents.

No definition is given of "commercial agency by way of secondary activity" because it is impossible to lay down suitable criteria which apply in every case. All the surrounding circumstances must be considered in each individual case in deciding whether a commercial agent is carrying on business by way of secondary activity. Moreover, opinions on this subject vary from one country to another. The Directive here refers back to the usages of trade in the State whose law governs the contract. Where the commercial agent does carry on his business by way of secondary activity the provisions of the Directive, in principle, apply. The Member States may allow the parties to derogate only from those mandatory provisions which are specified in this Article.

The provisions in question would in point of fact involve the principal in financial burdens which would be unreasonable in relation to the economic importance of the business carried on. To make these provisions compulsory would have the effect of restricting substantially the entry into and carrying on of the business of commercial agent by way of secondary activity for a large number of people who derive appreciable revenue from it, e.g. persons who collect group orders for mail order establishments—very often they are married women who normally do not carry on any trade or business.

*Explanatory Memorandum*

## CHAPTER II—RIGHTS AND OBLIGATIONS OF THE PARTIES

Articles 5 to 10 deal with the rights and obligations of principal and agent.

They must help each other to achieve the objects of the contract of commercial agency. The contract relates to the economic interests of both parties. Each of them is bound, within the framework of the contract, to protect the interests of the other. The basic principle is that each must act fairly and in good faith. As there is no consensus in the Member States as to the applicability of that principle in this field, Article 5(1) and Article 10(1) expressly provide for it. The same principle applies concerning the commercial agent's conduct *vis-à-vis* third parties, especially where he brings about a commercial relationship between principal and third party.

### Article 5

The first paragraph sets out the general principle that the commercial agent must act fairly and in good faith *vis-à-vis* his principal and must protect his interests with all proper care. Paragraph (2) contains a non-exhaustive list of obligations which flow from that principle and which are incumbent upon the commercial agent. In the first place there is the obligation not to act as intermediary in relation to, nor to conclude transactions with, third parties whom the agent knows to be insolvent. He must accordingly (sub-paragraph (*a*)) inform the principal concerning the solvency of third parties with whom transactions are in course of negotiation or execution. Sub-paragraph (*c*) requires the agent to keep certain accounts which must, if appropriate, include accounts relating to moneys owed by customers. Sub-paragraph (*e*) emphasises the commercial agent's obligation to comply with all instructions given him by the principal within the framework of the agency. It is for the principal alone to decide, for example, whether and on what terms a commercial transaction is to be entered into and performed. In this respect therefore the agent's independence is limited.

### Article 6

Even after termination of the contract the commercial agent is bound to exercise special care as regards the commercial or industrial secrets communicated to him or of which he became aware during the currency of the contract. In no case is he at liberty to disclose them to third parties. As a general rule he must not exploit those secrets for purposes of his own business. This principle cannot, however, be always rigorously applied. The commercial agent cannot be prohibited from turning to account trade or professional information, or information which is special in his field of activity, acquired by him before termination but during the currency of his contract with the principal. The dividing line between what is permissible and what is prohibited has to be determined in accordance with the notions of the sound businessman and commercial usage. Article 6 provides that the commercial agent must show that his exploitation of secrets is not inconsistent with those notions. Thus an agent who began to exploit secrets after termination of the contract would run the risk of not being able to discharge the burden of proof which lies upon him. This provision applies independently of the rules set out in Article 32 relating to agreements restricting competition.

*EEC Directive*

### Article 7

Notwithstanding that the commercial agent is self-employed, free to arrange his work as he thinks fit and to carry on, concurrently with the commercial agency entrusted to him, any other activity for his own account or for account of a third party, he must obtain the principal's consent if he wishes to engage in business on his own account, or for account of a third party, in goods or services which compete with those covered by his agency. Paragraph (3) provides that the parties may in this matter limit or increase the agent's freedom of action.

### Article 8

It can sometimes happen that the proprietor of a patent, trademark, design or model brings legal proceedings against the agent in order to prevent him from selling or using the protected product. The agent may be required to pay damages for infringement of the rights in question. National laws and international conventions allow action to be brought directly against the person who commits the infringement. In these circumstances it is of small importance whether the infringer of industrial, commercial or intellectual property rights acted in his own name or in the name of another, on his own initiative or at the request of a third party. As the Directive in no way purports to make changes in relation to the exercise of these rights of protection, it could not possibly prohibit the bringing of legal proceedings against commercial agents who act on behalf of their principals. The Directive does, however, expressly provide that the principal must indemnify the agent who suffers damage because one of those rights has been infringed in the course of carrying on the agency, if the infringement was attributable to the principal. Where the agent considers that he would be entitled to claim damages from the principal if, in the action brought by the proprietor of the right of protection against the agent, judgment were to be given in favour of the former, the agent shall be entitled to require the principal to be joined as a third party in an action on a warranty or guarantee, or in any other third party proceedings, in the court seised of the original proceedings pursuant to the national law (see Article 6(2) of the Judgments Convention of 27 September 1968 and Article V of the Protocol annexed thereto).

The position will be the same where the commercial agent infringes the fair trading laws e.g. if he disregards certain prohibitions relating to publicity, defamation etc.

### Article 9

By far the majority of commercial agents in the Member States are at the present time authorised only to negotiate on behalf of their principals, the conclusion of the actual agreement for the transaction being a matter for the principal himself. The Directive reflects this situation.

Paragraph (1) provides that the agent has, by definition, authority to negotiate commercial transactions for account of the principal. It also provides that the agent has no authority to conclude them unless the principal confers it on him.

Paragraph (2) sets out certain presumptions. The agent always has authority to receive notices of complaint from third parties concerning defective goods

*Explanatory Memorandum*

or services. Similarly he always has authority to receive notices to the effect that goods are available for collection, in cases where the person to whom they were supplied declines to accept them. Lastly, he always has authority to protect the principal's rights as regards the preservation of evidence.

Where a commercial agent describes himself as having greater authority than that arising by virtue of the various presumptions aforesaid, third parties must not rely upon his description even though they know, or it is actually proved, that the agent is working for a particular principal. Any authority in excess of that presumed must be proved. The Directive does not specify how such authority should be conferred. The matter is governed in each specific case by the relevant national law.

Paragraph (3) relates to the case where the principal reduces the agent's authority below that provided for in paragraphs (1) and (2). Limitations on the agent's authority cannot be invoked against the third party unless he was aware or ought to have been aware of them.

*Article* 10

The principal's general and special duties *vis-à-vis* the commercial agent are substantially the same as those which arise under the legislation, case-law and juristic writings in Member States. As regards the principles it expresses and its phraseology and form, this Article is the counterpart of Article 5 (duties of the commercial agent).

Paragraph (1) requires the principal to act fairly and in good faith, while paragraph (2) contains a non-exhaustive list of the principal's special duties. He must make available to the agent, in suitable quantity, such materials, information and documents as are necessary for the performance of his activities. In addition, the principal must provide the agent with all information concerning current and prospective production which is requisite for the performance of the contract. He must also inform the agent without delay of the acceptance, refusal or partial execution of commercial transactions. These items of information are important in view of the fact that, as provided in Article 15, the right to commission arises at the moment when the principal and the third party enter into the commercial transaction, and the execution of the transaction determines when the commission becomes payable.

*EEC Directive*

## CHAPTER III—REMUNERATION AND REIMBURSEMENT OF EXPENSES

The provisions of this chapter, namely Articles 11 to 20, are based on the principle that the commercial agent is entitled to be remunerated for his services. These Articles indicate also the various elements that go to make up his remuneration, the conditions under which the agent is entitled to commission on transactions entered into during the currency of the contract and after termination, the time at which commission is payable, the way in which the amount of commission is to be calculated, and the cases in which the right to commission is extinguished. These Articles confer on the commercial agent the following rights: the right to examine the principal's books for the purpose of verifying the correctness of the commission statement, the right to special commission for collecting payment of moneys, the right to be remunerated in cases where the principal does not make use of his services or where the principal makes less use of them than the agent could in the normal course of events have expected.

### Article 11

This Article adopts those forms of remuneration of commercial agents which are in use in the Member States. For the avoidance of doubt paragraph (1) provides that any variable item of remuneration which is calculated by reference to turnover is to be deemed to be commission. It is common for the agent's remuneration to consist not of a percentage of the amount of the invoice but of a payment calculated by piece, weight or volume.

Paragraph (2) deals with the amount of commission where no specific amount has expressly been agreed. It confirms the general rule which already applies in all Member States, namely, that the parties are free to determine for themselves the amount of commission.

### Article 12

This Article specifies at what point of time the right to commission arises for commercial transactions entered into during the currency of the contract. The right to commission arises in the following three cases (which are those generally accepted in the laws of Member States):

— where the transaction is procured by the commercial agent,
— where the transaction is entered into with a third party with whom the agent has previously negotiated or agreed a transaction on behalf of the principal,
— where the transaction is entered into with a third party in the geographical area or belonging to the group of persons covered by the agency.

Where a transaction is carried out during the currency of the contract the agreement to enter into it has, generally speaking, already been concluded. Where, however, entry into the agreement takes place after termination of the contract of commercial agency the commercial agent is entitled to commission if the transaction was negotiated by him or if it was entered into largely as a result of his work.

Paragraph (2) provides that a principal who, under Article 13, owes commission to a former agent for a transaction entered into after termination of

*Explanatory Memorandum*

the contract is not under obligation to pay commission to the new agent unless it was otherwise agreed.

### Article 13

As regards transactions entered into after termination of the contract this Article provides that the commercial agent is entitled to commission on transactions negotiated by him and on transactions prepared by him which are entered into mainly as a result of his efforts. These provisions follow the principles applied in a number of Member States. The right to commission exists, however, only where the transaction is entered into within a reasonable period after termination of the contract. The time required for examination of offers and for making the various calculations which have to be made can vary considerably from one transaction to another. It appeared undesirable to fix a specific period of time applicable in all cases. It was considered more important that the rule here should be fair rather than that it should be precise.

### Article 14

Under this Article the commercial agent is entitled to special commission for collecting payment of moneys, such commission being dealt with separately in the contract and recorded separately in the books and in the commission statement.

### Article 15

The agent's right to commission arises at the moment when the principal and the third party enter into the commercial transaction. The Directive thus advances the time at which the right comes into being, for this is not the position in those legal systems under which the right to commission arises only if, and in so far as, the principal carries out the transaction. It follows from this Article that where the principal is declared bankrupt, is in liquidation, makes an arrangement or composition or is the subject of similar proceedings before the commercial transaction has been executed, even if executed only in part, the commercial agent may prove in those proceedings for the amount of his claims. This is the main advantage of the provisions set out on this subject in the present proposal as compared with the legal systems in which the right to commission arises at some later time.

The commission is payable at the latest when the third party executes his part of the transaction. Any agreement to the contrary is void. Moreover, commission is payable if the principal has performed his part of the transaction but the third party has not yet executed his part. The parties may, however, agree that in such cases the commission will be payable at a later time; but the time for payment is not to be extended beyond the last day of the third month following that in which the principal completes the performance of his obligations *vis-à-vis* the third party. Here the agent is entitled to a payment on account, of suitable amount, payable on the last day of the month following that in which the principal performed his part of the contract. If the third party discharges his obligations *vis-à-vis* the principal before the end of the period agreed between them the commission becomes payable as soon as he has discharged them. In any event, commission is payable on a sum equal to the

*EEC Directive*

value of that part of the transaction which has been executed by the principal or third party. Where the principal or third party fails to perform his part of the transaction in full, the amount of commission is to be calculated on the basis of the value of that part performed which is the higher.

There are six advantages in regulating the matter in this way:

1. The general rule is that the principal is not bound to pay commission unless the third party performs his part of the transaction.

2. Where the principal performs his part of the contract first, payment of commission in full may be postponed for so long as the third party fails to perform his part. A suitable payment on account must, however, be made to the agent.

3. The agent knows that where the third party has not performed his part of the contract, and however long that state of affairs continues, commission will be paid as a general rule at the end of the third month following that in which the principal performs his part. The exceptions to this are set out in Article 16.

4. The period of three months which is allowed for preparation of the commission statement will facilitate the accounting involved.

5. The commission statement must include not only commission which is actually payable but also commission earned though not yet payable, so as to give the agent the opportunity of proving his debt, if necessary, in insolvency proceedings (see Article 22).

6. The wording of the Article makes it clear that in the event of partial performance of the transaction by one party, only a partial commission is payable. Where both parties perform only part of their obligations, the amount of commission will be proportionate to that part whose value is the higher. But where one party performs in full and the other only in part, commission will be payable on the whole value of the transaction.

*Article* 16

The right to commission, which arises when principal and third party enter into the commercial transaction, can in certain circumstances be extinguished. Some legal systems already specify to some extent what these circumstances are and provide either that no right to commission arises, or that the right is nullified with retroactive effect, in cases where those circumstances occur.

Where subparagraph (a) applies, the transaction was entered into with a customer who was insolvent and, because the agent failed in his duty under Article 5 and omitted to inform the principal thereof, the principal was unaware of the insolvency. In addition, the customer has not performed his part of the contract. Here the loss of entitlement to commission is due to the negligence of the agent. The only cases intended to be caught by this subparagraph are those in which the agent fails to exercise his duty of care, with consequent loss to the principal or potential loss to him if he had executed the transaction.

Where subparagraph (b) or (c) applies the transaction was validly entered into but was not executed for some such reason as *force majeure,* or because the customer's business has ceased to exist or has ceased payment, so that the principal cannot perform his part of the transaction or is unwilling to do so. It will be mainly for national law to determine which cases are covered by these two subparagraphs. In any event it is impossible to spell out in the Directive the precise meaning of such concepts as "impossibility" and "serious grounds", the scope and significance of which have been settled by the law or by the case-law or in juristic writings in the Member States.

## Article 17

This Article gives some degree of protection to the commercial agent as regards the calculation of his commission. It specifies in particular how discounts and incidental expenses are to be dealt with in preparing the commission statement. These provisions are not mandatory.

## Article 18

This Article entitles the commercial agent to obtain information and, if necessary, to examine the principal's books of account. He may exercise this right to the extent necessary for verifying the correctness and completeness of the commission statement. It is supplementary to Article 15(5).

Items of information of which the agent becomes aware as a result of the exercise of his right to examine the books of account must not be divulged to third parties nor exploited by the agent (Article 6 applies by analogy). Such items are to be regarded in the same way as commercial or industrial secrets belonging to the principal.

## Article 19

The commercial agent is entitled under Article 11 to be remunerated for his work. In certain circumstances he is entitled to be paid even though he does no work for the principal or less work than anticipated. This would be the case, for example, where the commercial agent has begun to negotiate transactions for the principal or where the agent has done whatever is necessary to enable him to carry out his part of the agency contract but, as regards the sector entrusted to the agent, the principal has not developed his business to the extent that the agent could reasonably have expected having regard to the economic development of the undertaking and to market movements.

Some legal systems classify these cases under the heading of "non-acceptance by the principal". But there is no fault on the part of the principal if his conduct is attributable to circumstances beyond his control. The circumstances in which no remuneration should be paid will be determined by the national law and the relevant case-law. Yet again it was necessary to confine the Directive to fundamentals.

Paragraphs (2) and (3) relating to calculation of commission indicate what is meant by suitable remuneration. The amount of remuneration is to be determined by reference to all the material circumstances e.g. the amount of any lump-sum payment agreed between the parties or of any commission already earned. Account must also be taken of expenditure not incurred and of sums which the agent has earned by doing other work, or of sums he could have earned because he had less work to do for the principal.

*EEC Directive*

Of course the amount of remuneration will. be increased if the commercial agent has for the benefit of both parties opened up sale or distribution establishments that remain wholly or partly unused.

### Article 20

The proposal adopts the general rule which currently obtains in the Member States that the commercial agent is not entitled to reimbursement of expenses incurred in the normal course of his activities unless the parties agree otherwise or unless there is a custom to the contrary.

It is, however, expressly provided that expenses incurred in connection with some special activity undertaken on the instructions or with the consent of the principal shall be reimbursed e.g. the cost of an advertising campaign.

*Explanatory Memorandum*

CHAPTER IV—DEL CREDERE

*Article* 21

This Article defines the *del credere* agreement whereby the commercial agent guarantees in favour of the principal that a third party will pay for goods or services supplied in execution of commercial transactions which the agent has negotiated or agreed. It also protects him when he gives a *del credere* guarantee. The protection afforded-is about on a par with the average throughout the various Member States. The written form is mandatory. *Del credere* agreements concluded by cable, telex or telegrams are treated as satisfying this requirement. The draft proposal for a Directive on suretyship contains a like provision in keeping with developments in modern business. *Del credere* agreements may be in the form of a suretyship agreement or of an indemnity agreement.

*Del credere* agreements are to be made by commercial agents only in relation to transactions which they themselves have negotiated or agreed. As he plays no part in those transactions which are arranged directly between principal and third party it appears to be entirely proper that his liability should not extend thereto. Furthermore, the Article provides that *del credere* agreements which impose on the commercial agent unlimited liability for all transactions are void. This is based upon considerations of social policy and is intended to show clearly that the commercial risk lies on the principal.

By analogy with the commission payable under Article 14 for collection of moneys, the commercial agent is entitled to be paid a separate commission, of reasonable amount, on all transactions covered by his *del credere* undertaking.

It appeared to be reasonable to allow the parties to derogate from certain of these provisions. They may do so in cases where the principal or the third party is established outside the Community, for in such cases the agent's knowledge of the market is extremely relevant. They may derogate also in cases where the agent is given unlimited authority to agree and to execute commercial transactions.

*EEC Directive*

Chapter V—Bankruptcy or Winding-up of the Principal Execution and Assignment

*Article 22*

Most commercial agency businesses are from the economic point of view small-scale and accordingly depend heavily on the principal. For this reason they should for certain purposes be treated in the same way as employees. This Article confers on them the same protection as employees have where bankruptcy or winding-up proceedings are opened against the principal, where he makes an arrangement or composition with his creditors or is the subject of similar proceedings, where an order is obtained by a third party for payment to him of sums of money held by the principal representing debts due from the principal to the agent, or where the agent assigns debts due to him from the principal. As regards the bankruptcy, winding-up and other similar proceedings hereinbefore referred to, Member States may fix maximum figures of income beyond which the protection would no longer apply. In the other fields covered by this Article such maxima have already been fixed in most of the Member States.

*Explanatory Memorandum*

CHAPTER VI—MAKING OF THE CONTRACT AND CESSATION OF THE CONTRACT

## *Articles* 23 *and* 24

The Directive does not require every commercial agency agreement to be in writing, although one Member State does impose that rule and a number of trade associations of which commercial agents are members would like to see that requirement adopted. Each party is, however, entitled to receive from the other, upon request, a written statement signed by that other setting out the terms of the contract and any terms subsequently agreed. The same applies, *mutatis mutandis,* where the contract is terminated by mutual agreement. After careful consideration of the advantages and disadvantages of·a compulsory written contract and bearing in mind particularly that in cases where the contract was not reduced to writing the result would be nullity of the contract, it was decided that the Directive should not impose a requirement of writing. The rule now proposed avoids useless complication and unnecessary paper-work and will no doubt be in the best interests of both parties.

## *Articles* 25, 26, 27 *and* 28

A contract for a fixed or determinable period, known in some States as a contract for a specific purpose, terminates upon the expiration of the period for which it was concluded. The Directive provides (but the parties are free to agree otherwise) that where a contract for a fixed or determinable period continues to be performed after that period has expired, it shall be deemed to be converted into a contract for an indeterminate period. All doubt is thereby removed and the parties are at liberty to agree otherwise.

The parties are entitled to agree upon the period of notice to be given in order to terminate a contract concluded for an indeterminate period. Certain minimum periods must, however, be observed for reasons of social or competition policy as well as for the sake of certainty as to the law.

In order to avoid any misunderstanding the Directive provides that periods of notice are to coincide with the end of a calendar month.

Article 27 deals with the two common cases in which the parties may terminate the contract without observing any period of notice or waiting for the contract to run its normal term. First there is the case where one of the parties has in relation to the contract committed a fault such that the other party cannot be required to keep it in being until the end of the period of notice or until the end of the agreed period of duration of the contract. Secondly there are the cases of *force majeure,* inevitable accident, change in the surrounding circumstances, etc., which substantially undermine the commercial basis of the contract. An example would be the case where the commercial agent finds it impossible to continue in business for reasons of health, old-age or serious and unforeseeable family circumstances.

Certain technical requirements are imposed in relation to these provisions. Thus the party who wishes to terminate because of the fault committed by the other party must do so as soon as he becomes aware of it. Where Article 27(1)(*b*) applies, termination must take place within a reasonable time after the occurrence of the event which justifies termination. In both cases the reasons for termination must upon request of the other party be communicated to him in writing.

*EEC Directive*

Article 28 provides that where the contract is terminated by reason of the fault of one of the parties, the party who is at fault is liable in damages to the other. However, to lighten the burden of proof the Directive provides that the agent may claim a lump-sum indemnity instead of damages where the contract is terminated by the principal or is declared by the principal to be at an end. This will apply where the principal terminates either by notice of improper length or before the contract has run its full term, in circumstances where there is no fault on the part of the agent, no *force majeure* and no inevitable accident. The indemnity is to correspond to the remuneration which would have been earned during the unexpired period of the contract, but with a maximum period of two years. If the agent decides to claim damages instead, he must prove his loss.

### Article 29

This Article reflects the law as it stands generally in the Community at the present time. Upon termination of the contract all samples, materials and documentation which were made available by the principal to the agent must be returned to the principal.

In order however to secure the agent's claims for remuneration and reimbursement of expenses he is given a lien. The lien does not apply to secure his entitlement to goodwill indemnity.

### Article 30

This Article requires the Member States to provide in their law that commercial agents shall be entitled to goodwill indemnity. Some Member States already do so; the others will have to introduce it as a law reform measure affecting commercial agents.

After termination of the agency contract the agent or his heirs are to be entitled to payment of a goodwill indemnity provided the three following conditions are satisfied:

1. the agent has brought new customers to the principal or has appreciably increased the volume of business with existing customers,
2. the principal will after termination of the contract continue to derive substantial benefits from the increase in custom or turnover,
3. because of termination the agent is no longer in receipt of the remuneration to which he was entitled during the currency of the contract.

All three conditions must be satisfied.

The amount of indemnity must be reasonable having regard to all the circumstances. As a general rule it would be reasonable that the agent receive in respect of each year of the agency at least one tenth of the average annual remuneration received by him during the preceding five years. In making this calculation account is to be taken of the entitlement to commission under Article 13 following termination. The agent can never require an indemnity of more than twice the average annual remuneration. Usually he will be entitled to the maximum indemnity after twenty years. Exceptionally, either party may request that the rule fixing the amount of the indemnity at one tenth of the average annual remuneration over the preceding five years, for

*Explanatory Memorandum*

each year of the agency, be waived if it would be equitable to do so. The amount of indemnity arrived at is not, however, to exceed an amount which is equal to twice the average annual remuneration. Below that figure the waiver may operate to the advantage of the agent, so that he receives more, or to the advantage of the principal, so that he pays less. If the parties cannot agree, the amount of indemnity will be determined by the Court.

Paragraph (4) is based on the idea that the agent is entitled to the indemnity even in those cases where he has terminated the contract by notice of the proper duration required under the contract or by law. This paragraph limits the amount of the indemnity to not more than one tenth of the average annual remuneration for each year during which the contract has subsisted, as provided in paragraph 2, where the agent terminates the contract but not in reliance on any of the grounds specified in Article 27(1). The object here was to avoid the situation where the agent would exercise his right of termination during the early years of the contract in order to obtain the maximum indemnity specified in paragraph (3). On the other hand the agent will be able to obtain the maximum indemnity where he has proper grounds for terminating the contract, where the principal terminates without proper grounds or where the contract comes to its end in the normal fashion. The fact that the provisions contained in paragraph 4 are rather more finely drawn than the existing national law provisions is explained by the adoption, in paragraph 2, of a uniform method of calculating the indemnity.

For the avoidance of doubt, Article 30 provides that if the agent dies during the term of the contract, his heirs are to be entitled to the goodwill indemnity. The indemnity is, of course, payable *inter alia* to the agent because on his side he provides a consideration which is not fully paid for by the normal remuneration.

*Article 31*

This Article sets out three situations in which the goodwill indemnity is not payable.

The first is where the principal terminates the contract under Article 27(1)(*a*) because of a fault committed by the agent.

Secondly there is the situation where the principal continues to contract with the agent's successor by agreement either of the agent or of his heirs, the new agent succeeding to all the rights and duties of the old. One would no doubt be justified in supposing that in these circumstances the old agent will receive a lump-sum payment from his successor which will include the goodwill indemnity.

The third case is the situation where the agent terminates the contract without having proper grounds under Article 27(1)(*a*) or (*b*) and, in addition, fails to observe the contractual or other legal provisions concerning the length of the period of notice or, otherwise, the period of the contract itself. It appeared to be equitable to provide that in such circumstances the agent would have no claim to goodwill indemnity.

*Article 32*

The question of restraint of competition after termination of the contract is

*EEC Directive*

dealt with in very different ways in the legislation, case-law and juristic writings in the various Member States. This proposal for a Directive provides that agreements restricting competition must be expressed in writing and must not subsist for more than two years after termination of the contract. They must not be wider in scope than the geographical area or group of persons covered by the agency and must be limited to the type of goods or services which formed the subject-matter of the agency at the time of termination. After termination of the contract the principal must pay to the agent a suitable indemnity throughout the whole period of currency of the agreement restricting competition. The amount is to be calculated on the basis of the agent's remuneration having regard to all the surrounding circumstances. Up to a point it is open to the principal to bring the agreement restricting competition to an end and thereby extricate himself from the obligation to pay the indemnity.

The present proposal specifies in which cases the obligations arising under an agreement restricting competition may be modified. The cases mainly in point are those where the principal terminates the contract on the ground of fault committed by the agent, where the agent terminates on the ground of fault committed by the principal, where either party terminates because of *force majeure,* inevitable accident or for some personal reason, which makes it impossible for him to continue with the contract.

*Explanatory Memorandum*

### Chapter VII—General and Final Provisions

*Article* 33

The parties are free in certain cases to derogate from some of the mandatory provisions in the Directive. Those provisions are:

"Article 15(4):   Agent's right to receive a suitable payment on account.

Article 19     :   Agent's right to remuneration where the principal has not made use of his services or has made less use of them than the agent could ordinarily expect.

Article 21     :   Agent's right to separate commission for giving *del credere* guarantees.

Article 26(2):   Agreement as to minimum period of notice for termination of an agency contract concluded for an indeterminate period.

Article 30     :   Agent's right to goodwill indemnity."

The parties may vary the provisions on the foregoing matters where the agent is a company or legal person whose paid-up capital is more than 100 000 EUA. The parties may exclude entirely the rights provided for in Articles 19, 21 and 30.

This Article reposes on the basis that commercial agents who are economically strong enough to carry on business in the form of a company or legal person are not under disadvantage in negotiating the terms of a contract. Accordingly they do not require any special protection.

*Article* 34

This Article is concerned with limitation periods in relation to rights which flow from the provisions of the Directive. The periods of limitation vary in length from one Member State to another, depending on the particular subject-matter, from six months to thirty years. Article 34 fixes a uniform period of four years calculated from the end of the year in which the right arises. Derogations are, however, allowed as regards rights which arise during the period of ten years preceding termination of the contract to sums of money which have been omitted from the commission statement referred to in Article 15(5) or to reimbursement of expenses under Article 20. In these cases the period of limitation begins to run from the end of the year during which the contract expires, the object being to obviate the difficulty which the agent would experience if he had to commence legal proceedings during the currency of the contract. In proposing a period of ten years prior to termination it is considered that certainty as to the law would thereby be assured whilst at the same time taking account of the fact that in all Member States a limit is imposed upon the length of time during which books of account and relevant documents have to be preserved.

*Article* 35

This Article is based on the principle that principal and agent are not entitled to derogate from the mandatory provisions contained in the Directive, or more precisely from the mandatory provisions of national law adopted in application of the Directive. They are prohibited from doing so only in so far

*EEC Directive*

as the derogation would be inconsistent with the provisions which are designed to protect the agent. Member States will thus have to ensure that terms agreed between the parties are void under the national law if they are contrary to the mandatory provisions.

The relevant provisions are as follows[57]:

Article  5(1):   Duty of the commercial agent to act fairly and in good faith.

Article  8    :   Agent's right to damages from the principal where the agent has had to meet a claim for infringement of industrial, commercial or intellectual property rights, the infringement being attributable to the principal.

Article 10(1)
and
Article 10
(2)(*b*) and (*c*):   Duty of the principal to act fairly and in good faith, especially to provide the agent with all the information he requires in order to carry out the contract, and to inform him of the acceptance, refusal or partial execution of commercial transactions.

Article 11(1)
and (3)       :   Agent's right to be remunerated for his services.

Article 12(1):   Conditions governing the right to remuneration.

Article 13    :   Right to commission on transactions entered into after termination of the contract.

Article 14    :   Right to special commission for collection of moneys.

Article 15    :   Time at which the right to commission arises.

Article 16(1):   Cases in which commission does not become due.

Article 18    :   Agent's right to examine the books of account.

Article 19(1)
and (2)       :   Right to remuneration where principal does not make use of agent's services to the extent expected; basis of calculation of remuneration in these circumstances.

Article 20(2):   Right to reimbursement of expenses.

Article 21(1)
(2) and (3)   :   The *del credere* provisions, which as provided in paragraph 4 may be derogated from only where the principal or the third party is established or is habitually resident outside the Community, or where the agent has been given full authority to conclude contracts.

Article 23    :   Right to receive a signed written statement of the terms of the contract.

Article 26    :   Formal requirements relating to notice and minimum period of notice.

Article 27    :   Notice in case of serious fault or undermining of the commercial basis of the contract.

---

[57] Some of the mandatory provisions in the Directive (*e.g.*, Articles 1, 2, 3 and 22) do not relate to the contract itself and in this respect are different from the provisions listed here.

*Explanatory Memorandum*

| | | |
|---|---|---|
| Article 28 | : | Right to damages or lump-sum indemnity for wrongful termination, at the agent's option. |
| Article 29(2) | : | Agent's right of lien. |
| Article 30 | : | Goodwill indemnity. |
| Article 32 | : | Agreements restricting competition—formal requirements, scope and duration. |
| Article 34 | : | Limitation periods. |

Paragraph (2) provides that the rule prohibiting derogation from the mandatory rules does not apply where and in so far as the agent carries on business as a commercial agent outside the Community. Thus where the agent carries on business partly inside the Community and partly outside it the parties may derogate from the mandatory provisions so far as concerns that part of the business which is outside. The important thing is that within the Community all commercial agents be placed on an equal footing and have the benefit of the protection conferred by the Directive. In this way, moreover, the conditions of competition to which principals who appoint agents within the Community are subject will be in balance. On the other hand, where agents carry on their business outside the Community they and their principals must be free to derogate from the mandatory provisions because, in order to be able to compete successfully, they must have full scope to adapt to prevailing market conditions.

*Articles 36 and 37*

It is recognised that as the subject-matter of the Directive is complex a relatively long period of time will be required for it to be introduced into the national laws.

*EEC Directive*

**Proposal for a Council Directive to
coordinate the Laws of the Member States relating to
(self-employed) Commercial Agents**

The Council of the European Communities,

Having regard to the Treaty establishing the European Economic Community, and in particular Articles 57(2) and 100 thereof;

Having regard to the Proposal from the Commission;

Having regard to the Opinion of the European Parliament;

Having regard to the Opinion of the Economic and Social Committee;

Whereas the restrictions on freedom of establishment and freedom to provide services in respect of activities of intermediaries in commerce, industry and small craft industries were abolished by Council Directive 64/224/EEC of 25 February 1964[58];

Whereas the differences in national laws concerning commercial representation substantially affect the conditions of competition and the carrying on of that activity within the Community and can be detrimental both to the protection available to commercial agents *vis-à-vis* their principals and to the security of commercial transactions; whereas moreover those differences are such as to inhibit substantially the conclusion and operation of commercial representation contracts where principal and commercial agent are established in different Member States;

Whereas trade in goods between Member States should be carried on under conditions which are similar to those of a single market, and this necessitates approximation of the legal systems of the Member States to the extent required for the proper functioning of the common market; whereas in this regard the rules concerning conflict of laws do not, in the matter of commercial representation, remove the inconsistencies referred to above, nor would they even if they were made uniform, and accordingly the proposed harmonisation is necessary notwithstanding the existence of those rules;

Whereas in this matter the legal relationship between commercial agent and principal must be given priority of treatment;

Whereas in many cases commercial agents are as a rule, though in differing degrees, economically in a weak position *vis-à-vis* their principals, and it is accordingly appropriate that in harmonising and improving the minimum rules in the laws of the Member States relating to commercial agents there be alignment upon the principles set out in Article 117 of the EEC Treaty,

Has Adopted this Directive:

---

[58] OJ No. 56, 4.4.1964, P. 869/64.

*Text of the Directive*

CHAPTER I—SCOPE OF APPLICATION

**Article 1**

1. The harmonisation measures prescribed by this Directive apply to the laws, regulations and administrative provisions of the Member States governing the relations between self-employed commercial agents and their principals.

2. National laws and trade usages which are not inconsistent with the provisions of this Directive shall continue to apply to the relations referred to in paragraph 1.

**Article 2**

For the purposes of this Directive the expression "commercial agent" means a self-employed intermediary who has continuing authority for a fixed or indeterminate period to negotiate and/or to conclude an unlimited number of commercial transactions in the name and for account of another person (who is hereinafter called "the principal").

**Article 3**

This Directive does not apply:

—to intermediaries who are wage or salary earning employees within the meaning of Directive 64/224/EEC of 25 February 1964,

—to intermediaries who act in their own name,

—to intermediaries appointed to negotiate or to conclude in the name of the principal a specified transaction or a number of specified transactions only,

—to intermediaries who carry on their activities in the insurance or credit fields.

**Article 4**

The Member States are at liberty:

1. Not to apply Articles 15(4), last sentence, 19, 26(2), 30 and 31 to persons who act as commercial agents but by way of secondary activity only; the question whether the activity is carried on in that way being determined in accordance with commercial usage in the State whose law governs the relations between principal and agent.

2. To apply some or all of the provisions of this Directive, as the case requires, to persons who carry on other trades or professions and who, although they work for their own account and/or in their own name, can under the national law be assimilated to commercial agents.

*EEC Directive*

CHAPTER II—RIGHTS AND DUTIES OF THE PARTIES

**Article 5**

1.　The commercial agent shall in carrying out his activities act fairly and in good faith *vis-à-vis* his principal and third parties. He shall perform his duties with the care which a sound businessman would exercise.

2.　Without prejudice to and in pursuance of the general duty specified in paragraph 1 the commercial agent shall:

> (*a*)　at all times supply to the principal the information he needs in order to conduct the business satisfactorily, especially as regards the solvency of third parties in current commercial transactions of which the agent is aware,
>
> (*b*)　keep separately from his own moneys all sums received for the principal and pay them over to him without delay,
>
> (*c*)　keep proper accounts relating to the accounts receivable and assets of his principal,
>
> (*d*)　look after such property as is given into his possession with the care which a sound businessman would exercise,
>
> (*e*)　comply with all instructions given to him by the principal for attaining the object of the agency, provided they do not basically affect the agent's independence. The agent may arrange his activities and use his time as he thinks fit.

3.　Unless otherwise agreed the commercial agent may employ the services of commercial agents and commercial travellers.

**Article 6**

The commercial agent shall not, even after the contract has come to an end, divulge to third parties or turn to account any commercial or industrial secrets which were disclosed to him or of which he became aware because of his relationship with the principal, unless he proves that his doing so is consistent with the principles of a sound businessman.

**Article 7**

1.　The commercial agent may carry on business for his own account or for account of a third party provided that business is in goods or services which do not compete with those for which he was appointed to represent the principal. In particular he may undertake to act as commercial agent for another principal or work for an employer as a salaried or wage-earning representative.

2.　The commercial agent shall obtain the consent of his principal for the carrying on of any activity for his own account or for account of a third party if that activity involves goods or services which compete with those for which he has been appointed to represent the principal.

3.　The parties may derogate from the provisions of paragraphs 1 and 2 and, in particular, agree that the commercial agent shall not carry on other activities for account of another principal, for his own account or as an employee.

*Text of the Directive*

## Article 8

1. Where the commercial agent has had to meet a claim for breach of industrial, commercial or intellectual property rights over goods or services forming the subject-matter of his agency he may claim damages from his principal if the breach was caused by the principal.

2. The provisions of paragraph 1 shall apply *mutatis mutandis* in the event of breach of the rules of fair competition.

## Article 9

1. The commercial agent shall have authority to negotiate commercial transactions for account of the principal. He shall have authority to conclude agreements in respect thereof only where the principal empowers him to do so.

2. The agent shall be presumed to have authority:

—to receive complaints from third parties where goods or services supplied are defective, and, where goods are not accepted, notices that they are available for collection;

—to protect the principal's rights to have the means of proof preserved.

3. Limitations of the agent's authority shall be ineffective as against third parties unless they were aware or ought to have been aware thereof.

## Article 10

1. The principal shall in his relations with the commercial agent act fairly and in good faith. He shall make available to the commercial agent all the assistance he needs, having regard to the circumstances, for the performance of his part of the contract.

2. Without prejudice to the general duty specified in paragraph 1, the principal shall make available to the agent in suitable quantity such materials, information and documents as are necessary for the performance of his activities. He shall in particular:

(*a*) supply the agent with samples, designs, price lists, printed advertising material, conditions of contract and other documents relating to the goods and services for which he has been appointed agent;

(*b*) provide the commercial agent with all information which is requisite for the performance of the contract, particularly as regards current and prospective production, and inform the agent without delay when the principal foresees that the volume of commercial transactions that the principal will be able to execute will be considerably lower than the commercial agent could normally expect;

(*c*) inform the commercial agent without delay of the acceptance, refusal or, in appropriate cases, the partial performance of a commercial transaction.

*EEC Directive*

### CHAPTER III—REMUNERATION AND REIMBURSEMENT OF EXPENSES

**Article 11**

1. The principal shall remunerate the commercial agent by paying him commission or a fixed sum or both. Any variable item of remuneration which is calculated by reference to turnover shall be deemed to be commission.

2. The amount of commission shall be agreed between the parties. In the absence of agreement the agent shall be entitled to the commission that is customarily allowed to agents appointed for the goods or services which form the subject-matter of his agency in the place where he carries on his activities. If there is no custom as to the commission the agent shall be entitled to a fair commission.

3. Agency contracts which exclude the agent's right to be remunerated shall be void.

**Article 12**

1. The commercial agent shall be entitled to commission on commercial transactions entered into during the currency of the contract:

   (*a*)  where the transaction is procured by the commercial agent, or

   (*b*)  where the transaction is entered into with a third party with whom the agent has previously negotiated or agreed a transaction falling within the terms of his agency, or

   (*c*)  where the commercial agent is appointed to cover a specific geographical area or a specific group of people and the transaction is entered into in that geographical area or with a person belonging to that group, notwithstanding that the transaction was negotiated or agreed otherwise than by the commercial agent.

2. The commercial agent shall not be entitled to the commission referred to in paragraph 1 if by virtue of Article 13 that commission is payable to another agent.

**Article 13**

The commercial agent shall be entitled to commission on commercial transactions entered into after the contract has come to an end:

   (*a*)  where the transaction was negotiated by him, or

   (*b*)  where, the preparatory work having been done by him, the transaction was entered into mainly as a result of his efforts during the currency of the contract; in these cases, however, he shall be entitled to commission only if the transaction was entered into within a reasonable period after the contract came to an end, a "reasonable period" being one which is proportionate to the type of transaction in question and to the volume thereof.

**Article 14**

Where the commercial agent is under duty to the principal to collect payment of moneys, the commercial agent shall be entitled to a special commission therefor.

*Text of the Directive*

## Article 15

1. The right to commission arises at the moment when the principal and the third party enter into the commercial transaction.

2. The commission shall be payable upon the happening of either of the two following events:

   (*a*) as soon as and to the extent that the principal has performed his part of the transaction, even if he fails to carry out his obligations fully in the manner agreed or satisfies some of them only partially, or

   (*b*) as soon as and to the extent that the third party has performed his part of the transaction.

3. If the principal or the third party fails to perform his part of the transaction in full the amount of commission due shall be calculated by reference to the value of that part performed whose value is the higher.

4. The parties may agree that so long as the third party has not performed his obligations the commission shall be payable at a later time than that provided for in subparagraph (*a*) of paragraph 2 above. The commission shall, however, be payable in all cases not later than the last day of the third month following the month during which the principal completed the performance of his part of the contract. Where the parties agree as aforesaid the agent shall be entitled to receive a payment on account, of suitable amount, not later than the last day of the month following the month during which the principal completed the performance of his part of the contract.

5. The principal shall each month supply the commercial agent with a statement of the amount of commission earned and the amount of commission payable. The statement shall set out the essential data used in calculating the amounts of commission. The statement shall be prepared promptly and in any event not later than the last day of the month following that in which the commission in question was earned. The parties may agree that this period shall be extended to three months.

## Article 16

1. The right to commission shall be extinguished:

   (*a*) Where the commercial agent has not fulfilled his obligations under Article 5(2)(*a*), the principal having entered into the commercial transaction without being aware of the third party's insolvency and it being established that the third party has not or will not perform his part of the transaction, or

   (*b*) if and to the extent that it has become impossible to perform the transaction, this being in no way attributable to the principal, or

   (*c*) if performance of the transaction cannot reasonably be required of the principal, particularly where there exist in relation to the third party serious grounds for non-performance.

2. Any commission which the commercial agent has already received for these commercial transactions shall be refunded.

*EEC Directive*

**Article 17**

Unless otherwise agreed commission shall be calculated on the gross amount of the invoice without deduction of cash discounts, fidelity rebates or reductions allowed unilaterally by the principal after entry into the commercial transaction, and without deduction of incidental expenses such as costs of transport, packaging, insurance, taxes and customs charges, unless these incidental expenses are invoiced separately to the customer.

**Article 18**

1. The commercial agent shall be entitled to be supplied with all necessary extracts from the copies of the principal's books of account, together with explanations thereof, to enable him to check the amounts of commission to which he is entitled. Article 6 shall apply *mutatis mutandis*.

2. If there exist proper grounds for thinking that the items referred to in paragraph 1 which the principal has supplied are incorrect or incomplete, or if the principal refuses to supply them, the agent shall be entitled to require that either the agent himself or some person designated by the agent (being a person qualified for that purpose in accordance with the requirements of the national law applicable in the State where the books of account are kept), at the option of the principal, be given access to the books of account and the accounting documents for the purpose of examining them. This right may be exercised to the extent necessary for checking the correctness or completeness of the commission statement or of the said items.

**Article 19**

1. The agent shall be entitled to remuneration if he has already fulfilled his obligations under the agency contract or if he has already taken steps to meet those obligations, even though the principal has made no use of his services or has used them to a considerably lesser extent than the agent could normally have expected, unless the principal's conduct is due to circumstances beyond his control.

2. Usually, in calculating the remuneration referred to in paragraph 1, account shall be taken of all the circumstances, the basis being the average monthly remuneration of the commercial agent during the twelve months before the circumstances described in paragraph 1 arose. If the contract was concluded less than twelve months previously the remuneration shall be calculated on the basis of the average monthly remuneration paid during the currency of the contract.

3. In applying paragraph 2 the following shall be taken into account:

   (*a*) the expenses incurred by the commercial agent for the purpose of setting up the agency and preparing to commence business,

   (*b*) the amounts which the commercial agent has saved on expenses, the amounts which he has earned in carrying on some other activity and those which he has deliberately not earned because he has declined some activity which was nevertheless suitable.

**Article 20**

1. The commercial agent shall not be entitled to reimbursement of expenses

*Text of the Directive*

incurred in the usual course of his activities unless the parties have agreed otherwise or there is a custom to the contrary.

2.   Where, however, the agent incurs expenses in connection with special activities undertaken on the instructions or with the consent of the principal, he shall be entitled to be reimbursed.

*EEC Directive*

### CHAPTER IV—DEL CREDERE

**Article 21**

1. Every agreement whereby the commercial agent guarantees in favour of his principal that a third party will pay the price of goods or services forming the subject-matter of commercial transactions which the agent has negotiated or agreed, shall be evidenced in writing or by cable, telex or telegram. This type of agreement is hereinafter referred to as a *del credere* agreement.

2. (*a*) A *del credere* agreement covering transactions which were not negotiated or agreed by the commercial agent shall be void.

   (*b*) A *del credere* agreement shall be concluded in relation only to a particular commercial transaction, or in relation to a series of such transactions with particular third parties who are specified in the agreement.

   (*c*) Any *del credere* agreement which amounts to an unlimited guarantee on the part of the commercial agent for transactions falling within the first sentence of paragraph 1 shall be void.

3. The commercial agent shall be entitled to be paid a separate commission, of reasonable amount, for transactions entered into to which his *del credere* guarantee applies.

4. The parties may derogate from the provisions of paragraphs 1 to 3 as regards transactions:

   (*a*) in which the place of business of the principal or of the third party is outside the territory of the Community or, if the principal or third party has no place of business, then his place of habitual residence is outside that territory, or

   (*b*) which the agent has been given full power to agree and to carry out.

*Text of the Directive*

CHAPTER V—BANKRUPTCY OR WINDING-UP OF THE PRINCIPAL, EXECUTION AND ASSIGNMENT

**Article 22**

1.   Natural persons whose income is mainly derived from a commercial agency shall as regards sums owing to them for remuneration and reimbursement of expenses be treated as employees of the principal where bankruptcy or winding-up proceedings have been opened in respect of the principal or an arrangement, composition or other procedure is in progress with the principal's creditors.

2.   The natural persons to whom paragraph 1 applies shall in relation to sums owing to them by the principal on account of remuneration and reimbursement of expenses enjoy those rights to which employees are entitled as regards the amount of income for which execution cannot issue where third parties obtain an order for execution against the principal.

3.   The provisions of national law relating to employees shall apply *mutatis mutandis* to the natural persons referred to in paragraph 1 as regards assignment of sums owing to them by the principal for remuneration and reimbursement of expenses.

4.   The Member States may fix maximum figures of income for purposes of the application of paragraph 1.

*EEC Directive*

CHAPTER VI—MAKING OF THE CONTRACT AND CESSATION OF THE CONTRACT

**Article 23**

Each party shall be entitled to receive from the other a signed written document setting out the terms of the contract and any terms subsequently agreed. Any purported waiver of this right shall be invalid.

**Article 24**

Article 23 shall apply *mutatis mutandis* where by mutual agreement the agency contract is terminated.

**Article 25**

Subject to Articles 27 and 28 a contract for a fixed or determinable period shall terminate upon the expiration of the period for which it was made. Unless otherwise agreed a contract for a fixed or determinable period which continues to be performed after that period has expired shall be deemed to be converted into a contract for an indeterminate period.

**Article 26**

1.  Where the contract is concluded for an indeterminate period either party may terminate it by notice. Notice shall be given in writing. The period of notice shall be the same for both parties.

2.  During the first year of the contract the notice shall be of not less than two months. After the first year the period of notice shall be increased by one month for each additional year which has begun. The Member States may prescribe a maximum period of notice which shall in no case be less than twelve months. Periods of notice shall coincide with the end of a calendar month.

**Article 27**

1.  Either party may terminate the contract at any time:

    (*a*)  where the other party has in relation to the contract committed a fault such that the party who terminates cannot be required to keep it in being until the end of the period of notice or until the end of its agreed period of duration, or

    (*b*)  where some circumstance arises which makes it impossible to perform the contract, or which seriously prejudices its performance, or which substantially undermines the commercial basis of the contract, so that the party who terminates cannot be required to keep it in being until the end of the period of notice or until the end of its agreed period of duration.

2.  Termination must be effected *vis-à-vis* the other party as soon as the fault becomes known or as soon as the events which justify termination have occurred. The party who terminates shall upon request of the other inform him in writing of the reasons therefor.

3.  Where the contract is terminated under paragraph 1(*a*) the party who is at fault shall be liable in damages to the other.

*Text of the Directive*

**Article 28**

1.   Where one of the parties terminates the contract or declares that it is at an end, without in either case observing the proper period of notice provided for by the contract or by law, and neither of the grounds for termination set out in Article 27 applies, that party shall be liable in damages to the other.

2.   In the cases referred to in paragraph 1 the commercial agent shall be entitled to claim a lump-sum indemnity in lieu of damages where the contract is terminated by the principal or declared by him to be at an end. The indemnity shall be calculated on the basis of the average remuneration paid to the agent during the period of twelve months preceding the declaration or termination. If the contract was concluded less than twelve months previously the indemnity shall be calculated on the basis of the average remuneration received during the currency of the contract up to the time when the relevant event took place. The indemnity shall be paid for the unexpired period of the contract but subject to a maximum period of two years.

**Article 29**

1.   Upon cessation of the contract the commercial agent shall deliver up to the principal the materials and documents referred to in Article 10(2) unless he has disposed of them in the normal course of business.

2.   To secure the rights of the commercial agent as regards remuneration and reimbursement of expenses, he shall have a lien over such movables and other property of the principal as are in his possession pursuant to the contract, which lien shall continue after cessation of the contract.

**Article 30**

1.   After cessation of the contract the commercial agent or his heirs shall be entitled to require payment by the principal of a goodwill indemnity:

   (a)   where the agent has brought new customers to the principal or has appreciably increased the volume of business with the existing customers, and

   (b)   where as a result thereof substantial benefits will continue to accrue to the principal, and

   (c)   where, notwithstanding Article 13, the cessation of the contract results in his not receiving remuneration for transactions negotiated or agreed, after the contract has come to an end, between the principal and the customers referred to in subparagraph (a) above.

2.   The goodwill indemnity shall be reasonable in amount having regard to all the circumstances. It shall be equal to not less than one tenth of the annual remuneration calculated on the basis of the average remuneration during the preceding five years, including transactions on which commission arises under Article 13, multiplied by the number of years for which the contract has been in existence. If the contract was concluded less than five years previously the indemnity shall be calculated on the average remuneration received during the period which has actually run.

3.   The amount of the indemnity shall not exceed twice the average annual remuneration calculated in the manner provided in paragraph 2. Subject always

to this maximum, either party may request that the amount of the indemnity be calculated otherwise than as provided in paragraph 2 where, having regard to all the circumstances, it would be equitable so to calculate it.

4.   Where the agent terminates the contract by notice the period of which is consistent with the period of notice required by the contract or by law, he shall be entitled to an indemnity not exceeding the amount provided for in paragraph 2. If such termination is justified having regard to the principal's conduct, or for reasons which are particular to the agent, such that the agent cannot be required to continue his activities, the indemnity may be fixed at the maximum amount provided for in paragraph 3 if this is equitable.

5.   The right to goodwill indemnity shall not by prior agreement be contracted out of or restricted. It may be exercised only during the period of three months following cessation of the contract.

6.   The right to indemnity provided for in Article 28 shall not affect the right to goodwill indemnity.

**Article 31**

No claim to goodwill indemnity shall arise:

> (a)  Where the principal terminates or could have terminated the contract under Article 27(1)(a),
>
> (b)  where the principal maintains the contract on foot with the agent's successor who was introduced by the agent himself or by his heirs, the successor being from the legal point of view substituted entirely in the place of the agent,
>
> (c)  where the agent terminates the contract without giving notice of the proper duration required by the contract or by law and without proper grounds under Article 27(1).

**Article 32**

1.   Any agreement restricting the business activities of the commercial agent following cessation of the contract shall be in writing, and in default thereof shall be void. This type of agreement is hereinafter referred to as an agreement restricting competition.

2.   An agreement restricting competition shall apply only in relation to the geographical area or group of persons entrusted to the commercial agent and to the goods and services covered by his agency at the time when the contract came to an end.

3.   An agreement restricting competition shall be valid for not more than two years after cessation of the contract.

4.   Subject to the provisions of paragraph 5 the principal shall pay to the commercial agent a suitable indemnity so long as the agreement restricting competition is in force. The indemnity shall be calculated on the basis of the remuneration of the commercial agent and shall have regard to all the circumstances of the case.

> 5.  (a)  Where the principal terminates the contract under Article 27(1)(a) the agreement restricting competition shall continue effective but the agent shall not be entitled to the indemnity.

*Text of the Directive*

(b) Where the commercial agent terminates the contract under Article 27(1)(a) the agreement restricting competition shall apply unless terminated by him. Such termination shall be effected in writing.

(c) Where either party terminates the contract under Article 27(1)(b) or thereunder declares it to be at an end, the other party may terminate the agreement restricting competition. Such termination shall be effected in writing.

6.   Before the contract has come to an end the principal may terminate the agreement restricting competition and, if he does so, shall after the expiration of six months from the time when he gave notice of termination no longer be under obligation to pay the indemnity referred to in paragraph 4.

*EEC Directive*

### CHAPTER VII—GENERAL AND FINAL PROVISIONS

**Article 33**

1.  Where the commercial agency is undertaken by a company or legal person whose most recent annual accounts show that it has a paid-up capital exceeding the equivalent of 100 000 European Units of Account, the parties may derogate from the provisions of Articles 15(4), 19, 21, 26(2) and 30.

2.  The European Unit of Account (EUA) means the unit of account defined in Commission Decision No. 3289/75/ECSC of 15 December 1975[59].

**Article 34**

1.  Claims which arise under the foregoing provisions shall be subject to a limitation period of four years. The limitation period shall begin to run from the end of the year during which the claim arose.

2.  As regards claims which arise during the last ten years of the contract for commission which has not been included in the statement referred to in Article 15(5), or for reimbursement of expenses under Article 20, the limitation period shall begin to run from the end of the year during which the contract came to an end.

**Article 35**

1.  Any stipulation whereby the parties derogate, to the detriment of the agent, from the provisions next hereinafter mentioned shall be void: Article 5(1), 8, 10(1), 10(2)(*b*) and (*c*), 11(1) and (3), 12(1), 13, 14, 15, 16(1), 18, 19(1) and (2), 20(2), 21(1) (2) and (3), 23, 26, 27, 28, 29(2), 30, 32 and 34.

2.  In addition to the cases of derogation permitted under Article 21(4) and Article 33, the parties may derogate from the compulsory provisions specified in the foregoing paragraph in relation to those activities which the commercial agent carries on outside the Community.

**Article 36**

1.  The Member States shall before 1 January 1980 adopt and publish the provisions which are necessary to comply with this Directive and shall inform the Commission thereof immediately. They shall apply those provisions from 1 July 1980.

2.  From the time of notification of this Directive the Member States shall inform the Commission, in good time to enable it to communicate its observations, concerning the draft laws, regulations and administrative provisions which they plan to adopt in the field governed by this Directive.

**Article 37**

This Directive is addressed to the Member States.

---

[59] OJ No. L 327, 19 December 1975, p. 4.

## ANNEX B

**Law amending the German Commercial Code**[60]

*(Commercial Agents)*

August 6, 1953

¯BGBl. 1953 I Nr. 45, p. 771

The Bundestag has enacted the following:

### Article 1

The Seventh Part of the First Book of the German Commercial Code is to be amended as follows:

### Seventh Part

*Commercial Agents*

#### §84

(1) A commercial agent is he who is permanently entrusted as an independent person engaged in business to negotiate transactions for another person engaged in business (the principal) or to conclude transactions in the principal's name. A person is independent if he is in general permitted to arrange his activities freely and to determine his own hours of work.

(2) Any person who, without being independent within the meaning of subsection (1), is permanently entrusted with the negotiation of transactions for a principal or to conclude transactions in his principal's name, is deemed to be an employee.

(3) The principal may himself be a commercial agent.

#### §85

Either party is entitled to demand that the terms of the contract together with any subsequent additional agreements thereto shall be set out in writing and signed by the other party thereto. This right may not be excluded by agreement.

#### §86

(1) It is the duty of the commercial agent to concern himself with the negotiation or conclusion of transactions; he must act therein in the best interests of the principal.

(2) It is his duty to keep the principal properly informed and in particular to advise him immediately of each negotiation and the conclusion of any transaction.

(3) He must carry out his duties with the diligence of a prudent businessman.

---

[60] Based on "Commercial Agency and Distribution Agreements in Europe", British Institute of International and Comparative Law; Special Publication No. 3 (1964), pp. 56–75.

## §86a

(1) The principal must make available to the commercial agent all those materials which are necessary for the performance of his duties, such as samples, drawings, price lists, promotional literature, and the terms and conditions of business.

(2) The principal is under a duty to give to the commercial agent all necessary information. He must keep him immediately informed of the acceptance or refusal of all transactions negotiated by the agent or concluded by him without authority. The principal must notify the agent of cases where the principal is only able or willing to execute an appreciably smaller order than was to be expected in the circumstances; this right may not be excluded by agreement.

## §86b

(1) Where the commercial agent himself undertakes to guarantee the fulfilment of the obligation arising out of a transaction he is entitled to a special remuneration (*del credere* commission); this claim may not be excluded by agreement. The undertaking may only be assumed with respect to a specified transaction or to transactions with specified third parties which are negotiated or concluded by the commercial agent. Such undertaking is required to be in writing.

(2) The claim to the *del credere* commission arises at the conclusion of the transaction.

(3) Subsection (1) does not apply where the principal or the third party has his establishment or failing that, his residence, abroad. Nor does it apply to transactions for the conclusion and execution of which the commercial agent has unlimited authority.

## §87

(1) The commercial agent is entitled to commission on all transactions concluded during the term of the contract which are the result of his activity or are concluded with third parties which he has introduced as customers for business of a similar nature. He is not entitled to commission where this is due to his predecessor in accordance with subsection (3).

(2) Where the commercial agent is allotted a particular district or a particular *clientèle,* he is also entitled to commission on transactions concluded without his intervention with persons within his district or among his *clientèle* during the term of his contract. This does not apply where the commission is due to his predecessor under subsection (3).

(3) For a transaction which is not concluded until after the term of the contract has expired, the commercial agent is only entitled to commission where he has negotiated it or has initiated and so prepared it that its conclusion is preponderantly due to his activity and provided that the transaction is concluded within a reasonable time after the expiry of his contract.

(4) In addition to the entitlement to commission for concluded transactions, the commercial agent is entitled to commission in respect of all sums collected by him in accordance with the terms of his instructions.

## §87a

(1) The commercial agent is entitled to commission from the time when, and to the same extent as, the principal has executed the transaction. A contrary

agreement may be made but the commercial agent is nevertheless on the execution of the transaction by the principal entitled to an adequate advance which is payable at the latest on the last day of the succeeding month. Apart from any agreement, however, the commercial agent is entitled to commission from the time when, and to the same extent as, the third party has performed the transaction. The right to partial commission on a transaction partly executed may be excluded, so long as it is agreed that the principal shall pay to the commercial agent commission on the whole transaction as soon as a defined proportion thereof has been executed.

(2) Where it is established that the third party fails to perform, entitlement to commission is extinguished; any sums already paid by way of commission must be repaid.

(3) The commercial agent is also entitled to commission when it is established that the principal has not executed the transaction either in whole or in part, or has executed it in a manner otherwise than in accordance with its terms. This does not apply where, and in so far as, the execution of the transaction has become impossible, without the principal being responsible for such impossibility, or in circumstances where it was not reasonable to expect him to fulfil it, in particular on the ground that the conduct or position of the third party has provided a sufficient reason for its non-execution.

(4) The commission is payable on the last day of the month in which in accordance with §87c(1) the accounting for the commission is to take place.

(5) No agreements may be made which place the commercial agent in a less favourable position than he would otherwise enjoy under subsections (3) and (4).

§87b

(1) Where the amount of the commission has not been fixed, the customary rate is deemed to have been agreed.

(2) Commission is to be calculated on the amount which the third party or the principal has to pay. Discounts for cash are not to be deducted; the same applies to subsidiary charges, particularly in respect of transport, packing, customs duties and taxes except if such subsidiary charges are separately invoiced to the third party. Turnover tax which is separately invoiced solely by reason of the provisions of the tax laws is not regarded as separately invoiced.

(3) In respect of agreements relating to rental and uses intended for a period of certain duration, commission is to be calculated on the basis of the amount payable in respect of the duration. In the case of contracts of uncertain duration, commission is to be calculated on the basis of the amount payable in respect of the time between the commencement up to the time from which it is first possible for the third party to determine the contract; the commercial agent is entitled to further commission as appropriate in the event of the contract continuing.

§87c

(1) The principal must account monthly in respect of the commission to which the commercial agent is entitled; the period of accounting may not in any event be extended beyond three months. The account must be rendered immediately, and in any event before the end of the succeeding month.

(2) The commercial agent is at the rendering of the account entitled to an extract from the books relating to all transactions in respect of which he is entitled to commission in accordance with §87.

(3) The commercial agent is also entitled to information in respect of all matters relating to his entitlement to commission, when it becomes payable, and its calculation.

(4) In the event of a refusal to supply extracts from the books or where there is a reasonable doubt as to the accuracy or completeness of the account or the extracts from the books, the commercial agent is entitled to demand that either himself or an auditor or an "under oath" accountant nominated by him, at the option of the principal, shall be entitled to inspect the books and other relevant documents to such an extent as may be necessary to establish the accuracy or completeness of the account or the extracts from the books.

(5) These rights of the commercial agent may not be excluded or limited.

### §87d

The commercial agent is only entitled to reimbursement of his expenses incurred in the proper course of business where this is customary in the trade.

### §88

The rights arising out of the contractual relationship shall become barred after four years, commencing from the determination of the year in which they accrued.

### §88a

(1) The commercial agent may not in advance abandon his claim to any legal rights of lien or retention.

(2) After the determination of the contractual relationship the commercial agent has in accordance with general legal provisions an existing right of lien on all material placed at his disposal (§86a(1)) but only in respect of such claims as have fallen due in respect of commission and reimbursement of expenses.

### §89

(1) If the contractual relationship has been entered into for an indefinite period, it may be determined during the first three years of the contract by six weeks notice to expire at the end of any calendar quarter. Where any other period of notice is prescribed, there must be a minimum period of one month; the period of notice must be such as to expire at the end of a calendar month.

(2) After the contract has subsisted for more than three years such contract may only be determined by notice of at least three months in length expiring at the end of a calendar quarter.

(3) Any period of notice agreed upon must be the same for both parties. Where such periods differ the longer period shall apply to both parties.

### §89a

(1) The contractual relationship may be put an end to by either party without notice for important reasons. This provision may not be excluded or limited.

(2) Where the ground of termination by one party is conduct for which the other is responsible, the latter is liable in damages for any loss thereby occasioned to the other party as a result of the cessation of the contract.

### §89b

(1) The commercial agent is entitled to demand from the principal after the termination of the contractual relationship a reasonable compensation for loss of goodwill provided and as far as:

1. the principal has derived after the determination of the contractual relationship substantial advantages from his business relations with new customers which have been introduced by the commercial agent

2. the commercial agent has, by reason of the termination of the contract, lost rights to commission which he would have had on transactions already concluded, or to be concluded in the future with customers introduced by him if the contract had continued and

3. the payment of compensation in respect of loss of goodwill is fair and reasonable in all the circumstances.

It is the equivalent of the introduction of a new customer if the commercial agent so appreciably expands the principal's commercial relations with an existing customer that this amounts as a matter of business to the introduction of a new customer.

(2) Such compensation shall not exceed the average of the annual commission or other annual remuneration for the last five years of the activity of the commercial agent; for a shorter period of duration of the contractual relationship the average during the period of activity is to apply.

(3) The claim does not arise where notice to determine the contractual relationship has been given by the commercial agent unless justified by the conduct of the principal. The same rule applies where the principal has given notice to determine the contractual relationship and has given notice for an important reason arising out of any "fault" of the commercial agent.

(4) This claim may not be excluded in advance. It must be asserted within three months of the determination of the contractual relationship.

(5) [Refers to insurance agents and is not relevant to this paper.]

### §90

The commercial agent may not exploit or divulge any commercial or industrial secrets which have been confided to him or which have come to his notice in the course of his activity on behalf of the principal, even after the termination of the contractual relationship, in so far as this would in all the circumstances be contrary to rules of behaviour of a decent businessman.

### §90a

(1) Any agreement whereby the commercial agent is after the determination of the contractual relationship restricted in his business activity (agreement for restriction on competition) is required to be in writing and a document containing the agreed restrictions signed by the principal is to be delivered to the commercial agent. Such an agreement may only extend for a maximum of two years from the determination of the contractual relationship. The principal

is bound to pay to the commercial agent a reasonable compensation in respect of the period of the restriction on competition.

(2) The principal may, in writing, up to the termination of the contractual relationship, renounce the restrictions on competition with the result that after the expiry of six months following upon such declaration, he shall be relieved of any obligation to pay compensation. Where the principal determines the contractual relationship for an important reason arising out of any "fault" on the part of the commercial agent, the latter has no claim to compensation.

(3) Where the commercial agent determines the contractual relationship for important reasons arising out of any "fault" on the part of the principal, he may within one month after such termination, in writing declare himself free from the restrictions on competition.

(4) No agreement may be made which is less favourable for the commercial agent.

§91

(1) §55 also applies to a commercial agent authorised to conclude transactions on behalf of a principal who is not normally engaged in business.

(2) A commercial agent even though he has no authority to conclude transactions is regarded as authorised to receive complaints in respect of defective goods, declarations that the goods are available for collection as well as similar declarations whereby a third party claims or reserves his rights in respect of defective performance; he may act on behalf of the principal in respect of the principal's rights in connection with perpetuating testimony. A third party is only to be bound by the limitation of such rights where he knew or ought to have known of such limitation.

§91a

(1) Where a commercial agent who is only engaged to enter into negotiations has concluded a transaction in the name of the principal, and the third party was not aware of such want of authority, the transaction is to be regarded as being made with the consent of the principal provided he does not give notice terminating the transaction without delay on being informed by the commercial agent or the third party of the conclusion and the substantial content of the transaction.

(2) The same rule applies where the commercial agent who is engaged to conclude transactions concludes a transaction in the name of the principal which he is not authorised to conclude.

§92

[Refers to insurance agents and is not relevant to this paper.]

§92a

(1) In respect of the contractual relationship of a commercial agent who is under an obligation not to act for other principals or who is not able to do so by reason of the nature and extent of the duties demanded of him the Federal Minister of Justice in conjunction with the Federal Ministers for Economics and Labour, after having heard the associations representing the commercial agents and the principals may make orders, which do not require the assent of

the Bundesrat, laying down the minimal contractual obligations of the principal in order to ensure the required social and economic needs of the commercial agent or of a particular group of commercial agents. Such obligations as therein laid down may not be excluded or limited by the terms of the contract.

(2) [Refers to insurance agents and is not relevant to this paper.]

### §92b

(1) §§89 and 89b are not applicable to a part-time commercial agent. Where the contractual relationship is for an indefinite period, it may be determined by one month's notice to expire at the end of a calendar month; in the event of any other period of notice being agreed, such period must be the same for both sides. The claim to an adequate advance under §87a(1), second sentence, may be excluded by agreement.

(2) Subsection (1) hereof may only be applied by a principal who has engaged the commercial agent expressly as part-time commercial agent to negotiate or conclude transactions.

(3) Commercial usage determines whether a commercial agent is a part-time commercial agent only.

(4) [Refers to insurance agents and building society agents and is not relevant to this paper.]

### §92c

(1) In the event of a commercial agent having no establishment in Germany any agreement deviating from any of the provisions of this Part may be concluded.

(2) The same applies where the commercial agent is authorised to negotiate or conclude transactions having as their object the chartering or equipping of vessels or the carriage of passengers in vessels.

## ANNEX C

### Inconsistencies and confusions in terminology

See Part III, paragraph 39—

(1) *Use of a number of different words (or phrases) to express the same idea*

   (*a*) A commercial_agent may (like an English agent) make a contract between a principal and a third party. This is described by the following phrases: "conclude . . . transactions" in Article 2, "conclude agreements" in Article 9, and "agreed a transaction" in Article 12(1)(*b*) as well as (in effect) in Articles 21(2)(*a*), 21(4)(*b*) and 30(1)(*c*).

   (*b*) The commercial agent is generally called "commercial agent" but sometimes just "agent". There seems to be no system behind these different uses: for example, in Article 10(2), line 2 and in 10(2)(*a*) we have "agent" but in 10(2)(*b*) and (*c*) "commercial agent"; in Article 12(1), line 1, 12(1)(*a*) and (*c*) we have "commercial agent" but in 12(1)(*b*) "agent". These are random examples. There is no ambiguity, but this is very untidy drafting.

   (*c*) The relations between a principal and a third party are generally called "commercial transactions" but sometimes just "transactions". For example, in Article 12, lines 1–2, we have "commercial transactions" but in 12(1)(*a*), (*b*) and (*c*) "transaction"; in Article 21(2)(*a*) and (*c*) we have "transactions" but in 21(2)(*b*) "commercial transaction". Again the usage seems random and untidy. The description of the relations between a principal and a third party as "agreements" in Article 9 and as "the contract" in Article 15(4) is even more objectionable. Usually in the draft Directive "contract" refers to the relations between a principal and a commercial agent: see note (2)(*a*) below; as to "agreement" see notes (1)(*d*) and (2)(*b*) below.

   (*d*) A particular term of the contract between a principal and a commercial agent is in Article 32 called an "agreement" (*cf.*, also Articles 21 and 30(5)), but a "stipulation" in Article 35.

   (*e*) Article 15(1) refers to the time when the right to commission "arises". The reference to commission being "earned" in Article 15(5) seems to be to the same point (since "earned" is there contrasted with "payable"). Whether "due" in Article 15(3) means "earned" or "payable" is totally unclear.

   (*f*) The relations between a principal and a commercial agent are generally referred to as "the contract" (see note (2)(*a*), below), but in Articles 11(2), 12(1)(*b*) and 32(2), the draft Directive uses "his agency" (*cf.*, also 5(2)(*e*)). Article 19(1), line 2 and Article 24 have the best of both worlds by using "the agency contract". ("The agency" is also used in another sense: see note (2)(*d*), below).

   (*g*) Normally, where the commercial agent does not make a contract between a principal and a third party he is said to "negotiate" a transaction (for example, Articles 2 and 9), but Article 12(1)(*a*) says that in this situation the transaction is "procured" by the commercial agent, presumably meaning negotiated.

(*h*) In Article 15(2)(*a*) both the principal and the third party "perform" their "part". In Article 15(4) the principal still "performs" his "part"— but the third party "performs" his "obligations". In Article 16(1)(*a*) the commercial agent has "not fulfilled his obligations"—while the third party does not "perform his part".

(*i*) There seems to be no difference between "without delay" in Articles 5(2)(*b*) and 10(2)(*b*), and "promptly" in Article 15(5). "As soon as" in Article 27(2) seems to mean much the same thing.

(*j*) For collecting payments, the commercial agent gets a "special" commission (Article 14), but as *del credere* agent he gets a "separate" commission (Article 21(3)).

(*k*) There is probably no difference between what Article 11(2) calls "a fair commission" and what Article 21(3) calls "a . . . commission of reasonable amount".

(*l*) There probably is meant to be some difference between "terminating" a contract and "declaring it to be at an end" (Article 28) but it is not easily discernible to an English lawyer.

(*m*) "Cessation" in the Chapter VI heading, and in Articles 29, 30, 32(1) and (3) seems to mean the same thing as "came to an end" in 32(2) and 32(6): whether "termination" in Article 27(2) also means the same thing is not clear: the draftsman may be drawing the same distinction that is suggested in the previous note.

(*n*) Article 30 sometimes refers to "goodwill indemnity" (30(1), (2), line 1, (5) and (6)) and sometimes just to "indemnity" (30(2), line 7, (3) and (4)). There is no ambiguity but it is untidy.

(*o*) Under Article 5(2)(*a*), the commercial agent must "at all times supply" information; under Article 10(2)(*b*) the principal must "provide" information. Do the two verbs mean different things? Is the omission of "at all times" in 10(2)(*b*) significant?

(*p*) Article 30(1)(*c*) refers to transactions "negotiated *or agreed*". One would suppose that the words in italics refer to the situation in which a commercial agent has made a contract between a principal and a third party (see note (1)(*a*), above). But in that case they have no counterpart in Article 13, so that the cross-reference to Article 13 is meaningless. Perhaps "or agreed" here means something else, but this is totally unclear.

(2) *Use of the same word to express a number of different ideas:*

(*a*) "Contract" in Article 6 seems to mean the totality of the relations arising between a principal and a commercial agent out of the contract between them; it also seems to mean this in Article 12(1) and in Article 13, in the Chapter VI heading, and throughout Chapter VI (that is, Articles 23–32). Yet in Article 11(3) "contracts" seems to mean particular terms in contracts.

(*b*) "Agreements" in Article 9 appears to mean the whole of the contract between a principal and a third party; in Article 32 it means a term of the contract (in the sense of note (2)(*a*)) between the principal and a commercial agent; it seems to have the same meaning in Articles 21 and 30(5). "Agreement" throughout Article 21 appears to mean one of the terms of the contract between a principal and a commercial agent, whereas the word "agreed" in the same article is used to refer to the contract between a principal and a third party.

(*c*) "Contract" generally means the relations between a principal and a commercial agent (see note (2)(*a*), above); but in Article 15(4) it appears to mean the totality of the relations between a principal and a third party; so also in 10(2)(*a*) ("conditions of contract").

(*d*) "The agency" sometimes means the relationship between a principal and a commercial agent: see note (1)(*f*), above. But in Article 19(3)(*a*) it seems to refer to the commercial agent's business establishment.

Printed in England for Her Majesty's Stationery Office by McCorquodale Printers Ltd., London
HM 7924   Dd. 293916   K24   10 77   McC 3336/2

# Appendix 5

# House of Lords Select Committee Fifty-First Report

WEDNESDAY 27 JULY 1977

By the Select Committee appointed to consider Community proposals whether at draft or otherwise, to obtain all necessary information about them, and to make reports on those which, in the opinion of the Committee, raise important questions of policy or principle, and on other questions to which the Committee consider that the special attention of the House should be drawn.

Ordered to Report:—

1. R/3/77: draft council directive to co-ordinate the laws of the member states relating to (self-employed) commercial agents

1. The proposed Directive deals with the legal relationship between "commercial agents" and their principals. For the purposes of the Directive a "commercial agent" is, broadly speaking, an independent person acting on a continuing basis in the name of a manufacturer or trader and negotiating or concluding contracts on his behalf for the supply of goods or services. The Directive if adopted would require standardised rules to be implied into the agency contract under which the commercial agent acts for the manufacturer or trader; in many instances departure from these standardised rules to the detriment of the commercial agent would not be permitted; the rules concern the rights and duties of the agent and of his principal, the remuneration of the agent, the agent's rights in the insolvency of the principal, and the making and cessation of the agency contract. Some of the Member States already have statutory codes, the content of which varies, concerning the legal relationship between these parties; the other Member States, including the United Kingdom, have no such code. One of the main purposes of the Directive is to introduce harmonised rules in the Member States about this kind of agency, since it is considered by the Commission that the existing differences are detrimental to the functioning of the Common Market; the other main purpose is to strengthen the position of the commercial agent vis-à-vis his principal by requiring the existence in all Member States of rules which favour the agents.

2. At the outset, those concerned in drafting the Directive seem to have encountered difficulty in defining the expression "commercial agent". Article 2 of the draft defines the expression to mean "a self-employed intermediary who has continuing authority for a fixed or indeterminate period to negotiate and/or to conclude an unlimited number of commercial transactions in the name and on account of another person (who is hereinafter called 'the principal')." This is a wide definition, and the draftsmen seem to have

299

been so much impressed by its width that in Article 3 they proceed to exclude from the definition two classes of persons who in any case would not have been within it. The exact area that could be covered by the definition is very indeterminate; it has been suggested that it could include such persons as travel agents, advertising agents, stockbrokers, loading brokers, and forwarding agents to the extent that they act for particular principals over a period of time. It could cover buying agents, though later articles suggest that this is not intended. Agents in the insurance and credit fields are expressly excluded. It becomes clear, at a late stage in the draft, that it is intended to cover companies acting as agents as well as individuals so acting. Generally speaking, the Committee found the drafting of the Directive loose and uncertain.

3. The Committee take the true intended effect of the Directive to be to protect independent commercial agents who are engaged to canvass for orders for the principal's goods or services as distinct from "commercial travellers" who are employees of the persons whom they serve. The draft Directive contains rules concerning commission which considerably favour the commercial agent. Of the other detailed rules which compliance with the Directive would cause to be implicit in the agency contract, the most important would be those which would confer on the agent (a) the right on cessation of the contract to be paid a "goodwill indemnity" where he has brought new customers to the principal or appreciably increased the volume of business with existing customers, and as a result substantial benefits will continue to accrue to the principal (Article 30); (b) the right, where the commercial agent is for a period after cessation of the contract bound by an agreement restricting his business activities, to be paid remuneration during that period (Article 32); and (c) a right to preferential treatment in the insolvency of the principal. The inclusion in the agency contract of rights of the kind mentioned under (a) or (b) above, though required by the laws of some of the Member States, is not compulsory according to the law of the United Kingdom; in that country they are a matter for negotiation between the parties, and the inclusion of (b) would, it is thought, be very unusual. If the Directive were adopted in its present form these rights would, under the law in each of the Member States, have to be conferred on the agent, save that the right to the goodwill indemnity would be excluded if the agent were a company with a paid-up capital exceeding 100,000 European Units of Account ("EUA") (about £67,000). It would not, however, be difficult to avoid being excluded on this ground; the company could operate on loan capital, or several companies each having a capital less than 100,000 EUA could be formed.

4. While therefore the law of the United Kingdom includes, at present, no special rules governing the relationship between commercial agents and their principals, the laws of the continental Member States do include rules for the protection of these agents, but these it appears vary very considerably from country to country. Thus the Sub-Committees (B and E) which have considered the Directive were informed in evidence that the degree of protection for agents in France goes much further than that provided for in the Directive, and had been raised so high that "principals were not interested in entering into contracts with French agents." The rules in Germany are evidently less favourable to the agents, and it is said that even after the protective law was introduced "the commercial agency was still the cheapest means of marketing goods in Germany."

5. The purpose of the present report is not to review the Directive in detail and to criticize its drafting, but to consider whether there is any justification in principle for introducing a Directive on this subject at all. The justification put up by the Commission is summarised as follows in the Commission's Explanatory Memorandum at page 2.

"Basically, the proposal has two objectives. The first is to remove the differences in law which are detrimental to the proper functions of the common market. They affect the conditions of competition and create considerable legal uncertainty. This applies, for example, in relation to the goodwill indemnity, which is known in some Member States but not in others. It is more expensive for the principal to have an agent in those countries in which the goodwill indemnity is already compulsory by law, and this operates very much to the economic advantage of principals who are not under an obligation to pay any indemnity after the contract has terminated. The second objective is to safeguard or improve the protection that already exists for commercial agents. Although they are self-employed, most commercial agents are economically in a weak position vis-à-vis their principals. In so far as the proposal envisages minimum rules it does not affect those provisions of national law which are more favourable to the commercial agent and does not stand in the way of progress. From a more general point of view the proposal is aligned on the principles set out in Article 117 of the EEC Treaty, and, in harmonising the law, endeavours to achieve a levelling-up."

6. This statement on the part of the Commission is notable for the boldness of its assertions. It is, for example, insupportable to lay down as a general proposition that "it is more expensive for the principal to have an agent in those countries in which the goodwill indemnity is already compulsory by law, and this operates very much to the economic advantage of principals who are not under (such) an obligation . . .". Obviously, the question whether the one principal has a competitive advantage over another depends as much, if not more, on the rates of remuneration which they each pay during the period of the contract, to say nothing of the other terms of the contract. It may suit both principal and agent to dispense with a provision for goodwill indemnity in favour of a higher rate of commission during the currency of the contract. There would seem no justification for prohibiting them from making what bargain they please about this. The statement that "most commercial agents are economically in a weak position vis-à-vis their principals" appears to be simply a matter of assertion. The preamble to the Directive is couched in more cautious terms and states that "in many cases commercial agents are as a rule, though in differing degrees, economically in a weak position vis-à-vis their principals." The evidence given on the part of the Manufacturers' Agents' Association of the United Kingdom was that there are twenty thousand agents in this country. It is difficult to believe that the Commission knows the conditions under which "most" of these persons work, and their economic strength. The evidence of the Association was that "the agent used to have to get the best terms he could from his principal, today we have a form of agreement which is ever increasingly being accepted by British principals". The evidence further was that the standard form of contract "goes rather further than the directive which you are now considering, particularly in respect of the goodwill compensation clause"; and that "there is no question . . . whatever that there is now a greater demand, especially in the economic situation in which we live today, for manufacturers' agents than ever before." The Association stated in its written submission that "it is generally conceded that the commercial agent is invariably the weaker party as between himself and his principal." Dr R A Haumann, a German lawyer who gave helpful evidence about the law of that country, stated that "in general, the manufacturer's agent is in a weaker position and this weaker position is a bad thing for him. It leads to insecurity." But he went on to say that "we are not in favour of compulsory provision overall in Germany . . . there must be some

compulsory provisions in agency law, but in my opinion there is a little too much in this respect in the EEC draft Directive." On the other hand, the Confederation of British Industry stated that "the realities of commercial and industrial life being what they are, it is probable that proper investigation would show that principals are very often at the mercy of commercial agents and in at least equal general need of 'protection', and that the relative economic positions (which in effect means sizes and physical or financial resources) are very frequently irrelevant in determining which party is the dominant one in practice." The Association of British Chambers of Commerce, in their submission, said:

> "The guiding principle behind the Commission's proposals is that commercial agents are believed to be in a weaker negotiating position than their principals, and thus need protected and inalienable rights. The ABCC does not believe this premise is correct. The Commission claims that in countries where a preferential regime has been introduced for commercial agents (for example Belgium) there has been a resulting increase in their numbers. This is evidence of nothing more than the fact that the people take advantage of a preferential status if it is offered to them. It does not mean that in the absence of this preferential status those who might otherwise act as commercial agents would be severely disadvantaged. On the contrary, the ABCC considers that an agent is frequently in a reasonably strong position and is not therefore always in need of the extended protection proposed.
>
> The Commission is particularly keen to impose protection where a principal in one country appoints a selling agent in another country. The ABCC believes that this relationship will most frequently occur when a comparatively small manufacturer wishes to break into an export market and, having neither the resources nor the immediate sales potential for setting up a full time distributor or his own office in the country, hires an agent with specialised and local knowledge to do the job on his behalf. In this type of situation, there is very little likelihood of the principal being in such a strong negotiating position that the agent is in need of special protection.
>
> In the UK, at least, there exist various established trade associations, most notably the Manufacturers' Agents' Association, who protect the interests of members, and presumably provide their membership with clear advice and guidelines as to acceptable conditions of agency contracts."

7. In the result therefore, the facts, so far as they are ascertainable at all, seem to emerge very much as might be expected. At one end of the scale it seems that there are agents who are at the mercy of their principals; at the other end, principals at the mercy of their agents; in the middle, there appears to be a substantial body of agents whose services, according to the evidence of their Association, are much in demand and who are steadily improving their position. To impose, on this variegated pattern of agents, one body of inflexible legal rules seems to the Committee to be incapable of justification. What is needed is a flexibility which enables the parties to the agency contract to arrange terms which suit their respective needs.

8. In general, the Committee question the desirability of imposing strict standards in these commercial matters. If terms which favour the commercial agents are imposed, then the principals will find other means of selling their goods, by employing their own travellers, by employing commission agents who act in their own names, or by forming subsidiary companies. Distortions of business are a common result of imposing inflexible rules.

9. The Commission's other justification for the Directive is that it would remove "a continuing and quite definite inequality of the conditions of competition." Here, again, the Committee feel the lack of any supporting evidence. In so far as a manufacturer wishes to sell his goods in a particular country there seems to be no room for distortion of competition. Each manufacturer will be in the same position, according to whether or not the country in question has adopted rules resembling those in the Directive. The notion that a manufacturer will be positively debarred from selling in a country where agencies are so favoured seems to the Select Committee to be fanciful.

10. It should be observed that the Directive is not intended only to govern international transactions in which the manufacturer is in one Member State and the agent in another. The Directive would apply to trade which is being carried on entirely in one Member State, so that an English manufacturer dealing through English commercial agents entirely with English customers in the domestic market would have to accord to his agents the terms laid down in the Directive. For this, the Commission relies on the proposition that "trade in goods and the provision of services should always be effected under conditions which are similar to those of a single market." The Committee do not entirely accept this far-reaching proposition; but if there is to be a single market of the size of the Community, the need for flexibility in the ways in which commercial transactions can be carried out seems to be all the greater.

11. The Committee have recently noted with concern a tendency on the part of the Commission to interfere, in ways which are not altogether judicious, with particular segments of the national legal systems. They instance, in particular, the draft Directive on liability for Defective Products on which they reported in their 63rd Report of last Session, and the draft Directive on Contracts negotiated away from Business Premises ("Doorstep Selling") on which they are about to report. No doubt the operation of the Community requires the steady, though not hasty, development of some uniformity of general law in the commercial field throughout the Community. But caution is needed. The present Directive, for example, would, if adopted, apply to a particular and relatively small section of the field of agency, some hard and fast rules quite unknown to the general agency law of the United Kingdom. As to product liability, paragraph 8 of the Committee's 63rd Report points out that "the two legal systems of the United Kingdom, like those of the majority of the other Member States, accept as a general rule the principle that non-contractual liability for loss or damage caused to others should be based on fault—in the case of product liability the tort or delict of negligence. To incorporate into such a legal system a special rule whereby liability for loss or damage of a particular kind from a particular cause is made independent of all fault raises legal and practical problems of great complexity . . .". The draft Directive on Doorstep Selling might jeopardise many sales activities in the United Kingdom which are open to abuse only to a very limited extent, and which can provide a valuable service to the consumer. The Committee are unconvinced that these interferences are, as the Commission contends, called for so as to prevent competition from being distorted. The general law of a nation is not something which has come into existence by accident; it arises from the local circumstances, habits, and sentiments of the people' changes in it must be effected only with care and where real need can be demonstrated.

*Recommendation*

12. The Committee are of the opinion that this draft Directive raises important questions of policy and principle. They recommend that this Report should be debated by the House.

# Appendix 6

# Council Directive 86/653

**On the coordination of the laws of the member states relating to self-employed
commercial agents**
(18 December 1986, OJ 1990 L382/17)

*The Council of the European Communities*

Having regard to the Treaty establishing the EEC, and in particular Articles 57(2) and 100
thereof,

Having regard to the proposal from the Commission,

Having regard to the opinion of the European Parliament,

Having regard to the opinion of the Economic and Social Committee,

Whereas the restrictions on the freedom of establishment and the freedom to provide
services in respect of activities of intermediaries in commerce, industry and small craft
industries were abolished by Directive 64/224/EEC;

Whereas the differences in national laws concerning commercial representation substantially affect the conditions of competition and the carrying-on of that activity
within the Community and are detrimental both to the protection available to commercial agents vis-à-vis their principals and to the security of commercial transactions;
whereas moreover those differences are such as to inhibit substantially the conclusion
and operation of commercial representation contracts where principal and commercial
agent are established in different member states;

Whereas trade in goods between Member States should be carried on under conditions
which are similar to those of a single market, and this necessitates approximation of the
legal systems of the Member States to the extent required for the proper functioning of
the common market; whereas in this regard the rules concerning conflict of laws do
not, in the material of commercial representation, remove the inconsistencies referred
to above, nor would they even if they were made uniform, and accordingly the proposed harmonisation is necessary notwithstanding the existence of those rules;

Whereas in this regard the legal relationship between commercial agent and principal
must be given priority;

Whereas it is appropriate to be guided by the principles of Article 117 of the Treaty and
to maintain improvements already made, when harmonising the laws of the Member
states relating to commercial agents;

Whereas additional transitional periods should be allowed for certain Member States
which have to make a particular effort to adapt their regulations, especially those concerning indemnity for termination of contract between the principal and the commercial agent, to the requirements of this Directive,

*has adopted this Directive:*

CHAPTER I—SCOPE

## Article 1

1(1)   The harmonisation measures prescribed by this Directive shall apply to the laws, regulations and administrative provisions of the Member States governing the relations between commercial agents and their principals.

1(2)   For the purposes of this Directive, '**commercial agent**' shall mean a self-employed intermediary who has continuing authority to negotiate the sale or the purchase of goods on behalf of another person, hereinafter called the 'principal', or to negotiate and conclude such transactions on behalf of and in the name of that principal.

1(3)   A commercial agent shall be understood within the meaning of this Directive as not including in particular:

—a person who, in his capacity as an officer, is empowered to enter into commitments binding on a company or association,

—a partner who is lawfully authorised to enter into commitments binding on his partners,

—a receiver, a receiver and manager, a liquidator or a trustee in bankruptcy.

## Article 2

2(1)   This Directive shall not apply to:

—commercial agents whose activities are unpaid,

—commercial agents when they operate on commodity exchanges or in the commodity market, or

—the body known as the Crown Agents for Overseas Governments and Administrations, as set up under the Crown Agents Act 1979 in the United Kingdom, or its subsidiaries.

2(2)   Each of the Member States shall have the right to provide that the Directive shall not apply to those persons whose activities as commercial agents are considered secondary by the law of that member state.

CHAPTER II—RIGHTS AND OBLIGATIONS

## Article 3

3(1)   In performing his activities a commercial agent must look after his principal's interests and act dutifully and in good faith.

3(2)   In particular, a commercial agent must:

(a)  make proper efforts to negotiate and, where appropriate, conclude the transactions he is instructed to take care of:

(b)  communicate to his principal all the necessary information available to him;

(c)  comply with reasonable instructions given by his principal.

## Article 4

4(1)   In his relations with his commercial agent a principal must act dutifully and in good faith.

4(2)   A principal must in particular:
    (a)   provide his commercial agent with the necessary documentation relating to the goods concerned;
    (b)   obtain for his commercial agent the information necessary for the performance of the agency contract, and in particular notify the commercial agent within a reasonable period once he anticipates that the volume of commercial transactions will be significantly lower than that which the commercial agent could normally have expected.

4(3)   A principal must, in addition, inform the commercial agent within a reasonable period of his acceptance, refusal, and of any non-execution of a commercial transaction which the commercial agent has procured for the principal.

## Article 5

5   The parties may not derogate from the provisions of Articles 3 and 4.

CHAPTER III—REMUNERATION

## Article 6

6(1)   In the absence of any agreement on this matter between the parties, and without prejudice to the application of the compulsory provisions of the Member States concerning the level of remuneration, a commercial agent shall be entitled to the remuneration that commercial agents appointed for the goods forming the subject of his agency contract are customarily allowed in the place where he carries on his activities. If there is no such customary practice a commercial agent shall be entitled to reasonable remuneration taking into account all the aspects of the transaction.

6(2)   Any part of the remuneration which varies with the number or values of business transactions shall be deemed to be commission within the meaning of this Directive.

6(3)   Articles 7 to 12 shall not apply if the commercial agent is not remunerated wholly or in part by commission.

## Article 7

7(1)   A commercial agent shall be entitled to commission on commercial transactions concluded during the period covered by the agency contract:
    (a)   where the transaction has been concluded as a result of his action; or
    (b)   where the transaction is concluded with a third party whom he has previously acquired as a customer for transactions of the same kind.

7(2)   A commercial agent shall also be entitled to commission on transactions concluded during the period covered by the agency contract:
—either where he is entrusted with a specific geographical area or group of customers,
—or where he has an exclusive right to a specific geographical area or group of customers, and where the transaction has been entered into with a customer belonging to that area or group.
member states shall include in their legislation one of the possibilities referred to in the above two indents.

## Article 8

8   A commercial agent shall be entitled to commission on commercial transactions concluded after the agency contract has terminated:
(a) if the transaction is mainly attributable to the commercial agent's efforts during the period covered by the agency contract and if the transaction was entered into within a reasonable period after that contract terminated; or
(b) if, in accordance with the conditions mentioned in Article 7, the order of the third party reached the principal or the commercial agent before the agency contract terminated.

## Article 9

9   A commercial agent shall not be entitled to the commission referred to in Article 7, if that commission is payable, pursuant to Article 8, to the previous commercial agent, unless it is equitable because of the circumstances for the commission to be shared between the commercial agents.

## Article 10

10(1)   The commission shall become due as soon as and to the extent that one of the following circumstances obtains:
(a) the principal has executed the transaction; or
(b) the principal should, according to this agreement with the third party, have executed the transaction, or
(c) the third party has executed the transaction.
10(2)   The commission shall become due at the latest when the third party has executed his part of the transaction or should have done so if the principal had executed his part of the transaction, as he should have.
10(3)   The commission shall be paid not later than on the last day of the month following the quarter in which it became due.
10(4)   Agreements to derogate from paragraphs 2 and 3 to the detriment of the commercial agent shall not be permitted.

## Article 11

11(1)  The right to commission can extinguished only if and to the extent that:
—it is established that the contract between the third party and the principal will not be executed, and
—that fact is due to a reason for which the principal is not to blame.
11(2)  Any commission which the commercial agent has already received shall be refunded if the right to it is extinguished.
11(3)  Agreements to derogate from paragraph 1 to the detriment of the commercial agent shall not be permitted.

## Article 12

12(1)  The principal shall supply his commercial agent with a statement of the commission due, not later than the last day of the month following the quarter in which the commission has become due. This statement shall set out the main components used in calculating the amount of commission.
12(2)  A commercial agent shall be entitled to demand that he be provided with all the information, and in particular an extract from the books, which is available to his principal and which he needs in order to check the amount of the commission due to him.
12(3)  Agreements to derogate from paragraphs 1 and 2 to the detriment of the commercial agent shall not be permitted.
12(4)  This Directive shall not conflict with the internal provisions of member states which recognise the right of a commercial agent to inspect a principal's books.

CHAPTER IV—CONCLUSION AND TERMINATION OF THE AGENCY CONTRACT

## Article 13

13(1)  Each party shall be entitled to receive from the other on request a signed written document setting out the terms of the agency contract including any terms subsequently agreed. Waiver of this right shall not be permitted.
13(2)  Notwithstanding paragraph 1 a member state may provide that an agency contract shall not be valid unless evidenced in writing.

## Article 14

14  An agency contract for a fixed period which continues to be performed by both parties after that period has expired shall be deemed to be converted into an agency contract for an indefinite period.

## Article 15

15(1)  Where an agency contract is concluded for an indefinite period either party may terminate it by notice.

15(2)  The period of notice shall be one month for the first year of the contract, two months for the second year commenced, and three months for the third year commenced and subsequent years. The parties may not agree on shorter periods of notice.

15(3)  Member States may fix the period of notice at four months for the fourth year of the contract, five months for the fifth year and six months for the sixth and subsequent years. They may decide that the parties may not agree to shorter periods.

15(4)  If the parties agree on longer periods than those laid down in paragraphs 2 and 3, the period of notice to be observed by the principal must not be shorter than that to be observed by the commercial agent.

15(5)  Unless otherwise agreed by the parties, the end of the period of notice must coincide with the end of a calendar month.

15(6)  The provisions of this Article shall apply to an agency contract for a fixed period where it is converted under Article14 into an agency contract for an indefinite period, subject to the proviso that the earlier fixed period must be taken into account in the calculation of the period of notice.

## Article 16

16  Nothing in this Directive shall affect the application of the law of the Member States where the later provides for the immediate termination of the agency contract:
   (a)  because of the failure of one party to carry out all or part of his obligations;
   (b)  where exceptional circumstances arise.

## Article 17

17(1)  Member States shall take the measures necessary to ensure that the commercial agent is, after termination of the agency contract, indemnified in accordance with paragraph 2 or compensated for damage in accordance with paragraph 3.

17(2)  (a)  The commercial agent shall be entitled to an indemnity if and to the extent that:
   —he has brought the principal new customers or has significantly increased the volume of business with existing customers and the principal continues to derive substantial benefits from the business with such customers, and
   —the payment of this indemnity is equitable having regard to all the circumstances, and, in particular, the commission lost by the commercial agent on the business transacted with such customers. member states may provide for such circumstances also to include the application or otherwise of a restraint of trade clause, within the meaning of Article 20;
   (b)  The amount of the indemnity may not exceed a figure equivalent to an indemnity for one year calculated from the commercial agent's average annual remuneration over the preceding five years and if the contract goes back less than five years the indemnity shall be calculated on the average for the period in question;
   (c)  The grant of such an indemnity shall not prevent the commercial agent from seeking damages.

17(3)   The commercial agent shall be entitled to compensation for the damage he suffers as a result of the termination of his relations with the principal.

Such damage shall be deemed to occur particularly when the termination takes place in circumstances:

—depriving the commercial agent of the commission which proper performance of the agency contract would have procured him whilst providing the principal with substantial benefits linked to the commercial agent's activities,

—and/or which have not enabled the commercial agent to amortise the costs and expenses that he had incurred for the performance of the agency contract on the principal's advice.

17(4)   Entitlement to the indemnity as provided for in paragraph 2 or to compensation for damage as provided for under paragraph 3, shall also arise where the agency contract is terminated as a result of the commercial agent's death.

17(5)   The commercial agent shall lose his entitlement to the indemnity in the instances provided for in paragraph 2 or to compensation for damage in the instances provided for in paragraph 3, if within one year following termination of the contract he has not notified the principal that he intends pursuing his entitlement.

17(6)   The Commission shall submit to the Council, within eight years following the date of notification of this Directive, a report on the implementation of this Article, and shall if necessary submit to it proposals for amendments.

## Article 18

18   The indemnity or compensation referred to in Article 17 shall not be payable:

(a)   where the principal has terminated the agency contract because of default attributable to the commercial agent which would justify immediate termination of the agency contract under national law;

(b)   where the commercial agent has terminated the agency contract, unless such termination is justified by circumstances attributable to the principal or on grounds of age, infirmity or illness of the commercial agent in consequence of which he cannot reasonably be required to continue his activities;

(c)   where, with the agreement of the principal, the commercial agent assigns his rights and duties under the agency contract to another person.

## Article 19

19   The parties may not derogate from Articles 17 and 18 to the detriment of the commercial agent before the agency contract expires.

## Article 20

20(1)   For the purposes of this Directive, an agreement restricting the business activities of a commercial agent following termination of the agency contract is hereinafter referred to as a restraint of trade clause.

20(2)   A restraint of trade clause shall be valid only if and to the extent that:

    (a) it is concluded in writing; and

    (b) it relates to the geographical area or the group of customers and the geographical area entrusted to the commercial agent and to the kind of goods covered by his agency under the contract.

20(3)   A restraint of trade clause shall be valid for not more than two years after termination of the agency contract.

20(4)   This Article shall not affect provisions of national law which impose other restrictions on the validity or enforceability of restraint of trade clauses or which enable the courts to reduce the obligations on the parties resulting from such an agreement.

CHAPTER V—GENERAL AND FINAL PROVISIONS

## Article 21

21   Nothing in this Directive shall require a Member State to provide for the disclosure of information where such disclosure would be contrary to public policy.

## Article 22

22(1)   Member States shall bring into force the provisions necessary to comply with this Directive before 1 January 1990. They shall forthwith inform the Commission thereof. Such provisions shall apply at least to contracts concluded after their entry into force. They shall apply to contracts in operation by 1 January 1994 at the latest.

22(2)   As from the notification of this Directive, Member States shall communicate to the Commission the main laws, regulations and administrative provisions which they adopt in the field governed by this Directive.

22(3)   However, with regard to Ireland and the United Kingdom, 1 January 1990 referred to in paragraph 1 shall be replaced by 1 January 1994.

    With regard to Italy, 1 January 1990 shall be replaced by 1 January 1993 in the case of the obligations deriving from Article 17.

## Article 23

23   This Directive is addressed to the Member States.

# Appendix 7

# 1996 Commission Report on the Application of Article 17 of Council Directive 86/653

This Report is made under Article 17(6) of Council Directive on the co- ordination of the laws of the Member States relating to Self-Employed Commercial Agents 86/653/EEC.[1] Article 17 of Directive requires Member States to take the measures necessary to ensure that the commercial agent is, after termination of the agency contract, indemnified or compensated.

Article 17 represents a compromise between the Member States. It was therefore agreed that Member States should have the choice between the indemnity system and the compensation system and that the Commission would undertake a report to the Council on the practical consequences of the different solutions.

This report is made on the basis of responses to a questionnaire which was sent out, inter alia, to organisations representing agents and principals, chambers of commerce and federations of industry and legal practitioners specialising in agency law. The authorities of Member States were also invited to contribute with their views and experience.

THE TWO SYSTEMS

## 1. The Indemnity System

Under the indemnity system, the agent is entitled, after cessation of the contract, to payment of an indemnity if and to the extent that he has brought new customers to the principal or has significantly increased the volume of business with existing customers and the principal continues to derive substantial benefits from such customers after the cessation of the contract. The payment of the indemnity must be equitable having regard to all the circumstances and, in particular, the commission lost by the commercial agent on the business transacted with such customers. Finally, the Directive provides a ceiling on the level of indemnity of one year calculated from the agent's average annual remuneration over the preceding five years and if the contract goes back less than five years the maximum is to be calculated on the average for the period in question.

The indemnity represents the continuing benefits to the principal due to the efforts of the agent. The agent, however, will only have received commission during the duration of the contract, which will not typically reflect the value of the goodwill generated for the principal. It is for this reason that the payment of a goodwill indemnity is commercially justified. An indemnity will only be payable if the agent has brought to the principal new customers or increased business with existing customers. If no goodwill has been generated

[1] OJL 382 p 17 of 31.12.1986

or there is a group of customers whom the principal can derive no benefit from, no indemnity need be paid. Therefore, a principal should not be forced to pay an unreasonable amount of indemnity.

The indemnity system was modelled on Article 89b of the German Commercial Code which had provided for the payment of a goodwill indemnity since 1953 and concerning which a large body of case-law has developed regarding its calculation. This case-law and practice should provide invaluable assistance to the Courts of other Member States when seeking to interpret the provisions of Article 17(2) of the Directive.

First it is necessary to ascertain whether an agent has a right to an indemnity having regard to the circumstances in which the agency contract was terminated An indemnity is payable on termination of the contract except where one of the circumstances in Article 18 of the Directive applies. Clearly, the indemnity is payable on the end of a fixed term contract and in principle, an indemnity or limited indemnity is payable on the bankruptcy of the principal.

Secondly, the conditions set out in Article 17(2)(a) of the Directive have to be met, namely that either the agent has brought new customers or has substantially increased the volume of business with existing customers. As regards the volume of business with old customers, the German courts look to see if the increase in volume is such that it can be considered to be economically equivalent to the acquisition of a new customer. In relation to new customers, the addition of one new customer is sufficient. However, new customers from outside his territory for which the agent is not entitled to commission are excluded as there is no loss of commission for which the agent needs to be compensated. The agent must have acquired the new client and in this respect the instrumentality of the agent is crucial. A small level of involvement is sufficient and it is enough that the agent has merely contributed to bringing the new customer. However, the agent must have played an active role and therefore the existence of a new customer who falls within the territorial scope of an exclusive agency agreement will not automatically suffice

Thirdly, the principal must continue after the end of the agency contract to derive substantial benefits with such customers. This is presumed to be the case even if the principal sells his business or client list if it can be shown that the purchaser will use the client base.[2] If the agent continues to meet the needs of the same clients for the same products, but for a different principal, the agent is prevented from seeking an indemnity.[3] It is also possible for the court to consider a fall in the turnover of the principal's business. Fourthly, the payment of an indemnity must 'be equitable.

As to the actual calculation of the indemnity, it is undertaken in the following way:

### Stage 1

(a) The first stage in line with the second indent of Article 17(2)(a) is to ascertain the number of new customers and the increased volume of business with existing customers. Having identified such customers the gross commission on them is calculated for the last 12 months of the agency contract. Fixed remuneration can be included if it can be considered to be remuneration for new customers.[4] Special circumstances may justify departing from this, for example, where is a long start up period.

---

[2] Case 18 U 162/76 Oberlandesgeticht Hamm of 14.3.1977
[3] Case BB 605/60 Bundesgerichtshof of 25.4.1960
[4] Case VII ZR 194/63 Bundesgerichtshof of 15.2.1965

(b) An estimate is then made as to the likely future duration of the advantages to the principal deriving from business with the new customers and such old customers with whom the business has been significantly increased (intensified customers) which is calculated in terms of years. The aim is to predict the likely length of time the business with the new and intensified customers will last. This will involve considering the market situation at time of termination and the sector concerned The fact that sales drop after termination of the contract does not automatically lead to a corresponding reduction in the level of indemnity as sales may decline due to lowering s in quality of goods or competition.[5] The usual period is 2–3 years, but can be as much as 5 years.

(c) The next factor to consider is the rate of migration. It is acknowledged that over time customers will be lost as customers naturally move away. The rate of migration is calculated as a percentage of commission on a per annum basis and is taken from the particular experience of the agency in question. This clearly varies, but in one case the Bundesgerichtshof held that the rate of migration was 38%.[6]

(d) The figure is then reduced in order to calculate the present value taking into account that there is an accelerated receipt of income. Such a calculation based on average interest rates is a concept found in other jurisdictions

## Stage 2

It is at this stage that the question of equity is considered as set out in Article 17(2)(a) second indent of the Directive. The figure is rarely adjusted for reasons of equity in practice. The following factors are taken into account:

—Whether the agent is retained by other principals;

—The fault of the agent;

—The level of remuneration of the agent. For example, did the principal recently reduce the rate of commission e.g. because he felt that agent's earnings were becoming too high or pay to the agent a large amount of commission on contracts with customers which the agent did not introduce or had little to do with? Also, did the agent receive special compensation for keeping a consignment inventory, special bonuses for new clients, del credere commission, any special allowance for trade fairs or extra payments for sub-agents? Did he incur costs regarding loss of sub-agents?

—Decrease in turnover of the principal;

—Extent of the advantage to the principal;

—Payment of pension contributions by the principal;

—The existence of restraint of trade clauses. Clearly, a principal will be required to pay a higher indemnity for this.

## Stage 3

The amount calculated under Stages 1 and 2 is then compared with the maximum under Article 19(2)(b) of the Directive. This provision provides that the amount of the indemnity may not exceed a figure equivalent to remuneration for one year calculated from the

[5] BB 227/70 Celle of 13.1 1.69

[6] Case VIII ZR 94/93 Bundesgerichtshof of 23.2.1994

commercial agent's average annual remuneration over the preceding five years and if the contract goes back less than five years the indemnity shall be calculated on the average for the period in question. The maximum is in fact therefore a final corrective, rather than as a method of calculating the indemnity.[7]

In calculating the maximum, remuneration includes all forms of payment not just commission and is based on all customers, not only new or intensified customers.[8] If the sum under stages 1 and 2 is less than the maximum then this sum is awarded. If however, the sum exceeds the maximum, it is the maximum which is awarded. It is unusual for the maximum to be reached unless the agent has procured all or most of the customers

**An example of stages 1 to 3 is set out:**

| | | | |
|---|---|---|---|
| Commission on new customers and/or intensified customers over last 12 months of agency | | | 50,000 ECUs |

Anticipated duration of benefits is
3 years with 20% migration rate

| Year 1 | 50,000–1,000 | = | 40,000 ECUs |
|---|---|---|---|
| Year 2 | 40,000–8,000 | = | 32,000 ECUs |
| Year 3 | 32,000–6,400 | = | 25,600 ECUs |

| | |
|---|---|
| Total lost commission | 97,600 ECUs |

| | |
|---|---|
| Correction to present value say 10%. This figure being equal to the actual indemnity | 87,840 ECUs |

This figure might be adjusted
for reasons of equity (stage 2 above)

A final correction must be made should
the amount exceed the maximum
under Article 17(2)(b) of the Directive.

Article 17(2)(c) states that the grant of an indemnity shall not prevent the commercial agent from seeking damages. This provision governs the situation where the agent under national law is entitled to seek damages for breach of contract or failure to respect the notice period provided for under the Directive. Annex B attempts to identify these provisions.

It can thus be seen that the method of calculation of the indemnity is extremely precise and should lead to a predictable outcome. Principals should therefore be able to ascertain their risks in advance and to be able to enter into agency contracts with some degree of assurance. From the agent's perspective, clearer rights make it easier for the claim to be made and established.

---

[7]  Case VII ZR 47/69 Bundesgerichtshof of 19.11.1970
[8]  Case VII ZR 23/70 Bundesgerichtshof of 3.6.1971

## 2. The Compensation System

Under Article 17(3) of the Directive the agent is entitled to compensation for the damage he suffers as a result of the termination of his relations with his principal. Such damage is deemed to occur particularly when the termination takes place in circumstances:

—depriving the agent of the commission which proper performance of the agency contract would have procured him whilst providing the principal with substantial benefits linked to the agent's activities.

—and/or which have not enabled the agent to amortize the costs and expenses he had incurred for the performance of the agency contract on the principal's advice.

There is no maximum level of compensation.

The compensation system was based on French law, which dated from 1958 and whose aim was to compensate the agent for the loss he suffered as a result of the termination of the agency contract. As for the indemnity system in Germany, a body of case-law has developed in France concerning the right and level of compensation. Various judgments of the French courts have justified the payment of compensation on the ground that it represents the cost of purchasing the agency to the agent's successor or on the ground that it represents the time it takes for the agent to re-constitute the client base which he has been forcefully deprived of.

By judicial custom the level of compensation is fixed as the global sum of the last two years commission or the sum of 2 years commission calculated over the average of last three years of the agency contract which conforms with commercial practice. However, the courts retain a discretion to award a different level of compensation where the principal brings evidence that the agent's loss was in fact less, for example, because of the short duration of the contract or where, for example, the agent's loss is greater because of the agent's age or his length of service.

The indemnity is calculated on all remuneration, not just commission. It is based on the gross figure. No distinction is made between old and new customers and it includes special commission. There is no practice to reduce for professional costs. Finally, outstanding commissions must also be included in the calculation.

The indemnity represents that part of the market lost to the agent and his loss is fixed at that moment. Accordingly, future occurences are not taken into account, such as the principal ceasing to trade, the agent continuing to work with the same client or developments in the market place. Similarly, the agent is not required to mitigate his loss.

The Directive has brought about a greater interest in claiming damages for failure to respect the proper notice period. The amount awarded is the highest of the period not respected calculated on commission received for the last two years or the commission received during the identical period the previous year.

Further, more specific comments on the system in France can be found in Annex B.

POSITION IN MEMBER STATES

All Member States have implemented the Directive and a list of the laws is annexed to this Report as Annex A. With the exception of France, the UK and Ireland, Member States have incorporated the indemnity option into their national law. The UK has permitted the parties to choose the indemnity option, but if they fail to do so, the agent will be entitled to compensation. Ireland has failed to make any choice at all in its legislation and accordingly the Commission has opened Article 169 proceedings. The Commission has also opened infraction proceedings against Italy for failure to implement Article 17 of the Directive correctly. Further details can be found in Annex B concerning Irish and Italian law.

In most Member States there has yet to be any reported court decision, whilst in other Member States there are only a small number of cases. This is explained by the fact that the laws in most Member States are still very new and that these laws have only applied to all contracts in operation as from 1 January 1994. In addition, in France and Germany where there are cases, many agencies are not international in nature and the law follows long established traditions.

The second reason for the lack of reported cases is the tendency for the parties to settle cases before the court hearing. Agents are not always in the financial position to pursue their claims through the courts and therefore are forced to accept settlements. In addition, the uncertainty linked to court proceedings, invariably in a different jurisdiction deters agents from pursuing their claims through the courts.

The cases in Germany and France show a continuity with the existing jurisprudence in these countries. In Portugal, where the Directive represents a change to the previous situation the case-law shows an approach which is different to that of the German courts with an attempt by the judge to apply directly the principle of equity. In Italy, where there has only been one judgment under the new Article 1751 of the Civil Code, the Viterbo Magistrate Court has ruled, that having regard to the lack of criteria for calculation of the indemnity in Article 1751 of the Civil Code, it would apply the collective agreement. The collective agreement follows a system of calculation based on the duration of the agency and is not related to the number of new customers brought. Thus, it also takes a different approach to the German courts. However, this is a single judgment of the Italian courts and has yet to be confirmed. In Denmark, only three judgments have been reported. A fourth judgment is now subject to appeal. The reported cases reveal a tendency to take over and follow German jurisprudence.

Having regard to the relative lack of jurisprudence and the nature of the subject matter, the Commission in its preparation for this Report sought to ascertain the practical as well as the legal situation. An outline of the legal and practical position is set out in more detail in Annex B.

There are no statistics available in any of the Member States. The International Union of Commercial Agents and Brokers have now started to collect data. This is a helpful development, as IUCAB should be able to collect a good level of data through its member organisations in Member States and IUCAB has offered to present these statistics periodically to the Commission. The Portuguese authorities have also established a centralised method of collecting information from all courts on the nature and outcome of cases which involve EC law or the Lugano Convention, which of course, includes the Directive on Commercial Agents.

BUSINESS PRACTICE

The Commission sought to ascertain whether, as a result of the Directive and in particular the right to an indemnity or compensation, there had been any change in business practice. The Commission also wanted to establish whether, as a result of the different options, distortions in competition had arisen. The lack of statistics makes it more difficult to reach conclusions in this regard.

Overall, the Commission found that there had not been any change in business practice. There was some evidence that principals were moving to distributorship contracts in France, Germany, Luxembourg and Belgium. This can be partially explained by the fact that on lawful termination of distributorship contracts no indemnity or compensation is payable or a reduced level. In the UK, Ireland and Sweden it was reported that principals were now considering much more carefully whether agency contracts were the most appropriate business arrangements and were therefore taking a much more cautious approach. However, principals were not always actually moving away from agency contracts.

In the UK there appears to have been a specific reaction. First prior to the coming into force of the UK Regulations implementing the Directive, principals terminated their agency contracts and on the whole re-negotiated new contracts. There were, however, occasions where new agency contracts were not entered into or the agents were taken on as employees. This reflects the fundamental change brought about by the Directive to UK law and the fear of principals of the unknown. It is too soon to determine whether there will be a permanent shift away from agency contracts in the UK.

Under French law and practice, compensation awarded in the vast majority of cases amounts to 2 years commission which is twice the legal maximum provided for under the indemnity option. This clearly makes the appointment of an agent in France under French law a much more costly enterprise. This has led some principals seeking when appointing an agent in France to seek to apply a law other than French law or to avoid entering into agency contracts altogether. There is no evidence of any widespread problems or distortions in trade as regards those Member States who have opted for the indemnity system and those who have opted for the compensation option.

## REACTIONS OF PRINCIPALS AND AGENTS

It can generally be said that agents have given a positive considered to have increased their rights. This would be the case in Austria, Denmark, Finland, Ireland, Luxembourg, Sweden and the UK. French agents continue to feel positively about the system of compensation in France and do not wish for change.

The reaction of principals has been mixed. To some extent, principals are bound to feel negative about change as they now have to grant greater rights to agents. For other principals it is not that they are against paying an indemnity on termination, but rather there is a degree of discontent in that the system lacks clarity. French principals appear to support the compensation system and have not raised any objections regarding it.

There is no tendency amongst either agents or principals in the Member States who have implemented the indemnity option to favour anything other than the indemnity system. In the UK, where the parties are able to opt in favour of payment of an indemnity, no clear preference emerges although most contracts do not contain an indemnity provision. Principals are still unclear about what the differences between the two systems are. There is a certain level of interest in the indemnity amongst some principals because of the maximum limit, but other principals prefer the compensation option as agents must prove actual loss.

A number of difficulties have arisen in relation to Article 17 of the Directive.

## (1) Interpretation difficulties

Many commentators and lawyers have pointed to the imprecise and uncertain nature of Article 17, which causes difficulty ill trying to advise clients on the extent of an agent's rights on termination. This was reported in particular in Denmark, Ireland, Italy, Spain, Sweden and the UK.

### (a) Indemnity

As regards the indemnity option, there has been a tendency in some Member States to seek reliance on the maximum figure whereas under the German system, which influenced the Directive, the maximum has no bearing on the actual method of calculation of the indemnity. It is merely used at the end of the process as a final adjuster. In some Member States attempts are made to try and establish an equitable amount taking into account various different factors, which again is not the approach taken by the German courts. Denmark and Austria appear to follow the German model but in the case of Austria, the maximum limit is often reached, whereas in Germany it is very rarely reached except when all the customers have been brought by the commercial agent.

In Italy, it appears, at the moment, that the previous system continues to apply even though a new law was introduced. This has been re-enforced in the ruling in the Pretura Viterbo case in which the court held that the provision of Article 1751 of the Italian Civil Code, which implements Article 17(2) of the Directive, was so uncertain as to the method of calculation of the indemnity it would apply the collective agreement. The method of calculation under the collective agreement does not correspond with the German model, but is based on the length of the contract, the level of commission and the percentages set out in the collective agreement.

It therefore appears there is a divergence of approaches. However, there is of course still only a very limited jurisprudence of the courts of Member States concerning Article 17 outside Germany.

### (b) Compensation

As regards the compensation option, clearly this has not presented problems of interpretation in France where pre-existing jurisprudence has continued to be applied. However, as regards the UK which applies the compensation option in default of the choice of the parties, there is a fundamental difference in approach. At this stage, there is no UK case-law but the parties in practice are attempting to apply common law principles. These common law principles are directly opposed to the well-established method of calculation of compensation in France. For example, the English system will take account of future developments after termination of the contract and this results in the need to for the injured person to mitigate his loss. Whereas, under French law, events after the termination of the agency contract have no bearing on the compensation to be awarded. Under French Law, the standrd award is two years commission which represents the value of the purchase of an agency or the period it will take the agent to re-establish his client base. It is difficult to see how the UK courts will reach this figure. This, no doubt, derives from the previous legal position in the UK, that agency contracts could be terminated on notice without any payment being due. This naturally has had consequences for business practices. There was no real concept of goodwill attaching to an agency to which the agent had a right to a share in. It is not possible to predict how the UK courts will interpret the Directive, but it seems likely that they will have regard to existing common law principles.

The same difficulties are likely to arise in Ireland if Ireland opts for the compensation option.

### (c) Consequences of uncertainty

The difficulties in interpretation have had an effect on the reactions of agents and principals to the Directive. For both it has entailed increased time being spent on negotiation since rights and levels of rights are not clearly established. This benefits neither party. It has also led to different amounts being awarded. Uncertainty and divergence also lead to a reluctance to create agencies and act as a barrier to principals to take on agents in other Member States. It is important that the Directive is uniformly interpreted and leads to predictable and clear results.

## (2) Position of Agents

The Directive has led to an improvement in the position of agents vis-à-vis their principals. Nevertheless it appears that agents are not always able to enforce their rights to the full because they lack the resources to take court action. This is a problem of a general nature and not specific to the Directive Possible remedies lie outside the remit of this Report. However, it is the view of the Commission that clarification of the provisions of the Directive and methods of calculation will be of assistance to agents and make the enforcement of rights easier.

## (3) Choice of Law

Finally, certain problems have been encountered with regard to choice of law clauses in contracts and attempts have been made to avoid the application of certain laws by choice of law clauses or jurisdiction clauses. The Directive does not lay down any rules concerning private international law. The parties are therefore free to choose the law which is to govern the agency contract, subject to the rules contained in the Rome Convention 1980 on the law applicable to contractual obligations. In the Commission's opinion Articles 17 and 18 of the Directive are mandatory rules and accordingly, the courts of the Member States can apply the law of the forum in accordance with the 1980 Rome Convention and thereby ensue the application of the Directive. The 1968 Brussels Convention on jurisdiction and enforcement of judgments in civil and commercial matters will also assist in ensuring, that in so far as Community cases are concerned and the agent is carrying on his activities in the

EC, that a court of a Member State will have jurisdiction.[9] Accordingly, there does not appear to be any need to amend the Directive in this regard.

CONCLUSION

The Commission notes that the indemnity option has been chosen by the vast majority of Member States and that this has received the support of agents and principals in those Member States. The Directive provides for a ceiling on the level of indemnity, but does not give precise guidance for its method of calculation. A clear and precise method of calculation would lead to greater legal certainty, which would be of advantage to both parties. As regards the compensation option, which has been maintained by France, it does not appear to have caused problems for agents and principals in France. The level of compensation in France is generally much higher than the level of indemnity. The implementation in the UK whereby the parties have the choice of the system has led to uncertainty, particularly as neither of the two options is known to the British legal system.

At this stage, there is very little jurisprudence concerning the Directive. Having regard to the information received, it appears that there is a need for clarification of Article 17. Any more further far-reaching conclusions are premature. The Commission considers that this Report, which gives detailed information, particularly concerning the method of calculation of the indemnity as it is carried out in Germany, provides further clarification of Article 17 of the Directive and secondly, by so-doing should facilitate a more uniform interpretation of Article 17 of the Directive.

---

[9] *Arcado Sprl v Haviland SA* Case No 9/87 [1988] ECR 1539 the court held that right to compensation was contractual in nature and therefore Article 5(1) of the 1968 Brussels Convention applied thus opening the possibility of an additional basis of jurisdiction

# ANNEX A

LIST OF MEMBER STATES LAWS IMPLEMENTING THE DIRECTIVE
ON COMMERCIAL AGENTS (86/653/EEC)

Expiry of implementation period: 31.12.89
(United Kingdom and Ireland: 31.12.93)
(Italy, concerning article 17: 31.12.92)

1. *Belgium*   Law of 13.4.1995
published in Moniteur Belge of 2.6.1995, pg. 15621
entry into force: 12.6.1995

2. Denmark   Law no 272 of 2.5.90
publication: Lovtidende A. 1990 p. 922
entry into force: 4.5.90
application to contracts in operation: 1.1.92

3. *Germany*   Law of 23.10.89
publication: Bundesgesetzblatt 1989 I 1910
entry into force: 1.1.90
application to contracts in operation: 1. 1.94

4. *Greece*   Presidential Decree no 219 of 18.5.1991
publication: OJ of the Greek government no 81 of 30.5.1991 and no 136 of
11.9.1991 as amended by Decrees no 249/93, 88/94 and 312/95.
entry into force: 30.5.1991
application to contracts in operation: 1.1.94

5. *Spain*   Law 12/1992 of 27.5.1992
publication: BOE no 129 of 29.5.1992
entry into force: 19.6.1992
application to contracts in operation: 1.1.94

6. *France*   Law no 91–593 of 25.6.1991
publication: OJ of the French Republic 17.6.1991 p. 8271
entry into force: 28.6.1992
Decree 92–506 of 10.6.1992
Publication: OJ of the French Republic 12.6.1992 p. 7720
entry into force: 1.1.1994
application to contracts in operation: 1.1.94

7. *Ireland*   Statutory Instrument: SI No 33 of 1994 of 21.2.1994
Entry into force: 1.1.1994
application to contracts in operation: 1.1.94

*8. Italy*          Legislative Decree no 303 of 10.9.1991
                    publication: Gazetta ufficiale no 57 of
                    20.9.1991.
                    entry into force: 1.1.1993
                    application to contracts in operation: 1.1.94


*9. Luxembourg*     Law of 3 June 1994
                    publication: Memorial A-No 58 of 6.7.1994, p. 1088
                    application to contracts in operation: 1.1.94


*10. Netherlands*   Law of 5.7.89
                    publication: Staatsblad 1989 no 312
                    entry into force: 1.11.89
                    application to contracts in operation: 1.1.94
                    Re-enacted by Law no 374 of 1993 as Articles 400–445 of Title 7 of the
                    Burgerlijk Wetboek


*11. Austria*       Federal Act of 11.2.1993
                    published in Federal Gazette 88
                    entry into force: 1.3.1993
                    application to contracts in operation: 1.1.1994


*12. Portugal*      Decree no 178/86 of 3.7.86
                    publication: Diário da República, I série, 1986, p. 1575
                    entry into force: 2.8.86
                    application to contracts in operation: 2.8.86
                    amended by law No 118/93 of 13.4.93 published Diario da
                    República No 86 p.1818 of 13.4.93
                    application to contracts in operation: 1.1 94


*13. Finland*       Law no 417 of 8.5.1992
                    published in Gesetzblatt of 14.5.1992
                    entry into force: 1.11.1992
                    application to contracts in force: 1.1.1994


*14. Sweden*        Law no 351 of 2.5.1991
                    entry into force: 1.1.1992
                    application to contracts in force: 1.1.1994.


*15. UK*            Statutory Instrument SI 1993 no 3053 of 7.12.93
                    and SI 1993 no 3173 of 16.12.1993
                    entry into force: 1.1.94
                    application to contracts in operation: 1.1.1 994
                    Northern Ireland:
                    Statutory Rules of Northern Ireland 1993 no 483 of 17.12.1993
                    entry into force: 13.1.1994
                    application to contracts in operation: 13.1.1994

## ANNEX B

BELGIUM

The law on Commercial Agent Contract only came into force on 12 June 1995. Accordingly, there are no cases decided by the courts on the new law.

Article 20 of the law introduced the right to a goodwill indemnity. Prior to the new law, the right to a goodwill indemnity had been rejected by the main decisions of the Belgian courts as goodwill was considered to attach to the principal more than to the agent. Accordingly, the new law has brought about an important change to the law.

The law contains no guidance as to how the indemnity is to be calculated, but it is argued by most commentators that is for judge to determine the amount taking into account various factors such as level of commission in last years of the contract, level of development of customers, extent to which principal will continue to derive benefits, duration of contractual relations, level of involvement of the principal, existence of a pension financed by the principal or whether the agent's contract with the principal is his sole agency. One author has specifically drawn on the German method of calculation.

Practising Belgian lawyers considered that regard would be had to the law on commercial representatives and to the German experience. Under the Law on Commercial Representatives of 3 July 1978, however, the indemnity is calculated on the basis of 3 months wages for a commercial representative who has acted for the same principal for a period of one to five years. This period is increased by one month for each further five years.

Under Article 18(3) of the Belgian law, it is possible to claim damages for lack of notice, which amounts to lost commission in accordance with method of calculation set out in this Article.

Finally, under Article 21 of the Belgian law, an agent who has a right to an indemnity can claim in addition damages for the harm actually suffered. It is not clear in what circumstances is this payable and whether entitlement to an indemnity gives automatically a right to seek damages. In the view of the Commission this latter interpretation would be contrary to Article 17(1) of the Directive as the effect of such an interpretation would be that the two options would apply cumulatively.

DENMARK

With the implementation of the Directive in Denmark and the introduction of the right to an indemnity under Section 25 of Law No 272 of 2 May 1990, a new right was granted which had not existed under the previous law.

To date, only three judgments have been reported.[10] In *Lope Handel* the principal was ordered to pay losses for the failure to respect the contractual period of notice and to pay an indemnity of 1 years commission on the new customers acquired for the principal by the

---

[10] *Lope Handel v GE Lighting* (Commercial Court of Copenhagen of 25.9.1995); *S&L Eskimo* (High Court, Western Division of 14.11.1995); *Cramer v B&B* (Commercial Court of Copenhagen of 15.12.1995)

agent. It was proved that the new customers were lost one year after termination of the agency contract. In *S&L*, the principal was ordered to pay an indemnity equivalent to the maximum. It was proved that practically all the customers were brought by the agent. In *Cramer,* the court found that a substantial number of customers were once-only customers with whom the principal could expect no further business. The principal was ordered to pay an indemnity amounting to DKK 150,000. For comparison the maximum would have been 400,000.

In practice it appears that agents seek the maximum amount and principals try to argue the figure down. At present, although there is no set picture, there is no tendency to pay the maximum figure. Calculations appear to follow the German model.

As for other Member States, no useful statistics are available.

Section 6 of the law implements Article 17(2)(c) of the Directive and provides that if an agent or principal is in breach of his obligations to the other, the other is entitled to compensation for any damage caused thereby.

## GERMANY

Article 89b of the Handelsgesetzbuch sets out the agents right to an indemnity. The method of calculation is set out in the Report itself.

In practice it appears that there has been no change in Germany as to the method of calculation of the indemnity following the implementation of the Directive in Germany as the indemnity provision of the Directive did not require change to German law. The change noted by industry was in relation to contracts with other EU countries, which prior to the Directive did not provide for an indemnity.

## GREECE

The implementation of Article 17 of the Directive by Article 9 of Presidential Decree 219 of 18 May 1991 did not conform with the Directive, in particular, in that it did not implement the second indent of Article 17(2)(a) which requires that the indemnity be equitable. Greece has following correspondence with the Commission introduced a new law in 1995 which implements Articles 17(2)(a).

Article 9(1)(c) states that the right to seek an indemnity does not prevent an agent from seeking damages under the Civil Code. Damages are payable and awarded according to whether the contract was fixed term or of indefinite duration.

An agent may also seek damages for lack of proper notice.

## SPAIN

Article 28 of law No 12/1992 of 27 June 1995 provides for the payment of an indemnity Article 29 of the law provides for the award of damages if the principal unilaterally breaks an agency contract which is for an indefinite period. The Directive has filled a legal gap in Spanish law in that prior to the law implementing the Directive there was no specific law covering commercial agents or commercial agency contracts. However, Article 29 is not restricted merely to breach of contract and by virtue of this Spain has seemingly implemented both options contained in Article 17 of the Directive unless the Court interprets the scope of Article 29 narrowly.

Owing to the recent coming into force of the law there is a lack of jurisprudence in this area. The case-law prior to the new law may be of relevance for the future since some of the principles may act as guidance for future judgment by the Spanish courts.

Under the old law, it was also possible to claim both damages and a goodwill indemnity and agents used to cumulate both claims. The difference between both remedies was sometimes blurred in practice. The Supreme Court has repeatedly recognised the possibility of obtaining an indemnity for goodwill. The judge is given a wide discretion to fix the level of the indemnity and in general it is calculated depending on the agent's earnings.[11] As regards damages, the courts considered a number of different matters in arriving at the award, including the level of the last commission, the nature of the activity, loss of prestige and whether the contract was exclusive or not.[12]

Finally, damages are payable for failure to respect the correct notice period which is the amount of commission the agent would have received if the notice period had been respected.[13]

However, despite these judgments it is still difficult to reach general conclusions, particularly as in Spain the level of indemnity is fixed after the hearing and the decision is not published.

FRANCE

Unlike for many other Member States, the Directive has not brought about radical change to the pre-existing law in France. Under Article 12 of Law No 91/593 of 25 June 1991, French law continues to give a right to compensation on termination of the agency contract. The change brought about relates to the circumstances in which compensation is payable and not in its calculation. The right to compensation now exists for the nonrenewal of the contract and termination by the agent for reasons of old age, sickness or infirmity and on death.

Compensation is calculated as before according to the jurisprudence as neither the old law or the present law sets out the method of calculation. In the vast majority of cases it amounts to two years gross commission which is calculated from the agent's average remuneration over the preceding three years or the global sum of the last two years commission. This sum has become the customary award and is confirmed with court decisions applying the new law.[14]

The indemnity is calculated on all remuneration, not just commission. It is based on the gross figure. No distinction is made between old and new customers and it includes special commission. There is no practice to reduce for professional costs. Finally, outstanding commissions must also be included in the calculation.

---

[11] Supreme Court judgments of 22 March 1988 and 19 September 1989

[12] Judgment of Court of Appeal of Lugo of 4.6.1994; Court of Appeal Valence of 14.7.1993 and Court of Appeal Barcelona of 30.1.1995

[13] Judgment of Supreme Court of 19.9.1989

[14] See for example: Court of Appeal Toulouse 20.12.1994 Les Annonces de la Seine, No 39 1.6.1995 p 28; Court of Appeal Dijon, 16.6.1994 Les Annonces de la Seine, No 39, p 26; Court of Appeal Paris, 17.1.1995, Les Annonces de la Seine 1.6.1995; No 39. p 8.

The indemnity represents that part of the market lost to the agent and his loss is fixed at that moment. Accordingly, future occurrences are not taken into account, such as the principal ceasing to trade, the agent continuing to work with the same clients or developments in the market place. Similarly, the agent is not required to mitigate his loss.

The French courts do not order the payment of two years gross commission as compensation where it can be shown that the loss suffered by the agent is less, for example, because of the short duration of the contract. Similarly, the level may be increased, where, for example, an agent's loss is greater because of his age or length of the agency contract.

The Directive has brought about a greater interest in claiming damages for failure to respect the proper notice period. The amount taken is the highest of the period not respected calculated on commission received for the last two years or the commission received during the identical period the previous year.

IRELAND

Ireland has not implemented this provision and therefore agents do not have either a right to compensation or an indemnity. Under the common law, an agent can seek damages for breach of contract. In a fixed term contract, this will allow the agent to claim the commission he would have received until the end of the contract, subject to the agent's duty to mitigate his loss. However, this is not sufficient for the purposes of implementing the Directive. In cases of contracts of indefinite period the claim is usually for remuneration during the notice period to be respected. In addition, in both cases, he may claim for the economic loss suffered as a result of the breach of contract.

To date there are no reported cases.

ITALY

Italy amended Article 1751 of the Civil Code by Article 4 of legislative Decree No 303 of 10 September 1991 to introduce the indemnity system set out in the Directive. However, in the view of the Commission the implementation by Italy is incorrect in that Italy has treated the two indents in Article 17(2)(a) of the Directive as alternative conditions whereas they are in fact cumulative. Accordingly the Commission has opened infraction proceedings.

It appears that the old system of collective agreements continues to apply. The Enasarco agreement of 30.10.1992 was agreed to by both principals and organisations representing agents. By doing so they have de facto re-introduced the criteria which were applicable under the previous text of Article 1751.

In its judgment of 1 December 1994, the Viterbo Magistrate Court applied the collective agreement. The court held that Article 1751 of the Civil Code could not be applied in practice as it does not fix any criteria for calculating the indemnity except the maximum. Accordingly, the court considered it appropriate to apply the collective agreement. The Court also stated that the circumstances in Article 1751 were not intended for calculating the amount of indemnity, but for determining whether an indemnity was justified if at least one of the circumstances applied. Further, the court considered that wisely the social partners, in order to avoid practically insoluble problems, had replaced the old collective agreement thereby enabling Article 1751 of the Civil Code to be applied in practice. It is not clear at this stage whether this judgment will be followed.

The system of the collective agreement is based on level of commissions and duration of the agency contract and the set percentages laid down in the agreement.

Under the collective agreement, the agent in most cases receives an amount which is much less than the maximum envisaged under the Directive.

LUXEMBOURG

Luxembourg's law implementing the Directive of 3 June 1994 applies to all contracts existing before 1 January 1994 as well as to contracts entered into force after that date. Article 19 provides for an indemnity to be paid on termination. The new law introduced a right which did not exist under the pre-existing law. Those consulted thought it was too soon to develop a theory about how the law would be interpreted.

Article 23(1) sets out the right to damages for unjustified failure to give due notice and Article 23(2) provides for damages to be paid for a serious breach of contract. Article 24 states that this amounts to a sum equal to the remuneration that would have been received in the period between the breach and the normal end of the contract. To calculate this sum regard is to be had to the previous level of commissions and to other relevant matters. This sum can be reduced if the judge considers it too high in the circumstances of the case.

THE NETHERLANDS

Article 7:442 of the Civil Code provides for an indemnity to be paid on termination of the agency contract. Under Article 7:439 damages are payable for unjustified failure to respect the correct notice period and Articles 7:440 and 7:441 provide for damages to be paid for breach of contract. This covers the period from actual termination to the date on which the agency would have been terminated had proper notice been given. This amount is the amount of remuneration which would have been received and is based on the commission received prior to termination and other relevant circumstances. The judge can reduce the amount if he considers that it is too high having regard to the facts of the particular case. Under Article 7:441.3, the party can seek in place of the sum under Article 7:441.1 and 2., compensation for the actual damage suffered and he bears the burden of proving his loss.

There is not any reported case to date concerning the new law and nor are there any statistics.

AUSTRIA

The Austrian law of 11 February 1993 came into force on 1 March 1993. Under Article 24, the agent has a right to an indemnity. To date there are no reported cases concerning the amount of indemnity or damages payable on termination of an agency contract under the 1993 law. The Directive has lead to a change in the previous law and in particular to a doubling of the maximum limit. Therefore, previous case-law is not useful guidance. Under the old law, there was a digressive reduction in the upper limit of compensation of aggregate amount of one year's commission calculated as a yearly average over the previous three years according to the length of the relationship.

In practice, it appears that commercial agents calculate the indemnity on the basis of the average income of the last five years taking into account the fluctuation of customers by computing a digression of income on the basis of 5 years. In most cases, this exceeds the upper limit set by law. On this basis, the parties negotiate in order to find a reasonable settlement. The method of calculation is based on German experiences.

It was considered too soon to make any judgment about the average level of indemnity paid. A claim for damages or performance of the contract can be made if a party terminates the contract prematurely without just cause under Article 23. Article 23 also applies to a breach of Article 21 which is concerned with notice periods. Any other claims for damages are dealt with in accordance with the provisions of the General Civil Code and the Commercial Code.

### PORTUGAL

Portugal adopted its law in 1986 which followed to a large extent the proposal for the Directive and included at Article 33 the right to an indemnity. The law came into force on 2 August 1986. It has been amended by Articles 33 and 34 of Decree No. 118/93 to bring Portugese law in conformity with Article 17 of the Directive.

In Portugal there have been a number of court judgements.[15] The courts have calculated the level of indemnity taking into account the importance of new clients, the increased development of existing customers, the advantages to the principal after the termination of the contract and the loss of commission by the agent. The courts consider the indemnity as a measure of compensation for the agent for the benefits to the principal existing at the end of the contract with the clients developed by the agent.

Under Article 32 of the law and under Articles 562–572 of the Civil Code, there is also a right to be indemnified for the damages suffered for breach of contract. Article 29 specifically provides for damages for failure to respect the notice period or alternatively to damages for lack of due notice. The agent can seek, as an alternative to damages, a sum calculated on the basis of the average monthly remuneration over the previous year multiplied by the time remaining if the contract had continued to run. If the contract is of less than one years duration then the whole contract period is to be used.

### FINLAND

Under section 28 of Act No 417 of 8 May 1992, the right to indemnity on termination of an agency contract was introduced. The Directive has brought about a change in the pre-

---

[15] Accórdão da Relação de Coimbra of 14.12.1993 Court of Appeal in Colectānea de Jurisprudéncia, Year XVIII, 1993, Volume V, P 46; Accórdão do Supremo Tribunal de Justiça of 4.5.1993 in colectānea de Jurisprudéncia—Accordrãos do Supremo Tribunal de Justiça, Year I, Volume II, 1993, p 78 and also same court, judgment of 27.10.1994 in Year II, Volume III, 1994, p 101; Acórdão da Relação do Porto of 18.10.1994 in Colectānea de Jurisprudéncia, Year XIX, Volume IV, 1994, p 212.

existing law. The law came into force on 1 November 1992 and there has been no court decision to date.

In practice, it appears that agents seek the maximum amount and the principal makes a counter-offer. The negotiations result in an amount which is not based on any specific calculation, rather it is the outcome of bargaining. Generally, the indemnity is in the region of 3–6 months average commission. It was felt by the agents federation that the amount of indemnity period was slightly higher under the new law than under the old law, but no statistics are available to support this.

Under Section 9 of the law, the right to damages for harm caused by a violation of the agency contract is laid down or for when a party has neglected one of his obligations. Further, Sections 26 and 27 of the Act provide for damages where notice periods are not respected

SWEDEN

Article 28 of Law No 351 of 2 May 1991 introduced a right to receive an indemnity which did not exist under the previous law, which only sought to ensure that an agent received commission on orders concluded after the withdrawal of the agents authority provided that the orders were brought about through the acts of the agent during the currency of the agreement.

As for other Member States, there has yet to be any court decision. In practice agents seek the maximum amount permitted under the law and the parties negotiate on this basis to reach an equitable sum. In doing so, the parties take into account, inter alia, the duration of the contract, the agent's promotional activities, the number of new customers, orders given after termination, the possibility of a new contract for the agent and the costs incurred and investments made by the agent.

There are no statistics but the Swedish authorities estimated that awards were typically between 6 months and 1 year commission calculated as an average over the last years of the contract. This would represent an increase in the amount of compensation.

Article 34 of the law provides for damages for breach of contract.

UNITED KINGDOM

The UK has a opted its own particular system in that under Regulation 17 of Statutory Instrument No 3053 of 1993 the parties may choose whether an agent will have the right to an indemnity or compensation.[16] It is only in default of a contractual provision that the law requires compensation to be paid. This method of implementation has of itself produced uncertainty, particularly since neither of the two options are familiar to the UK legal systems.

The law has only recently come into force in the UK and has caused a certain amount of confusion as parties and lawyers attempt to apply concepts with which they are unfamiliar and which are a certain degree alien to UK traditions. Various different approaches have developed.

---

[16] Regulation 17 of SI No 483 of 1993 for Northern Ireland

In relation to compensation, lawyers try to apply traditional common law principles which does not work well since under the common law, termination of a contract in accordance with its terms or at the natural end of a fixed term contract does not give rise to a damages claim. Under the common law, the court tries to put the agent in the position he would have been in if the contract had been properly performed, but the injured party is expected to mitigate his loss and the court will have regard to future events. Typically for a fixed term contract, this would give the agent the right to claim commission for the duration of the contract. In the case of a contract for an indefinite period, the agent could seek damages for the notice period amounting to the remuneration he would have received in this period. The agent could also seek compensation for costs incurred in pursuance of the agency. Lawyers therefore have difficulties in reaching a view as to the level of compensation where the agent has died, become ill or retired. Typical compensation payments are between 3–6 months with some payments of 15 months depending on the level of service.

Some lawyers have therefore tried to apply by analogy the law relating to unfair dismissal or redundancy which is determined by age, length of service and the weekly wage.

As regards the indemnity provision, agents claim the maximum amount and then through negotiations a smaller sum is agreed. Typical payments appear to be between 3–6 months commission based on what would have been earned rather than the average of the last 5 years.

Most contracts do not contain a provision providing for an indemnity, but this does not necessarily reflect a preference for the compensation option rather than the indemnity option.

To date, there have been no cases and parties are reluctant to litigate since lawyers are unconfident in advising what their clients' rights are and consequently what the courts will award. However, there are likely to be cases in the near future.

# Index